Political Science in Africa

Africa Now

Africa Now is published by Zed Books in association with the internationally respected Nordic Africa Institute. Featuring high-quality, cutting-edge research from leading academics, the series addresses the big issues confronting Africa today. Accessible but in-depth, and wide-ranging in its scope, Africa Now engages with the critical political, economic, sociological and development debates affecting the continent, shedding new light on pressing concerns.

Nordic Africa Institute

The Nordic Africa Institute (Nordiska Afrikainstitutet) is a centre for research, documentation and information on modern Africa. Based in Uppsala, Sweden, the Institute is dedicated to providing timely, critical and alternative research and analysis of Africa and to co-operation with African researchers. As a hub and a meeting place for a growing field of research and analysis the Institute strives to put knowledge of African issues within reach for scholars, policy makers, politicians, media, students and the general public. www.nai.uu.se

Forthcoming titles

Stephen Marr and Patience Mususa (eds), *DIY Urbanism in Africa: Politics and Practice*

Titles already published

Cecilia Navarra and Cristina Udelsmann Rodrigues (eds), *Transformations of Rural Spaces in Mozambique*

Diana Højlund Madsen (eds), *Gendered Institutions and Women's Political Representation in Africa*

Jesper Bjarnesen and Simon Turner, *Invisibility in African Displacements*

Fantu Cheru and Cyril Obi (eds), *The Rise of China and India in Africa*

Ilda Lindell (ed.), *Africa's Informal Workers*

Iman Hashim and Dorte Thorsen, *Child Migration in Africa*

Prosper B. Matondi, Kjell Havnevik and Atakilte Beyene (eds), *Biofuels, Land Grabbing and Food Security in Africa*

Cyril Obi and Siri Aas Rustad (eds), *Oil and Insurgency in the Niger Delta*

Mats Utas (ed.), *African Conflicts and Informal Power*

Prosper B. Matondi, *Zimbabwe's Fast Track Land Reform*

Maria Eriksson Baaz and Maria Stern, *Sexual Violence as a Weapon of War?*

Fantu Cheru and Renu Modi (eds), *Agricultural Development and Food Security in Africa*

Amanda Hammar (ed.), *Displacement Economies in Africa*

Political Science in Africa

Freedom, Relevance, Impact

Edited by
Liisa Laakso and Siphamandla Zondi

LONDON · NEW YORK · OXFORD · NEW DELHI · SYDNEY

THE NORDIC
AFRICA INSTITUTE
NORDISKA AFRIKAINSTITUTET

Zed Books
Bloomsbury Publishing Plc
50 Bedford Square, London, WC1B 3DP, UK
1385 Broadway, New York, NY 10018, USA
29 Earlsfort Terrace, Dublin 2, Ireland

BLOOMSBURY and Zed Books are trademarks of Bloomsbury Publishing Plc

First published in Great Britain 2024 in association with the Nordic Africa Institute, PO Box 1703, SE-751 47 Uppsala, Sweden

Series design by Alice Marwick
Cover image © AJ_Watt/Getty Images

A catalogue record for this book is available from the British Library.

Library of Congress Cataloging-in-Publication Data
Names: Laakso, Liisa, editor. | Zondi, Siphamandla, editor, author.
Title: Political science in Africa: freedom, relevance, impact / edited by Liisa Laakso and Siphamandla Zondi.
Other titles: Political science in Africa (Zed Books) | Africa now (Zed Books)
Description: New York: Zed Books, an imprint of Bloomsbury Publishing, 2024. | Series: Africa now | "Most of the chapters in this book are based on papers presented at a conference "The Political Science Discipline in Africa: freedom, relevance, impact" jointly organized by the Nordic Africa Institute, Association of African Universities (AAU) and CODESRIA in Accra between October 31 and November 2, 2019." | Includes bibliographical references and index.
Identifiers: LCCN 2023019787 (print) | LCCN 2023019788 (ebook) | ISBN 9781350299504 (hardback) | ISBN 9781350299498 (paperback) | ISBN 9781350299511 (epub) | ISBN 9781350299528 (pdf) | ISBN 9781350299535
Subjects: LCSH: Political science–Africa. | Political science–Study and teaching–Africa.
Classification: LCC JA84.A35 P65 2024 (print) | LCC JA84.A35 (ebook) | DDC 320.096–dc23/eng/20230424
LC record available at https://lccn.loc.gov/2023019787
LC ebook record available at https://lccn.loc.gov/2023019788

ISBN: HB: 978-1-3502-9950-4
PB: 978-1-3502-9949-8
ePDF: 978-1-3502-9952-8
eBook: 978-1-3502-9951-1

Series: Africa Now

Typeset by Deanta Global Publishing Services, Chennai, India
Printed and bound in Great Britain

To find out more about our authors and books visit www.bloomsbury.com and sign up for our newsletters.

Contents

Illustrations

Figures

Tables

Acknowledgements

This collection was compiled as an outcome of the conference 'The Political Science Discipline in Africa: Freedom, Relevance, Impact' held from 31 October to 2 November 2019 in Accra, jointly organized by the Nordic Africa Institute, Association of African Universities (AAU) and Council for the Development of Social Science Research in Africa (CODESRIA). We are very grateful to the two organizations for bringing together researchers to share their insights on the challenges and opportunities facing scholars of political science in Africa today. We wish to thank all the participants who agreed to submit papers and go through the publication process. A few authors were added as the review process identified major gaps that would undermine the quality of this book. Some were identified at the 2021 Conference of the African Association of Political Science (AAPS).

We wish to thank Anna Mattsson for her sterling editorial assistance and two anonymous reviewers whose critique and advice helped strengthen this collection. Juliet Gillies helped with substantive language editing and Naledi Ramontja prepared the index.

Olivia Dellow and Nick Wolterman from Bloomsbury and Henrik Alfredsson from the Nordic Africa Institute provided crucial publishing support.

The responsibility for the content remains that of the editors and contributors, of course.

Contributors

Isa Adamu holds a master's degree in political science from the University of Buea in Cameroon.

Olugbemiga Samuel Afolabi is Professor of Democratic and Security Studies at the Department of Political Science, Obafemi Awolowo University in Ile-Ife, Nigeria, where he obtained a PhD, MSc and BSc in Political Science. He was a former head of department of Political Science, Obafemi Awolowo University, a research fellow at University of Johannesburg, South Africa, and DAAD senior fellow at University of Zambia, Lusaka, Zambia. His research interests include democracy, elections, security, conflicts and peacebuilding. He is well-published in these research areas.

Adigun Agbaje is Professor of Political Science at the University of Ibadan, where he also served as Dean at the Faculty of the Social Sciences and Deputy Vice-Chancellor. He was Director at the Centre for Social Science Research and Development, Ikorodu, and Director-General of the Obafemi Awolowo Institute of Government and Public Policy, Lagos. He is the author and co-editor of over ten books, including *Institutions and Popular Will in Africa's Search for Democracy, Development and Peace: Essays in Honour of Professor Oyeleye Oyediran* (2023).

Olumuyiwa Babatunde Amao is a research fellow at the Centre for Gender and Africa Studies at the University of the Free State, South Africa. He obtained doctorate degree in politics from the University of Otago in New Zealand. His research focuses on the decolonization of the foreign policy literature on Africa to reflect the role of 'agency' rather than 'structure'. Dr Amao is currently completing a book on the application of the meta-theoretical approach of analytic eclecticism to the understanding and interpretation of the foreign policy and intervention behaviour of regional powers in Africa.

Kwadwo Appiagyei-Atua is Associate Professor at the School of Law, University of Ghana, Legon, Accra, where he teaches public international law and international human rights law. He is also Adjunct Professor of Human Rights Law at the Centre for Human Rights, University of Pretoria, South Africa and the Centre for Human Rights, National University of Ireland, Galway. Kwadwo is a member of the Ghana Bar, a board member of the Global Observatory on Academic Freedom, Central European University in Vienna, Austria and Ambassador at the Magna Charta Observatory, University of Bologna, Italy. His research interests are post-colonial analysis of the historiography of international law, human rights and academic freedom.

Maame Adwoa Gyekye-Jandoh is a senior lecturer who also served as Head of the University of Ghana's Political Science Department from 2018 to 2022. Her teaching and research span the areas of development studies, comparative politics, gender and politics, political and economic reform and democracy in Africa, democracy and governance in Africa, government and politics in Ghana, and advanced comparative politics. Her publications and research interests cover a range of topics including African and Ghanaian politics, the role of civil society in a democracy, civil society-state relations (in Ghana), civil society and political extremism, democratization, gender and politics, migration both within and outside Africa, citizenship and migration, and politics of the developing world. She is an affiliate of the Center for Gender Studies and Advocacy (CEGENSA) at the University of Ghana and is currently a visiting scholar at the Institute of Economic Affairs (IEA-Ghana).

Göran Hydén is Distinguished Professor Emeritus of Political Science at the University of Florida. He has published books and articles on politics and development in Africa over the past fifty years, most recently *Africa and Democratization; Theorizing in Comparative Politics* (2023).

Christopher Isike is Professor of African Politics and International Relations at the University of Pretoria and Director of the African Centre for the Study of the United States, University of Pretoria (ACSUS-UP), South Africa. He is the president of the African Association of Political Science (AAPS), and member of the board of directors of Global Development Network (GDN). His research interests include African soft power politics, women, peace and conflict studies, women and political representation in Africa, rethinking state formation in Africa, politics in a digital era and African immigration to South Africa.

Liisa Laakso is Senior Researcher at the Nordic Africa Institute. She has served as Rector of the University of Tampere and as Dean of the Faculty of Social Science at the University of Helsinki. In 2004, she was nominated to Professorship in Development and International Cooperation at the University of Jyväskylä. Her publications cover topics like democratization, higher education, academic freedom and international development policies.

Ruth Mireille Manga Edimo is Associate Professor of Political Science at the University of Yaoundé II. She is a former PhD fellow of Sciences Po/CEVIPOF in Paris, France. Her research, teachings and publications cover digital political participation, public policies in Africa, migration and citizenship, democracy, expertise and culture. Manga Edimo is an executive member of the International Public Policy Association (IPPA).

Njekwa Mate is a lecturer in Governance and Public Management at the Department of Government and Management Studies, University of Zambia. He is also the regional manager of Southern Africa for the Varieties of Democracy (V-Dem) Project. His research interests include democracy, ethnicity, migration, governance and public management.

Hélène Amélie Molo is a PhD candidate at the Department of Political Science, University of Yaoundé II, Cameroon. Her thesis is on the relationship between law and politics in Africa. Her email is: ameliefr2002@yahoo.fr.

Lebohang Motsomotso is a senior lecturer in African Politics at the Department of Political Sciences, University of South Africa. She completed her PhD in political science at the University of Pretoria. Her PhD focused on self-writing through torture, authorization and liberation of the lived experiences of Winnie Madikizela-Mandela and Assata Shakur. Her thesis explored the intersectional structures of oppression that are formed by colonial, gendered, and racist systems. Her research interests are in decolonial thought, political theory, liberation movements, prison writing, African women's writings and narratives.

Shadrack Wanjala Nasong'o is Professor of International Studies at Rhodes College in Memphis, Tennessee. His research interest lies in the areas of democratization, identity politics, social conflict and governance, which are areas in which he is widely published. Nasong'o has been honoured with the Rhodes College's Clarence Day Award for Outstanding Research and Creative Activity, and the Ali Mazrui Award for Research and Scholarly Excellence from the University of Texas at Austin.

Fabien Nkot is Professor of Public Law and Political Science at the University of Yaoundé II in Cameroon. He holds a PhD from Laval University in Québec, Canada and currently is the head of the Department of Political Science at the University of Youndé II. He has been a visiting professor at Nanjing University in China, the University of Lausanne in Switzerland, as well as Columbia University in New York. His books include *Usages politiques du droit en Afrique: le cas du Cameroun* (2005) and *Dictionnaire de la politique au Cameroun* (2018). One of his last publications is 'Untold perspectives about Cameroon's Economy' in Célestin Monga, *The Oxford Handbook of the Economy of Cameroon* (2022).

Eghosa E. Osaghae, a tenured professor of Comparative Politics at the University of Ibadan, is currently Director-General of the Nigerian Institute of International Affairs, Nigeria's foremost foreign policy think tank. His research interests include the interface between state-level formations and global dynamics and the management of conflicts in Africa.

Matthew Sabbi recently joined the Otto Suhr Institute of Political Science, Freie Universität Berlin, Germany. Prior to that, he was a postdoctoral researcher in African Politics and Development Policy at the University of Bayreuth, Germany. He is interested in political sociology and development politics with a particular focus on the strategies of political actors in local institutional reforms in Africa. He has held fellowships at the Merian Institute for Advanced Studies in Africa (MIASA) at the University of Ghana, Accra, and the Bayreuth Academy of Advanced African Studies, University of Bayreuth, Germany.

Aili Mari Tripp is Vilas Research Professor of Political Science at the University of Wisconsin-Madison. Her research has focused on gender/women and politics in Africa, women's movements in Africa, and transnational feminism. She is the author of several award-winning books, including *Seeking Legitimacy: Why Arab Autocracies Adopt Women's Rights* (Cambridge University Press, 2019) and *Women and Power in Postconflict Africa* (Cambridge University Press, 2015). She has served as the President of African Studies Association and is an editor of the *American Political Science Review*.

Olajumoke Yacob-Haliso is Associate Professor of African and African American studies at Brandeis University, and Vice-President of the International Studies Association (ISA). Her research focuses on gender and women in Africa, African refugees, and African politics and international relations. Her most recent publications are *African Refugees* (2023) and *The Palgrave Handbook of African Women's Studies* (2021).

Siphamandla Zondi teaches politics at the University of Johannesburg and leads this university's Institute for Pan-African Thought and Conversation. He studied at the University of Durban-Westville and Cambridge University. His overriding research interest is on the decolonization of being, power and knowledge. This purview permeates his work on revolutionary political thought, political movements, knowledge politics and research methodology, Africa's agency in the world, and Global South solidarity. His most recent edited books are the *African Voices in Search of a Decolonial Turn* (2022) and *The Polticial Economy of Intra-BRICS Cooperation* (2022).

1

Political science in Africa

Freedom, relevance and impact

Liisa Laakso

Introduction

Links between political science and political struggles are complex but undeniable. This is particularly evident in societies going through dramatic socio-economic changes resonating in their political systems, too. Much of Africa is an example of that: before 1990, multiparty political systems were an exception, but by 1995, it was de jure one-party or non-party systems that had become rare. As these changes were sudden and took place under differing conditions, the outcomes have also differed. By 2023, political transitions had by and large stagnated if not reversed, which is manifest, for instance, in electoral disputes and 'constitutional coups' extending the tenure and powers of the executive. Variations between African countries and the discontents of democratization highlight the importance of local-level developments, but a large part of the literature analysing African politics builds on comprehensive 'grand theories' of African otherness. The focus has been on factors and contexts that distinguish Africa from the rest of the world and the West in particular: neopatrimonialism, weak state institutions and the political economy of dependency. While comparative perspectives and views from outside are valuable, they can only be complementary to the knowledge at the local level.

What then has been the role of political science discipline in Africa during the struggles for democratization? The question is most pertinent not only in terms of practical policies but also of academic curiosity. Yet, very little systematic analysis has been done on it. The most comprehensive collections of political science in Africa were published before the 1990s: *Political Science in Africa* edited by Yolamu Barongo published in 1983 and *The Teaching and Research of Political Science in Eastern Africa* edited by Walter O. Oyugi in 1989. In this regard, Africa is not an exception however. Studies of the state of political science per se are surprisingly few – and those that are available mostly concentrate on American political science. There are two exceptions: *Regime and Discipline: Democracy and the Development of Political Science* edited by David Easton, John G. Gunnell and Michael B. Stein in 1995, which includes also case studies outside the West, although none from Africa, and *Relevance of Political Science*, edited by Gerry Stoker, Guy Peters and Jon Pierre in 2015, which focuses more on thematic contents than regional experiences of the discipline.

It is thus high time to look at the state of the discipline in Africa. In accordance with the earlier literature, what we mean by political science stems from its definition across the continent, and gestures towards how the discipline has evolved in different departments. The analytical stakes involved in delimiting the term include political theory, the history of political ideas, political systems, public administration, public policy analysis, political sociology, comparative politics, political economy and international relations (IR). A survey of the forty years old discipline in South Africa revealed two major epistemological positions 'those favouring quantitative analysis and those favouring philosophical/historical approaches' (Gouws, Kotze and Van Wyk 2013: 394).

Next I will outline the history of political science in Africa, give an overview of earlier literature on it and describe its changing political context. Before conclusion, I will explain the structure and content of this book. First, however, it is useful to clarify our approach: Why freedom, relevance and impact?

Freedom, relevance and impact

In 2019, a Beninese political scientist Oswald Padonou wrote that intellectuals in Africa feature as analysts or commentators of Africa's ongoing historical political struggles rather than prominent participants in them (Padonou 2019). Provocative as it may be, Padonou's claim deserves a careful look at least by researchers of politics. What is at stake is no less than academic freedom, relevance of scientific research and its impact on political developments.

Freedom, relevance and impact of research are immensely important for science and its advancement. They are on the agenda of producers, supporters and users of research work all over the world and with regard to all disciplines. By 2021, only a glance at an internet search with keywords 'research impact' or 'research relevance' showed that workshops around these themes had been mushrooming, while international networks advocating academic freedom have become the more vocal the more internationally interconnected academics are (see SAR 2020).

At the same time, the relations between academic freedom, relevance of scientific research and its impact are maddeningly complex. They all are preconditions to each other. It is not possible to conduct relevant research without freedom to think, investigate and conduct experiments. The impact of research in any decision-making does not make sense if the research itself is irrelevant. Freedom to disseminate knowledge requires an audience, students or wider public that is listening so that the knowledge has an impact on their thinking and vice versa. On the other hand, these very same phenomena are frequently juxtaposed to each other. Too much academic freedom without social responsibility equals researchers not having to care about the relevance of their work. Those who are funding the research are not getting value for their money. Political scientists, however, have been increasingly concerned about the growth of the impact agenda subverting their roles 'only as responsive to policymakers' needs' (Bandola-Gill, Flinders and Anderson 2021: 233). Responding to the immediate demands of taxpayers, labour markets and business includes the risk of limiting theoretical research – not to mention the balancing between relevant and critical research and so on.

This complexity relates to the ways political science knowledge is produced, disseminated and utilized in society at large, and it also varies in different historical conditions. Academic freedom is not only about academic's freedom to express their opinions in political issues. It requires recognition and protection of the principle that disciplinary knowledge is determined by the disciplinary community itself. This takes place according to a rigorous mechanism involving university autonomy and peer review in the appointment of teachers, granting degrees, awards, research funding, accepting manuscripts for publication and so forth. Any outside interference in these practices can undermine the quality of knowledge and the substance it contributes towards public discourse and decision-making.

Academic freedom thus is not limited to the dissemination of expertise distinguishing good ideas from bad ones, but it concerns also the means to create and protect that expertise (see Post 2012; Appiagyei-Atua, Beiter and Karran 2016). By the same token, privileging disciplinary knowledge over patronage, ideology or populism is key to democratic competence and legitimacy. Yet, knowledge is never monolithic. Among other things, it involves disputes about democracy, decision-making and public opinion. Political science, which directly deals with all these questions, is a particularly interesting discipline in this regard. And Africa, a politically heterogeneous continent with rapid changes, a particularly interesting environment to study the freedom, relevance and impact of political science. And indeed, even if not active in political struggles as Padonou claimed, there is no doubt that political scientists have had a role in Africa.

Political science in Africa

Political scientists have been featured in pan-African, anti-colonial and anti-apartheid movements, the post–Cold War mobilization for political reforms, in the continuing and contested consolidation of multipartyism and among the voices of the 'Global South' in the debates of international political economy. Political science education, particularly administration, was useful already for colonial rule, although degree programmes became important only after independence. As the new nations needed capacity for their public service, university education expanded rapidly for instance in Legon, Ibadan and Makerere (Barongo 1983a: 1). The new states also needed research capacity. In Uganda, the Makerere Institute of Social Research (MISR) widened its disciplinary scope from anthropology to political economy, development and political science (Mbalibulha 2013: 127). Makerere soon became an important intellectual and ideological centre in independent Africa (Campbell 1989: 114; Miti 1989: 60).

By the 1960s, political science was still dominated by foreign scholars and Western research foundations. Britain and the United States, for instance, had specific 'study and serve' programmes for junior staff combining fieldwork with short-term teaching at the African universities. While universities wished the foreign teachers to remain longer and were in need of senior staff, too, there were also concerns about the lack of opportunities for local academics creating a vicious cycle affecting the local research competence (McKay 1968; Tettey and Puplampu 2000: 92). Vernon McKay reports that the flow of American and other foreign researchers to African universities in the 1960s was described as 'inundation' (McKay 1968: 1).

To some extent, governments attempted to control this inundation and also the content of the research done under research permits. Kenya and Uganda rejected projects that involved interviewing busy officials, and in Zambia in 1967, the government explicitly banned visiting scholars to study the ruling United National Independence Party. In many countries, it was also challenging for foreigners to get research permits in topics related to refugees and foreign policy (McKay 1968).

This foreign domination, however, did not represent any monolithic political science in Africa, but consisted of different academic traditions. In the French and continental European traditions, politics as a university subject originated from and was connected to philosophy or law, while the British tradition was divided into what Mackenzie called 'humanistic' and 'radical' ones, the former paying attention to cultural socialization and education of new leaders, and the latter to the rational scientific basis of the discipline. Later on, the picture was complicated by an American focus on practical training (Mackenzie 1971: 298–9).

Secondly, as much as political science was imported and applied in Africa, it was also developed there. According to Göran Hyden, 'Africa served as the prime focus for the pioneers as they embarked on defining the parameters and methods for comparative analysis in political science ... a discipline that was trying to free itself from an old-fashioned form of institutional analysis that was empirically tied to Western constitutional democracies' (Hyden 2019a: 2). The task was nothing less than that of understanding political mobilization in the non-Western and peripheral parts of the world, which was particularly critical to the hegemonic power of the United States (Mackenzie 1971: 282), not least 'to find an answer to the appeal of Marxism among nationalist leaders' (Campbell 1989: 119). And indeed, the instruments and modes to utilize, disseminate and develop US-led political science all over the world were many, starting from professional networks and exchange programmes to scholarships and research funding. Adele Jinadu (2000: 2) quotes a Finnish political scientist Erkki Berndtson: 'partly due to the early institutionalization, and partly because of the global hegemony of the United States after World War Two, American political science has influenced the institutionalization of political science around the world' (Berndtson 1991: 39–40).

But Africa soon became pivotal for the multidisciplinary field of development studies, too, guiding the industry of international development assistance with new connections between the North and South (Hyden 2019b). Thus, research cooperation widened beyond hegemonic US and old colonial powers to the Nordic countries and Canada, for instance. And in the early 1970s, liberal modernisation theories were challenged by new approaches to international political economy inspired by Latin American debates and African experiments of socialism. By the same token, Makerere as an intellectual centre was replaced by Dakar, Dar es Salaam and Nairobi.

The beginning of the 1970s was a time when the first generation graduated in political science in African universities and joined the university and research staff, and a time when most African governments had already introduced their first development plans (Miti 1989: 57). On the one hand, this meant an emphasis on applied research instead of basic or theoretical research, which was regarded as a luxury the African states cannot afford. On the other hand, it highlighted the need to determine the exact research needs of African governments for planning and development. To this end, the governments created research institutes under various ministries. According to Abdalla Bujra and Thandika Mkandawire, the more localized these institutes were in terms of personnel, the more confident the governments became in using their expertise (Bujra and Mkandawire 1980: 27). Such strong links between research and the state did not always support ambitious research. The authors continued:

> Like the early period when the *Universities* were under pressure to produce graduates, local researchers in research institutes also came under pressure from government to undertake many research projects and to produce results and reports as quickly as possible for government consumption. These researchers also had no alternative but to fall back to the conventional models and tools of research which they have learned from Europe and North America and which exists and dominates the African universities. (Bujra and Mkandawire 1980: 28)

Earlier literature

The first scholarly overviews of the role and content of political science in Africa did not appear before the end of the 1970s after scholars in Africa had already accused Western approaches, programmes and academic fora of directly or indirectly legitimizing the unjust world order along with the then prominent criticism of modernization theory and its methods. Prominent advocates of this critical thinking in Africa were Walter Rodney, who worked at the University of Dar es Salaam, and Samir Amin at the Institut Africain de Développement Economique et de Planification (IDEP) in Dakar (Tandon 1989: 100). Yash Tandon described this shift to political economy in Africa by a tendency 'to review international relations in holistic terms' rather than by 'pedantic exhibition of esoteric games modelling' (Tandon 1989: 101). Claude Ake argued that African scholars should abandon the Western seemingly objective behaviourist method because it totally ignored global inequality and Africa's dependency:

> In some disciplines such as political science, the turn to quantification has been given so much emphasis and considered so fundamental, that it was referred to as a revolution, the so-called behavioural revolution. Quantification has greatly reinforced the conservatism of Western social science; some fundamental issues

are glossed over . . . other questions are trivialized in the course of quantification.
(Ake 1982: 132–3)

According to Ake, the task of African scholars was to invent 'an appropriate model of
development' (Ake 1982: 193). But since this, by definition, would have challenged the
existing order, it was also something the African governments were concerned about.
He referred to the example of Nigeria, where the National Universities Commission
had noted that there are too many social scientists and that the number of social science
faculties, including also political science, was too high, even though the demand for
social science skills was also acknowledged to be very high (Ake 1982: 197).

Similar views were expressed in the aforementioned collections *Political Science in
Africa: A Critical Review* and *The Teaching and Research of Political Science in Eastern
Africa*. In the first one, Wang Metuge saw much of the teaching of political science in
African universities as ideologically biased and serving the interests of the existing
power structures (Metuge 1983: 50–4). Eme Awa noted that although political science
was a popular subject, and after having completed their studies students were likely
to get jobs, the content of education was not responding to the actual needs of public
administration and management (Awa 1983: 34–5). Henry Ejembi criticized political
science as lacking knowledge of the 'normative foundations' of governance in Africa
(Ejembi 1983: 24).

In the latter collection, Göran Hyden claimed that the whole discipline had 'missed
the boat in the sixties with regard to analyzing, explaining and predicting the future of
development in Africa' (Hyden 1989: 45). According to him, the swing from political
science to the political economy did not improve the situation, because 'its principal
couriers were expatriates. Thus, when governments grew impatient with what they
viewed as "irrelevant ideas" or "unfair criticism" and took steps to discipline the
academics, political science was one of the first subjects to suffer. Thus, in the late
1970s, political science in Africa had lost both its identity and prestige. It was a
shattered discipline' (Hyden 1989: 23).

The experiences from Dar es Salaam, where Hyden himself worked, were mixed. On
the one hand, President Nyerere's 'education for self-reliance' provided good grounds
for critical thinking (Chikwendu 1983: 38–9). The University of Dar es Salaam became
an important academic environment for some of the leading African intellectuals:
Claude Ake, Archie Mafeje, Mahmood Mamdani and Issa Shivji among them. Walter
Rodney's book *How Europe Underdeveloped Africa* with a postscript by a former
Tanzanian Minister of Economic Affairs and Development A.M. Babu, published
in Dar es Salaam in 1972, became influential. According to Rodney, in Tanzania,
development concerns were 'accompanied by a considerably more positive action' than
elsewhere in the continent (Rodney 2012: xi). In the words of Horace Campbell, Dar es
Salaam 'emerged as one variant of "nationalist" ideas in the era of decolonization, but
with the added impetus of a society which aspired towards a different path than the
neo-colonial route' (Campbell 1989: 105). Not surprisingly, it also became a safe haven
for Southern African liberation movement academics in exile.

On the other hand, as Tanzania along with many other African states faced
deepening economic problems spreading to political life, too, the government became

wary of all 'foreign' and critical views. It demanded education useful for the ruling party and research supporting the government programmes like Ujamaa villagisation (Campbell 1989: 122–3). To the extent that such conformity became the order of the day, international interaction across African borders became redundant (Bujra and Mkandawire 1980: 29; Mujaju 1989: 78).

One of the consequences was that ambitious theoretical research in political science remained marginal both in teaching and research. The focus of the discipline, often in the name of relevance, was in public administration and in international relations (Miti 1989: 58; Mujaju 1989: 70). In Nigeria, Adele Jinadu expressed concern over the splitting of the discipline to different departments, faculties and professional associations threatening its coherence:

> Thus, if disciplinary development and institutionalization are tied to 'relevance', as has been the trend in Nigeria, it can be argued that such cognate areas of political science as public administration, local government and international relations that potentially have a demonstrable, instrumental value for developmental purposes and that have ministerial 'constituencies' (external affairs and local government) should detach themselves from political science. In this way the coherence of the discipline is undermined and, as a complementary development, rival professional associations of public administration and international affairs have emerged in opposition to the Nigerian Political Science Association. (Jinadu 1987: 66–7)

But as it turned out, political science, too, became instrumental to the rule in Nigeria. Jibrin Ibrahim did not spare his words:

> The professors of political science who designed a transition programme aimed at frustrating the democratic aspirations of the Nigerian people and enabling President Ibrahim Babangida to perpetuate his tyrannic and corrupt rule for eight years, have clearly betrayed the deontology that guides their disciplines. (Ibrahim 1998: 123)

In balance, however, one has to note that all over Africa, there were also political scientists who reflected the frustrations of the public and increasingly vocal civil society (see Eyoh 1998). The political upheaval in Africa in the late 1980s and early 1990s was even more profound than the earlier similar one in Eastern Europe. It was not only about shifting from socialist states to multiparty democracies but also about dismantling authoritarian rule in the market-oriented states. An important debate analysing these upheavals centred around the ideological premises of the International Monetary Fund (IMF) stabilization programmes in Africa (Campbell 1989: 109).

This was the heyday of the political science discipline in Africa. A good example is Zimbabwe, where mobilization against structural adjustment policies and the ruling ZANU(PF)'s plans to introduce a de jure one-party state witnessed the emergence of new kinds of civil society coalitions involving also the African Association of Political Science (AAPS). Jonathan Moyo's *Voting for Democracy: Study of Electoral Politics in Zimbabwe* by the University of Zimbabwe in 1992, became a best-seller, and not only in Zimbabwe. Moyo did not only question the government's official conclusion that the 1990 Zimbabwean general elections had been 'substantially free and fair', he also showed that a great majority of voters opposed the plans of a one-party state (Moyo 1992).

In 1990, a Council for the Development of Social Science Research in Africa (CODESRIA) and Africa Watch conference in Kampala on the role of intellectuals in African politics resulted in the 'Kampala Declaration on Intellectual Freedom and Social Responsibility' and a collection *Academic freedom in Africa* edited by Mamadou Diouf and Mahmood Mamdani (1994). According to the declaration, 'The intellectual community has the responsibility to struggle for and participate in the struggle of the popular forces for their rights and emancipation' (The Kampala Declaration on Intellectual Freedom and Social Responsibility 1990). In the concluding chapter of the collection, Diouf predicted that even if the political transitions in Africa did not enhance academic freedom, they did highlight its importance and the importance of African intellectuals' social responsibility (Diouf 1994: 335).

Context

Towards the end of the century, conditions for rigorous social science research in many African universities were compromised. And this affected its usefulness for policymaking. African governments became dependent on foreign expertise (Mkandawire 1997: 17). Apart from commissioned consultancy for donor-driven policies, there was not much demand for locally produced policy-oriented research (Rasheed 1994: 103; Zeleza 2002: 14). According to Raufu Mustapha, the ways in which the state, markets and civil society in Africa were conceived and related to each other were not only misleading but also part of the actual political problems there (Mustapha 2006: 189, 199). African academics faced increasing pressure to raise funding for their work. Mahmood Mamdani's *Scholars in the Marketplace* documented the consequences of the profound shift towards managerialism in the running of Makerere University. His own experiences reached the 1980s when, according to him, the government devalued higher education because it saw the university as too critical and later as not economically productive enough (Mamdani 2007: xiii). But what happened in the mid-1990s were transformations of the curricula to respond to the needs of the labour markets (Mamdani 2007: 52). Mamdani describes the general frustration by quoting a Makerere student: 'professional excellence has dropped in this University. There are no seminars, public addresses or debates, yet we have full-time professors in plenty. They are only seen in public when they are agitating for living wages' (Mamdani 2007: 118).

It needs to be noted that this experience was by no means limited to African universities. Rebecca Boden and Debbie Epstein describe the consequences of managerialism in Britain as 'tensions between traditions of the freedom of academics and the requirements of new corporatized organizational hierarchies' (Boden and Epstein 2011: 479). In a seminal collection covering different traditions and subfields of political science, Gerry Stoker, Guy Peters and Jon Pierre, too, discussed how judgements about the impact and relevance of political science posed threats of its marginalization (Stoker, Peters and Pierre 2015: 2–4). This then revealed conflicts over its basic values ranging from radical constructivist views that political science is a way to control social forces and, in that sense, harmful for their freedom, to the juxtapositions of empirical research on 'real world problems' vs. conceptual theorizing, social relevance vs. disciplinary relevance, quantitative vs. qualitative research and so on.

In Africa, the debates of the epistemological premises of political science have been particularly strong in the calls to decolonise universities – increasingly so in the aftermath of 'Rhodes Must Fall' student uprising in 2015 at the University of Cape Town. Africanization of the universities, of course, had been on the agenda since the 1960s but not in any uniform form (Mbembe 2019: 239). In his essay 'Decolonising Universities', Mahmood Mamdani goes back to the discussion between Ali Mazrui and Walter Rodney. While the latter called academics to support national struggles against imperialism, the former was concerned with authoritarianism in independent Africa (Mamdani 2019: 21). Another line of reasoning in decolonizing political science is focusing on methodology. In a collection entitled *Decolonising the University, Its Knowledge and Disciplines*, edited by Sabelo J Ndlovu-Gatsheni and Siphamandla Zondi, Fidelis Allen in a chapter – 'Decolonising African Political Science and the Question of the Relevance of the Discipline for Development' – resonates Claude Ake's criticism that the dominant American political science does not grasp the African reality (Allen 2016; see also Ojo 1983: 59). Adele Jinadu in his Presidential Address for the African Association of Political Science in 1999 formulated the tasks of the discipline by saying that 'Africa must be studied in terms of the conditions and possibilities for its own self-centred development, and the adaptation of its own indigenous institutions to the problems of governance' (Jinadu 2000: 11). One immediate objective in decolonization, thus, relates to the opportunities of researchers to co-operate continentally (see Bujra and Mkandawire 1980: 29).

In the end, it is not only the practical difficulties or methodological issues that frame the state of African political science but the dramatic trajectories in African politics providing unique opportunities and unique constraints for academics to play a role – and sometimes contradictory ones. The aforementioned detailed criticism of Jonathan Moyo in 1992 against the ruling party and President Robert Mugabe did not prevent him from becoming later a politician of the same party. One of his most detrimental legacies as a Minister of Information and Publicity (2000–2005 and 2013–2015) is the legislation restricting freedom of expression in Zimbabwe. In the aftermath of the ousting of Mugabe from power, Moyo wrote:

> There'll never be anyone like Cde RG Mugabe. I'm grateful for the opportunity to have served my country under and with him. I'm proud that I stood with and by this iconic leader during the trying moments of the last days of his Presidency. Democracy requires politics to lead the gun! (quoted in Chidza 2017)

Tempting as it is, one should not fall into the trap of historian's fallacy by assuming that Zimbabwean and Nigerian political scientists should have predicted events following their decisions to be in the service of incumbent regimes from the same perspective and with the same information that we have today. Politics is an art of uncertainties. Political science by definition is not for or against any particular regime. The regime can use political science, it can oppress political science, or it can be indifferent to political science. Political science can provide knowledge for discussion and dialogue for the rulers and their opponents. The function of political science can be to open up space for politics or alternatively to compensate for space that is constrained. The question 'What is the role and space of political science discipline in Africa?' is a genuine one.

About this book

Most of the chapters in this book are based on papers presented at a conference 'The Political Science Discipline in Africa: Freedom, Relevance, Impact' jointly organized by the Nordic Africa Institute, Association of African Universities (AAU) and CODESRIA in Accra from 31 October to 2 November 2019.

The first five chapters after this introduction focus on the paradigms and thoughts of African political science, debates that have over time shaped the evolution of the discipline and debates about the discipline and the quest for decolonisation. Shadrack Wanjala Nasong'o clarifies the problematic of development in the theoretical discussions both as far as the generation of empirical political knowledge and emancipation from oppression are concerned. He divides the theoretical approaches into developmentalist liberal and emancipatory critical ones and argues that the latter has been more relevant for analysing, interpreting, and explaining political phenomena in contemporary Africa. Göran Hyden identifies three 'critical junctures' in the history of political science in Africa when development management has joined it: namely modernization, economic policy reform and a focus on regime change. Referring to Tanzania as a case study, he asks if the current emphasis on investment rather than aid and coordination across national boundaries is bringing a fourth juncture stressing the importance of multilateral organizations. In his chapter, Eghosa E. Osaghae asks if political science is a 'Western' discipline and suggests that comparative politics, as the epistemological and methodological hub of the discipline, presents an appropriate context for mainstreaming decolonization in it. Siphamandla Zondi looks at the decolonization of university disciplines, political science among them, as part of the struggles of students, the poor and the excluded other, calling for a decolonial turn in the whole knowledge environment instead of cosmetic reforms only. To this end, it is necessary to unmask the coloniality of the discipline and of politics as practice. In her chapter, Lebohang Motsomotso clarifies the political experience of colonialism, apartheid and exile through the concepts of marginalization, vulnerability, violence and mourning, and their criticality for political sciences in Africa. She discusses the potential of occurrences such as the Truth and Reconciliation Commission of South Africa as spaces of recognition.

The chapters of the second section look at the teaching of political science and its sub-disciplines. Christopher Isike and Olumuyiwa Babatunde Amao provide a detailed analysis of the epistemological perspectives of the political science curricula by examining the content and course design of political science modules of six universities in Nigeria and South Africa. They show that these still are predominantly Western-centric and argue that decolonizing them can take place only if the state is decolonized as well. Ruth Mireille Manga Edimo shows the importance of policy studies and policy analysis in the Cameroonian context, where research and teaching are not autonomous from administrative engagement. Matthew Sabbi with reference to Ghana looks at how the epistemic claims and historical legacies of social science have framed teaching and research on local politics. Maame Gyekye-Jandoh overviews literature on the rising levels of ethnic conflict in the contexts of democratic transitions and identifies a gap in systematic comparative studies between countries. Her comparative analysis of Ghana and Nigeria highlights the importance of variables such as legal systems. Aili Mari Tripp and Olajumoke Yacob-Haliso's overview of the rapidly growing research on gender and politics in Africa focuses on the interdisciplinary roots, methodological innovativeness and activist-intellectual experiences of this subfield, making its overall contribution to African political science nothing but indispensable. Njekwa Mate investigates the linkage between political science research and education in Southern Africa and notes that the lack of adequate infrastructure is a major hindrance to the use of empirical data in teaching. Finally, Olugbemiga Samuel Afolabi in his analysis of political science research in three universities in South Africa, Nigeria and Zambia, takes a critical look at the 'over-reliance' on descriptive approach and limited resources of methodological teaching.

The chapters in the last section discuss academic freedom and the role of political scientists as public intellectuals in Africa. Adigun Agbaje's analysis of the interviews and self-reporting of thirteen African political scientists, highlights the importance of linkages between the discipline and African peoples where they live in their communities and civic terrains, as well as regional and global platforms for academic networking. Fabien Nkot, Molo Hélène Amélie and Isa Adamu differentiate between two opposed ideas of the role of intellectuals, one advocating practical action and the other keeping a distance from policy praxis. They show that both can explain the contribution of political science to the construction of the Cameroonian nation-state and also the ideological battles within it. Finally, Kwadwo Appiagyei-Atua shows the intrinsic linkage between academic freedom and democratization in Ghana through a detailed analysis of the legislation regulating different aspects of university work.

In the last chapter, Siphamandla Zondi reflects the enduring dynamics in the constitution of the political in Africa and the emerging dynamics arising from or responding to them, the local turn in African thinking included. He argues that rethinking African politics has become an imperative and has implications for how we think about political science alike. The future trajectories of the discipline or disciplines in Africa are tied to the necessity of decolonization and the necessity to have scientific impact.

Conclusion

The overall transformation of the higher-education sector in Africa has meant that the teaching in political science has expanded both in terms of the student numbers and contents of the curricula. Large number of classes requires time and resources often at the cost of research and creative thinking. But the transformation has also brought jointly defined standards and quality assurance advancing the profession both for training and research. Furthermore, datasets like Afrobarometer provide possibilities to comparative and longitudinal research like never before. The fact that research topics today are complex and approaches increasingly multidisciplinary means that much of the work that can be defined as political science is taking place in other departments like communication, psychology or sociology. Yet, division between empirical quantitative analysis and philosophical normative approaches has remained. Also, detailed epistemological analysis of the values and foundations of the discipline and attention to local questions contrasts the excessive specialization of its high-impact international journals and publishing industry.

It is our belief, however, that the observed gaps in political science to address the political realities in African societies continue to drive theoretical rigour in thought, empirical research, training and teaching. The discipline of political science in Africa has evolved through the colonial-postcolonial ruptures and continuities, development regime, dictatorship and struggles for democracy. It has been an integral part of African independence and public discussions about state, power and political economy. The discipline has contributed to the education of whole generations of civil servants of independent states and intergovernmental organizations. It has framed the competencies of decision-makers as well as civil society.

While the relations between the discipline and political power have been complex and contested, the underlying tone of the most influential African scholarship has been no doubt a critical one over time. Research has provided insights into instability and conflicts and contributed to political transitions and peace. Beyond different schools, sub-disciplines and methodological choices, there has also been an epistemological unity: imageries of society and the world as a hierarchy and politics as a competition of ideas (see Alasuutari and Qadir 2016).

Political science has also been marginalized, instrumentalized and suspected by various academic, political and commercial interests. It is a science that constantly needs to defend not only its own existence to those who are funding and using it but also the cause of the democratic struggles it is destined to study. And it is precisely because of those struggles that political science throughout its history in Africa has been relevant and is likely to be relevant also in the future.

2

Political science and the study of Africa

Mapping the theoretical and conceptual terrain

Shadrack Wanjala Nasong'o

Introduction

The main focus of much of political science research in and on Africa has been the problematic of development in its social, economic and political trajectories. Yet, the process of development has largely taken place within a context of political, economic and cultural oppression. Whereas the focus on the problematic of development gives epistemological priority to positivist approaches that are assumed to facilitate the generation of empirical political knowledge, research emphasis on the problematic of emancipation from oppression and exploitation calls for normative political epistemologies rooted in interpretivist or hermeneutic theoretical approaches that prioritize an epistemological conception of knowledge that facilitates grappling with evaluative issues such as the purposes of African governments, the nature of African regimes, the goals of their political actions and the moral-ethical foundations of African states. Many different theoretical approaches have been employed in the political study of Africa throughout the post-independence period both by Africanists in the Global North and by Africans on the continent. These approaches can be divided into two broad categories – developmentalist liberal approaches and emancipatory critical approaches. This chapter seeks to map out these multiple theoretical approaches and evaluate their analytical and explanatory potency.

The chapter begins with a broad survey of the developmentalist theoretical and conceptual approaches to the study of African politics that lie in the liberal research tradition. This is followed by a focus on the emancipatory theoretical approaches that are essentially critical in orientation. Finally, the chapter examines the efficacy of the dialectical method in the study of African politics. The main argument of the chapter is that the relevance and impact of political science epistemologies generated via critical theoretical lenses have been more profound than political science epistemologies generated via developmentalist liberal theoretical perspectives. The former epistemologies tend to be transformational in their intent and implications while the latter ones tend to be conservative and, ipso facto, pro-status quo. The chapter further argues that given its conceptual rigour and analytical potency, the dialectical method is most appropriate for analysing, interpreting and explaining political phenomena in contemporary Africa, particularly issues of democratization, social reform and development more generally.

Mapping the theoretical terrain I:
Developmentalist liberal approaches

From the time of independence, the political science approach to the study of Africa was dominated by developmentalist liberal theories. The key assumption of these theories was that African countries would develop along the same lines of political and economic development as the Western industrial liberal democracies. Among the most prominent theories in this developmentalist liberal tradition are modernization theory, political order approaches and public policy analysis perspective.

Modernization theory: The 1960s through the early 1970s

Modernization theory is based on Walt Rostow's (1960) exposition of stages of economic growth. All political systems, according to Rostow, develop through the same five stages of economic growth beginning with traditional society through the transitional stage, take-off stage, drive to maturity stage, to high mass consumption stage (see Nasong'o 2019). At the political level, modernization theory held that the key to political development was a rapidly growing electorate both willing and able to participate in the political process. As political participation grew, it was expected to generate corresponding growth and specialization of government agencies as leaders responded to the legitimate demands of citizens. It was envisaged that the economic, social and political trajectories of modernization would culminate in the establishment of modern industrial democracies in Africa. The macrocosmic level of modernization that focused on the empirical trajectories and manifest processes of the modernization of nations and their societies, economies and polities was dominated by Africanist scholars in the Global North (Almond and Coleman 1960; Huntington 1965, 1968; Anber 1967; Whitaker Jr. 1970). African scholars on the continent engaged in microcosmic evaluations of modernization that focused on the componential elements of social modernization such as urbanization (Obudho 1983), gender-based inequality (Kabira, Adhiambo-Oduol and Nzomo 1993; Nnaemeka 1998), the problematics of ethnicity (Nyangira 1987; Nnoli 1998), bureaucratic corruption (Chweya et al. 2005) and the prospects for democracy in Africa (Oyugi et al. 1988), among others.

Nevertheless, modernization theory, especially its macrocosmic aspect as conceptualized and applied by Africanist scholars, rested on four shaky assumptions. First is the a priori assumption that ethnic identity is, in and of itself, a hindrance to development, while industrialization is the ideal end of a modern political economy. Second is the assumption that modernization is a unilinear process in which traditional attributes like ethnic affiliations would ultimately erode away to be replaced by modern forms of affiliation to civic and professional associations. The reality, however, is that ethnicity and other forms of ordering societies including clan and caste systems are often revitalized and strengthened by the modernization process as evidenced by ethnic mobilization in the electoral processes in Africa in the context of democratization. Third is the assumption that the modernization process is a zero-sum game in which certain social and political advances along the modernity trajectory would inevitably result in an equal decline in traditional culture and values. On the contrary, it is apparent that traditional institutions often adapt to and co-exist with modern institutions. Whitaker Jr. (1970) demonstrated this in the case of northern Nigeria where the creation and expansion of modem political institutions were accompanied by the strengthening of the political roles played by traditional Muslim leaders (emirs). 'Far from modern institutions having simply driven out traditional ones, elements of the institutions of each type or origin coalesced to form a workable system of power and authority' (Whitaker Jr. 1970: 460). Fourth and finally, modernization theory assumed that traditional attitudes and institutions are inherently irrational and thus a hindrance to modernization or development. On the contrary, ethnicity historically provided the basis for the organization of resistance against colonial rule; it was a basis for adaptation to the uncertainties and insecurities caused by the rapid changes introduced by colonialism, and for mobilization of the nationalist struggle for political independence. In more contemporary terms, ethnicity functions to cushion the individual against the deleterious effects of alienation inherent in the rapidly modernizing societies of Africa by providing a sense of belonging and appreciation of one's social roots in a community. Even more importantly, ethnic movements demand justice and equity in the political and resource dispensation of the moment and thus effectively contribute to democratic practice (Nasong'o 2008: 24; 2005: 97).

Political order approaches: The late 1960s through the late 1970s

A number of developments in Africa and the United States beginning in the mid-1960s led to a shift from modernization theory in the political study of Africa, especially among Africanist scholars. First was the rise of secessionist movements, guerrilla insurgencies and the frequent military coups on the continent. This violent trend debunked the belief in democratic power transfer associated with modernization theorists. Second was the intensification of the Cold War and the commitment of the United States to contain the spread of Communism into Africa via means that were anathema to the optimistic assumptions of modernization theory. Third was the politics of the civil rights movement in the United States and its potential for violence as well as the protests against US involvement in Vietnam, both of which led to the mantra of 'law and order' as the political slogan for presidential campaigns in the United States beginning 1964. The impact of these three political developments resulted in a shift away from modernization's belief in benign political development to a pessimistic expectation of 'political decay' in Africa manifested in 'conflict and chaos'. The foremost exponent of this perspective was Huntington (1968) according to whom the modernization process, instead of contributing to democracy and stability, engenders political instability. It was now contended that democracy is not necessarily a natural or direct end-product of modernization; that modernizing states face six major crises, which, if not dealt with, threaten regime collapse and political decay. These were identified as the crises of identity, legitimacy, participation, penetration, distribution and integration (Huntington 1968). To these six, Rothchild and Curry Jr. (1979) added the crises of national survival and of foreign control.

Political order theorists prescribed political institutionalization as the remedy to these crises. By this, they meant the creation of strong governance structures capable of maintaining political order and stability. Such institutionalization had to be the top priority of African leaders. Paradoxically, this perspective was the antithesis of the modernization approach. Instead of the rising levels of popular political participation envisaged by the latter, the former gave African leaders the license to curtail popular participation in the name of securing stability and order. Huntington (1968: 7), for instance, argued that the most critical political difference among countries is not their *form* of government but their *degree* of government. He admired the Leninist vanguard single party, arguing that though such single parties may not provide liberty, they provide authority and create governments that actually govern. Zolberg (1966) went so far as to argue, in the case of West Africa, that the single-party system provided political order, the prerequisite for successful modernization of African societies. This political order perspective provided African leaders with a sound intellectual rationalization for the establishment of authoritarian single-party states viewed as the most viable political rubric for the onerous task of nation-building and economic development (Nasong'o 2005: 7–16; Nyong'o 1992a: 90–6).

Public policy process perspectives: The late 1970s through the 1980s

In the mid-1970s, critiques emerged to the effect that much of political science scholarship on Africa was too abstract to be of any practical relevance in addressing the day-to-day policy problems faced by Africans. Scholars were urged to descend from their lofty grand theorizing and make their research more policy-relevant. This was coupled by an increasing emphasis on the role of the state in Africa with scholars beginning to interrogate the relationship between the state and its domestic constituencies including ethno-regional groups, social movements, and classes; as well as the relationship between the state and external forces such as transnational corporations, international organizations, and agents of bilateral and multilateral interests. Hence, by the end of the 1980s, the state had become the focal analytical point for African and Africanist political scientists, seeking to understand and explain what Nyong'o (1992b) calls the 'lost decades' of Africa's political independence (see also Rothchild and Olorunsola 1983; Rothchild and Chazan 1988; Migdal 1988). These developments led to the emergence of two trajectories of public policy research that drew from political science and economics. First is the political economy approach whose main assumption is that politics and economics are so mutually interrelated that previous attempts to study each in isolation from the other offered solutions that did not capture real-world conditions (Schraeder 2004: 312). This approach appropriated rational choice models from economics whose essential thesis is that individuals are rational actors that make decisions on the basis of a cost-benefit analysis of the trade-offs between a variety of options. As rational actors, they seek to maximize utility and minimize cost. The political component of this approach emphasizes the importance of understanding the variety of policy alternatives available to policymakers and other interests in society as they bargain for an outcome that they perceive to be in their best interests. Bates (1981) applied this approach to explain why food production declined in Africa in the first decades of independence, contributing to vicious cycles of famine and starvation. In other words, why should reasonable leaders adopt public policies that have harmful consequences for the societies they govern? The answer, according to Bates, lies in the political calculations of African policymakers. Similarly, African scholars such as Ng'ethe (1977), Nyong'o (1987), Mkandawire and Olukoshi (1995), and Mkandawire and Soludo (1999) have utilized the political economy approach to explain the dynamics of national development and Africa's linkages with international political economy.

The second trajectory of the public policy process perspective focuses on public policy analysis. This entails evaluation of the outputs of government policies and programmes. The approach probes and explores the strategies available to policymakers for addressing the social, economic and political problems that characterize the quest for development. The approach is action-oriented and aims at problem-solving. Its main concern is to analyse policy options available to policymakers and evaluate which ones are most germane to the development process. Taking this problem-solving approach with a view to assisting African leaders tackle the constraints presented by inherited colonial institutions, resource scarcity and environmental degradation, Rothchild and Curry Jr. (1979) contend that African leaders are capable of adopting policy options from a variety of strategies each of which encompasses different trade-offs depending on the nature of the policy goals desired by the political leaders. It was against this background, for instance, that Kenya set up the Kenya Institute of Public Policy Research and Analysis as an independent think tank and staffed it with the country's leading political economists to provide advice on appropriate public policy.

Neoliberal theoretical eclecticism: Mid-1990s through 2010s

The end of the Cold War during the last decade of the twentieth century marked a new era dominated by neoliberal ideas. This reality has seen a shift within the liberal political science tradition in theorizing about politics in Africa and elsewhere in the developing world. The liberal tradition is now marked by a new theoretical and conceptual eclecticism. The first is the study of democratization, inspired by the so-called second liberation of Africa (see Bratton and Van de Walle 1997; Adar 1998; Nzongola-Ntalaja and Lee 1998; Olukoshi 1998; Ajulu 2000; Mbaku and Ihonvbere 2003; Oyugi, Wanyande and Odhiambo-Mbai 2003; Murunga and Nasong'o 2006). These scholars share the optimism of democratic consolidation in Africa with modernization theorists. However, they do not assume a priori that such consolidation would be easy or even assured.

The second trend in the liberal tradition, which is a corollary to the first one, focuses on the centrality of civil society in the politics of democratization in Africa.

The first crop of scholars who took this approach heralded civil society, defined in terms of social formations such as trade unions, professional associations, community organizations, women's organizations and religious groups among others, as the hitherto missing key to sustained political reform and insurance of political renewal on the continent (Harbeson, Rothchild and Chazan 1994; Gibbon 1995; Kleinberg and Clark 2000). Subsequent scholars in this trajectory took a more critical position, arguing that in spite of civil society's critical role in pushing authoritarian regimes to open up political space to competition, its democratic predisposition cannot be taken for granted as organizations within the realm of civil society exhibit contradictory possibilities (Callaghy 1994; Murunga 2000; Nasong'o 2004, 2007).

A focus on the role of ethnicity in African politics constitutes the third trend in the current liberal tradition. Herein some scholars contend that the resurgence of ethnic conflicts in Africa was inevitable after the end of the Cold War and these conflicts constitute the bane of African political development. Other scholars posit that the ethnicization of politics is inherently positive as it both engenders and calls for decentralization of authority from the contested national centre to the local levels, hence promoting democratic ethos (see Glickman 1995; Rothchild 1997; Adar 1998; Nnoli 1998). Fourth is the gender approach to the study of African politics. Scholars who take this approach argue that the classic themes on African politics need to be enriched by focusing on the hitherto marginalized women, whose empowerment has yielded more of their numbers in the political arena with serious implications for the nature of political discourse and policy formulation in Africa (see Tamale 1999; Boko, Baliamoune-Lutz and Kimuna 2005; Oyewumi 2005; Nasong'o and Ayot 2007).

The fifth and final trend is one that focuses on 'worst-case scenarios' of state collapse in Africa. With Somalia, Sierra Leone, Liberia and Congo Kinshasa as their analytical focus, this approach analyses the ability of warlords to use their control of valuable resources; including diamonds and gold, as a source of income to fund illicit activities, especially guerrilla wars against centralized state authority. Taking this approach, Reno (1995, 1998) notes that historically, external actors, particularly transnational corporations, have shown themselves to be more than willing to enter into financial arrangements with warlords as long as the said warlords control access to a valued resource or territory. Arguably, however, one must be wary of attempts to generalize from Reno's worst-case scenarios to the broader universe of the continent's states because, for every extreme case of state collapse such as Somalia, there exists other cases of effective conflict resolution and state-building such as Mozambique (Manning 2002). The state of the liberal tradition in the social study of Africa in the twenty-first century is thus characterized by a lack of unanimity on the specifics of which liberal theories are most apposite for the analysis of African politics and society. As the above five trends amply illustrate, the liberal approach entails myriad competing ideas, theories, and policy prescriptions. These differences notwithstanding, scholars in the liberal tradition are bound together by their common belief in the Western liberal democratic tradition as the model to be emulated by African leaders.

Mapping the theoretical terrain II:
Emancipatory critical approaches

Developmentalist liberal theories of African politics were influenced by the experiences of the Global North. They assumed that African countries could and should replicate the development models of the Western capitalist world. On the other hand, critical emancipatory theories were inspired by the socialist experiments of Eastern Europe, China and Cuba as well as the social-democratic systems of the Nordic countries. Critical perspectives emphasize the deleterious impact of external forces in African politics and contend that genuine development will be achieved in Africa only through emancipatory revolutionary struggles that facilitate the inauguration of socialist and people-centred modes of governance throughout Africa. Among these emancipatory critical perspectives are dependency theory, the African nationalist school, world-systems theory and Marxism.

Dependency theory: The late 1960s through the early 1970s

Despite the optimistic projections of modernization theorists, Africa experienced political authoritarianism, economic stagnation and social strife through the 1970s, 1980s and beyond. Modernization theorists explained these problems in terms of factors internal to Africa, especially poor governance and corruption. Dependency theorists focused on external factors and argued that the problem of underdevelopment in Africa was a product of the continent's incorporation into the global capitalist system from an unequal footing. This resulted in the extraction of resources from Africa and their transhipment to Europe hence the progressive underdevelopment of Africa. According to Rodney (2012 [1972]), the spread of international capitalism culminated in colonialism and the incorporation of Africa into the global capitalist system. This marked the end of autonomous development in Africa. European domination, Rodney argues, resulted in the development of underdevelopment, that is, the gradual impoverishment of the African continent as previous development was halted, blunted, and reversed. Instead, under the colonial economy, substandard wages were paid to African workers while no profits were reinvested in the colonies in the form of social services to benefit Africans. Profits were instead expatriated to the metropolises where they contributed to the material well-being of Europeans, a process that led to the development of Europe and the underdevelopment of Africa simultaneously (Rodney 2012 [1972]).

From the dependency perspective, governance in postcolonial Africa has less to do with the management of public affairs for the benefit of Africans, but more to do with the maintenance of the unequal relations between the postcolonial and the former colonial metropolises. The African political elite constitutes a comprador class that serves as the political, economic, and cultural agent of global capitalism. According to Nabudere (1977, 1979), transnational corporations constitute the neocolonial form of this type of imperialism. The local comprador class, who manage subsidiaries of these corporations, or sit on their boards, benefit from the survival and success of these businesses and thus influence domestic policymaking to protect these foreign interests. Such policies benefit only the foreigners and their local allies (see Frank 1970, 1972; Leys 1975). Hence, African governments preside over the impoverishment of local majorities and, as Nyong'o (1989) argues, have to be strong enough to master the tensions and conflicts generated among the masses by this process of underdevelopment. Inevitably, therefore, authoritarianism becomes the established mode of governance in this scheme of things, the process of democratization notwithstanding.

The African nationalist school: The early 1970s and beyond

At the time when modernizationists were shifting to law and order approaches, the African nationalist school of thought emerged out of the University of Dar es Salaam, Tanzania and founded the African Association of Political Science in 1973. Led by Arnold Temu, Isaria Kimambo and Walter Rodney (who took up a teaching position at the University of Dar es Salaam in 1969), this school of thought sought to interpret African history from African lenses and epistemes rather than the colonizers. It promoted a Pan-Africanism that was anti-imperialist and called for a socialistic ideology and front of the people and not just of states. Urging for the unity of the 'progressive groups', these scholars held that the African masses must be at the forefront of the African revolution and not post-colonial, neo-colonial states. This Dar es Salaam debate, together with its counterpart, the Kenyan debate, which occurred contemporaneously, had a great impact on the teaching and raising of political consciousness in East Africa (Kimambo 1971; Temu and Swai 1981; Tandon 1982; Nabudere 2006). The principal premise of this school of thought is that the traditional focus of the critical tradition on the negative impacts of the global capitalist system and national economic classes must be supplemented if not supplanted by a growing cognizance of the immense political power and autonomy enjoyed by African states and African peoples. 'Specifically, scholarships must reflect the indigenous power of African political institutions and actors in their relationship with domestic and international economic actors' (Schraeder 2004: 336).

A critical aspect of the African nationalist school of thought is the promotion of Africa-specific scholarship that builds on African research networks and the interests of African scholars and peoples. Accordingly, the Council for the Development of Social Science Research (CODESRIA) headquartered in Dakar, Senegal, was set up in 1973 as a Pan-African research organization charged with the mandate of promoting, facilitating, and disseminating social science research on Africa by Africans. Its first executive secretary was the critical scholar, Samir Amin. CODESRIA has since emerged as the flagship, premier institution, and principal outlet for critical scholarship on Africa by African scholars (see, for example, Mamdani and Wamba-dia-Wamba 1995; Mkandawire and Olukoshi 1995; Hountondji 1997; Ibrahim 1997; Murunga and Nasong'o eds. 2007). It is the direct product of the African nationalist school of thought.

The world-systems approach: The mid-1970s through the 1980s

The world-systems approach emerged in the mid-1970s and focused on the exploitative nature of the relations between the Global North and Global South. Wallerstein (1976,

1979), the theory's main exponent, analysed the emergence of the capitalist world system, which he saw as a system controlled by the major powers of the West. This system is characterized by alternating periods of economic boom and bust in which the metropolises progress and the periphery get impoverished. According to this perspective, European overseas imperialism epitomized by the scramble for Africa was a consequence of contraction in the capitalist world economy between 1873 and 1897 (Wallerstein 1976; Nabudere 1979). In place of the centre-periphery dyadic approach of the traditional dependency theorists like Frank (1967) and Cardoso (1977), Wallerstein conceptualized an intermediate class between the two, the semi-periphery. Countries in the semi-periphery are neither very powerful nor are they overly impoverished. These are states that wield economic and political power within their immediate regions, such as Nigeria in West Africa, Kenya in East Africa and South Africa in the Southern African region.

According to the world-systems approach, genuine socio-economic development in Africa can only occur with a shift from the capitalist ethos of the moment to a people-centred socialist form of governance. Otherwise, attempts by any given country to attain socio-economic transformation within the capitalist world system are doomed to fail. However, the possibility for the overthrow of the capitalist world economy is complicated by the existence of the semi-periphery. The revolution is supposed to be occasioned by extreme polarization between a small core of the richest countries and the vast majority of the poorest ones. However, semi-periphery countries delay the process of polarization by undermining the creation of a unified front against the centre countries. Semi-peripheral states see themselves as better off in economic and political terms than the countries of the periphery and thus wittingly or unwittingly serve as agents of the metropolises by seeking to strengthen their position in an otherwise exploitative global system (see Amin 1976).

Neo-Marxist approaches: The late 1970s

Drawing from the principles of classical Marxism, neo-Marxism emerged in the late 1970s and affected critical theory on Africa (see Botchwey 1977). First, whereas classical Marxism concurred with dependency theorists that capitalism is inherently exploitative, neo-Marxists contended that individual African countries could achieve 'dependent development' within the capitalist world economy by pursuing auto-centric development (see Amin 1990a). Neo-Marxists such as Amin (1976, 1990a), Nabudere (1977, 1979), and Sklar (1979) rejected the dependency theory's contention that only one mode of production – capitalism – characterized the international political economy. They posited that the fundamental socio-economic differences that exist both between and within African economies point to the simultaneous existence of both capitalist and non-capitalist modes of production at the international, regional, national, and even sub-national levels. Neo-Marxists thus preferred a more nuanced approach that took into account myriad developmental processes and results globally, regionally, and nationally. Second, neo-Marxists argued that it was wrong to assume that the spread of capitalism across the globe has had a permanent pernicious effect on Africa. On the contrary, they contended, in line with their classical Marxist precursors, that the spread of capitalism to Africa marked a major developmental stage in the inexorable march towards socialism, the ultimate end of sociopolitical development. In line with Wallerstein's postulation (1979), neo-Marxists posited that semi-periphery countries have witnessed rising levels of literacy, urbanization, agricultural mechanization, and industrial output; all of which constitute the requisite conditions for the crystallization of a proletariat, the class charged with leading the revolutionary struggle for the overthrow of capitalism and the realization of a classless society characterized by equality of all.

Richard Sklar (1979) went so far as to contend that fundamentally, class relations are determined by relations of power, not relations of production as classical Marxists presumed. Central to Sklar's thesis is the argument that the African state is not a mere reflection of the society's economic system, nor should it be viewed as a sheer instrument of its dominant classes. Instead, Sklar posited a perception of African politics in terms of class competition with varying degrees of class competition and conflict. In certain circumstances, the economic elite may control the activities of the ruling elite; while in other circumstances, the reverse may be the case. The point, according to this approach, is to eschew the notion that one particular class or combination of classes will always be dominant, nationally and internationally, and to focus on the reality of different class configurations and relationships latitudinally in each African country and longitudinally within each country.

New critical trends: The mid-1990s through the 2010s

In the twenty-first century, following the disintegration of socialist experiments across the globe, a shift has occurred in the critical political science tradition just as it has occurred in the liberal tradition. The critical approach has largely shifted away from prescriptions for the inauguration of socialist modes of governance to devolution of power to ensure a people-centred mode of governance. In the twentieth century, the Soviet Union had served as an ideological beacon of hope for African Marxists seeing a path to development that was independent of capitalism. Its demise ushered in a period of extreme pessimism among critical scholars (see Shaw 1991; Ajulu 1995, 2000). This pessimism engendered theoretical revisionism that resulted in a number of new research trends and perspectives. The first trend is a critical review of the process of democratization. Focusing on the role of external powers in promoting multiparty democracy in Africa, critical scholars contend that this is a form of neocolonialism that is contributing to the re-colonization of the continent. Claude Ake (1994) for instance, argues that for the most part, the adoption of multiparty politics in Africa has contributed to the 'democratization of disempowerment' in which the essence of electoral contests is the rotation of self-interested elites of different political parties in power while the majority of the citizens remain disempowered from the political system. Ake (1996) argues further that the true essence of democracy is social democracy wherein popular masses are guaranteed concrete social and economic rights beyond the abstract civil and political rights that are the hallmark of liberal democracy. Achieving social democracy, according to Sklar (see Falola 2002), requires the nurturing of 'developmental democracy' in which collective group interests as opposed to individual self-interest are protected and promoted; and the pursuit of social justice, and prioritization of economic rights. Sklar posits that such developmental democracy constitutes the best political option to the prevailing cruel choice between laissez-faire liberalism without social justice on the one hand, and authoritarian modes of statist developmentalism on the other.

The second new major trend in the critical political study of Africa is embodied in the political economy approach that critiques the increasing power and authority of international financial institutions, especially the World Bank and International Monetary Fund (IMF) over the economic decision-making of African countries. Following the end of the cold war, IMF/World Bank loans increasingly became tied to the conditionalities of economic liberalization in the name of structural adjustment programmes (SAPs). SAPs ran counter to the legitimate interests of the masses and, insofar as they were negotiated in closed-door boardrooms and needed force to implement, were inimical to genuine efforts at creating responsive and accountable governance in Africa (see Cheru 1989; Mkandawire and Olukoshi 1995; Mkandawire and Soludo 1999; Murunga 2007). Scholars in this research orientation argue the case for Africans to retake the initiative in the SAP debate, otherwise the processes of political democratization, economic liberalization and the simultaneous determination of Africa's economic policies by international financial institutions amount to shifting from political dictatorship to authoritarian economism (Nasong'o 2004).

The third critical trend is rooted in the dependency perspective and has two main trajectories, neo-imperialism and post-imperialism. Neo-imperialism proceeds from the premise that the granting of political independence to African countries did not alter the exploitative military, economic, political and cultural relations between Africa and the capitalist Global North in any meaningful way. Taking this view, Lumumba-Kasongo (1999) argues that indeed, the exploitation of Africa has increased and intensified in the post–Cold War period. The post-imperialism perspective, on the other hand, posits that as agents of Global North imperialism, transnational corporations can play both negative and positive roles depending on the nature of the relationship between the international wing of the corporations' managerial bourgeoisie headquartered in Global North countries and the local indigenous wing of the same managerial bourgeoisie in African countries. Sklar and Becker (1999) concur that such relations are not ideologically neutral as they transmit the capitalist values of the Global North to African countries. They argue, nonetheless, that such transmission of ideas, attitudes and values is not a unilinear process but a two-way traffic: 'Members of the corporate international bourgeoisie are just as likely to be sensitized to the developmental values of their host country partners as the other way round' (cit. in Schraeder 2004: 336; see also Falola 2002: 678).

The fourth new trend in the critical tradition focuses on the idea of engendering the social sciences by which is meant making gender an integral element in the analytical approach to various themes in African politics and society (Sall 2000; Murunga 2002). Parpart and Staudt (1990) and Nasong'o and Ayot (2007) for instance, argue that gender is critical to political development in Africa and to all scholarly efforts to conceptualize and theorize the modern African state whether in its historical origins, current composition, or the management of the extraction and distribution of resources. Some scholars in this realm focus on the collaboration between patriarchy and capitalism and the constraining impact of this on the role of women in socio-economic development. In this regard, April Gordon (1996) argues that although patriarchy and capitalism once collaborated to control and exploit women, their interests no longer coincide in contemporary Africa and, accordingly, women have the capacity to design new creative strategies to reform existing patriarchal structures and capitalist development to enhance their own status and improve their opportunities. This eventuality, according to Nasong'o and Ayot (2007), is contingent upon the facilitation of a critical mass of women representation in key policymaking state institutions.

The study of social movements and their contribution to the struggles for more inclusive governance in Africa constitute the fifth new research trend in the critical tradition. The work of Mamdani and Wamba-dia-Wamba (1995) is emblematic of this genre. The authors in this volume adopt a broad definition of social movements to encompass all group activity independent of the state; a perspective that enables them to examine such varied social formations as national liberation movements, religious revivalist movements, ethno-nationalist movements, and community-based organizations of self-empowerment among others. The thread linking the myriad movements examined in this work is a shared experience of past oppression and the perpetual struggle for survival and inclusion in the political process. The potential for the success of these social movements in achieving their objectives is dependent upon the types of objectives they set for themselves, and the strategies they devise for achieving them; the quality of their leaderships and followers; as well as the nature of their ideologies or organizing principles (see Nasong'o 2007: 22–3).

Just like their liberal counterparts, critical scholars are not agreed on any one single theoretical framework as possessing the requisite descriptive, explanatory, and predictive potency to serve as the main guiding frame of reference for scholars in this research tradition. Nevertheless, they are united by their common resolve to confront the deleterious effects on African peoples and social systems of the neoliberal models of development imposed by the dominant social classes working in cahoots with foreign capitalist interests; as well as their commitment to generating knowledge and policy prescriptions that reflect the lived experiences and daily realities of Africans as opposed to that which merely caricatures the experience and realities of the Global North.

Mapping the theoretical terrain III: The dialectical method

A unique and analytically powerful theoretical framework that has been utilized in the study of Africa is the dialectic method. Engels (1973[1940]) writes that the dialectic method is principally a science of the general laws of motion and the development of nature, human society, and thought. Three laws constitute the dialects: (1) The law of the unity and conflict of opposites, which states that the world in which we live is a paradoxical terrain characterized by a unity of contradictions – the integral vs. differential in mathematics; action vs. reaction in mechanics; positive vs. negative electricity in physics; fusion and fission of atoms in chemistry; spirit vs. flesh in religion;

and the elite vs. the masses, rulers vs. ruled, haves vs. have-nots in political science. (2) The law of the passage of quantitative change into qualitative change by which small quantitative changes take place that eventually add up to a major qualitative change – such as loss of a single hair at a time over time leads to baldness. (3) The law of the negation of the negation, which states that historical progress is achieved through a series of contradictions. Where the previous stage is negated, this does not represent its total elimination. The new stage does not completely wipe out the stage that it supplants, it represents the original stage at a higher level.

Ali Mazrui is the political scientist that has put this method, particularly the law of the unity of opposites, to great effect in his analysis of African political phenomena. As early as 1966, he wrote of Ghana's Kwame Nkrumah as 'the Leninist Czar'. He argued that Nkrumah strove to be Africa's Lenin, a revolutionary theorist, while at the same time he sought to be Ghana's Czar, an imperial ruler! In Mazrui's view, 'Nkrumah's tragedy was a tragedy of excess, rather than of contradiction. He tried to be too much of a revolutionary monarch' (Mazrui 1966: 9). Similarly, in a comparative study of South Africa and Nigeria, Mazrui (2006) employs the same dialectical law, arguing that the two countries represent alternative faces of Africa, mirroring the political and socio-economic contrasts inherent in the African condition: Nigeria is the Africa of human resources; South Africa is a land of mineral resources. Nigeria is repellent to European settlement; South Africa is a magnet for such settlement. Nigeria is a mono-racial society; South Africa is a multiracial society. Nigeria is grappling with the politics of religion; South Africa is preoccupied with the politics of secularism. Nigeria is Africa's largest exporter of oil; South Africa is the continent's largest consumer of oil. Nigeria is a paradigm of indigenization; South Africa is a paragon of Westernization.

Mazrui's penchant for the dialectical runs through most of his works, from diagnosing the African condition through juxtaposing Islam between globalization and counterterrorism to analysing the politics of gender and the culture of sexuality (Mazrui 1986, 2004a, 2014). He has analysed the crisis of habitation in Africa – Africa was the earliest habitat of mankind but the last to become truly habitable. He has focused on the basic paradox of Africa's location – the reality that despite the centrality of its geographical and cultural position, Africa remains the most marginal of all of the world's continents. Mazrui has also lamented the humiliation of African peoples; a humiliation that arises from the triple burden of slavery, colonialism, and racism (see Mazrui 1980, 1986). Mazrui (2004b) has explored the historical, cultural and economic significance of Africa to the development of the United States. He contrasts this demonstrated significance of Africa to the development of the West with the combination of neglect and malice directed at the African continent and to peoples of African descent by the West in general and the United States in particular. Throughout this study, Mazrui demonstrates that this is a tale of two Edens: 'Africa as the Eden of Lost Innocence' and 'America as the Eden of Current Power and Future Fulfillment'. People of African ancestry have, he argues, been part of the vanguard for the Edenization of America. But America is also influencing Africa, the first Eden. He observes that the United States is a major force in the liberalization of black people in Africa; but also, black people are a major force in the democratization of all people in the United States (see Nasong'o 2017).

The case for the dialectical method

Arguably, the dialectical method is a most fruitful approach to the analysis and explanation of Africa's political realities. Examples from Kenya help illuminate the explanatory potency of this method. The common idea that in politics there are no permanent enemies and permanent friends is indeed the exemplification of the first dialectical law at play – the law of the unity and conflict of opposites. For instance, Kenya's founding president, Jomo Kenyatta, and his vice-president, Oginga Odinga, were intimate friends in the nationalist struggle for independence, but they became sworn enemies a couple of years after independence. On the other hand, Kenya's fourth president, Uhuru Kenyatta, and his deputy, William Ruto, were sworn enemies on opposite sides of the 2008 post-election violence that pushed the country to the brink, but they became bosom friends in the aftermath of their indictment by the International Criminal Court and teamed up to win political power. To fully understand phenomena, therefore, we must seek out their internal contradictions.

The second dialectical law is the law of the passage of quantitative changes into qualitative changes. For instance, loss of one hair does not make one bald. But continuous loss of hair culminates in a qualitative change called baldness. Similarly, at the social level, change, development or progress is not unilinear. Sometimes one step forward is followed by two steps backwards and vice versa. Note the convoluted and messy decades-long process of democratization in Kenya that eventually led to the promulgation of a new constitution in 2010. Indeed, even when nothing seems to be happening, small quantitative changes are usually taking place that add up eventually to a major qualitative change. Note here the seismic ruling of the Supreme Court of Kenya that nullified the August 2017 presidential election, a first in Africa and perhaps only second in the world. This was preceded by periodic changes in the personnel of the Supreme Court: the retirement of Chief Justice Willy Mutunga brought in Chief Justice David Maraga; the dismissal of Deputy Chief Justice Nancy Barasa brought in Kalpana Rawal whose retirement brought in Philomena Mwilu; the retirement of Phillip Tunoi brought in Isaac Lenaola. It is hardly to be expected that without these little quantitative changes (not to mention the protracted changes that led to the new constitution that provided for a Supreme Court), the celebrated landmark ruling nullifying the presidential election would have occurred.

The third and final dialectical law is the law of the negation of the negation. This obtains in the repetition at higher levels of certain features and properties of the lower level and the apparent return of past features. For instance, when a grain of barley is put in fertile soil, it germinates into a plant. The original grain is negated. The plant grows, flowers and produces even more and better grains, which are harvested and processed in the making of beer – the negation is thereby also negated! Similarly, social development is a constant struggle between form and content and content and form, resulting in the eventual shattering of the old form and the transformation of the content. Like in the grain of barley case, this is a spiral process where the movement comes back to the position it started but at a higher level. In Kenya, for instance, a tendency towards authoritarianism has been noted on the part of President Uhuru Kenyatta raising fears of a return to the old KANU days – the denigration of civil society as 'evil society', the attack on Africog, the threats to the Supreme Court justices, and the deportation to Canada of Miguna Miguna, among others. Nevertheless, we may have spiralled back to some features of the past authoritarian order but we are at a higher level given the political and social changes that have taken place – it can never be the kind of authoritarianism of the single-party era.

The value of the dialectical method is its essential capacity to illustrate the fact that sociopolitical change and progress is achieved incrementally through a series of contradictions. In instances where the previous developmental stage is negated, the negation does not imply it is wholly replaced. The new stage does not completely wipe out its predecessor stage, the contradictory forces are renewed and the dynamic struggle continues. This reality is captured in the popular adage, 'the more things change, the more they remain the same' (see Nasong'o 2018).

Conclusion

This chapter has examined three broad strands in the theoretical approaches to the political study of Africa. Developmentalist liberal theories, informed by the momentous experiences of the Western world, assume that African countries can and should replicate the development models of the Western capitalist world. These approaches are overly internalist in outlook, tending to assume that African politics and development are essentially a function of factors internal to African states. On the other hand, critical theories were inspired by the socialist experiments of Eastern Europe, China and Cuba as well as the social-democratic systems of the Nordic countries. Critical perspectives emphasize the deleterious impact of external forces in African politics and contend that genuine development will be achieved in Africa only through emancipatory revolutionary struggles that facilitate the inauguration of socialist and people-centred modes of governance throughout the continent. For its part, the dialectical method seeks to explain African political phenomena by focusing on the contradictions inherent in all forms of organization that constitute the forces of change and continuity. In the final analysis, the epistemologies generated by the liberal tradition have tended to explain political phenomena within the extant status quo, whereas epistemologies generated by the critical tradition have tended to be transformational in terms of their impact and implications. For the most activist critical scholars, the point is not just to explain the political world, but, most importantly, to change it. The dialectical method, on the other hand, demonstrates the process for such change and transformation. Arguably, the latter is most apposite for analysing and explaining political phenomena in contemporary Africa.

3

Political science and development management

Parallel tracks and critical junctures in Africa

Göran Hydén

Introduction

The comparative study of politics and the international donor concern about managing development are products of the same critical historical juncture last century: decolonization and the need to assist the former colonies in Africa to 'catch up' with the rest of the world. Both started from the same platform – modernization – but on separate, yet parallel tracks. Development management has evolved largely as a policy concern, while political science, not surprisingly, has paid most attention to politics. There has been path dependency but also critical junctures when the two tracks have come together, either to clash over economic policy as in the 1980s or to join hands as in boosting regime change in Africa in the wake of the 'Third Wave of Democratization' (Huntington 1991). In the early 2020s, it is clear, the marginal value and strength of this singular focus on democracy or democratic development is past its peak. That is why there is reason to ask where development management and political science in Africa will move next. Given that they are linked together through funding, their destiny is likely to continue to be a story of how the two tracks are pursued independently yet in tension or support of each other. Thus, this chapter is looking backwards all the way to where it started and ends with turning the focus on the future.

The same platform

Critical junctures are brief spells of time when uncertainty prevails and human choices are contingent on factors that are little known, yet when made, have the impact of paving the way for a new and lasting social order. Critical juncture, therefore, tends to be linked with 'path dependency', the notion that development follows a steady path (Acemoglu and Robinson 2012). The brief period of decolonization in the late 1950s and early 1960s in Africa was indeed a time of contingent choices. Those who were in the position of contributing to shaping the new order included a team of political scientists who foremost wanted to improve the comparative study of politics but whose ideas also spilled over into how development policy and development management were to evolve once the international community made its choice to provide assistance to the new states in Africa. These pioneers of comparative politics were concerned about two things. The first was to develop a theoretical framework for analysis that made it possible to compare political systems regardless of the level of development or cultural orientation. In their search for objectivity, they landed in structural functionalism (Almond and Coleman 1960), a theory that had been initially developed by social anthropologists to compare political systems in pre-colonial Africa (Fortes and Evans-Pritchard 1940). Its main tenet is that functions are the same in every political system, be that a pre-colonial African society ruled by elders or a chief, or a modern society like the United States. What makes systems different is their structural differentiation. The more developed a society is, the more differentiated its structures are. This theory signalled a significant break with previous scholarship in political science which had treated African territories through a colonial lens and had followed an old form of institutionalism that was largely descriptive. Structural functionalism brought in a 'new' political science by laying the foundation for comparative politics as we know it today.

The second thing these pioneers were concerned with was rectifying the historicist scenario that left Africa helpless and subject to colonial exploitation. This was a challenge because it meant conducting inquiries about societies for which previously accumulated literature was lacking. A good deal of their attention, therefore, was devoted to the elaboration of conceptual schemes which in many respects came to serve as surrogates for extensive empirical investigations. They sought inspiration from the Western intellectual tradition of thinking about the nature of social change (Shils 1963: 11–12). They shifted the terminology towards a more dynamic analysis focused on the transition from 'tradition' to 'modernity'. These were the foundation stones of the platform from which the study of politics in Africa and the management of its development were both to take off on parallel tracks. We have come a long way since then. The story needs to be told.

The development management track

Development management is a practical task, but it is guided by theories with roots in economics and political science. It is an activity that has been largely shaped and driven by Western donors working together under the umbrella of the Organisation for Economic Co-operation and Development (OECD), more specifically its Development Assistance Committee (DAC). This committee defined early on, in the 1960s, what it calls Official Development Assistance (ODA) which translates into government-to-government transfer of funds to support non-commercial development projects in African countries. This definition lasted for several decades but more recently the lines between aid, business and trade have become less clear than they used to be. In donor definition today, development assistance (or cooperation, as it has been renamed) is no longer just a sub-sector in the foreign affairs ministry. It is meant to be a 'whole-government' approach, which means that assistance is spread out on many hands. For example, mixing public with private involvement in foreign aid has become legitimate – even among the Nordic donors who for a long time were the last bastion in defence of the original ODA concept.

In trying to support development in African countries, donors have had to address two basic questions: what to do, and how? None of them has a single and clear-cut answer as, for example, the perennial quest for a 'best practice' in the donor community illustrates. The search for *what* to do has been buffeted by factors at a high level of abstraction. One is the institutional parameter. Donors have shifted their view of what matters most: state or society? From a comparative international perspective, this is an issue that all nations have faced as they develop. The experience elsewhere is that society gives rise to the state but once institutionalized as a rational instrument, it is the latter that becomes the engine of social change (Krasner 2009). The other parameter of what to do centres on the regime: Does, for example, a society need democrats to produce democracy or do democratic institutions, once in place, produce democrats? The international experience is varied. In European countries, experience suggests that the evolution of democratic institutions may have been the independent variable while in the United States, the Founding Fathers, the architects of the 1787 Constitution, may be credited with the country's evolution into a democratic society. Their moment in history was indeed a critical juncture that laid the ground for a social and political order which has evolved and survived to this day.

When it comes to *how* to manage development, the donors have varied in their approach over the years between trusting the African governments to do the right thing and mistrusting them by setting conditions for their support, as well as finding a compromise position in the form of partnership (Edgren 2003). The development management track since it left the modernization platform may be sketched as demonstrated next.

As suggested in the Table 3.1, each phase has its own characteristics from strategic aim to operational method. To fully understand how development management has shifted over the past six decades, a little fuller portrait is in place.

Table 3.1 Development Management in Africa, 1960–2020

		⟶	
Years	1960s–1970s	1980s–1990s	2000s–2010s
Phase	Modernization	Neoliberalism	Good governance
Aim	Getting society right	Getting state right	Getting regime right
Approach	Ownership	Donorship	Partnership
Process	Institution-building	Institutional reform	Institutional consolidation
Method	Technical assistance	Economic conditionalities	Diplomatic pressure

Modernization

The first phase of development management is most appropriately labelled after the platform from which it took off. The philosophy underpinning it may have been ethnocentric, but it was not explicitly ideological. The focus was on society and in the African context, to help society transit from what was perceived as 'traditional' to 'modern' values. The objective, therefore, was to get African society to become more like those in the West. The premise was that the starting point must be the African reality. Local ownership was considered vital for progress. The challenge, therefore, was to build institutions from 'within', that is, from the foundational values in the African context. Members of the younger generation in African countries were sent to America or Europe to acquire the necessary scientific skills to carry on this task in their home country while Western experts at the same time were sent off to Africa to advise decision-makers in public and private institutions.

The Nordic countries played a prominent role by dispatching their own 'experts'. It is worth remembering who this first generation of aid workers were. They were typically drawn from the fields that had been key in the development of these countries: producer cooperatives, trade unions and adult education (e.g. Johnsson, Nyström and Sundén 1983; Hultin 1985). This Nordic aid personnel worked closely with African counterparts and helped in the modernization effort across vital economic and social sectors while also acquiring insights into how development assistance may be best organized as a more systematic and long-term activity. It is no coincidence that the new aid administration was largely built on their shoulders once they returned to their respective home country in the north.

Tanzania is a good case study of this first phase. Donors were generally favourable to local policy initiatives and President Nyerere's *ujamaa* experiment was exactly what they were looking for: a country-wide rural development initiative that also stressed the importance of equality. It was not only the Nordic countries that embraced this ideology. Even the others, not the least the World Bank, were at that time viewing this form of non-Marxian socialism as a step in the right direction. There was in fact great enthusiasm in the international donor community, and Tanzania, while turning increasingly to China for ideological inspiration, was generously rewarded with grants from Western sources. Steering a middle road between McNamara (the then World Bank President) and Mao, however, proved too much for Nyerere. From having originally taken the position that moving into communal villages – his main strategy – would be voluntary, he gradually shifted to a Maoist position and made it compulsory! Neo-Marxist scholars at the time (e.g. Cliffe and Saul 1973; von Freyhold 1979) were still critical of the Tanzanian socialist venture for not being radical or revolutionary enough. The real 'whistle-blowers', however, were the Nordic aid workers serving the cooperative movement in the country (Hyden 1974; 1975). They saw their own work and not the least that of their Tanzanian counterparts going to waste as the strong cooperative movement that had been the backbone of the country's rural development was now crashing under the burden of complying with ill-conceived directives from government bureaucrats, especially its regional and area commissioners. The latter half of the 1970s witnessed a clear decline in enthusiasm for Tanzania among Western donors, although it took almost a decade for the Nordic countries to extinguish the awe that they had developed for Tanzania earlier.

Neoliberalism

The Tanzanian story is instructive because it marked the end of the first period when donors were ready to support local initiatives without first questioning their feasibility. Donors had shared with their African government counterparts the political enthusiasm that accompanied independence. It was as if only the sky were the limit. The position, therefore, that the international donor community adopted after the World Bank had published its critical report on Africa in the early 1980s (World Bank 1981) became a rude awakening for African governments. Not only did the donors now ignore Africa's own effort to deal with the economic crisis that had developed in the late 1970s – the Lagos Plan of Action – but they also joined hands to insist on policy reforms as a precondition for aid. In other words, African governments went from having taken for granted that their policies were effective and legitimate to one where they were now rejected out of hand. As a policy cartel, the donors took over the African development agenda. A period of donorship had been started and it was to last until the end of the century.

This turn in development management occurred at the same time as a global ideological shift took place away from relying on the state to viewing the market as the prime driver of change. The new policy agenda that African governments reluctantly agreed to follow focused on 'cutting the state to size' and introduced institutional reforms aimed at reducing the power of governments. In one important respect, this new policy orientation made sense. It freed up markets to producers, not least the peasant farmers, who had been heavily taxed in the previous state-dominated system. Because it hit right at the heart of political power, however, African governments went along only half-heartedly. The introduction of the New Public Management (NPM) approach to running government was a poor fit in an administrative culture that was built on seniority and hierarchical authority (Hope 2001). Previous administrative reform efforts had been largely a matter of tinkering with existing organizational structures but the NPM involved a sharing of power between heads of government and public sector managers that was much more fundamental. The notion that public managers should enjoy institutional and professional autonomy has proved to be a hard nut to crack in the African context. Politically appointed or elected leaders have continued to interfere with these officially independent bodies to increase their access to patronage resources. This type of 'state capture' is a main reason why African countries tend to score low on Transparency International's Corruption Perception Index (CPI).

The period of donorship began to come to an end in the late 1990s when influential donors, like the Nordics in collaboration with the British, realized that conditionalities do not necessarily work in favour of greater aid effectiveness. Taking the 'moral high ground' in policy discourse with African governments had backfired in many instances and the new donor doubts pointed in the direction of a more even relationship. This reorientation took several years to materialize and was eventually confirmed in the 2005 Paris Declaration. It affirmed what had agreed upon in the years leading up to the Declaration: the value of partnership.

Good governance

While the shift from modernization to neoliberalism had been quite controversial in Africa, because it was viewed largely as a donor demand, the move to the phase of good governance was relatively non-conflictual. There was a built-up demand in African countries for better governance, especially free elections and multiparty politics, and even if this reorientation posed a potential threat to government, political leaders had little choice but to accept this new situation. Even old autocrats like Daniel arap Moi in Kenya were ready to accept the emerging democratization agenda – albeit hesitantly – which was supported as much domestically as internationally. Members of the donor community could afford to retreat into a position of partner where the leadership would be taken by local political actors. While donors, therefore, have confined their role to funding democratic development projects and programmes, their support has been directed primarily to civil society organizations since governments have shown less enthusiasm in adopting good governance. This has put them in an awkward position in many African countries, for example, Rwanda, which is doing very well in development terms by following its own top-down approach to policy implementation despite its marginalization of local democracy (Hasselskog and Schierenbeck 2015; Huggins 2017). By taking the position as partner, donors have less opportunity to directly influence the course of events in African countries. They have confined themselves to helping with consolidating institutions rather than reforming them as tried in the previous phase. This is fine when public institutions proceed on a good governance path, but it creates trouble especially if a government violates the fundamental tenets of foreign aid such as being free from corruption and being implemented with the public interest in mind. Western governments have had to deviate from being just partners in quite a few cases where corruption scandals have affected the trust they have placed in their African partners. The partnership ideology has also elevated the relation to the highest political level. Thus, any intervention has had to be conducted by diplomats – not just the aid administrators. This has obviously politicized the partnership relation to the point where African governments are increasingly claiming greater ownership of foreign aid and being free to allocate the external funds in accordance with their own priority. The result is that the partnership model is increasingly in question. With the new global situation in which bilateral foreign aid is less important, and in Africa increasingly overshadowed by government interest in attracting foreign investors, it looks more and more as if development management, as we have known it for sixty years, may lose its prominence, if not existence. One of the victims of this trend would be democracy aid. The future of democracy in Africa would be a matter for Africans alone to defend and promote in an uncertain political environment.

The political science track

The study of politics in Africa has been an integral part of comparative politics, one of the fields within the discipline. It has received theoretical input and inspiration from studies of other regions of the world, but it is important to remember that when this field emerged in the 1960s, the African region had the most prominent place. The birth of comparative politics was first and foremost about being able to incorporate into comparison countries like those in Africa which previously had been left out of attention and treated as just 'backward'. What we have learned over the years is that politics in Africa does not easily lend itself to comparison within theoretical frameworks that lay claim to universal application. At the same time, it is important to acknowledge that Africa is not different because of its 'essence', that is, culture, but because of its economic structures which are the outcome of a combination of colonialism and underdevelopment.

Like development management, the study of politics in Africa has gone through separate phases, largely coinciding in time with those identified earlier for donor engagement. The first phase was primarily devoted to exploring the region through empirical research. There were voids to fill and thus, it focused on a wide range of issues. Structural functionalism that provided the impetus for this new focus on Africa was too general to serve as an operational frame. Instead, other theories were used in an expedient fashion to help explain the fresh reality that was uncovered. The second phase was one of theoretical simplification, characterized by the divergence that existed between those that focused on agency by falling back on a rational choice theory, on the one hand, and those, on the other, who relied on a neo-Marxist theory to explain the structural forces that determine African politics and development. While development management brought the key actors together in a cartel to influence African governments, political scientists during this same second phase were more divided than ever. It was only in their third phase that a common ground began to emerge again as the field turned to the study of democratization. Even if differences remained, they were shared within one and the same discourse. The political science track over the past six decades is summarized in Table 3.2.

Each phase deserves a little more elaboration so that the evolution of political science on the continent is viewed not only in its wider disciplinary setting but also in how its track is parallel with the way development management has proceeded.

Table 3.2 Political Science in Africa, 1960–2020

Years	1960s–1970s	1980s–1990s	2000s–2010s
Phase	Modernization	Economic policy	Political regime
Aim	Exploring	Simplifying	Mainstreaming
Method	Case studies	General theory	Democratic theory
Effects	Spotty knowledge	Thin knowledge	Focused knowledge
Orientation	Africanist	Ideological	Professional

Modernization

Structural functionalism was a bold attempt to create a general framework for the study of politics by portraying it in the form of an input-output system that changes like an organism through the dynamic interaction of its parts. In this perspective, there was no single political model that was superior to others; theirs was placed neutral. This was a great leap forward from the days when students of government had focused their research on the pros and cons of parliamentarism and presidentialism. The world of political science was no longer just about Europe and the Americas; it included Africa too. The problem with structural functionalism was that it was difficult to operationalize. For that reason, it never really took off. Instead, it was roundly criticized for its weakness in explaining modernization.

One line of criticism questioned the tendency to treat social change as a cluster of internally compatible variables that 'keep the system going' regardless of challenges to its legitimacy. As Huntington (1965) was one of the first to point out, if one unpacks the concept and treat selective aspects of it, e.g. institutions, one finds that modernization may strengthen instead of weakening traditional institutions and values, and rapid social change in one sphere may serve only to inhibit change in another. A second line directed its attention to the notion that tradition and modernity represent two mutually exclusive, functionally interdependent clusters of attributes. Rudolph and Rudolph (1967) showed in their research in India that in many instances 'traditional' institutions and values may facilitate rather than impede social change. Modernization, therefore, cannot be equated simply with the destruction of tradition because the latter is not a prerequisite of modernization (Tipps 1973). Nisbet (1969: 190–1) summarized the problems with this first attempt at comparative analysis by arguing that it is hardly more than a shoring-up of the idea of progressive development generally and, more particularly, of the belief that the recent history of the West could be taken as evidence of the direction in which mankind as a whole *would* move, and flowing from this, *should* move. A prominent African scholar, Ali Mazrui (1968: 82), referred to the assertion of these ideas of social evolution as 'the self-confidence of ethnocentric achievement'. Despite this and other forms of criticism, the view of the political system as an organism that evolves using its own energy served to legitimize what became the main research aim during 1960–70 – the exploration of politics in Africa. It was typically performed as country cases, and it produced a much richer understanding of the nature of politics on the continent. Those were the years when such concepts as 'clientelism', 'neo-patrimonialism' and 'Big Man politics' were coined and became part of political science discourse not just in Africa but elsewhere as well (see e.g. Lemarchand 1972; Ekeh 1975). Another theme that received much attention from the early political scientists was national integration and nation-building. Two volumes that stand out from these years is Aristide Zolberg's work on Ghana and the Ivory Coast (Zolberg 1966) and Crawford Young's research on national integration in Zaire – today's Democratic Republic of the Congo (Young 1976).

There was generous funding available from American private foundations, especially Ford and Rockefeller, which supported 'area studies' around the world as part of America's growing role as an emerging world leader. This support included scholarships for young African scholars to study at US universities. Thus, the exploratory research that took place in the first phase was shared between young US and European researchers as well as those Africans who got their doctoral education at US universities. It was a massive enrichment of knowledge, but it was spotty in the sense that it was conducted largely as case studies with no dominant theory guiding it.

Economic policy

The second phase was a product of thinking about development in donor circles but also the result of the internal dynamics in the field of comparative politics. There was a growing sense in the late 1970s that African political science, as it had evolved in the first phase, was not policy-relevant enough. Economics was emerging as the discipline with a monopoly on development policy knowledge which scholars like Robert Bates challenged with his political analysis of economic policy in Kenya and Tanzania (Bates 1981). His analysis reflected the broader change that was taking place in the political science discipline at large and came to have an influence on scholars beyond the circle of Africanists who were forced to address his contribution to remain relevant. A majority was sceptical for two reasons. One was the oversimplification that his rational choice theory brought to the study of a region of the world where the institutions that make rational choice policy-relevant are largely missing or at least very weak (e.g. Young 1994; and Herbst 2000). The other was its overemphasis on agency and neglect of structure. One line of argument was that it completely negates the institutional reality on the ground in Africa, as argued by Chabal and Daloz (1999). Africa has its own dynamics and will not change merely because of policies based on rational choice. Another line pursued, for example, by Peter Anyang Nyong'o (1989) and Thandika Mkandawire (ed. 2004, ed. 2005), with a more radical perspective on policymaking in Africa, was critical of African governments. They did not believe that the answer was lying in the dynamic of indigenous society but instead in improving state performance. They pointed to a direction of political science research that has continued to be prominent: a distance to and critique of the political leadership on the continent.

The focus on economic policy inevitably brought ideology to the fore of political studies. The relative dominance that the donors had acquired in the field of development management exacerbated this trend. African scholars outside the mainstream economics discipline were uncomfortable with the neoliberal association of rational choice theory and ended up, therefore, in more radical positions, often inspired by Neo-Marxist theory. The fact that very few of them continued to interpret African politics in such a perspective suggests that a major reason for their embrace of it was opposition to the neoliberal/rational choice paradigm. Once its marginal value was gone, these scholars joined the mainstream in the field. The overall conclusion about the production of knowledge in political science during this second phase is that because it was ideological, it was thin and lacked enough depth to last.

Political regime

The last phase signals a coming together of sorts with a focus on regime change. The basic premise of the third wave of democratization has been accepted as the common foundation for political science research even though there remains variation in what aspects of regime change get primary attention. Some scholars, like Lindberg (2006), emphasize the role of elections in bringing about democracy while others argue that a vibrant civil society is the key (Monga 1996), and yet others maintain that raising civic consciousness is what matters most (Mamdani 1996; Bratton and Logan 2006). African scholars like Ninsin (1998) and Jinadu (2004) have contributed by highlighting the peculiarities of democratization in multi-ethnic societies through case studies of Ghana and Nigeria respectively.

The interesting thing about political science research in Africa since the turn of the century has been the effort to integrate it into the mainstream of comparative politics. This has led to a form of scholarship that stresses what Africa has in common with other regions of the world. This ambition is evident at two levels. The first is the integration of South African political science into the wider African political science community. This has taken place by opening borders that were once closed. Researchers from various African countries have been able to secure positions at South African universities and South Africans are taking a greater interest in the politics of other African countries. This means that the research agenda across the continent is increasingly identical focusing, as suggested above, on various dimensions of democratization.

The second level of integration occurs in professional publications where editors are looking for articles or books that focus on how African politics compare in an international context. Thus, for example, analysing African countries using global data, whether on democracy or corruption, has become an increasingly common research preoccupation. While this scholarship has been methodologically a notch above what was done earlier, the problem with trying to fit Africa into global comparative frames is that the knowledge which is produced is quite partial. It offers a portrait of the region that does not really do justice to the full complexity of governing regimes that are established to run multi-ethnic societies. Democratic theory is based on the historical experience of societies in Europe and America and the conditions that facilitated democratization in those countries are not present or replicated in contemporary African societies. Thus, while some criticism can be made of how African governments have responded to the call for regime change, brushing them off as merely interested in their own power is far too easy and rarely a fair assessment of what it means to govern an African country.

The marginal value of democratic theory has been in decline in the last few years as democracy itself has been backsliding in many parts of the world. Apart from the normative purpose it serves in activist circles, it is not a great aid to analysing governance in Africa. Countries in the region are still developing and democratizing which means that they need to be analysed in their wider socio-economic and political context, as Ake (1996) emphasized. Democracy needs to be treated not just as an independent but dependent variable too.

Critical junctures

Development management and political science research have largely been pursued independently of each other. There have been flows of ideas back and forth, but it is only on three occasions that they have come together in what is described in this chapter as 'critical junctures'. The first was at the very inception when both were anchored in modernization. The second was when the donor community turned around from accepting African ownership of the policy agenda to insisting on itself owning it. This 'donorship' phase was influenced by theoretical changes in both economics and political science. The early 1980s was a short spell in which uncertainty about the future prevailed and donors took advantage of research to pave the way for economic policy reform. Because it was such a drastic break with the previous phase, it split the political science research community in two groups: one going along with a new research agenda, and second, as we have seen, looking for a radical alternative rooted in structural explanations of Africa's development. The third such critical juncture was when researchers and donors found a common ground in a focus on regime change. The question in the early 2020s is whether this phase has run its course. Are we approaching a fourth critical juncture?

The donor community may already feel that the whole issue of development management is at such a juncture. Bilateral aid for development is losing much of its prominence as African governments increasingly insist on their political sovereignty and express their preference for investment rather than aid. There is also growing dissatisfaction with how African governments have responded to the calls for regime change. Tanzania is once more an interesting case study. Having been strongly embraced by the Nordic donors, Tanzania has more recently found itself a target of criticism from the West. The memory of President Magufuli's anti-corruption measures during his first year in power has become overshadowed by the more repressive measures his government has taken against the political opposition and other critics in society. It is experiences like these that make politicians in the West question the value of trying to reform African governments. To the extent that they wish foreign aid for development management to continue, they are increasingly stressing the importance of working through multilateral organizations to tackle, for example, climate change and human rights violations. The coronavirus pandemic has reinforced this inclination. Problems are increasingly global and need coordination across national boundaries.

The political science research community has its own challenges. While there is merit in the ambition to mainstream political science in Africa to make it an integral part of the wider field of comparative politics, there is also a pull in the direction of an African political science, that is, one that looks at research through an African lens. None of these alone would be helpful if allowed to dominate the field. As suggested earlier, mainstreaming thins the knowledge base; localizing or Africanizing it carries the risk of parochialism. Furthermore, as African political scientists learned in the 1980s, the 'ideologization' of the research agenda quickly turns into a blind alley rather than the road forward. Because democratic theory has lost much of its prominence in the discipline, there is room for students of politics in Africa to make an inroad of their own by focusing on the structural realities that determine the nature of politics in the region – without in advance prejudging it by 'heavy' theory. Pursuing such a middle road would be beneficial for both political science research in Africa at large and the promotion of a more African political science. It would contribute to a greater appreciation of the role that structures play in politics, a perspective that is lost in so much of the research on democratization that has stressed the importance of human agency and the rules that guide it. Such a middle road would also widen the space for African perspectives on politics in the region, a point that would be important for those who wish to strengthen the African voice in the discipline such as the Nairobi-based consortium of African universities, the Partnership for African Social and Governance Research (PASGR). Finally, since sponsorship of African political science has been, and continues to be largely external, pursuing such a middle road would be a way of exploring how such dependence might be reduced, if not completely ended in the years to come. In short, a final critical juncture?

4

Mainstreaming decolonization in political science in Africa

Eghosa E. Osaghae

Introduction

In over three decades of teaching introduction to political science courses to first years, I have found two topics to be of special interest because of how they elicit critical engagements on the discipline from as yet largely uninitiated students. The first is the topic 'steering problems of politics', which requires students to pinpoint the great issues and problems that they think have challenged human society everywhere and driven political inquiry over the ages. Many do well to name power, its uses and abuses, and how to keep its destructive propensities in check; inequality; oppression; domination; justice; freedom; human rights; government; conflict; and democracy. If these issues trouble all societies, then there is a basis for having a discipline that analyses them in a manner that can produce general or common ways of understanding and addressing them. The second topic is: What is a discipline? For this, we take as a point of departure, Roseman, Mayo and Collinge (1966) discussion of the 'ingredients of a discipline'. For them, a discipline is a specialized and systematic field of study whose distinctive status is recognized in the academe. The really interesting bit is the listing of the ingredients of a discipline, which they intended as a checklist for assessing the status of political science which, at the time they wrote, was still relatively a young, emerging and contested discipline (the cataclysm of the behavioural revolution was still raging). The ingredients included (1) a distinct subject matter with subfields; (2) founding fathers; (3) a body of classical works; (4) own concepts and 'technical' vocabulary; (5) own set of generalizations, theories, and methods; and (6) disciplinary self-consciousness that includes periodic assessments of standing in relation to related social science disciplines. Again, these ingredients are not a problem and students are quite pleased that political science is a discipline with solid foundations. Nonetheless, questions were raised about the absence of Africans in the honours role of founding fathers which has Plato, Aristotle, Weber, Marx, David Easton and several American pioneers, as well as in the listing of classical works that include Plato's Republic, Machiavelli's The Prince and Karl Marx's Communist Manifesto. This led some to argue that political science is a 'Western' discipline. Did this make it less valuable or worthy of study? This usually generated quite a debate, with the majority considering the discipline worthy of study but that its value will be higher if the African content was enhanced.

The foregoing provides a useful introduction to the subject of this paper, in which I consider how the discipline becomes more 'African' against the backdrop of recent movements to decolonize university education in Africa in general, and the increased questioning – and rejection – of 'Western', 'colonial', and 'White' scholarship and curricula. The whole idea of a global division of intellectual labour that assigns theory and theory-building to the Global North and data generation and theory extension and application to the Global South but more so to Africa has come increasingly under scrutiny (e.g. see: Engels and Müller 2019; Apata 2019). A leading scholar of ethnicity had 'explained' why most theories of ethnicity, for example, emanate from the USA in a rather condescending manner:

> Since the USA is virtually the modern ethnic equivalent of Noah's Ark on the one hand, while its sociology dominates Western social science on the other, any impeccable revelation on ethnicity in America, whether from Harvard or some other oracle, will predictably exercise extraordinary influence on sociological thinking about race and ethnicity elsewhere in Europe, Asia and Africa. (Smith 1982: 3)

It is such intellectual colonialism, which reproduces and keeps Western hegemony and domination alive in its assumption that Western experiences universally define the human that has drawn the ire of anti-colonial, post-colonial and decolonial scholarship and social movements (cf. Oyewumi 1997). The responses from the students' wing of this movement (Nyamnjoh 2016), which has been a lot more political, vehement and uncompromising, have been captured as follows:

> Over the past 5 years, student-led calls to 'decolonise the curriculum' at UK universities have become increasingly widespread, vocal, and insistent. These calls are part of a broader, global movement to 'decolonise the university', whose most prominent recent iteration has been the 'Rhodes Must Fall' campaign in South Africa. In the United Kingdom, high-profile campaigns at several institutions have demanded that the ways in which university syllabi embody and perpetuate the legacies of colonialism be acknowledged and addressed. Of all the sub-disciplines of the arts and social sciences, political theory is ripe for decolonisation, given that it is dominated by a canon of White thinkers, many of whom played significant roles in legitimating and promoting the colonial project (Omar 2016; Nyamnjoh 2016). (Choat 2020: 404)

And:

> The decolonisation of curricula has significance because as well as effecting changes *beyond* and outside the university, it could affect change *within* universities, which remain sites of the reproduction of racism and White privilege (Peters 2015: 643). (Choat 2020: 406)

The point in all this, that the time has come to decolonize academic disciplines and course offerings, is a valid one. But this cannot be only on account of decolonizing for its own sake. It is also and perhaps more because it has become abundantly clear that the universal frames and reaches of knowledge, theories and methodologies assumed in the disciplines are false: Western experiences and epistemologies do not define all humans, and the theories and perspectives that flow from them are not applicable to all formations, systems and societies.

How should African scholars and intellectuals respond to this situation? Reject all that is foreign, Western and colonial, and insist that only what is African is tenable and acceptable – in other words, build a uniquely African body of knowledge? Or critically engage extant dominant perspectives which define the state of disciplines and work through them to formulate and develop perspectives that reflect and are more relevant to African situations within larger comparative frameworks? I believe that the latter offers a more 'scientific' option for African political science. As my first-year students would say, it is the African content that needs to be enhanced. The notion of an African political science is as undesirable as it is impracticable. Notwithstanding the ethnocentricity of so-called universal paradigms, it cannot be denied that the paradigms are products of historical social, political, cultural and economic interfaces, exchanges and imbrications between the West and the rest of the world, of which globalization, colonialism, neocolonialism and postcolonialism represent significant forms. In fact, Fanon asserts that 'Europe is literally the creation of the Third World' (2001: 81). The very claim to (racial) superiority, for instance, developed in relation to non-Western societies. It is also well known that Greek philosophy which is often posited as the bedrock of Western civilization benefitted a lot from intellectual interfaces with Egypt and North Africa as well as Islamic philosophy. African and other non-Western formations and politics are, likewise, not self-contained. The point is not only about the intellectual interfaces and miscegenation, however. It is also about the African content and 'service to the world of learning', as Sklar (1983: 12) reminds us in relation to the highly Westernized scholarship on post-Cold War democracy and democratization:

> We should study this process [of democracy] not only to learn about Africa, but also to refresh our knowledge about the meaning of democracy itself. As the African philosopher, Edward Wilmot Blyden, might have said, in our time, these experiments in democracy constitute 'Africa's service to the world'.

From a slightly different perspective, Ekeh (1983) has also argued that because of the transformations of social structure that occurred under colonialism, especially the dehumanization that accompanied the violent destruction of selfhood and originality as emphasized by Fanon, very little remains of pristine, indigenous or autochthonous African formations. In any case, we know from oral and documented histories, traditions, folklore, arts and other sources that like societies elsewhere in the world, African formations – statehood, customary law, thought systems, economic systems and so forth – have continuously been open to and influenced by relations with other societies. Perhaps the best example is found in the contemporary body of thought taught as 'African political thought' in many universities today. It emphasizes the distinctiveness and originality of thought in Africa, but as Sklar (1985: 21) has pointed out, 'The veil of radicalism [of an anticolonial nature] enchants, mystifies, and ultimately deceives the unwary beholder. At this juncture in the development of African political thought, it hides the awful evidence of colonial descent'.

This being the case, scholars and students should be encouraged not only to consider what European thinkers have said about the non-European world but also to challenge the self-understanding of the 'West' and its claims to universalism (Choat 2020: 412; forthcoming). It is more dangerous to throw the baby out with the bathwater. This, I think, *is* the way to go. The rest of the chapter discusses how this can be done in political science through strengthening and mainstreaming the powerful construct of decolonization. I believe that the construct offers the necessary filters for engaging the universe of knowledge from grounded perspectives, thereby enhancing the relevance and responsibility of political science as a strategic discipline. As we will see, relevance and responsibility have been at the heart of the debate on the utility and heuristic value of the discipline in Africa. I argue that the subfield of comparative politics, which is the epistemological and methodological hub of the discipline, presents the appropriate context for mainstreaming decolonization, and then examine the core elements and merits of decolonization as an analytical framework.

What is decolonization, and what are we decolonizing?

Although decolonization has become a popular concept in African discourses and is used in ways that suggest consensus on meaning, it has quite a variety of meanings and could very well be regarded as a contested rather than settled concept. For a long time, decolonization was understood as the process of struggle against the forces of colonial rule that culminated in independence or what is now called formal decolonization. It encompassed the whole gamut of liberation (nationalism, independence) thinking and actions that crystallized in an ideological movement that had African personality, African nationalism, African socialism, African democracy and Pan-Africanism (which all sought to show that African formations were original and distinct from those of European and other civilizations) as major levers. This strand of decolonization was rekindled by South Africa's independence in 1994 that triggered the resurgence of assertions of African personality hinged on the concept of *ubuntu* (Thabo Mbeki's famous *I am an African* speech on the occasion of the inauguration of the country's new constitution in 1996 was one of the signposts of the resurgent movement). One key distinction of decolonization in South Africa was its use as a counter ideology of racial superiority and domination, as was evident in the #RhodesMustFall revolts against the 'House that Race Built'. This brought racism and its dehumanizing concomitants, which had somewhat disappeared from African decolonization discourses because they focused more on non-settler colonialism, back in.

Other popular notions and formulations of decolonization in Africa, which belonged to what I have described elsewhere as the replacement genre (Osaghae 1993), took their bearings from these foundations. After independence, decolonization became Africanization or indigenization, a process by which many countries sought to replace colonial (European) officials, institutions and practices with Africans and African equivalents. In the economic sector, this resonated as nationalization, a policy that encouraged state takeover of key industries and companies owned and controlled by foreign capital. Decolonization as 'replacement' encompassed the change of colonial names and references: Gold Coast became Ghana, Dahomey, Benin, Upper Volta, Burkina Faso, Congo Kinshasa, Zaire, Pretoria-Witwatersrand-Vereeniging, Gauteng and so on. In Mobutu's Zaire, the *authenticite* or Zairianization policy encouraged citizens to adopt indigenous names, culture, fashion and music in place of foreign ones, and KiSwahili was not only adopted as an official language in Tanzania and most of East Africa, but was considered for adoption as a lingua franca for the continent in the 1970s. The replacement genre of decolonization also found expression in the writings of leading African statesmen, nationalists and political elites who propounded African versions of universal and European models and thought systems to make the points that Africa had distinct and original forms and that, contrary to what may have been inferred in colonialism legitimating ideologies that had civilizing mission at the core, African thoughts, institutions and formations were not inferior to others. This was an integral part of the anti-colonial legitimating ideologies that underpinned the entire decolonization process (Osaghae 1993).

While the foregoing notions of decolonization set the frame for discussing the subject in Africa especially, they do not capture the essence of the concept as an epistemological and methodological tool, which is the sense in which it is employed in this paper. For us, decolonization denotes critical engagement with, and deconstruction of, dominant perspectives of knowledge in the discipline of political science which embody legacies of colonialism, reproduce unequal power relations between the global north and global south, and consign other forms and perspectives of knowledge especially from Africa to the margins of analysis by analogy and dependence. The African roots of decolonization as an intellectual movement can be traced back to Fanon (2001 [1963]) for whom decolonization meant not only complete overthrow of colonial power and structures, but also, more fundamentally, the forms of knowledge that underpin them. In terms of its current usage by global south scholars especially, the 'what' of decolonization covers the whole gamut of dominant perspectives (modernization, neomodernization, liberalism, neoliberalism, race, sexism) that lay claim to universal application and validity, and thereby colonize knowledge spaces (although I should warn that liberal and inclusive usages, which amount to a colonization of everything, poses the danger of deradicalizing the concept and obfuscating its historical contexts). The goal of decolonization is not so much to reject or replace extant knowledge, but to deconstruct claims to universalism, sameness and unilinear growth paths, and mainstream diversity and divergence as anchors of knowledge (Said 1978; Chatterjee 1986; Bhabha 1994; Ashcroft, Griffiths and Tiffin 1995, 1998; Narayan 1997; Chakrabarty 2000; Mbembe 2001, 2002). Put differently, Western and European narratives, perspectives and theories, no matter how highly developed they may be, constitute only one of the frames through which social reality can be analysed, explained and understood; there are, in addition, other perspectives – African, Asian, Latin American – that reflect different realities and offer alternative frames of analysis (see, for example, Houtondji 1997; Lauer and Anyidoho 2012). The object of decolonization, if you will, is to mainstream the 'other', not as a provincial other, but one that can be generalized and from which other formations including Western formations can also learn and be analysed (Amin 1990b; for 'deprovincialization' see Ndlovu-Gatsheni 2018). This genre of decolonization scholarship (also called postcolonial and decoloniality studies) represents an intellectual movement and approach that has become quite popular with Africanist scholars in the humanities, especially literature, linguistics, philosophy and history, who led the critical engagement with universal, global, scientific and Western texts of colonialism and hegemony. They have created the 'other' as alternative narratives the way the sociology of knowledge has generally failed to do. In particular, by emphasizing context-dependent theorizing, decolonization has gone beyond the dualism of (cultural) relativism and universalism which treats the relative and universal as not commensurable, and whose universal does not admit of 'others' (read as 'deviations').

Defined in these terms, decolonization is not unfamiliar territory in African political science and social sciences, which have been critical of the ideological underpinnings of what Oyovbaire (1983) referred to as the 'tyranny of borrowed paradigms', that is, Western and Eurocentric Western theories and perspectives. Employing borrowed paradigms, Zeleza (1997) was to argue much later, implied 'manufacturing' African studies and crises through lenses that did not always fit African circumstances. But a far greater problem was that borrowed and imported paradigms made political science, and other social sciences in Africa, tools of Western imperialism and hegemony (Ake 1982; Arowosegbe 2008). This clearly called for decolonization, but there was no consensus on what form this should take. While some advocated indigenization and Africanization of content, perspectives and curriculum, including the possible adoption of indigenous languages as mediums of scientific and scholarly discourse, in continuation of the replacement mould of decolonization (Wa Thiong'o 1986; Park 1988), others considered it a 'dubious and unpromising enterprise' to seek to replace 'the particularism and ethnocentricism of Western social sciences by slinking off into some higher particularism in the garb of "Negro-African [social science]" with its own specific and exclusive sets of principles and methodologies' (Wilmot 1973: 2).

But it was the methodology that provoked the sharpest divisions, which were akin to those between traditionalists and behaviouralists at the height of the reconstruction in political science. On the one side were the radical political economists who believed that Marxist and neo-Marxist approaches offered the only valid counter-colonial alternatives, and on the other, the so-called bourgeois scholars who stuck to the science of politics approach and were regarded as apologetics of Western paradigms. The two sides also differed on the involvement or responsibility of the political scientist. While the bourgeois scholars emphasized stability and orderly change and pursued 'objective' and scientific knowledge, the radical school advocated revolutionary change and national and global scholarly activism that combined theory and praxis because, as it was argued the responsibility was not only to develop scientific tools 'for achieving a better understanding of Nigerian society', but also to provide a 'practical guide to action on how to transform that society for the better' (Nkom 1993: 196; also Onoge

1977). But even among radical scholars, there were disagreements on the role of the state, modes of class analysis, and relations with external forces.

These issues underlay the famous debates in universities across the continent in the 1970s, 1980s and 1990s, most notably in Zaria, Dar es Salaam and Makerere, which were the hotbeds of radical scholarship (e.g. see: the debate between Oyovbaire (1980) and Bala Usman (1980) in Zaria, as well as among Mamdani, Bhagat and Nadubere in Makerere in Tandon (1982, 1984)). Although the end of the Cold War slowed down the ideological contests a bit and even witnessed a bridging of some gaps (as in the increased concern with issues of ethnicity and identity by radical scholars), the debates on decolonization have continued (the fierce debate provoked by Mazrui's (1994, 1995a, 1995b) advocacy of benign colonialism as a response to state failure in Africa, which Mafeje (1995, 1998) shot down as a continuation of neocolonial scholarship is a case in point). Beyond the debates, decolonization discourses blossomed in several writings on neocolonialism, dependency/underdevelopment and delinkage, which all admitted the impracticability of absolute autarchy whether in development or knowledge systems, but emphasized the need to neutralize the effects of external interests on internal choices (Barongo 1980; Amin 1989, 1990a, 1996). It is also important to state that the debates and writings influenced political science curriculums and curriculum reviews across Africa (see Barongo 1983b), and the adoption of canonical works on decolonization like Fanon's (2001 [1963]) *The Wretched of the Earth* and Rodney's (2012 [1972]) *How Europe Underdeveloped Africa* (which was written while Rodney was at the University of Dar es Salaam) as basic texts. In the final analysis, although the divisions and debates remained, there was some consensus that relevance and responsibility measured in terms of African realities, contexts and needs should drive decolonization discourses (Mafeje 2000), though it seems fair to say that decolonization was never fully developed as a coherent theory or methodological handle in African political science. This, I think, largely explains why the discipline lagged behind the humanities in the reconstruction of decolonization perspectives. Except for occasional spurts that tided with the ebbs and flows of evolving global processes and elicited African responses (such as the second independence perspective that located democratization in African contexts), decolonization took a long leave.

This was until the rise of decoloniality in South Africa in the 2000s. The resurgence of decoloniality as a social movement in South Africa was propelled by unresolved issues of anti-colonial struggles and the slow pace of post-apartheid transformation. The #RhodesMustFall and #FeesMustFall revolts by students denouncing continued racial domination and demanding accelerated transformation of universities as power spaces were high points of the movement, but it also had a bourgeoning intellectual arm that revived the analytical value of decolonization in robustly refreshing ways (Ndlovu-Gatsheni 2013, 2018; Ndlovu-Gatsheni and Zondi 2016; Nyamnjoh 2016; Zondi 2018; forthcoming). Although it retained elements of the old replacement trajectories for the fairly obvious reason that a matching of transformation with expectations was necessary, the value added by the South African revival was a theory of colonialism and decolonization that had racism, racial domination and dehumanization at the core. These vexed issues, which differentiated settler-colonial experiences where the race was a defining element from non-settler experiences, but were crucial to analysing colonialism as a system of domination as Fanon so clearly showed, had somehow disappeared from African decolonization discourses, rendering them more provincial as a result. By bringing these issues back in, South African scholars were reinserting African decoloniality discourses back into more comparatively global and general frames, and it is not surprising that the emerging themes resonated well with decolonialists in the UK ('Decolonising SOAS', 'Why Is My Curriculum White?', and 'Rhodes Must Fall in Oxford') and other parts of the world. The writings of Franz Fanon, Steve Biko and other Black Consciousness thinkers, as well as those of Latin American decoloniality scholars, provided useful anchors for the emergent South African school which was more far-reaching in combining theory and praxis at the levels of universities, knowledge systems and disciplines (Ndlovu-Gatsheni and Zondi 2016). The greater significance of the South African renaissance is not only that it rekindled interest in the analytical value of the concept of decolonization across the continent, but that it came at a critical juncture when African political and social sciences were showing signs of inertia and fatigue in engagements with a vicious form of neoliberal colonialism that had conformity and uniformity within new borrowed paradigms as key elements.

From the 1980s when structural adjustment programmes and reforms ushered in a new paradigm of neoliberal development thinking, the social sciences witnessed a rash of new concepts, analytical frameworks and theories. The paradigm has similar assumptions with those of modernization theory that colonized the field for a long time, especially with regard to Western-inspired universalisms and the location of dependent and peripheral countries of the global south at the receiving end of Western precepts and nostrums. But the colonization of the new neoliberal perspective is far more stringent. First, the economic, political and social reforms, which are its main drivers, are imposed mostly as conditionalities on indebted, weak and fragile states and governments, leaving them with very few if any options at all. The accent on regime change (the installation of compliant neoliberal regimes in receiving countries) ensures that this is the case. Altogether, these interventions seriously constrained whatever was left of notions or claims to sovereignty in the global south. The stranglehold on knowledge production and social scientific analyses was no less severe. Through strict terms and conditions attached to research grants and projects (and lockstep demands by journals and publishers), studies could only be undertaken within set assumptions, concepts, theories, designs and methodologies, and researchers hardly had the luxury to consider alternative frames or think outside the box.

The core of the new paradigm consisted of what can be called the 'fetish' of institutions: the hinging of the character of systems, their functionalities and effectiveness on institutions, for which reasonable adjustments and reforms were designed to build strong institutions (which were, of course, Western in origin and practice) to replace Africa's weak and ineffective institutions. As has been well acknowledged, the neoliberal paradigm shift gave impetus to the resurgence of institutional approaches in the methodological reconstructions of the 1990s and 2000s which saw the return of formal and informal institutions of state and government as the main units of analysis and development (Steinmo, Thelen and Longstreth 1992; Weaver and Rockman 1993; Peters 1999; Pierson 2000). The reconstruction was a major factor in the colonizing influences of neoliberal orthodoxies. An emphasis on institutions is not a bad thing in itself (after all advocates of social engineering repose great confidence in the efficacy of institutions), but doing so in a reductionist and de-contextualized manner that approaches institutions in isolation of historical, political, economic and social forces and one-size-fits-all fashion is problematic. The tendency is to operationalize institutions as apolitical empirical markers whose presence, growth and effectiveness can be easily tracked, monitored and evaluated. Thus, to take one example, elections are reduced to effective regulatory frameworks and so-called free and fair election variables in isolation of the complex factors that make them critical state legitimacy tests rather than routine free and fair elections. The fact that elections and their outcomes remain disruptive even when free and fair templates have been complied with raises the question of how far we can go with analysis of highly politicized societies where the legitimacy and functionality of the state are flawed while keeping out 'politics'. The 'fetish' of institutions has two other correlates with serious limiting implications. First is the renewed emphasis on 'evidence-based' empiricism and quantification, which requires scholarly works to 'say it with figures' and discourages qualitative and discursive analyses (which, evidently, the majority of African social scientists prefer). The works of Afrobarometer, Freedom House, MO Foundation and other primary quantitative data sources serve the purposes of the new paradigms very well, but it is not always certain that the statistics they provide reflect the realities. The second correlate is the reinvention of key concepts to fit the new paradigms. Civil society was reinvented as the vanguard of democratization and democracy and as a check and alternative to the state – at a point the replacement of 'impossible' states with civil society was contemplated; democracy and democratization were operationalized as processes of phased transitions and consolidation centred around elections; governance was defined in terms of transparency, participation and accountability; states were redefined in minimalist regulatory terms; elections, as we have said, were reduced to free and fair variables of voter orderliness, efficient counting of voters, effective security, and so on.

These were the kinds of templates and frames that set the boundaries for analysis. Many social science scholars in Africa especially simply became academic consultants within the frames, and technical and consultancy reports gradually replaced traditional scientific papers. This was most obvious in the field of economics which enjoyed generous funds from donor agencies to build capacities in the new-style science, but political science was not too far behind. In the course of time, the discipline was taken over by reinvented and ideologically slanted concepts and analytical frames that gave new meanings to basic concepts like civil society, state, governance, elections, democracy, leadership, transitions and so on. Even new buzzwords like 'big man' and state failure had similar slants. For example, Apata (2019) shows how narratives of corruption reinvented it as a problem with African patent (for the constructions and reconstructions of new buzzwords and fuzzwords, see Cornwall and Eade 2010). These were the frameworks within which the crises and challenges that confronted Africa in the period beginning from the late 1980s, especially those related to state fragility and failure, were analysed. As we have said, the African responses were feeble and the problem seemed to be the absence of a coherent framework for critically engaging the neoliberal onslaught. Uncharacteristically, the new false universals were uncritically embraced by political scientists including those who would minimally insist on the creed of 'concrete analysis of concrete situations'. Once again, the study of African politics was in the throes of an unprofitable mimicry of Western scholarship (Ekeh 1997: 83) and subordination to the experiences of supposedly superior experiences (Olukoshi 1999: 464).

This situation rekindled debates on the epistemology, content, relevance, priorities, autonomy and methodologies of the discipline of political science in the global South in general and Africa in particular. It is against the backdrop of the latest challenge in a series of what has been and is likely to continue as a recurrent challenge that I discuss the need to mainstream decolonization as a key methodological tool of political science in Africa, which I believe is best done within the subfield of comparative politics. It is to this that we now turn.

Comparative politics and the mainstreaming of decolonization

The emergence of decolonization as a methodological tool at both the global and sub-global levels has deep roots in comparative politics. As the following discussion will hopefully show, it emerged as an integral part of the movement away from the convergence of theories, perspectives and development trajectories to divergence and plurality. It is from these foundations that decolonization has surged in the mainstream of political science, and this provides the anchor for strengthening its methodological standing in the study of African politics.

The subfield of comparative politics is arguably the methodological hub of political science. According to Lijphart (1971: 682), 'Among the several fields or subdisciplines into which the discipline of political science is usually divided, comparative politics is the only one that carries a methodological instead of a substantive label'. Behavioural and post-behavioural reconstructions which demand more scientific approaches to the study of politics have made the comparative method, which is akin to the laboratory in the natural and physical sciences, the core of methodological growth and refinement. Thus, basic issues of concept formation, research designs, hypotheses testing, generalizations and theory formation across systems have been debated and addressed within the purview of the comparative method (Przeworski and Teune 1970; Lijphart 1971). This is the first reason that makes comparative politics the appropriate field for mainstreaming decolonization as a methodological tool for responding to generalizations that claim universal or law-like applicability. To what extent can postulates which describe or explain social reality in specific societies be generalized as universal postulates? Can concepts and their practice correlates be stretched across systems in spite of cultural relativity, differences in meaning, and contextual specificities? Are nomothetic generalizations which substitute variables for proper names, places, time and are system-blind possible – or desirable – in social science? Or, following the criteria of relevance and responsibility highlighted in the debates among African political scientists referred to earlier on, should we rather have idiographic or historically specific generalizations with proper names, places and time? How truly comparable are human societies even when they appear similar? Are there empirical and predictable regularities in human and societal behaviours, tendencies and formations that, irrespective of space and time, lend support to law-like generalizations? Are societies bound to follow the same trajectories, and can what works in some societies work for all? Can one size fit all?

The second reason, which is closely related and helps to address most of these questions, has to do with the substantive subject of comparative politics itself. For a long time, there have been debates on whether comparative politics should aim for convergence or divergence of perspectives and theories, and on what the most appropriate levels of analysis and theory formation should be: macro, micro, global, regional or nation-state. At the base of this debate was the possibility – or desirability – of all societies moving in the same direction, and through similar stages of growth, following processes and institutions used by the most advanced societies. Leading the convergence side were modernization theories which held that Western development was superior to all others and provided the model roadmap and image of future growth for other societies, and sought to formulate grand and universal theories and perspectives to support these claims. Modernization not only became the dominant perspective in comparative politics for a long time, but its ethnocentricity also gave it the face of 'colonial' domination. It was as such that modernization provoked counter, in effect decolonialist, theories and perspectives, notably dependency, underdevelopment and world systems. These all provided alternative historical, material and dialectical explanations and trajectories of growth and development that led the movement away from convergence to divergence and plurality of theories and perspectives. Most pointedly, the counter-theories held imperialism, colonialism and Western hegemony responsible for the underdevelopment of countries in the global south, and argued that their futures lay in delinking rather than convergence (Rodney 2012 [1972]; Amin 1989, 1990a, 1996). There were, in addition, other underlying methodological reasons for the shift from convergence and grand theories. These included problems of concept stretching (concepts meaning different things in different societies); too few cases, many variables (arising from the impracticalities of covering all cases, large N); and the loss of relevant contextual variables necessary for holistic explanations and applications due to the parsimony of general theories. Comparativists consequently became less ambitious and more realistic by settling for middle- to narrow-range (small-N) generalizations and theories that captured the nuances and specificities of different systems while at the same time providing the basis for further comparisons and higher-level generalization. This made the most similar systems design as tenable as the most different systems design not only for theory formation but also for policy and programme design and implementation (cf. Goggin 1986). Divergence and plurality also had other important methodological implications. One was that they made units and levels of analysis and focus of development more flexible and open-ended, ranging from within-system to system levels, to groups of (say regional) systems and, where possible, higher levels of generality. Secondly, they freed comparativists from the tyranny of quantitative scientification which at a point devalued qualitative approaches of the normative kind (Bond 2007). With divergence also came a plurality of (scientific) approaches that today include discursive analysis, narrative analysis, grounded theory, and so on.

It is within the context of the foregoing reconstructions, especially the displacement of the convergence trajectory that virtually colonized the field of comparative politics, that the seeds of decoloniality and decolonization – as drivers of divergent, alternative and plural perspectives – were sown. African social scientists, especially those of radical Marxist and political economy persuasions, embraced the decoloniality perspectives and aligned with scholars from Latin America and Asia to pursue and develop perspectives that were sometimes derisively described as third world or global south perspectives. However, in spite of the great analytical insights, it offered and the potential to serve as a relevance and responsibility filter for processing received and borrowed paradigms, decolonization was not fully developed as a methodological tool in African political science. For one thing, it did not become part of the mainstream curriculum at any level of study, and it was left to researchers and scholars to apply the precepts of decolonization as they deemed fit. Some of these, like the second independence and developmental state perspectives, turned out to be quite remarkable engagements with neoliberal orthodoxies that tended towards grand theorizing and global convergence and provided good examples of what form decolonization theory should take, but they were too fleeting and scattered to withstand the tyranny of neoliberalism.

The second independence perspective, which had the trappings of a social movement, pointed to the essence of democratization in Africa as not just another instance of democratic transition or replacement of authoritarian structures by democratic ones as the literature on democratization suggested at the time, but of a deeper engagement with the uncompleted process of state-building that made liberation a condition for democracy and development. More importantly, that democratization was not propelled by the forces of the so-called global democratic revolution and diffused through emulation and external support, but by domestic forces struggling to appropriate the state from captive colonial forces represented by the original colonizers and their post-independence agent-successors (Nyong'o 1987; Nzongola-Ntalaja 1987; Mamdani and Wamba-dia-Wamba 1995). Elsewhere, I have described second independence (also second liberation) as unique, and the most original and insightful African contribution to the scholarship on the democratization of the 1980s and 1990s, especially for showing that the state, its ownership, legitimacy and development agency, constitute the arena and object of democratic struggles (Osaghae 2005, 2015). Yet, despite its deep insights and potential to extend the theoretical frontiers and comparative frameworks of democratization beyond the limits of neoliberal orthodoxy, Ekeh (1997: 83) still considered second independence mysterious and presently lacking in analytical force. Thus, second independence ended up being one of the least acknowledged and interrogated concepts in the study of democratization in Africa, as none of what may be regarded as major works on the subject both by Western-Africanist scholars (cf. Diamond, Linz and Lipset 1988; Bratton and Van de Walle 1997; Joseph 1999) and by African scholars themselves (cf. Oyugi et al. 1988; Chole and Ibrahim 1995) considered the concept important enough to be a tool of analysis (compare, however, Nyong'o 1987; Ekeh 1997; Osaghae 2005).

Instead, the focus continued to be on what neoliberal perspectives that subjected all democratizing countries to the same conditions and stages of growth dictated: how the larger contexts of economic and political crises and reforms (e.g. governance and civil society), globalization, human rights, conflicts and so on, facilitated or complicated the process of democratization (cf. Gibbon, Bangura and Ofstad 1992; Chole and Ibrahim 1995; Ihonvbere 1996; Mengisteab and Daddieh 1999; Osaghae 1999).

A similar fate befell the developmental state perspective that emerged in response to the neoliberal stipulation of the Western-inspired minimalist state as the target of reforms in the Global South. The perspective questioned the tenability of the minimalist governance state whose major concern is market and service delivery efficiency when the pressing demands in Africa are for development and social transformation that require more not less state intervention (see Mkandawire 2001, 2005; Lumumba-Kasongo 2002; Khan 2004; and Mustapha 2006; for the governance state perspective as formulated by the World Bank, see Harrison 2004). According to Mustapha (2006: 199), what is needed is a 'type of state that is consistent with Africa's needs; not a minimalist state or a service delivery state but a transformative or developmental state'. One major difference between the two-state types as African experiments with them show is that whereas the pre-reforms developmental state gave African governments relatively wider latitude over policy and economic growth and enabled them to merge policy and social forces, the policy process in the reforms-driven governance state is externally controlled via conditionalities imposed by international financial institutions and donor countries and is aimed at installing market forces and further deepening dependence on global capital (Mengisteab 2008: 61). Experiences in the rest of the Global South were not different (see Bose 2004), and there is no gainsaying that insights from evolving Global South perspectives were good for interrogating the capacities of the state to function as development agents in comparative terms especially in the light of state fragility and failure discourses. Yet, once again, another veritable concept of decolonization floundered and fell to the stranglehold of neoliberal orthodoxy.

The sporadic rise and fall of such powerful conceptual frameworks and theories that grounded and reconstructed global perspectives according to Africa's realities and developmental imperatives showed that there was a lot more to be done to mainstream divergence in comparative politics. The dominance of neoliberal perspectives since the late 1980s, which marks a return to the convergence trajectory associated with modernization theories of old, backed this time by the captive forces of globalization, has made the rejuvenation of divergence- and pluralism-setting perspectives even more urgent and imperative (Osaghae 1995; Lushaba 2009). This is more so that decades of neoliberal reforms have not led to significant improvements in African conditions: states have sunken deeper into abysmal tunnels of fragility and failure, poverty levels have multiplied, development has remained at low levels, and dependency has reached unprecedented heights (Osaghae 2007). The failings and inadequacies of reforms and the perspectives that underlie them provoked critical reviews and engagements of methodological tools by African scholars, with most agreeing that more grounded Africa-centred and global south perspectives should be developed (Zeleza 1997, 2006a, 2006b; Soyinka et al. 2015; Osha 2018). I believe that decolonization offers the best framework for doing this and that the resurgence of decoloniality and decolonization discourses in South Africa provides a pedestal for further strengthening, consolidating and mainstreaming its rich insights. This is the argument that is elaborated in the next and concluding section of this chapter.

Conclusion

The case for decolonization in the study of African politics and development has been well made over the years. At the beginning of this chapter, the point was made that although the rejection of the colonial order and replacement of everything colonial by 'authentic' African paradigms is a popular conception of decolonization and an integral part of its pedigree, it does not capture the essence of decolonization as an analytical framework. A number of important delimiting points flow from this. First, that decolonization does not mean creating or focusing on African perspectives, worldviews, or interests to the exclusion of other perspectives. Delinking might be necessary, but it does not mean autarchy as every formation is, as Amin says, embedded within a larger polycentric world (Amin 1990a). This also means that adoption of local languages and scholarly works by African academics and publishers only, or replacement of Western thinkers by African thinkers in the curriculum of political thought may be symbolic or necessary, but they do not capture the essence of decolonization. Rather, decolonization denotes a rejection of universal or global world views and paradigms based on the supposedly superior experience of Western Europe and the global north, a view that was upheld by modernization theories that dominated the social sciences for a long time and most recently by neoliberal perspectives that have been dominant since the 1980s. To put this in proper perspective, we analysed the origins and mainstreaming of decolonization as a methodological tool of theory formation within the context of the subfield of comparative politics. Specifically, they are located in the movement away from convergence, that is, the linking of all societies and systems to one and same 'laws' and trajectory of growth and development that amounted to the colonization of knowledge, to divergence, that is, a plurality of 'laws' and trajectories of growth and development. Decolonization takes its bearings from divergence and plurality, for the purpose of difference as well as comparison. While convergence leads to one-size-fits-all frameworks, divergence insists that difference matters.

The importance of decolonization has been rekindled by the ravages of neoliberalism, the new colonial paradigm that has not been able to deliver on its set goals of growth and developmental targets in most of Africa and the Global South. Predictably, there have been critical decolonization engagements with neoliberalism that insist on divergence a la Africa-centred perspectives such as second independence and developmental state, but they were too fleeting and scattered to effectively challenge the new powerful convergence trajectories. These are the circumstances that precipitated a review of methodological tools and analytical frameworks in political science and other social science disciplines by African scholars. The main argument of this chapter is that strengthening decolonization, which has been in a state of incompleteness for so long, into a systematic framework presents the best response to not just neoliberal hegemony but future colonialisms as well. In this regard, the giant strides of decolonization studies, as well as the bourgeoning decolonial school in South Africa, offer very useful points of departure. To close this chapter, I shall briefly outline the elements that I consider pivotal to this rejuvenation. First, the comparative context that relates Africa-centred perspectives to others in the pluralist tradition has to be continuously emphasized. Decolonization implies that the production of scientific knowledge is not a one-way traffic and that no knowledge is superior to others. Second, decolonization is a multidisciplinary subject and framework. Insights and approaches from highly influential studies in the humanities (literature, history, philosophy, religion), social sciences and multidisciplinary disciplines and new schools (gender studies, cultural studies, development studies, indigenous knowledge, advanced studies) have to be harnessed into more systematic frameworks that would be continuously reviewed and updated. The subjects covered should however be substantive, relevant and discerning, to avoid a situation where decolonization becomes trivialized or hijacked by deriders of global south scholarship as 'decolonization of everything'. Thirdly, decolonization should be fully developed in a systematic way and integrated into the mainstream curriculum at undergraduate and graduate levels, and continuous research should be encouraged (Zondi's (2018) thoughts on how this can be achieved in the subfield of international relations provides a good guide).

5

What does the decolonial turn for political sciences in Africa entail? And where do we start?

Siphamandla Zondi

Introduction

The subject of the decolonization of social sciences and humanities (Hayes 2016) as well as natural science, of course, is not new, but it is now being increasingly connected to struggles of students, the poor and the excluded other (Ngcaweni and Ngcaweni 2018). It is that the call is being made emphatically as much in the streets as in the boardrooms and in academic conferences and publication such as during the student and staff protests in South African universities in 2015–2016, helping to put the issue of decolonization of education and knowledge on the world map. This has led to renewed academic discourses on the meanings of decolonization, Africanization and transformation in respect of university knowledge. Taken together these demands entail a call for a decolonial turn in our knowledge environment (Blaney and Tickner 2017). This is because the decolonial turn entails more than cosmetic reforms as we have seen in some post-colonial situations, but envisages a fundamental decommissioning of the colonial logics that frame knowledge today and how it is passed on from one generation to the next (Maldonado-Torres 2011). These discussions ought to happen at all levels of the academic discourse, including those working within specific disciplines such as political sciences and its sub-areas of politics, international relations, political economy, political sociology, gender and power, and foreign policy analysis. This chapter contributes to discussions taking place within political sciences by offering a perspective from the African decolonial family of perspectives on what the decolonial turn in the political sciences will entail and where we should start. It is far from a complete discussion of this subject, but it makes a suggestion about the broad frame of the debate and where we might start to deliberate shifting in the geography of reason in political sciences. The chapter is not an empirical analysis of what is happening in curricula of political sciences, but it is a reflection on debates in the discipline in Africa that represent a contribution to decolonization from a decolonial lens of analysis. The chapter suggests that we must first attempt to unmask the coloniality of the discipline and in politics as practice, identifying what specifically and fundamentally is colonial about them. Second, we must clarify what do decolonizing, Africanizing and transforming the discipline mean and entail for us.

This discussion is necessary because there is still confusion about exactly what is colonial about knowledge generally and political sciences in Africa, in particular, and what decolonizing it entails. Without explaining the colonial in specific ways, those who engage in decolonization may be doing cosmetic reforms instead of fundamental transformation. This is why too often in discussions about decolonization, the responses are that we have long been decolonizing and perhaps that we have already decolonized or that decolonizing is a discourse that blames outsiders only or that we must take responsibility for the science and practice of politics after independence now. We close with remarks on where the decolonial turn should practically start.

The author in political sciences: A conundrum

Since political sciences are a part of the Westernized idea of knowledge produced by epistemicide (Grosfoguel 2013), cultural murder (Diop 1991), ontological distortion and pedagogical deceit, it inherits from this tradition taken-for-granted ideas about what does it mean to speak or write in political sciences. It is now a well-established argument that Western knowledge is colonial in the first instance in that it de-centres the positionality of the author and speaker, requiring them to meet invented standards of objective scholarship. It invites the thinker and speaker into a fictitious position that critics call free-floating so that the thinker-speaker must hope to have a God's eye view of matter being studied and discussed. This objective position promises rationality gained only by the efforts of the thinker and speaker to extract themselves from that which they are studying or discussing, acquire a certain distance from the subject of study so that they can be trusted by the canon to offer what is called objective knowledge least contaminated with the subjective, which is assumed to be irrational and therefore not true knowledge. It assumes that there is a zero point of view, a sort of innocent and pure positionality, a sheer hubris we now know (Castro-Gómez 2005). This results in what Paulin Hountondji calls extraverted discourses (Hountondji 1997), what Ngugi wa Thiong'o likens to a dismemberment of the person from their knowing leaving them torn and apart (Wa Thiong'o 2009). This is what Archie Mafeje calls an illusion in a double sense (Mafeje 2011): that thinkers and speakers can divorce themselves from histories that produce them and that they speak from nowhere or anywhere when in fact they also speak from somewhere specific.

The discussion about decolonization cannot be discussed without defying and rebelling against this first law of colonial knowledge and euromodernity. It is a contradiction to use epistemically unjust tools of coloniality of knowledge to expose coloniality or dismantle it. This is a common mistake: the need to confirm to rebel; the thinking that you can rebel while complying with technologies of that which we rebel against. The hubris of point zero of knowing is fundamental to the coloniality of knowledge and it is, therefore, counter-productive to perpetuate it while arguing for decolonizing. Who we write and speak as and how we position ourselves in that process of writing and speaking is perhaps the first commandment in the decolonization process. Thus, we shall not be deceived into extraverted ways of discoursing about your ways of knowing and the ways of knowing you are thinking about. In eurocentrism, I am supposed to not speak about how I am speaking and not to speak or write in the first person, but hide in the third-person speech and conceal my positionality to participate in this great deceit about the rational and objective position. This implies that as I discuss the matter of decolonizing political sciences in Africa in this chapter, I must begin also by explaining how I intend to speak in this chapter. I need to explain as to who I speak as and where do I belong in the contested spaces about matters being discussed and what my ideological outlook is. I am required to be fully transparent in my authorship.

I write and speak from the perspective of those for whom the progress of modernity has brought much pain, injustice and scandals. I speak in a manner that identifies with the struggles of those who have been excluded, suppressed, denigrated, scorned, silenced, muted, suffocated exploited, killed, cursed and duped in the process of establishing modernity as the superior way of living, managing power, arranging statehood, knowing, worshipping and so forth (Ndlovu-Gatsheni 2013). I therefore consciously speak from the dark underbelly of a system whose friends extolled as a civilization and a success when in fact it was undergirded by the barbarity of epistemic violence, cultural murder and epistemicide (Ndlovu-Gatsheni 2007). The violence of the university, its knowledge and its disciplines is on record (Grosfoguel 2013). I identify with the biblical notion of a voice in the wilderness, a peripheral people, buried voices and a damned people, speaking the Canaan of freedom and prosperity into existence against the drowning voices of doubt and questions. I speak not out of the cold choice of topics that make sense to the academy or subjects that are new niches for those who want to stand out or themes that are sexy and today. But I speak because someone has got to convey the messages of the voices of those who live, work, study and think from the valley of the shadow of death including within the formal academy.

I am in this sense not intending to be 'reasonable' in response to the not-so-reasonable epistemic violence of exclusion, distortion and disparagement of ways of knowing from my work. I say this because my subject is about the unreasonable that has been normal under the guise of rationality. For Frantz Fanon says, the system asks the bruised, the hurt, the insulted, the cursed, the pained and wounded to be reasonable in their response (Fanon 2001[1963]). It asks them to be rational in the face of an irrational system of racism where the invented markers of race and gender become indicators of worth or ontological density, in the face of crude capitalism where workers including in universities are commodities placated by slave wages to numb their pain, crude patriarchy where women especially black and poor women are asked to be rational in the face of male violence. I am not rational and reasonable then. I speak from both my mind and my belly, my thoughts and my feelings.

The idea of a free-floating signifier, a thinker who occupies the position called objective is an illusion, now we know. Enough has been written to persuasively show that the objective is an illusion. Anyone who claims to think and speak from nowhere is like a person who is neutral in the face of injustice that Martin Luther King Jr called the friend of the oppressor. Second, a zero-point of rationality is an illusion (Castro-Gómez 2005) because we don't place on the table the issues that we deal with. Yes! there is a certain measure of historical determinism in the manner in which those living in the hellish zone of non-beings live. The mainstream has long ruled that historical determinism is wrong and not useful; we are unable to say the same because we don't arbitrarily choose what is in and what is out, but we are guided by voices and experiences in the wilderness.

It is the prior condition of what Sylvia Wynter calls the suffocating omnipresence of the imperial modern man and Eurocentrism that forces me into the combative mode. As Wynter explains, the act of shouting 'I can't breathe' made famous by the young black men suffocated by police officers in the United States is seen by the system as being unreasonable. The act of pushing the suffocating hand away is seen as unreasonable violence and reckless rebellion. I am at peace with the position of epistemic rebellion because it is, in essence, a negation of a prior negation. It is the pursuit of cognitive and epistemic justice, which is an important part of the principle of justice enshrined in international and national law and a big pillar of civilized life.

Epistemic disobedience permits the posing of deep and uncomfortable questions necessary in the oppressed and silence's liberation. It permits the posing of question against questions, method against method, negation of the negation. We need to be able to negate eurocentric negations. These are negations by which it has become normal to assume that Africa had no history, has no civilization, has science, has spirituality, and it is a dark continent.

In international relations, I am on the periphery where I come from. My sense of the world derives the vantage point from where I see things. My understanding of the key dynamics of the international system is shaped by the location from which I think. Eurocentrism as a perspective of the world that privileges the European experience, history, ways of knowing and illusions as superior to others creates the illusion that one can be physically on the periphery and yet think from the centre, that I can be in South Africa but borrow the lenses of fellow thinkers who are authentically thinking from Europe where they are also geographically located. This free-floating methodological positioning leads to the presentation of European perspectives as 'universal' and 'international', that murky cliche in our discourse today. It enables those who use it to hide their location behind notions of rationality, objectivity and universality. It enables them to avoid the scorn of being revealed to be unauthentic or to hide the fact that they are involved in mimicry.

The ability of eurocentrism to police our thoughts, decide who is rational and not, who is publishable or not, whose work can be passed or failed, is one of the worst injustices of our time. It lends credence to this idea that mainstream knowledge is imperialism. This means while we wish to choose to rebel against eurocentric illusions and negations (from the idea that disciplines have white fathers only or that international relations began in Europe and Europeans can declare its end or that race is a major concern for international relations etc.), there are terrible consequences from the centre, including its accessories within our universities. But if we don't rebel and shout, then let us just breathe. We will still suffer the suffocation from the omnipresence of the colonial order in our environments. There is, therefore, no real choice, but to try to live, which is to combat to survive. This is a real experience of junior black colleagues in departments across the country; it is about survival.

I have already referred to some detail as to how coloniality impinges on the positionality of subaltern scholars and their methodological option. This is a deeply personal dimension of the coloniality of knowledge that political science is also implicated in. I now wish to turn to show specific ways in which political science is implicated in the coloniality of knowledge. I use political science knowing that it is perhaps better used in the plural since there is no single political science since even what used to be sub-disciplines of international politics, comparative politics, foreign policy analysis have all since becoming disciplines in their own right.

Political sciences, coloniality of knowledge and eurocentrism

The simplest point to look at in unmasking the implication of the discipline in coloniality is to look at who speaks and who does not speak in its discourses. It is a discipline dominated and controlled by white men of a few European countries and other parts of the European diaspora. This is a problem. It masquerades as international when in fact it is regional at least or sectional in fact. The fathers of the discipline can be identified as those who are said to have been at the forefront of theory building. This implies we must credit the fathers, all from North America and Europe. The fathers of realism, from E.H. Carr and Hans Morgenthau to John Mearsheimer; fathers of liberalism or idealism from Immanuel Kant to J.M. Headley; fathers of liberalism, from Robert Keohane to Joseph Nye; fathers of constructivism like Alexander Wedt and Ted Hopf; and fathers of the International Society or English School from Headley Bull to Barry Buzan. It is not by accident that these white men come from the same region of the world that was also behind the demons of imperialism and colonialism. They share their location and culture with King Leopold, Otto Von Bismarck, Francisco Colom, Jules Grévy, Queen Victoria, Grover Cleveland, Alfonso Fransisco and Carlos Charles I. While the latter championed the colonization of territories for the political and economic benefit of Europe and its diaspora, helped establish the global power of Europe, the fathers of discipline helped colonize knowledge and enable the European perspective to also rule the world, both happening at the expense of others. The discipline remains in the hands of thinkers and writers from the white world to this day, while there has been growing participation of others. The frames of thinking, the theories, major decisions about the direction of the discipline, and terms of entry are still set from the white world to this day. It is in this context that European political scientists began a discussion in 2013, seeking to decide the shift from mega debates about theories of international relations to one of application and empirical validation (Dunne, Hansen and Wight 2013). The audacity to declare an end of mega debates on international relations theory before we have had inclusive debates is a clear example of coloniality at the heart of the discipline.

Eurocentrism lends this audacity to those who declared exhaustion of debates on certain issues, urging us to move on to a new one (Bell 1962) and intimate an end to contestations and battles for ideas and ideals (Fukuyama 1989). There are three obvious and prominent examples of this nature. Francis Fukuyama's *End of History* thesis is a declaration of end and a victory of the west over its enemies, both in political-ideological terms and, by implication, in epistemic terms. He declared that the Cold War contestation of ideologies, ideas and ways of politics had ended and that the west had scored a victory as its idea of liberalism had finally prevailed over all alternatives and therefore was now one narrow route to managing power, ensuring living well and thinking about the world. Fukuyama and others thus settled what Samuel Huntington called a clash of civilization (Huntington 1996) and validated what J. M. Headley called the successful Europeanization of the world through globalization and liberal democracy (Headley 2007). Daniel Bell spoke of the end of ideology, proclaiming the exhaustion of contestations on political ideas and ideologies about the world, relations among humans and the making of society in the 1960s. The imperial man arrogates to himself the power to say no one should think anymore because thinking on politics has been exhausted. These together with the end of international relations (IR) theory idea are a demonstration of the discursive power to invent and declare the end of things derives from the making of the imperial man who inherits the privilege and power to call things into existence and end things, to create space for human beings to speak and muzzle them because the time to speak has ended. When Europeans have resolved their internal differences and have reached some consensus they say the whole world has reached a consensus. It is because the other is absent right before the eyes of the imperial man; he is mute and cannot be heard. He cannot speak.

It is a conversation that begins with European fathers of political sciences and extends to their descendants today who hold the fort in defence of this privilege of the western epistemic lens. There is a mutually reinforcing interface between the biopolitics and the geopolitics of knowledge; the people who speak with authority in the discipline in the form of books prescribed and anchored, as well as in the location of their thinking, the locus of their enunciation. In this, the European and eurocentric are related.

Eurocentrism has the same audacity of self-belief as Kwasi Kwarteng found British imperialism and colonialism had during and after colonial rule (Kwarteng 2012). This is the courage to build the prosperity of the empire at the expense of the 'overseas' territory and to present this as modernity and civilization. This is the audacity to use barbaric means to build what is supposed to a civilization. Similarly, eurocentrism thrives on epistemicide and other forms of epistemic justice to maintain its hegemony, while preaching justice, rationality and humanity. This too is the proverbial ghost of the empire, an enduring impact of modern/colonial ways that have remained entrenched long after colonial rule ended. The discussion of political science is a discussion of how ways of knowing about the political have been managed often to achieve narrow political imperatives of the empire to this day. When seen from the belly of the periphery, especially in Africa of today, this too is one of the sorrows of the empire that continue to haunt us today (Johnson 2004). This situation enables some men from specific geopolitical locations central to euromodernity to declare the alphas and the omegas of thought such in the narrative of waves of democracy that are supposed to have beginnings and ends as well as the end of history thesis, both very prominent in political science discourses. This situation also enables these men from Europe and its diaspora to define what is proper political science, who is included and who is not, expecting all of us to mimic and align ourselves. This project is well-financed and resourced, including through the funding of political ideas, journals, publications and discourses. These trends give credence to the centre-periphery thesis, that is how the centre diffuses its ideologies, ideas, theories, methodologies and other agendas to the periphery thanks to the entanglement of the centre and periphery in unequal power relations (Wa Thiong'o 1993).

The second simple point is to look at the archive upon which the discipline is based. It has been shown that like other disciplines, political science suffers epistemological blindness, being built on the images of the world that occupied old white men ensconced within Eurocentric cosmic views of life (Jose and Motta 2017). The classics derived from the Mediterranean world through Greece and moved to Europe frame the modern narrative of history and the bulk of the material on which the political sciences discipline is built. Therefore, the memory on which African students are meant to remember their place in the world concerning the constitution of the political is, therefore, the memory of those who belong to the civilization that dismembered Africa and emptied Africans of their ontological weight. It is the memory of Europe and its diaspora in North America and Oceania in the main. Jack Goody shows how this memory of Europe was a nefarious invention actually in that it is a stolen memory, a product of a process by which Europe came to claim its pre-eminent place in the history of the modern (Goody 2006). Goody calls this a theft of history, a massively unjust process by which Europe and its diaspora placed themselves at the centre of a constructed world history. This is very evident in political science whose archive draws from this one view of the history of humanity, and therefore one view of the constitution of the political.

This gave political science epistemological blindness that enabled it to see selectively and therefore construct the political in ways that are now regarded as obviously unjust. Jim Jose goes to some length in exploring from a South perspective how this epistemological blindness manifests in the discipline, pointing out that, 'ever since its inception, political science has arguably been guilty of enacting numerous elisions and exclusions of subjects, objects and processes that are deeply political (and potentially democratic)' (Jose and Motta 2017: 652). The exclusionary logics of this epistemology functions through the binaries that remain enduring in how political science is framed; these include the theory versus facts, administration versus politics, political experts versus mass publics and so forth. All of these were attempts to distinguish between the political and the non-political, including the political versus the anti-political, but a lot of experiences of the political were excluded from the epistemological frame. Like its cognate disciplines, political science has been engaged in the practice of enforcing boundaries through markers that exclude and delegitimize other ways of constituting the political, thus helping to reinforce hierarchical notions of power and politics. As a result, it has had to contend over a long time with the challenging outsider perspectives, the views from the margins and voices in its wilderness pointing to what we might call the political-otherwise and political science-otherwise. This explains the fear of intrusion that has gripped political science (Hindess 1997), fear that slows down the process of transformation; a paranoia that has prevented its decolonization.

In this epistemological frame, we who are from the South – itself an invention of the West when it invented itself as the North – are expected to enter the knowledge of the political via the North. We are to abandon any prior knowledge falling outside the frame since such is both unknowable and unthinkable. Hountondji explains this forces us as African intellectuals into extraversion where we import theories and export data to validate them (Hountondji 2009). Thus, we are to abandon our memory and inculcate that of the West/North. As Table 5.1 shows, the literature that is the foundation of the whole discipline, its main debates, its main theories, does not include people who are not white. The inclusion of Sun Tzu, *The Art of War* written in 500 AD is only recent and is not fully embraced. As is evident in titles, but more so in the substance of discussions, the whole foundational archive is about what happened in and what was

Table 5.1 A Select List of Foundational Texts in Political Science

Political Science Classics	International Relations Classics
Nicolo Machiavelli, *The Prince*, 1512	Thomas Hobbes, *Leviathan*, 1651
Thomas More, *Utopia*, 1515	Norman Angell, *The Great Illusion*, 1910
Nicolo Machiavelli, *The Art of War*, 1520	Arnold Toynbee, *Prologue to the Survey of International Affairs, 1920–1923* (1925)
Francis Bacon, *New Atlantis*, 1626	Reinhold Niebuhr, *Moral Man and Immoral Society,* 1932
Gerrard Winstanley, *The True Levellers Standard,* 1649	E. H. Carr, *The Twenty Years' Crisis*, 1939
Thomas Hobbes, *De Cive*, 1651	Martin Wight, *Power Politics*, 1946.
James Harrington, *The Commonwealth of Oceana*, 1656	Hans J. Morgenthau, *Scientific Man Vs. Power Politics*, 1946
John Locke, *Second Treatise of Civil Government,* 1690	Hedley Bull, *The Control of the Arms Race* 1965
Charles de Montesquieu, *The Spirit of Laws*, 1752	Herbert Butterfield, Martin Wight, *Diplomatic Investigations*, 1966
Morelly, *Code of Nature, or True Spirit of Laws,* 1755	Andrew Linklater, *New Dimensions in World Politics,* 1975
Jean-Jacques Rousseau, *The Social Contract*, 1762	Michael Walzer, *Just and Unjust Wars*, 1977
Thomas Paine, *Common Sense*, 1776	Hedley Bull, *Anarchical Society*, 1977
Thomas Paine, *The Age of Reason*, 1794	Martin Wight, *Systems of States*, 1977
Mary Wollstonecraft, *A Vindication of the Rights of Woman*, 1792	Martin Wight, *Power Politics*, 1978
Fourier, *Theory of the Four Movements*, 1808	Kenneth Waltz, *Theory of International Politics,* 1979
Robert Owen, *A New View of Society*, 1816	Hedley Bull and Adam Watson, *The Expansion of International Society*, 1984
Hegel, *Philosophy of Right*, 1821	Hans J. Morgenthau, *Politics Among Nations*, 1985
Carl von Clausewitz, *On War*, 1827	Robert Keohane, *After Hegemony*, 1984
Alexis de Tocqueville, *Democracy in America*, 1840	Hans Köchler, *Democracy and the International Rule of Law*, 1995
Harriet Taylor, *The Subjection of Women*, 1869	Joseph Nye, *Soft Power: The Means to Success in World Politics*, 2004
George Washington Plunkett, *A Series of Very Plain Talks on Very Practical Politics*, c. 1923	J. Ann Tickner, *Gender in International Relations,* 1992
Vere Gordon Childe, *How Labour Governs*, 1923	Alexander Wendt, *Social Theory of International Politics* 1999

Source: Various sources assembled by the author.

in the interest of Europe and its diaspora. The implication is that what is then written and spoken about the political in the South is framed by the memory of the North, in response to or in reference to this epistemological canvass, whether on the state, on sovereignty, on governance, on democratic politics, on principles, on values, on theory, on political behaviour, on institutions, political community and construction of power. The foundational concepts and ideas being discussed in political sciences have a history, one that casts the discipline as implicated in epistemic violence when seen outside the North, the violence of exclusions, elisions, silencing, muting and willful deafness.

The third pillar of coloniality of knowledge in political sciences is concerning the pedagogical outlook in the discipline and its sub-disciplines. This is about what we teach and how we teach the political. In content and by rituals, we teach the knowledge included in the epistemological frame described above, which is the knowledge that is blind to knowledge about the politics that students from the South may have already encountered outside the set curriculum and syllabi, one that the professors in class do not consider knowledge since the texts on which teaching is based set markers about what is knowledge and what is not, what is the political and what is the non-political and the anti-political. We continue to discuss the political in classrooms and teaching materials in the manner derived from the memory of Europe and its diaspora. We teach Africa's national, regional and international politics fundamentally seen from the vantage point of Europe. We teach the subject matter framed by the epistemological prisms we describe that define for instance what is an introduction to political science or international relations, which is often about basic concepts like power, the state, political institutions, democracy, civil society, theories and ideologies as well as processes like participation, negotiations and elections. These often represent a heritage of epistemological domination for they are framed and derived from the Western archive about what is the political. Of course, in their innovative ways, teachers may elaborate on this, non-western experiences and even mount a challenge to mainstream interpretations of these selected ideas.

Three critical markers are crucial for understanding the coloniality of pedagogy in political science. The first, as we have discussed, is the taught knowledge often presented in the form of the textbook. It is well known that political science classes across the continent are taught based on so-called standard textbooks. Textbooks are universally accepted as the basis for first-year political sciences in most universities in Africa. Access to these Western-produced textbooks thought to be the easiest way to package the learning material on a variety of subjects for students is regarded as a critical success factor in teaching and learning. While textbooks aptly entitled 'introduction to politics' or 'political science' or 'international relations' are popular with teachers of first-year undergraduate degree programmes, other textbooks are prescribed in higher classes well. There are often added scholarly books, journal articles and other materials in higher classes. Yet Western books – both textbooks and scholarly books – remain entrenched as pedagogical tools in African universities and schools. The import of this is to entrench the epistemology of alterity that Western canons enforce across the world.

The second marker of coloniality of pedagogy is in the nature of classroom practices that shape teaching and learning in political science. These rituals and activities form part of the pedagogical strategy often decided by teachers who are either taught this from the compendium of Western didactic training material or is a behaviour learned by observation of previous teachers. Thus, the pedagogy of oppression is perpetuated as practices designed to pass the epistemology of exteriority gets passed on from one generation to the next. The predominance of traditional methods of teaching and learning based on paradigms that assume students are like sponges that must absorb the knowledge given to them through instructional tools is obvious. The focus on getting students to simply consume disputable facts helps to maintain the status by preventing the emergence on a mass scale of a radically empowered citizenry able to fundamentally transform the political everywhere it is found.

'Most professors have an intimate knowledge of what they do in their classrooms', surmised one study on the teaching of political science, 'while possessing very little knowledge of what other professors, even at their own institution, do in their classrooms' (Hartlaub and Lancaster 2008: 377). This is a crucial observation about the rituals that dominant pedagogical approaches permit, which allow excessive narrowing of boundaries of knowledge in political science by exalting the professor who has been approved by the epistemological traditions as a knower to set the frames of what gets known in classroom interactions. The learning process dominated by one knower standing in front of larger numbers of learners who are supposed to knowledge transferred to them is entrenched in the dominant politics of knowledge and how it is produced and transmitted. It is a key marker in the coloniality of knowledge. This enables the perpetuation of the epistemology of blindness and what Carter G. Woodson calls the miseducation of the other, which in his case was what he called the negro (Woodson 2012). In this order of things, teaching and learning happen through rectangular buildings, blackboards in front and podiums that reinforced teachers know and students do not.

What does decolonizing political science therefore entail?

Given what we have pointed out earlier as key markers of coloniality as a hidden underpinning of political science, it then follows that removing these markers constitutes decolonizing political science. It is so because having identified that what constitutes the virus of coloniality in modern political science, it is obvious that to decolonize in this case means finding vaccines to destroy the virus. It is about decommissioning the pillars on which coloniality entrench itself in political science long after the end of the colonial era. It is our submission that identifying the virus, dissecting it, explaining how it functions and infects us with an epistemology of blindness, the epistemology of exteriority is the first step in the decolonization process. This is so because coloniality thrives on concealing itself. We know from research that its endurance comes from the fact that it concealed itself as modernity and thus continued to infect the systems of power, being and knowledge hidden underneath modernity. This enables the political science founded on this epistemology to grow by conceit and deceit, infecting unsuspecting others who think they are interacting with modernity and common sense when in fact there is a hidden virus of coloniality in it.

Therefore, the primary strategy of epistemic decolonization in political science is both to expose the coloniality of its epistemological foundations, patterns and parameters and to be transparent about our positionality as political scientists committed to epistemic justice. This twin strategy is designed to end the conceit and deceit perpetrated by the culture of hiding the positionality of thinkers, speakers and writers in political science, using the principle of objective rationality. The whole archive of material we deal with to think through political questions across the world and in our localities needs us to unmask its colonial framing since its authors may not be alive anymore or if they are alive they may not be willing to come clean on their own volition. The task to unveil is a key strategy for decommissioning that which makes political science implicated in epistemic colonization. It is about exposing the hidden dark underbelly that political science inherits from eurocentrism. Exposing coloniality or other forms of injustice in the manner in which political science knowledge is produced and used, especially related to how choices about paradigms, theory, cultural location, epistemic location, values and ethics, an act of justice that is needed right now. This ranges from critiquing dominant perspectives and epistemic choices in political sciences to simply describing how these choices are made.

By the same token, the decision by us to be transparent about our loci of enunciation, our paradigms of thought, our philosophy of knowledge, the cultural imports of our positions, helps to ensure that those who read are not fooled into thinking we are writing from a God's eye view, an objective rationality location of thought. This is a decision not to replicate the myths of eurocentrism, including a particularly Eurocentric reading of objectivity and rationality governed by rules and conventions all designed to let the writer, thinker and researcher conceal the biases they bring to scholarship (Quijano 2000). This extends to the emergence of the new attitude where thinkers outside the mainstream are encouraged to insist on writing and thinking from where they are rather than via the euromodern cosmic arena. It is about combative ontology where the biography and geopolitics of knowledge are inverted in order to enable all of us to think authentically from where choose to (Mafeje 2011). The strategy frees those of us who have been detained by the conventions, rules and traditions of objective rationality that require us to be free-floating signifiers when researching, thinking and writing about deeply complex political questions of our time (Mignolo 2009). It is conscious disobedience against this expectation, a liberated attitude and even a combative posture on our part.

Second, and extending from the first strategy, the decolonization of political science requires us to consciously and practically shift the epistemology on which it is built by at least de-centring Eurocentrism. This entails re-centring all parts of the world simultaneously that may bring us closer to epistemic plurality. Shifting the centre in the discipline's epistemology entails allowing all parts of the world, all cultures, all geopolitical positions to equally legitimate sources of the epistemological frames that guide how we know in political science and other mainstream disciplines (Wa Thiong'o 2012). It makes it legitimate also to seek fundamental epistemic plurality in the discipline and the whole of knowledge, this is a diversity that takes us from political science as an epistemic monologue towards a multilogue, from political science as a discipline of knowledge towards one that is an ecology of knowledges (Zondi 2018). To this, we would need to move towards banishing silences that characterize political science and the rest of Eurocentric knowledge (Zeleza 2005a). Our task will be to unmute the silenced voices and let ignored experiences, by deliberating identifying those voices in archives and real life and let them be included in the conversation. We also need to deprovincialize Europe and its claims to universal perspective to enable epistemic freedom to come to regions of the world that disadvantaged by the universalizing of Eurocentrism and for cognitive justice for the victims of the actions of the cognitive empire that invaded the mental universe of peoples outside Europe and its diaspora (Ndlovu-Gatsheni 2018). This will let the questions that are pertinent and even primary from the viewpoint of regions other than Europe and its diaspora to be raised again and made central to conversations in political science. Shifting the centre also means transcending disciplinary knowledge and stretching even further the ability of the discipline to be undisciplined, to defy artificial disciplinary boundaries and escape disciplinary decadence that so far limited how we know the political (Gordon 2011). This is practically working to correct the theft of history (Goody 2006) by which Europe placed itself at the centre of world history to explain its cognitive domination of others and rationalize the continuation of this domination. This includes correcting the narratives about the origins of the political and its constituent parts such as democracy, notions of power, modern political institutions and so forth.

Space does not permit us to discuss how shifting the political science epistemological confines affects its research methodology and pedagogy, two critical entry points for the decolonization of the discipline. Save to say here that we are talking about shifting how we understand and use positionality and paradigms in methodology, how we identify and interpret research problems for this determines what gets researched, and how we choose to understand research designed and how we choose methods and research strategies for these determine how what is chosen is researched. Many of our challenges arise from the coloniality in how research methodology is understood, explained and used in political science often to preserve the tools and paradigms of the cognitive empire. Who we are in research processes; what we research; how we research and write about it; and whether we disseminate it, are all subject to the distorting technologies of the cognitive empire that continues to reign in our cognitive universe long after the physical empire was forced to grant limited independence to our territories.

Similarly, pedagogy relates to paradigms, practices and tools used to transmit knowledge in classrooms and other teaching and learning platforms including virtual platforms that have become popular during the COVID-19 pandemic. The paradigms, practices and tools flow from the epistemological frames of this area of knowledge. For instance, the embedded hierarchy of people, power, values, principles and so forth that underpin the mainstream epistemology is handed down to how teaching and learning reinforce rather than challenge or disrupt these hidden structures. Decolonizing political science requires unlearning the paradigms of alterity, the practices that miseducate, and tools like assessment techniques that re-establish coloniality through pedagogy. Central also to this process is to jettison the textbook since it has functioned as control and disciplining measures chisel mimics out of students.

Conclusion

The call to decolonize knowledge generally and political science as a discipline, its sub-disciplines and practices will demand much more of us and the knowledge system than it is assumed. This is coloniality as a model of power in the world including coloniality of knowledge established Eurocentrism as the top of the hierarchy of knowledge or as the only knowledge where all others have been erased or killed. There are many imports of this predicament including coloniality that is evident in the epistemologies, methodologies, pedagogies, and archives that underpin political sciences. This chapter has argued that the decolonial turn will come from the shifts in the epistemology, pedagogy, archive and epistemic attitude. It is a transformation that requires the transformation of the thinker and their attitude to knowledge, and it requires the thinker to also be an agent of change in pursuit of cognitive justice. The chapter proposes practical measures that can be taken in at least three areas: positionality of a political scientist; the canonical foundations of the discipline; and briefly research methodology and pedagogy. The latter deserves a lot more attention than space in this chapter permits, but what might be considered in explaining that in fuller ways as suggested earlier. Indeed, the time to decolonize political science has come and the ways of doing it are diverse. Not enough has been done to fully explore and discover these ways. This chapter seeks to contribute to this task in a small way.

6

A neglected subject

The politics of mourning the (de)humanized

Lebohang Motsomotso

Introduction

It is critical that political sciences as a field of study, particularly African political studies, should consider the importance of acknowledging the loss and grieve of those who are silenced and neglected through means of oppressive mechanisms. Especially because Africans have lived in mourning for centuries now, due to physical and social death, exploring the conditions of mourning and grieve assists in understanding the trappings of the current era. The dismemberment of Africa's experience from coloniality haunts the continent to this day, it manifests in high levels of stress, anxiety, pain, shame, low self-confidence, Afrophobia and a perpetual state of mourning and oppression. Moreover, such oppression is reproduced and results in prolonged aftermaths of colonialism such as civil wars, massacres and apartheid. Such aftermaths are the product of ontological terror which challenges the claim that black people are human and exist as well as experience life as humans (Warren 2018). When questioning whether black people are human or not, it leads to a deliberation of noting how black people experience life and death. Therefore, it requires exploring the divide between the living and dead. Mbembe's (2003) work on necropolitics provides a notable argument in understanding the status of life and death. Necropolitics is concerned with the subjugation of life to the power of death and how death can reconfigure relations among resistance, sacrifice and terror (Mbembe 2003: 39). Mbembe, notes that in the world, there are those who are able to maximize their power to cause destruction in the lives of others. This results in new and different forms of social existence whereby populations exist in conditions of 'death-in-life'. This condition explains the unequal and paradoxical relationship between death and life – it translates to a condition in which one is alive, but dead simultaneously. The consequence of such 'death-worlds' is that one cannot really die, therefore they cannot be mourned. Essentially, it translates to a position of not being fully alive, hence, it dismisses the possibility of being mourned.

Mourning is associated with loss and it exposes the human condition to vulnerability. The symbolism of mourning announces damage and harm – that something or someone has been taken away. Mourning is an expression of sorrow that is universal and is not limited to a particular race or gender. But when mourning is labelled as an act that is exclusively for those who are deemed human and it becomes a process of experiencing human vulnerability, it begins to exclude others, who are not valued as human. Mourning thus becomes only about those who are regarded as human. Hence, it is critical to closely examine how mourning is perceived, especially because it forms a critical part of dealing with loss. Evidently, on the African continent, loss has become an unavoidable result of the violent atrocities, such as massacres, civil wars and laws of segregation, that Africans have experienced. Therefore, an analysis of what underpins grievable lives should be undertaken, for the purposes of understanding the dynamics of human vulnerability and, more significantly, how human vulnerability can possess an unequal and biased understanding of grievable lives. This chapter explores how mourning converts an exclusive moment and event to an aftermath that has affected and uncovered human vulnerability. Human vulnerability occurs and is experienced through the body and mind, and humans experience violence through the mind and body. Accordingly, the body and mind become sites of violence and invariably mourning. Butler (2004: 20) asks a pertinent question, 'What makes for a grievable life?' From this question, more questions arise, 'Whose life?' and 'Why is life grieved upon?'. In these questions, one should consider the dimension of the human condition in relation to its exposure to violence, its vulnerability to loss and the consequence of mourning that follows. This dimension of the human condition foregrounds human vulnerability. Perhaps then it is unarguable that mourning constitutes vulnerabilities to the body and mind, as sites exposed to violence. The discussion here focuses on how exposure to violence in political life results in mourning and, evidently, dehumanization of neglected subjects. When mentioning the dehumanized, these are subjects that are neglected, silenced, excluded and unrecognized. In Africa's modern history the neglected subjects have experienced melancholy and death by way of enslavement during the precolonial era, genocide, massacres, civil wars during the colonial rule and a continued oppression that transcends and haunts an ongoing continuum of repression.

Hence, the purpose of this chapter is to extract meaning and understanding in how significant happenings that are unknowable and knowable in political life create grievable moments. For this reason, it is central to this discussion to explain what constitutes a political life. To begin with, there is no universal definition of what constitutes a political life, but, in an effort to understand the concept, the term, 'political', is explained as referring to achieving and exercising positions of governance; it is an organized control over a human community. What constitutes as 'political life' can, therefore, be understood to refer to how people live in groups and make decisions. Therefore, politics and life cannot be separated, political decisions are made in the spectra of life and are about life. Hence, in this discussion, the spectacle of life, in itself, will be examined as a political entity. To be politicized is to be made controversial, it encompasses branding certain groups' needs as though they are unnatural and undeserving, or certain actions as unjust and unlawful. A politicized life is often expressed through any action that is about affirming oneself and one's humanity and, thus, maintaining and restoring dignity becomes a politicized action. Persons, who undertake such actions, are often, if not always, regarded as threats to the status quo. Throughout history, these persons' are categorized as ill-disciplined, unruly, illegitimate and rebels, and they end up indicted as those that need to be humanized, because they lack human capabilities, such as discipline. This discussion will delve into the link between a politicized and depoliticized, as well as a humanized and dehumanized life, and explain how mourning is perceived in such circumstances. At the centre of this discussion is the question: How do you mourn a life that has been dehumanized? A life that has been deemed as not worthy and not recognized as legitimate. This discussion then considers how the dehumanized can be mourned when their humanity is already in question.

The first section explains how humanization and dehumanization transpire; the second section is an interpretation of exile as a tool of dehumanization, particularly in the content and context of oppression; and the last section provides a critical argument of how the dehumanized and the exiled are subject to violent mourning especially as neglected subjects that are silenced through the experiences of colonial rule such as apartheid in South Africa and the genocidal colonial era.

Interpreting the vulnerability for the humanized and dehumanized

> The body implies mortality, vulnerability, agency: the skin and the flesh expose us to the gaze of others, but also to touch, and to violence, and bodies put at risk of becoming the agency and instrument of all these as well. (Butler 2004: 26)

Butler explains that the body is exposed to vulnerability; the body is predisposed to judgement. With that in mind, various struggles have arisen for rights over bodies. But she still acknowledges the body as invariably a public dimension (Butler 2004). This means, in a social setting, the body exists within a public domain; hence, your body is subjected to the world. The body is exposed to a world of others; it is further exposed to inscriptions informed by others. Only later, and possibly with uncertainty, would one claim their body as their own – if, in fact, it does occur. In the formation of agency and will of the body, Butler (2004) posits a critical question, if one were to deny body proximity of others and exclude it from the position of an unwilled physical interaction, would that result in a body that enjoys autonomy without being exposed to social conditions? To be human is to have reason, agency and superiority; it is to live freely and, above all, it is to embody freedom; it is to be vulnerable to the conditions of life; and it is to be susceptible to mourning. Humanity is having wholeness and autonomy (McRobbie 2006). To be human is to be consistent in the ways in which life is valued, it is to have the freedom to move and thrive, without being subjected to a coercive force (Yancy and Butler 2015). There is a hierarchy of humanity that results in a discourse of dehumanization; it produces the effects of dehumanization and establishes the boundaries of humanity. The dehumanized are removed from the realm of reality. There is a restrictive conception of what is human, it is based on an exclusion of an established ontology. Those who are excluded are categorized as unreal; they suffer the violence of derealization. Butler (2004) understands derealization as a discourse that considers certain lives as disposable and not human. These are lives that do not fit into the frame of being human – their dehumanization occurs at this level, first, and, at the following level, it gives rise to physical violence, which unfolds and exposes itself through a physical manifestation of dehumanization, such as exile. Dehumanization ends up forging a culture that perpetuates the violence of exclusion and oppression.

Human lives are grievable lives: lives that are deemed worthy of being mourned. There is an epistemic underpinning and capacity that apprehends what it means to be human and have a grievable life. It creates the normative production of ontology that recognizes and unrecognizes injury and violence towards human lives. Butler (2016) mentions that there are normative schemes that emerge and are interpreted, based on the operations of power that determine who comes to be known as 'subjects' and who are not quite recognized as subjects, and 'lives' that are not recognized or will never be recognized as lives. In essence, operations of power, such as colonialism, apartheid and segregation, are founded on prejudice principles that create a divide and hierarchy between recognizable and unrecognizable lives. Consequently, it causes an ethical problem, where there is a hierarchy as it relates to grief, just as there is a hierarchy in regard to mourning. Butler (2004) notes that grievable lives are lives that are acknowledged. These are lives that are considered a loss; lives that are summarized and humanized in obituaries. These are lives that are worth noting, preserving and qualifying of recognition. Butler refers to an obituary as an action that functions as an instrument in which grieving is publicly distributed. She makes an example of the war casualties during the Gulf War, wherein 200,000 Iraqi children were killed; however, there were no obituaries for the casualties; if there were obituaries, it would mean these lives were worth preserving, acknowledging and grieving. Similarly, during the apartheid era in South Africa, many lives were lost during protests, but in newspaper articles, only lives that mattered would be accounted for. Lives that matter are publicly grievable lives and these would include white security personnel or white citizens – lives that matter, because they are human. The dehumanized are those who do not have obituaries, whose passing is not acknowledged as a loss; whose life is not grievable; whose life does not qualify as life. The dehumanized cannot have obituaries, because they never really died, because, to die means to have lived and only humans live; hence, the dehumanized never lived – they existed in a present-absent continuum. Thus, this informs how you cannot mourn those who are not human and you cannot mourn those who never lived.

Essentially, the dehumanized suffer disenfranchised grief – this is 'grief experienced by those who incur a loss that is not or cannot be openly mourned or socially supported' (Doka 1999: 37). Doka (1999) notes that humans can experience significant loss and, as a result of that loss, grief is experienced, but grief is acknowledged differently – basically, it is acknowledged in a hierarchical manner. Doka's work focuses on how societies have different sets of norms concerning grief: there are certain 'grieving rules' and these rules are codified as personal. He explains several reasons why grief is disenfranchised. His reasons warrant a closer examination, because they express how grief is justified differently and, by that virtue, these reasons help determine and account for how grieving, attached to loss, can promote dehumanization. Firstly, Doka mentions that grief can be disenfranchised in situations where a relationship is not recognized, whereby the relationship between the bereaved and deceased is not based on recognizable ties.

Secondly, when the loss is not recognized, it is not socially defined as significant. This second reason is highly significant in how Bulter (2004) explains grievable lives, since loss and grief account for the vulnerability of humans; it thus means loss is highly associated with vulnerability. Yet, vulnerability has to be recognized and perceived to have an ethical and authentic encounter with grief. However, there is a possibility that vulnerability is not recognized, and when it is not recognized, the loss experienced by the unvulnerable becomes disenfranchised loss. A loss that is unrecognized is a loss experienced by the dehumanized. This is because vulnerability is a precondition for humanization, and humanization takes place differently, depending on varying norms of recognition. Doka noted that grief, as a result of vulnerability, is acknowledged differently, based on varying norms. Butler, similarly, attests that vulnerability depends on existing norms of recognition. Therefore, vulnerability acquires another meaning: it is something that can be recognized or unrecognized and, significantly, it is an application of power, particularly by those who decide on whether vulnerability is recognized or not. This makes vulnerability operate in a particular framework in the precondition for experiencing loss and grief, that is to be human; thus, loss and grieving become an exclusively human condition. By that, it limits grief and loss to be determined by a set of conditions that fluctuate between recognized and unrecognized vulnerability.

The third reason Doka mentions is that the griever is not recognized. This reason ties in well with the former, which makes reference to that when the loss is not recognized, it is not socially defined as significant. He explains that there are institutions that do not recognize the loss or need to mourn.

The last reason to consider is when grief is disenfranchised because the individual's method of grieving is not validated – when grieving occurs in a manner that is deemed not socially acceptable. Yet, grieving or mourning can never really be measured, since it is a subjective expression of emotions. But, if the precondition of vulnerability has to exist for grief and loss to be recognized, and only humans experience vulnerability, then the period of validation for loss is only known by the human. It is only the vulnerable that are subjected to loss and mourning, and that predisposes them to their humanness. Those outside of the framework of vulnerability are subjected to unending dehumanization. These individuals are excluded from the norms of recognition: they can be deemed as banished or exiled – as unrecognizable lives.

Exile as the perpetual condition for the dehumanized

Exile is a political condition that is painful and unjust. Said (1999) reveals that exile is a political condition and a critical concept. Exile is banishment; it is political action that forces a person or group of people to depart from their own country and to seek refuge in another country; however, being in exile resembles, but is not the same as being a refugee. Living in exile means living in a space where you are always aware that it is not your home. Being in exile means constantly feeling an absence of belonging. Barbour (2007) warns that exile should not be thought of as a humanistic element, because, by so doing, it trivializes the suffering it causes. Said (2000: 174) notes that 'exile is irremediably secular and unbearably historical; that it is produced by human beings for other human beings; and that, like death but without death's ultimate mercy'.

He explains the intensity of exile and likens it to death, but death seems more bearable and merciful, because it has an ending; whereas the ending of exile is uncertain. This makes life in exile provisional and temporary, and the exiled vulnerable, because one cannot know when it will end. It gives rise to a life that is not static. Life in exile is nomadic and lived on the periphery – those in exile have to create their own structure and meaning (Barbour 2007). Said (2000) notes that living in exile fosters a conscientious subjectivity, an independence of mind, a critical perspective and originality in vision. This is because one has to construct and imagine a life outside of exile, while simultaneously interpreting the potential value of exile. Those who are in exile have to look beyond the existential and epistemological nature of their existence. Exile has an alienating and desolate feeling associated with it (Zeleza 2005b: 3).

Narratives of oppression are eminent through exile. Adesanmi (2004: 22) notes that these narratives are created by what he refers to as 'territorial integrity of oppression'. He explains this as how oppression has moulded itself into occupying territory and aspires to an insidious notion of spatial and temporal schematics. Thus, exile becomes a tool of oppression. It marks lines that separate the exiled and nonexiled. The exiled are marked by a discontinuous state of being, solitude and loneliness, and efforts of acculturation and community are difficult to establish (Zeleza 2005b: 9). Exile is marked by the tension between absence and presence; exile is thus also forged between this tension. When in exile, you are groundless; hence, you foster a careful subjectivity and critical perspective on independence, because you are decentred and nomadic. Zeleza (2005b: 9) argues that the exiled therefore find themselves in a

> perpetual deferment of constructing home in the hostland, of turning the exilic condition into diasporic condition in which the 'here' and 'there' of the original rupture are inverted as the new homeland assumes existential primacy and the old retains ontological affinity.

This condition that Zeleza speaks of forces one to drift between becoming and being. The notion of becoming explains a state in which the exiled are in a continuous process of becoming. This is a position of never achieving one's full potential; instead, one is always on a journey to attain belonging and acceptance in the host land. The exiled are forced to pursue acceptance, because the host land labels them as outsiders. The exiled find themselves within an ontological dimension of oppression (Freeman 2015). Exile is persistently being in a place that immerses one into loneliness and creates an urge for continuous attainment of belonging.

The exiled suffer attunement, according to Heidegger (1962). Attunement (*Befindlichkeit*) is 'an ontological structure that constitutes both how we find ourselves (*sich befinden*) in the world and how we are faring in it' (Freeman 2015: 25). Heidegger's (1962) conception of attunement describes how an individual perceives and experiences themselves and, fundamentally, how the world perceives and experiences the individual. Attunement explains a condition in which one cannot be isolated or experience the world separate from the context; basically, one experiences the world within a particular context. Although Heidegger's writings were not particularly concerned with interpreting exile, his explanation of attunement is critical, because it provides a valuable resource in mapping how the experiences of the exiled cannot be isolated from the nonexiled. Heidegger's attunement serves as a point of reference in explaining that there is a fundamental manner in which one exists in the world and it is structured by how you perceive yourself and how the world perceives you. According to Heidegger's way of thinking, one cannot exist in the world isolated from others' perceptions and, as a result, it makes one's existence rely upon others. Thus, it can be said that the nonexiled cannot exist without the exiled. There is an exaggerated sense of group cohesion among the exiled, and it is accompanied by a passionate hostility towards those who are nonexiled. For the exiled it prompts creating a 'new world', because they are already removed from their homeland and are simultaneously rejected by their host land; therefore, those who are in exile have a constant urge to (re) create. It is for this reason that Said (1993) acknowledges exile as an ontological and political space of freedom.

Freedom for the exiled is expressed through ontological grounds by assuming the position of attaining a way of becoming part of the group or attaining a feeling of belonging in the host land. Yet, through that process, a secondary process emerges: the exiled (re)create a new world in their efforts of attaining acceptance in their host land and, as a result, they occupy political space. Hence, exile becomes an ontological and political space of freedom. Yountae (2017) explores the unfortunate gap between the ontological and political spaces, and proclaims it as the abyss. Yountae (2017) provides a detailed explanation of the origins of the term 'abyss'. In his explanation, he mentions that the Oxford English Dictionary defines abyss as 'the bottomless chasm that bears a direct association with the primal formless chaos and the subterranean source of water in ancient Hebrew cosmology' (Yountae 2017: 8). Younate explains that the abyss is often associated with the terms, 'void' or 'nothingness', although he does mention the importance of distinguishing the two terms. A void indicates a state of being that is unoccupied either by a person or by any other visible content, it is empty, lacking and destitute. A void can mean both the 'space' is empty and the emptiness itself. The etymological root of a void, is *vacuus*, which also means empty and nothingness; thus, in this sense, the meaning of void is closely associated with nothing. Yountae (2017: 9) further verifies that 'if *nothing* points to the null state of existence, whether a person or a thing/matter, *void* presumes a previously occupied or filled state, if not an expectation of presence'.

Since the abyss is associated with a void and nothingness, it therefore points to an absence. Yountae provides various contextualizations of how the abyss presents itself. The abyss is connected with moving through a passage, a self's passage into and out of the abyss, essentially moving from loss to possibility and from finitude to infinity. The definition of the abyss has philosophical implications on human existence. By this, it means the abyss represents a symbolic and metaphorical explanation in various contexts. In the context of exile, the abyss represents a philosophical interpretation of exile. Yountae (2017: 11) explains that the abyss 'indicates the indeterminate – if not finite – structure of being, the precariousness of the human epistemological and ontological foundation'.

Essentially, when in the abyss, one experiences infinite solitude, and this experience resembles that of exile. Both exile and the abyss resemble a space of groundlessness. Both spaces convey the pain of the colonial wound and a state of the self, in which one lives in a suspended presence, not knowing what will unfold. This is the reality of exile and the abyss: it creates conditions that leave the self in a matrix of not belonging anywhere and consistently being in a state of anguish. When in exile, one loses your material and political grounding – material loss of the self occurs in that there is a metaphysical condition of absence. The political loss of the self occurs as a result of historical and politico-economic ground within a context of oppression, particularly since exile is a tool of oppression (Yountae 2017: 8–12, 92).

Since exile is a tool of oppression, it means there is an oppressor involved in enacting the oppression of exile. There is a known agent that enforces and monitors exile upon others. The distinction between the exiled and nonexiled has to be noted when interpreting the power dynamic relations between those who are exiled and nonexiled, because, through these relations of power, the relationship of the oppressor and oppressed emerges. It is through this relationship that an opportunity to unmask the exiled and nonexiled is granted. This reveal is granted by understanding who is subjected to exile and who is not. Exile is the condition of the oppressed, according to Said (1993). It further pronounces that exile unfolds as psychological, existential and physiological, and is an embodied dimension of oppression. In form and practice, the oppressed are denied personal autonomy, the oppressor imposes a worldview paradigm onto the oppressed, which denies them the power to direct their own lives. Freire in his seminal work on oppression, 'Pedagogy of the Oppressed' (1968), explains the link between oppression and dehumanization. He attests that the oppressor is dehumanized by the act of oppression, while the existential reality of oppression and the internalization of the image of the oppressor dehumanize the oppressed. Hence, exile is interpreted as a condition of the oppressed and the dehumanized.

The oppression is enacted through loss, nothingness and void. Among the consequences of exile is a loss, the entanglement of being groundless is caused by loss. Loss takes place when one has a conscious encounter with the other (Younta 2017: 75). According to a Hegelian understanding, the other is directly symbolic of the loss. Hegel (1971[1894]: 3) posits:

The knowledge of Mind is the highest and hardest, just because it is most 'concrete' of sciences. The significance of that 'absolute' commandment, *Know thyself* – whether we look at it in itself or under the historical circumstances of its first utterance – is not to promote mere self-knowledge in respect of particular capacities, character, propensities, and foibles of the single self.

By his interpretation of the self, the subject can only *know thyself* when it sees it in another self-consciousness or another subject (Hegel 1971[1894]).

Hegel (1971[1894]) explains that self-knowledge cannot be attained by way of introspection alone; one cannot examine a single self and reach significant conclusions. Instead, introspection must include an examination of one's relationships with others. This is because the self does not exist in complete isolation of other selves, but the self exists among other selves. By this understanding, a self that is aware of other selves, and the importance of recognizing others' selves, is part of self-knowledge. But, in the context of exile, when selves are separated and examined on the different paradigms, a distinction of selves emerges. A distinction of understanding the self emerges. Thus, there is significance in understanding who is deemed as human and who is not and what warrants humanity in an individual, because the status of the human and dehumanized distinguish the possibility of being exiled or not. It is therefore important to consider and interpret the conducts of humanization and dehumanization.

The violence of mourning

Violence is the order in which the dehumanized live, it is the living condition of the dehumanized. The state of violence is the aftermath of dehumanization. Violence is how human vulnerability unfolds as a control, without limit, over the will of others and expands itself as a way of life upon those who do not experience vulnerability. It enacts itself through acting on others, putting others at risk, causing damage to others and threatening to erase others (Butler 2004: 28–29). Violence aims at eliminating those who fall outside the framework of humanness, it is the tool of separating the human and dehumanized. Violence is enacted against those who are unreal. But it can be argued that violence fails to exclude, threaten or remove the dehumanized from recognition or reality, because they are already negated and removed. The dehumanized are confined to peculiar positions; they are encountered with violence again and again: firstly, as the dehumanized, who do not have vulnerability; and, secondly, as those who cannot be grieved, because they never lived and they were never human. They cannot suffer death, because they never lived and, therefore, they cannot be mourned. In the life of the dehumanized, violence renews itself. Violence then becomes a destabilizing effect, caught in a 'boomerang perception', meaning it is self-generative and continuous. Hence, violence becomes inexhaustible for the dehumanized; it is endless. The dehumanized are neither dead nor alive; thus, violence does not end. As such, violence is much like living in exile: it is a position that denies one humanity along an unending continuum. To illuminate the experiences of those living in exile and with violence, and who are denied vulnerability as the dehumanized, a great example is the Truth and Reconciliation Commission of South Africa, which details how mourning is violent for the dehumanized.

In 1995, the negotiations between political parties in South Africa reached a pivotal moment in the pursuit towards political transformation and the establishment of a new, lawful, nonracial society. This period is marked by a period of ambivalence and, to assist in bringing healing to the country, the Truth and Reconciliation Commission was established in 1995. This was a nonjudicial body, aimed at providing a temporal and material space for victims and perpetrators of all forms of violence generated through and by apartheid. The Commission was composed of three committees: The Human Rights Violations Committee (for the victims), Amnesty Committee (for hearings on amnesty applications); and the Reparations and Rehabilitation Committee (for identifying criminal cases and determine compensation for victims). The purpose of the Commission was to encourage confessions of politically motivated violence. The Commission was set as 'a place as they say, for the work of mourning to take its time' (Christianse 2003: 373). Essentially, the Commission was designated as a place where those who had experienced losses during the apartheid era could come forward and mourn publicly, in the guise of confessions and amnesty. Apartheid was constitutionalized racism: it defined social, political and economic relations based on racial boundaries. Christianse (2003) explains that individuals were racially defined: individuals could only be individuals in their capacities as representatives of defined categories. By apartheid's logic, their individuality was statistical. They were dehumanized, reduced to a numerical object. This occurs as an ideological structuring process of which the human – in this case the apartheid security police, the white man, the white woman, the superior – and the dehumanized – the black man, the black woman, the inferior – are deemed opposites in the ontological hierarchical structure of being (Yancy 2008).

The hierarchical structure of being is intensified by the colonial gaze: this is the gaze that discerns, with clarity, how the relationship between the human and dehumanized should unfold. Yancy (2008) acknowledges that the gaze reinforces the truth of racist categories and that racist categories reinforce the gaze. The gaze draws clarity, based on a racially discursive interpretation of superior and inferior relations. Moreover, the gaze warrants related interpretation of how the humanized and dehumanized will emerge, although the latter is explained excluding racial categories, but, in essence, it is embedded in prejudicial parameters. Fundamentally, the colonial gaze is understood to account for the dichotomy of black/dehumanized/unrecognized vis-a-vis white/human/recognized and it creates boundaries of inclusion and exclusion. By explaining the colonial gaze, it provides valuable knowledge of how existential phenomenology is bounded on discourses that are interpreted as advanced and recognized, and that follow good and civilized methods of investigation, as defined and measured in Western terms. Moreover, the theoretical amplification of vulnerability, exile, mourning and, more significantly, the humanized vis-a-vis the dehumanized provides a pretext to the violence of mourning.

As evident by the example of the Truth and Reconciliation Commission, it was a commission aimed at providing a public and recognizable space for mourning. Even so, it yields violence: it assumes that, before the establishment of the Commission, there was no loss and grief experienced, particularly because the loss and grieving were not officially recognized. It also presumes the notion that, if the loss is not recognized, then mourning cannot occur. The aims of the Commission then become questionable – how can mourning only begin in 1995, when it was established? Were people [the dehumanized] not allowed to mourn or be mourned before the TRC hearings? Did their mourning end when the Commission hearings ended? How do they mourn now, when they are still dehumanized? These questions probe the notion of vulnerability as something that requires recognition from another. These questions are pertinent when examining the answer to the question posed by Butler (2004), What makes for a grievable life? Because lives that are grievable are those that are mourned; those who are not mourned encounter mourning that is violent. The dehumanized are denied mourning, they suffer a structural denial of mourning, since mourning has to be recognized by a hierarchical structure of being, whereby humans are those who can be mourned and the dehumanized cannot be mourned. This is when mourning becomes violent for the dehumanized, because their mourning is not recognized: that in itself is an act of violence. The dehumanized experience mourning in a discriminatory manner, because their necessity to mourn is turned into violence (Das 2001). For the dehumanized, mourning is lived in real-time: meaning the reality of a (dehumanized) mother and her (dehumanized) son is that, at any moment, they might lose each other, for the mother if she loses her son, she might lose her reason for living. Although the human/white liberal's imagination feels temporarily bad about black suffering, there is no mode of empathy that can replicate the daily strain of knowing that, as the dehumanized/black person, you can be killed for simply being black or not following spurious notions such as: no hands in your pockets, no playing music, no sudden movements, no driving your car, no walking at night, no walking in the day, no turning onto this street, no entering this building, no standing your ground, no standing here, no standing there, no talking back, no playing with toy guns, no living while black, no grieving while black. What is more is that the dehumanized suffer.

Wilderson (2008: 97) asks: 'What does it mean to suffer?' It means to be ontologically positioned to be incompatibly different to the humanized; in which their actions are perceived as justifiable. For instance, when states are involved in protecting citizens [humans] against insurgency and terrorism, they are likely to enforce power, similar to the actions undertaken by the security forces in the apartheid era, when security forces did everything in their power to protect the status quo. Such violence is acknowledged as attesting to the vulnerability of human life. This is a clear instance in which state power and its violence are acceptable, because of the claim of vulnerability. Foucault (1979: 9) notes that 'justice no longer takes public responsibility for the violence that is bound up with its practice'. This is when power becomes a dominant mode of production in normalizing the nature of relations between the humanized and dehumanized.

Hence, occurrences such as the Truth and Reconciliation Commission of South Africa should perhaps be thought of as spaces of recognition. Butler (2004: 44) pronounces that 'when we ask for recognition for ourselves, we are not asking for an Other to see us as we are, as we already are, as we have always been, as we were constituted prior to encounter itself'. When asking for recognition it does not solicit asking to become part of the humanized; instead, it is an act of becoming; it instigates transformation; it petitions one's life as worthy, as vulnerable in relation to the other. It presents a (re)claim to one's humanity. Then, perhaps, organizations of the nature of the Truth and Reconciliation Commission can represent a space that begins the process of restoration for the dehumanized.

Concluding remarks

In conclusion, mourning is about grieving loss, and it is experienced through vulnerability. But when mourning is made an exclusive feeling and act, by virtue it excludes certain individuals. Mourning then is reduced to a discriminatory measure, that is based on boundaries of the relation between the humanized vis-a-vis the dehumanized. Moreover, for the dehumanized, it results in the manifestation of violence, because the notion of vulnerability is not extended to them. The experiences of the dehumanized are not accounted for and recognized with the value and morality as would apply with the humanized; hence, violence prevails in their being. But, of course, this cannot be an accurate understanding of how mourning manifests. For this reason, vulnerability, as a precondition for being human, should be re-examined, because of its underlying marginalization between those whose grieve is recognized and those whose grieve is not recognized. Hence, it is necessary for further analysis concerning how vulnerability is perceived. This analysis by its nature should be vigilant, because mourning and vulnerability are subjective experiences. Nonetheless, analysing mourning, grieve, as well as how and why the dehumanized are subjected to silencing and unrecognition of their loss contributes to why African Political Studies should acknowledge the loss and grieve of those who are dehumanized. It is a critical area of study because of the political traumas such as the precolonial, colonial and post(current)-colonial eras that Africa has experienced, and these traumas still haunt the continent. Therefore, dialogues, debates and literature centred on acknowledging and recognizing mourning and grieving for the black man and women should be highly considered within the field of political sciences. Especially because, unrecognition of mourning and grieve has resulted in long-standing effects of marginalization. Therefore, more research requires a delicate historical account of knowledge on how mourning and vulnerability are understood and how it is expressed in the past, present and future.

7

Political science for whom?

Reflections on teaching and learning political science in selected African universities

Christopher Isike and Olumuyiwa Babatunde Amao

Introduction

Over sixty years of post-colonial African university education has not produced African epistemologies that inform teaching and learning at its higher education institutions. For example, the curriculum in post-colonial African education is still reflective of the legacy of colonial education which was hegemonic and disruptive to African cultural practices, indigenous epistemologies and ways of doing. As Isike (2019) has argued, this partly explains why Africa remains locked outside the core of world affairs, given the nexus between knowledge creation and power. This becomes clearer when we examine the relationship between Western epistemology[1] and intended learning outcomes in colonial Africa which, for example, produced and continue to produce jobseekers instead of job creators who delude themselves as educated elites (see Ayandele 1974; Nwauwa 1997; Achebe 2009).

Indeed, several attempts have been made to examine the nexus between knowledge creation, its relevance to development and impact on African scholarship. Writing on the place of knowledge production and publishing in Africa, Zegeye and Vambe (2006) have argued that knowledge production and publishing in Africa continues to be dominated by Western experts, whose interests do not serve that of Africa, and that publishing in Africa ought to be controlled by its peoples if its African renaissance agenda is to be realized. Relatedly, Oloruntoba (2015) has argued for a Pan-African approach to knowledge production if Africa is to be liberated from the shackles of the global matrix of power, as manifested in the perverse forms of knowledge production, economic theory and praxis, and political system. Lumumba-Kasongo (2017) has argued that 'for higher education in Africa, especially the university system, to sustain

[1] We borrow from Livsey's (2017) caveat that: 'the "west" and the "western world" are problematic terms that misleadingly imply a homogenous, clearly bounded region that has been seen as the cradle of modernity'. Therefore, the term 'western epistemology' is used here to refer to the theory of knowledge which is rooted in western worldviews, beliefs and the learning methods they produce.

its legitimacy (trust, support, and acceptance) and its curriculum, and continue to promote its transformative mission within the existing world system, it must be socially and economically relevant; politically progressive; philosophically open, creative and inclusive; and culturally unifying' (Lumumba-Kasongo 2017: 43–4). This resonates with the Afrocentric approach espoused by Asante (1991: 171) which seeks in every situation the appropriate centrality of the African person in the curriculum and classroom, and wherein phenomena are viewed from the perspective of the African person.

In his contribution to the discourse, Maringe (2017) has raised three critical, but often unanswered questions about knowledge transformation in the African university. These include the imperatives behind knowledge production and transformation in post-colonial African universities; challenging why the knowledge production systems in research, curriculum design, teaching and learning, and the training of doctoral students have remained unchanged; and third, how the prevailing *eurocentric* knowledge production systems in Africa can be transformed to better serve the needs of universities in the era of decolonization (Maringe 2017: 1–2). These questions echo the more radical perspective of scholars such as Ake (1982) who explained the imperialistic and capitalistic character of Western scholarship on economic development in the Third world. In *Social Sciences as Imperialism: The Theory of Political Development*, Ake (1982) argued that Western social science scholarship in developing countries amounts to imperialism in the sense that

[It] foists on the developing countries, capitalist values, capitalist institutions and capitalist development, shapes the learning outcomes in social sciences towards addressing questions of how to make the developing countries more like the West and more importantly, it propagates mystification, and modes of thought and action, which inevitably serves the interest of capitalism and imperialism. (Ake 1982: xiii)

Ake went a step further by pointing out the seemingly imperialistic nature of social sciences in Africa in what he calls the 'capitalist bias in Western social science' (Ake 1982: 134). Western epistemology and social science as he argues promote capitalist values and ideologies through the socialization process, and that a social scientist who grows up in a capitalist society is likely to be indoctrinated with values that are supportive of the capitalist mode of production (Ake 1982: 135). These values, he notes, have the propensity to influence the paradigms he/she uses, the concepts he/she employs in teaching in the classroom and the way he/she formulates his/her research problems (Ake 1982: 135).

Thus, by treating a Western society as being the highest form in the evolutionary process of development, Western social science tends to become conservative, by deliberately ensuring the maintenance of the existing social order. This is reflected in concrete terms in the nature of research we undertake in Africa, in the values that political sciences seek to maximize, in the concepts that are being thought, and in the unit of analysis that must be employed. A classic example in this regard is the indoctrination of the Estonian model (Systems theory) and the structural-functionalist approach, which seem to have become the defining standard and the unit of analysing a state in the disciplines of economics, sociology and most notably political science. This has largely motivated the re-emergence of the debate and sometimes violent calls for the decolonization and Africanization of the higher education curricula in Africa, as most evidenced in the #FeesMustFall protests in South Africa in 2015.

This debate and the advocacy it has generated, among others, have generated germane questions around the relevance of extant social science curricula to the socio-economic and political challenges faced by the continent. In the context of this chapter, the key question addressed is: What are the epistemological perspectives shaping the political science curricula in Africa? And how relevant are these political science curricula to the continent's political and developmental realities? To answer these questions, a qualitative approach was employed to examine the content and course design of political science modules of six selected universities in Nigeria and South Africa. The selected universities are the University of Benin, University of Ibadan, and Obafemi Awolowo University in Nigeria, and the University of KwaZulu-Natal, University of Pretoria and the University of Zululand in South Africa. Nigeria and South Africa were selected as country and analytical case studies as they both have the highest concentration of universities compared to other countries on the continent.[2] A thematic content analysis technique was employed to analyse the teaching curricula of the six political science departments under study in line with the key research questions posed.

A content analysis of political science course content of selected universities

The purpose of this section is to present and analyse the course design and content of the political science programmes of the six universities selected for this study. This is with a view to answer the key questions on the epistemological perspectives shaping the political science curricula in Africa, and their relevance to the socio-economic and political realities of the continent and its peoples in a fast digitizing world. As aforementioned, the selected universities include the Obafemi Awolowo University (OAU), the University of Benin (UNIBEN) and the University of Ibadan (UI) in Nigeria and the University of KwaZulu-Natal (UKZN), the University of Zululand (UZ), and the University of Pretoria (UP) in South Africa.[3] The political science course curricula of these universities studied are presented in Tables 7.1–7.6 per university.

---

[2] Nigeria has 92 public universities and 79 private universities making a total of 171 universities, the highest in Africa. South Africa has twenty-six public universities and thirty-five private universities making sixty-one universities in total, the second-highest in the continent.

[3] Both authors have studied and worked in a number of these universities. For instance, one of them studied in two of these universities (UNIBEN and UKZN) and taught political science in 4 of them; UNIBEN, UKZN, UZ and UP in the last 18 years between 2002 and 2020. The other author studied while also teaching at UKZN. This positionality is useful in giving some experiential insight into the analysis made.

Obafemi Awolowo University, Nigeria

Table 7.1　Political Science Courses at the Obafemi Awolowo University

S/N	Course Code	Description	Course Load in Units
		First Year: Semester One	
1	PHIL 101	Introduction to Philosophy 1	3
2	SSC 101	Man, and His Social Environment	3
3	SSC 103	Man's Environmental Relations	3
4	SSC 105	Mathematics for Social Scientists 1	3
5	SSC 111	Foundations of Psychology 1	3
		Semester Two	
6	SSC 102	Elements of Economic Principles and Theory	3
7	SSC 104	Introduction to Political Science	3
8	SSC 112	Foundations of Psychology 2	3
9	SSC 106	Mathematics for Social Scientists 2	3
10	PHIL 104	Introduction to Philosophy 2	3
		Second Year: Semester One	
11	POL 201	Political Enquiry and Analysis	3
12	POL 203	Political Thought – From Plato to Machiavelli	3
13	POL 207	Elements of Political Economy	3
14	POL 209	Introduction to International Relations	3
15	SOC 203	Nigerian Traditional Social Structure	3
16	SSC 201	Statistical Sources and Methods 1	3
17	CSC 221	Computer Appreciation	2
		Semester Two	
18	POL 204	Introduction to African Politics	3
19	POL 206	Principles of International Relations	3
20	POL 202	Nigerian Constitutional Development and Politics	3
21	DSS 202	Introduction to Population Studies	3
		Third Year: Semester One	
23	POL 301	Contemporary Political Analysis	3
24	POL 303	Administrative Theory and Practice	3
25	POL 305	Public Policy Analysis	3
26	POL 307	The State and Economic Life	3
27	POL 313	Theories of International Relations	3
28	POL 315	Comparative Research Methodology	3
		Semester Two	
29	POL 308	Comparative Government and Politics	3
30	POL 312	Military in Politics	3
31	POL 310	Comparative Foreign Policy	3
32	POL 314	Marxist, Leninist Thought and Practice	3
33	POL 318	Comparative Public Administration in Nigeria	3
		Fourth Year: Semester One	
34	POL 401	Political Ideas	3
35	POL 405	Nigeria's Foreign Policy	3
36	POL 407	Political Parties and Pressure Groups	3
37	POL 409	State and Economy	3
38	POL 413	Public Finance Administration	3
39	POL 415	Research Project 1	3

Table 7.1 (Continued)

S/N	Course Code	Description	Course Load in Units
		Semester Two	
40	POL 402	Political Development and Modernization	3
41	POL 406	Comparative Federalism	3
42	POL 408	Comparative Public Administration	3
43	POL 414	Human Rights and Fundamental Freedom	3
44	POL 420	International Politics of Mass Communication	3
45	POL 416	Research Project 2	3

Source: Extracted from the section on the Department of Political Science, *Faculty of Social Sciences Academic Curriculum Handbook* (2012a) of the Obafemi Awolowo University, Nigeria.

University of Benin, Nigeria

The course design of the Political Science Department of the University of Benin specifically aims to achieve the following:

- Prepare students for the acquisition of sound knowledge to know the focus, scope and content of Political Science as an academic discipline.
- Offer instructions, training and social consciousness in courses that are relevant to the developmental needs and problems of Nigeria, Africa and other developing countries.
- Prepare students for administrative, managerial and policymaking positions in the public service, commerce and industry, international organizations, academic and foreign service.

Table 7.2 Political Science Courses at the University of Benin

SN	Course Code	Description	Credit Load
		First Year: Semester One	
1	POL111	Introduction to political science	3
2	POL 112	Introduction to Nigeria Government I	3
		Semester Two	
3	POL 121	Basic forms and organization of government II	3
		Second Year: Semester One	
4	POL 211	Concepts and scope of political science	3
5	POL 212	Pre-independent Nigerian government and politics	3
6	POL 214	Introduction to African government and politics	3
		Semester Two	
7	POL 221	Introduction to Public Administration	3
8	POL 222	Basic statistics for Political Science	3
9	POL 223	Post-independent Nigerian govt and politics	3
10	POL 224	Public Personnel Management	3

(Continued)

Table 7.2 (Continued)

SN	Course Code	Description	Credit Load
		Third Year: Semester One	
		Compulsory Courses	
11	POL311	Issues in African Government and Politics	3
12	POL 3I4	Theory and practice of Public Administration	3
13	POL315	Logic of Political Inquiry	3
14	POL318	Intro to Public Financial Management and Budgeting Process	3
15	POL312	Introduction to International Relations	3
16	POL313	Public Policy Analysis	3
		Elective Courses	
17	POL317	Classical and Medieval Political Theory	3
18	POL 319	Comparative Political Systems (Developed)	3
19	POL 320	Intro to Political Behavior	3
		Semester Two	
		Compulsory Courses	
20	POL 310	Research Methods	3
21	POL321	Modern Political Theory (Liberalism)	3
22	POL322	Modern Political Theory (Marxism)	3
23	POL 323	Nigerian Public Administration.	3
24	POL 320	Nigerian Local Government Administration	3
25	POL 324	International Organizations	3
26	POL327	Comparative Political Systems (Developing)	3
27	POL 325	Comparative Public Policy Analysis	3
28	POL 326	Topics in Political Behavior	3
		Fourth Year: Semester One	
		Compulsory Courses	
29	POL 411	Contemporary political analysis	3
30	POL 412	Nigerian Politics and Society	3
31	POL413	Nigerian Foreign Policy	3
32	POL 416	Public Personnel Administration	3
33	POL419	Development Administration.	3
34	POL480	Original Research Essay (Two Semesters)	3
		Semester Two	
35	POL421	Contemporary Political Analysis II	3
36	POL422	Foreign Policy of African States	3
37	POL429	Administrative Law Inter-Governmental Relations	3
		Elective Courses	
38	POL423	Comparative Federal Systems	3
39	POL424	Comparative Public Administration	3
40	POL427	Black Political Thought (In Diaspora)	3
41	POL428	International Law	

Source: Extracted from the section on the Department of Political Science, *Faculty of Social Sciences Academic Curriculum Handbook* (2012b) of the University of Benin, Nigeria.

University of Ibadan, Nigeria

Among other objectives, the Department of Political Science of the University of Ibadan seeks to achieve the following:

- Expand the frontiers of knowledge and transform the society through innovation;
- Be a world-class institution where conditions for learning are excellent and researchers are outstanding.

Table 7.3 Political Science Curricula at the University of Ibadan

SN	Course Code	Description	Credit Load
		First Year: Semester One	
1	POS 111	The Study of Politics	3
2	POS 112	Nigerian Constitutional Development	3
		Semester Two	
3	POS 113	The Organization of Government	3
4	POS 114	The Citizen and the State	3
		Second Year: Semester One	
5	POS 211	Political Analysis	3
6	POS 212	Political Ideas	3
7	POS 213	Politics in Africa I	3
		Semester Two	
8	POS 214	Politics in Africa II	3
9	POS 215	International Political System and Africa I	3
10	POS 216	International Political System and Africa II	3
		Third Year: Semester One	
11	POS 311	Statistical Method in Political Science	3
12	POS 312	Logic and Methods in Political Science	3
13	POS 313	History of Political Thought	3
14	POS 314	International Relations Theory	3
15	POS 315	Theory and Practice of Administration	3
		Semester Two	
16	POS 316	The Methodology of Comparative Politics	3
17	POS 321	Marxism	3
18	POS 322	African Political Thought	3
19	POS 323	Foreign Policies of The Superpowers	3
20	POS 363	Political Behavior	3
		Restricted Electives	
21	POS 324	Issues in International Politics	3
22	POS 333	The Government and Administration of Urban	3
23	POS 343	Public Administration in Nigeria	3
24	POS 344	Comparative Federal System	3
25	POS 345	Politics in Western Europe	3
26	POS 352	Politics in Communist Party States	3

(Continued)

Table 7.3 (Continued)

SN	Course Code	Description	Credit Load
		Fourth Year: Semester One	
		Compulsory Courses	
27	POS 411	Comparative Politics Of West Africa	3
28	POS 412	Contemporary political analysis	3
29	POS 421	Government and Politics of Nigeria	3
30	POS 431	Comparative Public Administration	3
31	POS 432	The Theory and Practice of Local Government	3
31	POS 433	Policy Analysis	3
33	POS 443	Principles of Administrative Law	3
		Semester Two	
34	POS 444	Politics of Underdevelopment	3
35	POS 451	Comparative Civil Relations	3
36	POS 453	Principles of International Law	3
37	POS474	International Institutions	3
38	POS482	Problems of Political Philosophy	3
39	POS471	Long Easy	3
40	POS454	Theory of the State	3
41	POS455	Foreign policies of African States	3
		Elective Courses	
42	POS466	Insurgency and Counter Insurgency	3
43	POS467	Rebellion and Revolution	3
44	POS470	20th Century Marxism	3

Source: Extracted from the section on the Department of Political Science, *Faculty of Social Sciences Academic Curriculum Handbook* (2012c) of the University of Ibadan, Nigeria.

University of KwaZulu-Natal, South Africa

The undergraduate programme in South Africa is designed as a three-year degree with an optional fourth year for an honours degree. This is slightly different from Nigeria where the BSc (Hons) degree is offered for a minimum period of four years. Therefore, to achieve uniformity with Nigeria, the courses offered at the Honours level (fourth year) in political science have been collapsed with those offered at the bachelor's level in the Universities of KwaZulu-Natal, Zululand and Pretoria presented in Tables 7.4, 7.5 and 7.6, respectively.

As shown in Table 7.4, the political science programme at the University of KwaZulu-Natal, which prides itself as a premier African university, was developed to serve as a launchpad for students who are interested in the systemic study of power and its exercise at the global, regional, national and local levels.

Table 7.4 Political Science Course at the University of KwaZulu-Natal

SN	Course Code	Description	Credit Load
		First-Year Courses	
1	POLS 101	Introduction to Political Science	16c
2	POLS102	Introduction to Global Politics	16c
		Second-Year Courses	
3	POLS 201	Issues in International Affairs	16c
4	POLS 203	Politics and Public Policy in Southern Africa	16c
5	POLS 204	Politics and Law in South Africa	16c
6	POLS 206	Contemporary African Politics and Development	16c
7	POLS 207	History of Political Thought	16c
		Third-Year Courses	
8	POLS 301	Modern Political Thought	16c
9	POLS 302	Political Communication	16c
10	POLS 303	Political Change in Developing Regions	16
11	POLS 304	Comparative Government and Politics	16
12	POLS 305	Wealth of the World, Poverty of Nations 1	8
13	POLS 306	Wealth of the World, Poverty of Nations 2	16
14	POLS 307	South Africa: Apartheid and After	16
15	POLS 308	International Relations	16
16	POLS 309	Comparative Asian Politics and Development	16
17	POLS 310	Policy Issues and Community Service	16
18	POLS 311	Independent Research1	8
19	POLS 312	Independent Research 2	8
20	POLS 314	Human Rights and Conflict Resolution	16
21	POLS 316	The Politics of Modernization: Institutions and Economic Growth	16
22	POLS 317	Political Economy of International Trade	16
23	POLS 318	African Political Thought	16
24	POLS 319	Seminal Issues in Political Ethics	16
		Fourth Year: Honors-Level Courses	
25	POLS 701	State and Justice in Modern Political Theory	32
26	POLS 702	International Relations and Global Politics	32
27	POLS 704	Cities, States and Politics of Urban Management	32
28	POLS 705	The Political Economy of Southern Africa	32
29	POLS 706	Political Philosophy in Context	32
30	POLS 707	Women and International Relations	32
31	POLS 708	Women and State	32
32	POLS 712	Corruption Sleaze and Politics	16
33	POLS 714	Ethics of Conflict, Diplomacy and Peace	16
34	POLS 716	Foundations of Political enquiry	16
35	POLS 720	New Theories of Democracy	32
36	POLS 721	International Political Economy	32
37	POLS 722	Political Change in Africa	32
38	POLS 723	Advanced Studies in International Relations 1	32
39	POLS 724	Advanced Studies in International Relations 2	32
40	POLS 730	Issues and Themes in Peace Studies	16

Source: Extracted from the section on Political Science in the *College of Humanities Academic Curriculum Handbook* (2013) of the University of KwaZulu-Natal, South Africa.

University of Zululand, South Africa

Table 7.5 Political Science Curricula at the University of Zululand

SN	Course Code	Description	Credit Load
		First-Year Courses	
1	APOL 111	Introduction to Political Science	16
2	APOL 112	Introduction to South African Politics	16
3	APOL 121	Introduction to International Relations	16
4	APOL 122	Introduction to International Organizations	16
		Second-Year Courses	
3	APOL 211	African Political Thought	16
4	APOL 212	Introduction to Political Sociology	16
5	APOL 221	Politics & Public Policy in Southern Africa	16
6	APOL 222	Themes in Contemporary Middle East Politics	16
7	APOL 231	African Politics and Development	16
8	APOL 232	Corruption & Development in Africa	16
		Third-Year Courses	
9	APOL 311	Foreign Policy Analysis	16
10	APOL 312	Geopolitics	16
11	APOL 321	Comparative Politics	16
12	APOL 322	Research Methodology	16
		Fourth Year: Honors-Level Courses	
13	APOL 501	Intergovernmental Relations in South Africa	30
14	APOL 502	Scope & Theories of International Relations	30
15	APOL 503	Political Change and Development in Africa	30
16	APOL 504	Gender and International Relations (SADC)	30
17	APOL 505	South African Foreign Policy Analysis	30
18	APOL 506	Research Paper in International Relations	30
19	APOL 507	Corruption & Sleaze in African Politics	30
20	APOL 508	Independent Research Paper	30

Source: Extracted from the section on Political Science in the *Faculty of Arts Handbook* (2015), the University of Zululand, South Africa.

University of Pretoria, South Africa

The Department offers two streams of undergraduate degree packages in the Faculty of Humanities, BPolSci in Political Studies and BPolSci in International Studies. The core of these two packages consists of two subjects namely political science (STL) and international relations (IPL).

Table 7.6 Political Science Curricula at the University of Pretoria

SN	Course Code	Description	Credit Load
		First Year	
1	PTO 101	Introduction to Politics	24
2	PAD 112	Public Administration	10
3	PAD 122	Public Administration	10
		Second Year	
4	IPL 210	International Relations Theory	20
5	IPL 220	Foreign Policy and Diplomacy	20
6	STL 210	Micro Political Dynamics	20
7	STL 220	Macro Political Dynamics (African state & governance)	20
8	PAD 212	Public Administration	16
9	PAD 222	Public Administration	16
		Third Year	
10	IPL 310	International Political Economy	30
11	IPL 320	Security and Strategic Studies	30
12	STL 310	Political Theory	30
13	STL 320	Political Analysis	30
14	PAD 312	Public Administration	20
15	PAD 322	Public Administration	20
		Fourth Year Honours: Political Science	
16	STL 751	Political Theory	20
17	STL 770	Research Report: Political Science	40
18	PTO 751	African and Regional Politics	20
19	PTO 752	Peace, Conflict and Mediation	20
20	PTO 753	Jean Monnet European Studies	20
21	STL 752	Political Policy Studies	20
22	STL 753	South African Politics	20
23	STL 754	Comparative Politics	20
		Fourth Year Honours: International Relations	
24	IPL 752	International Relations Theory	20
25	IPL 770	Research Report: International Relations	40
26	IPL 751	International Political Economy	20
27	IPL 753	Foreign Policy	20
28	IPL 754	Security and Strategic Studies	20

Source: Compiled by one of the authors, October 2019.

Discussion of findings

Epistemological perspectives shaping the political science curricula in Africa

It is clear from a reading of the course outlines and content of the six universities presented in the tables that there is a relatively strong presence of neo-colonialist tendencies in their curricula design and offerings. There is an almost *copy and paste*, and thus uncritical, adoption of Western epistemologies and their higher education models which have not fit Africa's transformation and development realities. This argument is premised on the following analysis:

Case study 1: Obafemi Awolowo University

- At the Obafemi Awolowo University, Nigeria, a prospective student studying towards a BSc (Hons) degree in political science will be required to undertake a total number of forty-five courses;
- Only six of the courses (SOC 203, POLS:303, 312,318, 405, 418) have a direct relationship with the prevailing Nigerian socio-economic and political environment;
- Four other courses (POLS: 204, 307, 402 and 409) are either directly or indirectly related to Africa's prevalent socio-economic and political realities;
- Another four courses (SSC:105, 106, 201, 202) are largely quantitative in nature (although still Western-centric, they can be excused);
- Two courses are designed as independent research dissertations (POL 415\416),
- The remaining twenty-nine of the forty-five courses offered are intrinsically rooted in Western social science and modes of learning.

Case study 2: University of Benin

- At the University of Benin, Nigeria, a prospective student studying towards a BSc degree in political science will be required to undertake a total number of thirty-nine courses;
- Only eight of the courses (POLS: 111, 112, 212, 223, 323, 320 412 and 413) have a direct relationship with the prevailing Nigerian socio-economic and political environment;
- Four other courses (POLS: 214, 311, 422, and 427) are either directly or indirectly related to Africa's prevalent socio-economic and political realities;
- Two courses are designed as either research-oriented or independent research dissertations (POLS: 310 and 480).
- The remaining twenty-five out of the courses offered are intrinsically rooted in Western social science and modes of learning.

Case study 3: University of Ibadan

- At the University of Ibadan, Nigeria, a prospective student studying towards a Bachelor of Science (Hons) degree in Political Science will be required to undertake a total number of forty-four courses;
- Thirty out of the courses offered were found to intrinsically rooted in Western Social Science
- Only five of the courses (POS: 112, 114, 333, 343, and 421) have a direct relationship with the prevailing Nigerian socio-economic and political environment;
- Six other courses (POS: 213, 214, 215, 216, 322 and 455) are either directly or indirectly related to Africa's prevalent socio-economic and political realities;
- The remaining three courses (POS: 311, 312 and 471) are designed as either research-oriented or independent research dissertations.

Case study 4: University of KwaZulu-Natal

- At the University of KwaZulu-Natal, South Africa, a prospective student studying towards a BSc degree (Hons) in political science will be required to undertake a total number of Fortycourses.
- Twenty-eight of the courses offered were found to be intrinsically rooted in Western social science and mode of learning.
- Only six of the courses (POLS: 203, 204,307, 704 and 705) have a direct relationship with South Africa's prevailing socio-economic and political environment.
- Four other courses (POLS: 206, 3186, 318 and 722) are either directly or indirectly related to Africa's prevalent socio-economic and political realities;
- The remaining two courses (POLS: 311 and 312) are designed as either research-oriented or independent research dissertations.

Case study 5: University of Zululand

- A prospective student studying towards a BA degree with a political science component will be required to undertake eight political science courses.
- Three of the courses offered were found to be intrinsically rooted in Western Social Science.
- Two of the courses (APOL 112 and 212) have a direct relationship with South Africa's prevailing socio-economic and political environment.
- Three other courses (APOL 312, 312 and 321) are directly related to Africa's prevalent socio-economic and political realities.
- One course (APOL 322) is designed as a research-oriented or independent research project.

Case study 6: University of Pretoria

- A student studying towards a BA (Hons) degree in political science takes twenty political science courses.
- For the three-year bachelor degree, students are required to do fifteen undergraduate courses out of which only one (7 per cent) had a clear African focus. The others were broadly rooted in Western epistemology although with latitude for individual lecturer agency to incorporate an African component to the themes thought.
- At the fourth year level for an BA (Hons) degree in political science, out of eight courses from which students are required to choose 5, 1 (STL 753) has a direct relationship with South Africa's prevailing socio-economic and political environment.
- Another 1 (PTO 751) is directly related to Africa's prevalent socio-economic and political realities.

- One (20 per cent) course (STL 770) is a research-oriented or individual research project.
- The remaining two (40 per cent) are global-centric and generally rooted in Western epistemology.
- For the Honors in International Relations, one (IPL 770) is an individual research report and the remaining four (80 per cent) are global-centric and generally rooted in Western epistemology.

It is also clear from the analysis of these curricula that there is no provision for digital politics as both a subject of learning and research given the impact of digitalization on Africa's politics since 2011. Relatedly, there is generally a low usage of digital technologies for teaching. What do these all mean in terms of relevance to Africa's lived realities given the nexus between knowledge and development?

Relevance to Africa's political and developmental realities

A close reading of the political science course syllabi of the selected universities indicates that the political science taught in Nigeria and South Africa is not relevant to the political realities of these states, their peoples, and the continent generally. The content of the curricula does not address themes on core issues and challenges of Africa's political realities and study of politics even when they are occurring in the continent. This continues what Hountondji (1990) described as the scientific dependence of Africa on Western gatekeepers for scientific activity which in many ways constrain the continent's development. His postulation still holds true:

> scientific and technological activity, as practiced in Africa today, is just as 'extroverted' as externally oriented, as is economic activity; its shortcomings are, therefore, of the same nature. That is, they are not cognate or consubstantial with our systems of knowledge as such. On the contrary, they derive from the historical integration and subordination of these systems to the world system of knowledge and 'know-how' just as underdevelopment as a whole results, primarily, not from any original backwardness, but from the integration of our subsistence economies into the world capitalist market. (Hountondji 1990: 7)

This is indeed the inevitable, and structural shortcomings of scientific activity in Africa which political science is not immune from. As noted earlier, the epistemological standpoint and worldview from which political science in Africa is taught is Western-centric and driven by the teleologic thought of European society as the ideal model and measure of a developed society. The purpose of this narrow thinking is to realize the capitalist goal of the Western liberal society which was and continues to be extended to Africa and the rest of the Global South through knowledge imperialism. In this sense, education from its basic to tertiary forms in Africa is imperialism as Ake (1982, 1996) has argued. This keeps the continent locked in a dependency on Western liberal ideas of state, governance and politics as the ideal to aspire to. This dependency limits Africa's capability to diagnose and solve its political challenges through its education systems as they are exogenous and out of tune with its political realities. For example, apart from UKZN, none of these institutions offer service-learning modules that engage with government and civil society at a practical level, and which also teaches students good citizenship values. Impliedly, there is hardly an interface with political stakeholders as visiting resource persons and neither is there an opportunity for students to experience the real world of politics that service-learning gives.

Second, in 2019, just under 40 per cent of the course content of the selected political science courses is directly related to Nigeria and South Africa and Africa in general. This is curious as a reading of the political science curricula of universities in North America, Europe and Asia show between 65 per cent and 80 per cent of content devoted and directly related to the sociopolitical realities of their states and continent[4]. It raises the question of how Africa effectively deals with its sociopolitical problems if it does not sufficiently study them and from its own lenses? This highlights the marginalization of Africa's worldviews, cultures and indigenous knowledge systems in global political science knowledge creation in ways that perpetuate Western epistemic hegemony. For instance, apart from Unizulu where one of the authors was head of department and introduced new courses on corruption and its development effects, none of the other universities except UKZN (also developed by this author) had a course on corruption which is a defining feature of African politics and development.

Third, as Nyoka (2013) argued, the exogenous nature of epistemology in African universities gives a peek into why its curricula are ineffective in explaining and resolving local African contexts and challenges. In the case of political science, the courses offered are not designed to address the fundamental causes of political instabilities of many African states making it difficult if not impossible to address national question issues around equal citizenship and their implications for nation-building. For example, universities are a microcosm of the larger macrocosm of the state, and unless the state and society itself are transformed both in purpose and character, it may be a mirage to expect universities to transform in the ways they should. Therefore, Africa's political science curricula should have content that interrogates the colonial origins of state formation in the continent, their essence and continued relevance in the light of post-colonial realities with a view to draw attention to the need to rethink and redesign the state in Africa to make them African states.

Clearly then, the imperative of decolonizing the political science curricula in African universities is not in doubt. What is unclear is what that means in terms of implementation, how it can be done and where responsibility for such decolonization lies. In the context of the chapter, decolonization refers to the process of challenging and dismantling the Eurocentric and colonial assumptions, theories, and perspectives that dominate political science in the continent. It involves a shift towards a more diverse and inclusive curriculum that recognizes the contributions of African cultures,

---

[4] The authors randomly compared political science curricula in the University of Minnesota, and Rutgers University in the United States, University of Hildesheim in Germany, University of Warmia and Mazury in Poland, the Rissho University in Japan, Seoul National University in South Korea. Also, between 2017 and 2019, one of the authors got information from personal communication with colleagues in these and a number of other universities across these countries and continents which have helped to make this argument.

perspectives and voices in ways that will disrupt the coloniality of knowledge, power and being which continue to undermine the worldviews, perspectives and voices of the continent. This implies decolonization should be beyond merely changing or Africanizing content to making such content relevant to the political realities and needs of Africa. Therefore, while where knowledge comes from is important, what is more important is how knowledge is applied to produce desired outcomes and impact. This is where teaching methods and the agency of the political science teacher come in. Besides what (the content) we teach, how do we teach? What teaching philosophy and pedagogical tools do we use? The question of how we teach is critical to the decolonial project of decolonising the political science curricula in Africa in terms of relevance and impact. Otherwise changing the content alone with regard for how it is taught will amount to pouring new wine in old bottles. The result will not necessarily change as the bottle (structure/culture) will still affect the taste of the new wine (content/ outputs). As we shall see in the next section, in a fast digitizing world, the use of digital technology offers an opportunity for decolonizing the political science curricula in Africa, and this is where the agency and responsibility of the political science teacher is paramount.

Political science faculty in African universities have to start engaging in the scholarship of teaching and learning to enable self-reflection and reflexivity on their teaching practices with a view to redesign course content to make them more relevant to the political realities of their societies and states. This will entail embracing epistemological diversity and inclusivity to incorporate Afrocentric curricula rooted in pre-colonial African worldviews and political value systems that defined society and governance in different ways from those of the West. In line with critical pedagogy, it will also entail making the African person/student the centre of teaching and learning as Asante (1991) espouses. However, decolonizing the political science curricula in African universities is not the responsibility of political scientists alone as the universities and the larger society and state under which they function also have a role to play.

Caught up in a rat race of pursuing the Western logic of capital accumulation for the survival of the fittest, states and university institutions in Africa are increasingly driven by liberal/profit imperatives which imperil the public good essence of universities. Relatedly, the craze for higher education certification in the continent as a result of the high premiums placed on higher education qualifications for employment has increased applications for studies without a corresponding increase in state funding of higher education. This has resulted in dire consequences for teaching and learning. For example, most public universities in Africa have very high student-to-staff ratios that compromise quality in order to cope with the increasing demand in the face of less state funding. Impliedly, there is an imbalance between teaching load and research output as research takes the back seat. This compromises teaching given the link between research and teaching, bringing the argument right back to the nature and essence of Africa's state systems, the governance ethos they produce and their overall impact on societal and state development.

Digitalization as a decolonial pedagogical tool

Back to the question of the relationship between digitalization[5] and decolonization of curricula in political science, pedagogical tools are important. If decoloniality is about addressing the coloniality of being, knowledge and power, it must necessarily go beyond content to include teaching methods. For example, how can decoloniality address knowledge creation in the post-colonial African classroom which still operates from a colonial mindset of the teacher as all-knowing giver of knowledge and the student as the passive blank slate who receives knowledge?

Digitalization offers some answers as it can support decolonization of the political science curricula in several ways. For example, it can help to democratize the classroom and allow for student participation in knowledge creation in political science since students come with knowledge based on their local experiences of politics and sense of the world. Apart from helping to foster critical pedagogical approaches to teaching, a democratic classroom also breaks down the traditional colonial hierarchies of power between the teacher and students which inhibits deep learning. Second, it offers access to diverse knowledge and resources from different cultural and linguistic backgrounds, which can help to challenge the dominance of Eurocentric/Western-centric perspectives in political science. Third, it enables collaboration and exchange between lecturers and students from different parts of Africa and the world, allowing for the sharing of diverse perspectives and experiences. This provides for new forms of expression and creativity in class that challenge traditional forms of representation, and enable the inclusion of diverse cultural and political expressions. Overall, digitalization can support the decolonization of curricula by promoting diversity, inclusivity and the recognition of African worldviews, social histories, experiences, voices and geographies as locus of enunciating politics and political science.

A cross-cutting issue in terms of relevance of the curricula that emerged from the content analysis of the course outlines is that digitalization is not sufficiently covered in the political science curricula of the selected universities, and this is generally the case across the other public universities in both Nigeria and South Africa. For example, none of the six universities studied had any courses that focus on the digital revolution as an issue of study or on the interface between digitalization and politics[6]. This is problematic given the profound impact of digitalization on the conduct of both domestic and international politics. According to Isike (2019: 277):

> the dearth of digitalization could be traced to a number of factors including the
> absence of dedicated professorships in politics and the digital revolution/internet,

---

[5]   Digitalization refers to the use of technology to transform traditional forms of communication, such as printed text, into digital formats that can be easily accessed and disseminated through electronic devices. In the context of education broadly, digitalization can enable the sharing of knowledge and resources across geographic and cultural boundaries, which can contribute to decolonization of curricula by promoting diversity and inclusivity in educational materials.

[6]   Three of the universities in South Africa (Unizulu, UKZN and UP) have one international relations course each that speaks to the role of social media in political change which was developed after the Arab Spring in North Africa in 2011. However this is not good enough.

scant research on politics and the digital revolution by political science researchers within departments, the bureaucracy associated with changing course contents and names, dearth of younger researchers in the discipline who are more likely to embrace the use of digital tools as well as general ignorance on digital technology.

These constitute some of the institutional challenges to digitalizing the study of politics in African universities. A corollary of this is low investment in digital learning technologies which in turn limits the potential of digitalization for decolonizing teaching and learning not only political science but also other disciplines across universities in Africa. For example, apart from the University of Pretoria whose investment in digital learning technologies paid off with the advent of the coronavirus pandemic that forced universities globally to transition into a full online learning,[7] the other five universities, especially the Nigerian ones struggled with this transition.[8] Overall, low investment in digital technologies for teaching and learning has adversely affected the use of digitalization as a decolonial pedagogical tool in both countries.

On the research side of digital politics, studies on the state of political science as a discipline in Africa have often focused on epistemological and pedagogical issues, and not much on teaching and learning methods. For example, not many political science experts or departments have researched the impact of the digital revolution on political participation, political processes, policymaking and public institutions (Isike 2019). Furthermore, fewer are engaging in research on the impact of the digital revolution on their teaching practice and content. An overview of article titles and abstracts of two key political science journals in South Africa (Politikon and Politeia) over a ten-year period (2009–2018) indicate that very little research has been done in these areas. A similar overview of titles and abstracts in *Studies in Politics and Society: Journal of the Nigerian Political Science Association*[9] over the same period show the same trend of low engagement with research on digital politics. We however note Politeia had more research on digital politics as it contained titles by political scientists in both Nigeria and South Africa on the impact of digitalization on the conduct of politics; electoral democracy and political participation even though they are on Nigeria and on the link between decolonization, Africanization and digitalization.

Conclusion

This chapter has argued that the political science curricula taught in Nigerian and South African universities are ineffective in explaining and resolving their local

---

[7] The University of Pretoria is one of the first in Africa to transition from in-person classes to full online classes in Africa and it took the university just over a month to do this transition which it maintained for two years (April 2020 and June 2022) with varying degrees of hybrid learning in the last year.

[8] The situation in Nigeria is made worse with poor internet infrastructure.

[9] This is the official journal of the Nigeria Political Science Association (NPSA) and it is Nigeria's equivalent of South Africa's Politikon which is the official journal of the South African Association of political Studies (SAAPS).

contexts and challenges. The analysis of the political science course outlines and content of the selected universities indicates the political science taught in Nigeria and South Africa is not relevant to the political realities of these states, their peoples and the continent generally. A discussion of the relevance of the political science curricula in Africa also includes the use of teaching and research methods that make use of modern technology in an era of digitalization. Our analysis of digital politics show that the mutually reinforcing impact of digitalization on the practice, research and teaching of politics is still emerging in Nigerian and South African universities as digital politics is not covered in the curricula in spite of its potential to revolutionize not only the conduct of politics but also research, teaching and learning. This is important given that digitalization can support the decolonization of curricula by promoting diversity, inclusivity and the recognition of African perspectives and voices in the study of politics.

We therefore agree with others who have made the argument before us that there is an urgent need for decolonizing, Africanizing and digitalizing the political science curricula in African universities. As we have shown in the cases of both Nigeria and South Africa, a situation where an average of over 60 per cent of the political science curricula in the universities studied are Western-centric does not bode well for Africa as it is a form of cultural imperialism which perpetuates Western epistemological and geopolitical hegemony in Africa. However, unlike others before us who have made the argument for decolonizing, Africanizing and digitalizing the curricula, we acknowledge that none of these can take place if the African state is not decolonized and Africanized. Universities are a microcosm of the larger macrocosm of the state, and unless the state and society itself are transformed both in purpose and character, it may be a mirage to expect universities to transform in the ways they should. This notwithstanding, as ivory towers, universities and academics have the agency to contribute to rethinking and redesigning the state in Africa. Political science teachers can leverage their individual agency using academic freedom, no matter how limited it is for now, to begin including content in their political science courses that interrogates the colonial origins of state formation in the continent, their essence and continued relevance in the light of post-colonial realities. This is with a view to draw attention to the need to rethink and redesign the state in Africa to make them African states. In essence, decolonizing the state in Africa before decolonizing and Africanizing the curricula is not a chicken or egg scenario as they can happen mutually. Our point here is to introduce the state component to the discussion because we believe a conducive state environment is critical to epistemological diversity and inclusivity in our universities.

8

Policy studies as a subdiscipline of political science in Africa

Teachings, research trends and professional expertise in Cameroon

Ruth Mireille Manga Edimo

Introduction

Policy studies operate as a sub-branch of political science that focuses on the governmental outputs that attempt to solve societal problems. It migrated from the United States to Europe in the 1980s (Eboko 2005: 4; Kubler and Maillard 2009: 9). The research area pinpoints '*what* policies governments pursue but also *why* governments pursue the policies they do, and *what* the consequences of these policies are' (Dye 2013: xi). It also addresses what governments concretely do by referring the field to the study of public action.[1] Meanwhile, policy studies have emerged in Africa on the eve of the 2000s as one of the political scientists' need to question the implementation of development policies and raise social, economic and cultural stakes (Eboko 2005: 4). In public universities in Cameroon, political scientists referred it to as 'a critical tool that should contribute to transforming society through the analysis of governmental actions and policies' (Interview with Cameroonian policy scholars). The strong relationship between political science's activities in Africa challenges the definition of policy studies. Political scientists refer to policy studies interchangeably to either 'public policies', 'policy analysis' or 'public policy analysis'. There is no clear-cut between policy studies and policy analysis. Policy studies point out both the academic arena and 'an autonomous field of expertise within the state apparatus' (Halpern, Hassenteufel and Zittoun 2018: 3) in which civil servants also attempt to map out state interventions in various social areas and suggest how to enhance states' actions.

The introduction of distinct curricula in policy studies in 2008 in public universities in Cameroon densified the political science's area of scientific production and expertise. Likewise, in Cameroon, policy studies have occurred as a specific topic

---

[1] Such an approach has been largely influenced by French studies of governmental action since 1970.

within administrative science, public administration, local government and foreign policy in public universities. Many political scientists who analyse the state's action and its relations to society and cultural groups also consider doing policy studies. If this has demonstrated the relationship between policy studies and other subfields of political science, it also highlights the role policy studies play within society.

This chapter questions the role of policy studies within the broad discipline of political science in Africa by highlighting the relationship between policy studies and political science programmes at the public universities in Cameroon. It relies on course and research contents, the background of policy studies' experts, and their activities. Activities allude to the use of expertise by political scientists who hold a minimum of a master's degree in public policy and those who teach, research or work within a public administration, a think tank, or a non-governmental organization. Such correlations are fundamental to understand how 'the division of labour' manifests itself within the discipline of political science in Cameroon and the manner through which policy studies do the work of a distinct scientific sector (Durkheim 1902 [1893]; Hausner 2019), as well as 'know-how' into a public utility.

The chapter implements a qualitative method that serves to identify the position and the content of policy studies into universities' programmes and activities and apprehend the different actions through which policy studies impact the development of political science in Cameroon. However, the review of the literature helps to clarify the research question and the paper's objective.

Literature debates on policy studies in Africa

Recent literature supports the argument that public policies have been formulated and implemented in Africa. Authors from this domain argue that international organizations and programmes have played essential roles in the process (Lavigne Delville 2017; Lavigne Delville and Ayimpam 2018) and situate policy studies in-between political science, socio-anthropology and international relations.[2] Accordingly, to speak of public action and policy studies in Africa broadly means to study countries 'under an aid regime' where international aid, its institutions and its funding play a structuring role (Lavigne Delville and Ayimpam 2018: 8). An evaluation of the literature also defends the argument that policy analysis has expanded on the continent and that French scholars influenced such process (Darbon et al. 2019). The implication is the definition of policy studies as a branch of political science that looks at states' development policies and public health (Eboko 2005; Braimah, Kilu and Annin-Bonsu 2014). The need to de-compartmentalize and differentiate policy studies from social anthropology of development, political sociology and political science is

---

[2] From their origins, policy studies have been confronted by two main competing approaches: the first, which emerged in the 30s, under policy sciences with a State-centered approach to public policy that prevailed until the 90s and the second, upheld by French political science traditions since the 70s and which instead, advances the "public action" concept to describe a multi-stakeholder process of policy design and implementation.

also present in the literature (Lavigne Delville 2017) despite the activities' growth in the African public universities.[3]

The use of concepts such as 'international public policies' (Petiteville and Smith 2006), 'international public action', 'global public policy and transnational administration' (Stone and Ladi 2015; Stone and Moloney 2019) in international relations influence the growth of the subdiscipline across the world and on the African continent.[4] Although the study of challenges constitutes part of that literature (Juma and Clark 1995: 121), the latter is still silent of such growth and policy studies' position within Africa's broad discipline. Such regard triggers this chapter's perspective, which seeks to look at how policy studies situate itself in Africa's political science through teaching, research, and use of expertise. It aims to understand how policy studies play a role within society as a sub-branch and a political science resource.

In a report, Darbon et al. (2019) capture the external influence on policy studies' local practices. They assume that policy analysis occurs far more in education, health, land and the management of resources or environment (Darbon et al. 2019: 3). However, there is no mention of policy studies' impact on expanding political science's activities.

The chapter addresses policy studies beyond its different qualifications by asking how policy studies' practice influences Cameroon's political science development. One distinct area of expertise within Cameroon's political science involves actors in various manners. It relies on political scientists' role through teaching, research and advisors inside organizations and public universities. We argue that policy studies operate as an academic course and contribute to political science development by expanding political scientists' activities in society.

About this research and its approach

The methodology uses the qualitative data that we obtained from the observations we made in Cameroon, Senegal, Benin and the Ivory Coast. We conducted fieldwork in Cameroon, which included interviews, focus groups discussions and content analysis of political science programmes in public universities, publications and PhD theses. The period covered 30 September 2019 to 7 October 2019. The objective aimed to identify policy studies curricula and position the subfield inside academies, political science programmes and Cameroonian society.

We interviewed ninety political scientists among public policy lecturers, researchers, students and practitioners. In the sample, there were: forty lecturers in political science; twenty PhD candidates; nine postgraduate students and practitioners of public policies; seventeen non-recruited doctors (PhD) in political science; and

---

[3] For instance, Cameroon and Senegal are two countries in which activities in policy studies are quickly expanding.

[4] For instance, there are two books that were just published by two political scientists' scholars of the University of Yaoundé II in the field of policy studies. One title mentions the term 'Global Public Action', while the other one talks about 'International Sports Events and Public Policies'.

three public policy readers from Benin, the Ivory Coast and Senegal who teach and research in public policies.

We considered seven[5] out of eight[6] public universities for their programmes and specialized degrees in public policies. The University of Bamenda is included in this list, although its political science programme is relatively new. The interviews and focus group discussions have engaged lecturers, researchers, postgraduate students and practitioners who occupy positions in public administrations or other types of organizations in society and carry out roles in policy studies and policy analysis. Lecturers in public policies answered a series of questions related to their course content in policy studies, the university's programme, their academic background and curricula, and their research focus and social activities. The fieldwork considered political scientists with qualifications in the discipline regarding the PhD thesis domain, the degree, and academic titles that they hold from universities and CAMES *(Conseil Africain et Malgache pour l'Enseignement Supérieur)*. According to a snowball sampling method, we contacted them at the university and over the telephone while we sometimes used networked communications technologies.

We applied the same method to postgraduates and professionals that work inside public administrations and organizations (universities and laboratories included, international organizations and NGOs, and lecturers and researchers not excluded). But we focused mainly on their activities. PhD candidates and other categories embraced in the sample were foreign lecturers and practitioners from Benin, Senegal and the Ivory Coast who read or hold titles and degrees in public policy. Interviews focused on teaching, research trends, and curricula that universities offer. Nevertheless, we had a look into the complexity of academics and practitioners' work inside public universities, public administrations, NGOs, and think tanks.

The institutionalization of policy studies in Africa: Case study of Cameroon

Cameroon counts eight state-run or public universities. Two of them are in the English-speaking regions (North-West and South-West) and six in the French-culture zones Dschang, Maroua, Ngaoundéré, Douala Yaoundé. In terms of education, the number of students, political scientists and research policies, Yaoundé and Douala's universities stand among the major universities. Their characteristics reflect both Anglo-Saxon and French systems of higher education. A presidential decree appoints vice-chancellors and pro-chancellors, while the minister of higher education is the chancellor for all higher learning institutions. The eight universities host political science programmes

---

[5] They include: the University of Yaoundé II, the University of Douala, the University of Ngaoundéré, the University of Maroua, the University of Bamenda, the University of Dschang and the University of Buea.

[6] The University of Yaoundé I was excluded.

regarding specialization and research areas, but this does not occur with the same orientations and intensity.[7]

Policy studies have not appeared as a distinct field of learning and research in Cameroon until the 2000s. International institutions undermined the breakdown in Africa's social sciences, and only anthropologists were interested in studying the development policies (Eboko 2005: 4–5). Interest in health issues, the introduction of Licence (Bachelor's Degree), Master, Doctorate (LMD) programmes in Cameroonian universities and interdisciplinary research groups in political science contributed to the institutionalization of policy studies as a distinct subfield of political science. It happened in public universities, research arenas and public administrations through specific programmes and public policies courses. At the university level, the LMD system expanded political science programmes within faculties of law and social sciences across Cameroon. Similarly, the increased needs for policy analysis expertise influenced the organization and identification of groups of political scientists in policy studies.[8]

However, there is an unequal distribution of political scientists' lecturers across public universities in Cameroon. Public policy courses are part of all political science's programmes in seven of the eight universities. The number of political scientists that teach the course varies between zero and eight per university. Out of total 156 political scientists that we identified in public universities in Cameroon, 15 teach a course on public policy. Some have a background in public policy, and others do not. In some public universities such as the University of Buea and the University of Yaoundé II, there are specific programmes in policy studies within the broad discipline of political science.[9] However, the University of Buea is more straightforward because policy studies constitute an area of study within public administration courses.

Teaching and research in public policies inside political science programmes have existed in Cameroon since 1971. Earlier orientations focused on foreign policy analysis with objects such as Africa's development challenges in the Cold War period.[10] The primary beneficiaries of such programmes were diplomats.

Introducing LMD programmes in 2005 in Cameroon[11] has reinforced the collaborative organization of existing research groups in political science. It also invigorated the creation of new research laboratories on the field and the identification

---

[7] For instance, compared to other public Universities in which the course was introduced in 2007/2008 at the same time with the LMD system, in the Universities of Maroua and Ngaoundéré, it was introduced in 2015/2016 and 2009/2010, respectively.

[8] We make reference to one common sentence that repeatedly occurs during the interviews: 'in public policy, we are', 'there is only one specialist who is recognised as such'. This last sentence is the response of one female lecturer in public policy analysis at the Department of Political Science of the University of Douala.

[9] At the University of Buea, the previously known Department of Political science and public administration was split to the department of International relations and conflict and the department of public administration.

[10] See for example one of the first special issues of the Institute's journal *Cameroonian Review of International Studies* (CRIS) published in 1996 and in which there are at least three articles that focus on development diplomacy.

[11] The system was introduced formally in 1999 through the ministerial decree no. 99/0055/Minesup/ Ddes of November 16th, 1999 on General Applicable Dispositions in the Organisation of Teachings and Evaluation in Cameroonian Universities.

of political scientists regarding their sub-disciplines. Research groups such as the Group of Social, Political, and Administrative Research (GRAPS)[12] influenced policy studies' institutionalization by promoting scientific collaboration with local political scientists and policy researchers from abroad.[13]

Faculties of law and political science in public universities such as the University of Yaoundé II have developed specialized degrees in policy studies since 2008. They have been delivering bachelor's and master's degrees in public policy. Such development enhanced the defence of master's and PhD theses and research as well, in policy studies. Compared to other public universities in Cameroon, the University of Yaoundé II leads the subfield by its number of lecturers, students and researchers in policy studies. The University of Douala follows by contributing to knowledge transfer, training and expertise delivery with other public universities.

Lecturers, PhD students and postgraduates in policy studies do consultancy for think tanks and non-governmental organizations. They participate in policy campaigns as volunteers and write policy briefs for private organizations such as the Nkafu Policy Institute.[14] However, programmes' evaluation is nevertheless the most practised by political scientists in Cameroon, particularly inside public administrations and ad-hoc committees. Compared to other public universities, Yaoundé II, Douala and Dschang Universities develop more vivid policy studies programmes because of their higher rate of lecturers and postgraduate students in that domain.

By separating political science from law and other social sciences in 2009, the African and Malagasy Council for Higher Education (CAMES) gave political scientists the possibility to run qualifications in policy studies and other sub-disciplines.[15] Such action resulted in the recruitment of four associate professors in policy who contribute to expanding knowledge in policy studies in different African universities since 2011.[16]

In universities, the identification of political scientists of the domain of policy studies as policy studies' 'specialists'[17] and the advocacy for a distinct subarea nurtures the institutionalization of policy studies in Cameroon. Alongside, PhD candidates contribute to international research programmes[18] as said by some of them.

---

[12] The GRAPS was founded in 1994 by a Cameroonian political scientist who is a full professor in political science at the University of Yaoundé II. He put together many political scientists with different backgrounds in social sciences through the GRAPS. Those came both from the Faculty of Arts and Humanities of the University of Yaoundé I, and the Faculty of Law and political science of other Cameroonian Universities from which they graduated. They had either collaborated or been PhD students of the leading professor who, himself, has a background in political sociology and comparative politics as areas of specialisation within political science.

[13] For instance, we think about its partnership with the Institute of Research for Development (IRD) with which it conducted research on the fight against HIV/ AIDS in Africa between 2006 and 2010, as well as the holding of seminars for political science's students of the University of Yaoundé II between 2006 and 2008.

[14] The Nkafu Institute is a think tank which is based in Yaoundé, Cameroon and which regularly organizes seminars and training on public policy.

[15] The result was the recruitment of associate professors of political science that specialized in policy studies and identified at the University as 'specialists'.

[16] Most of those associate professors teach the course in Benin, Senegal and participate in different African research groups in policy studies.

[17] It has repeatedly occurred during our interview as we mentioned earlier above in the text.

[18] Those programs were led by Cameroonian political scientists in the Diaspora in the early 2000s. They worked in international research centres such as the centre of International Research for Development (IRD) and had close relationships with the PhD's supervisor.

My PhD thesis focused on Comparative politics, but I can say that policy studies have been a primary area of my research training because, during my thesis preparation, I worked as a research assistant on an HIV research program. Political scientists and anthropologists doing their fieldwork in Cameroon and other countries in sub-Saharan Africa carried such programs. However, I was proposed to the program by my PhD supervisor whose primary research domain is political sociology, comparative politics and international relations.

(Source: a political scientist, assistant professor
at the University of Yaoundé II)

When I started my job in University in Cameroon after my education in France, I decided to only focus on policy studies, not to teach something else than public policies keep doing every day.

(Source: a lecturer in political science at the
University of Yaoundé II)

Holding a summer school on public policies in Cameroon in April 2019 comforted the subdiscipline place within political science in Cameroon and Africa.[19] Also did the membership and high positions of Cameroonians within the International Public Policy Association (IPPA).

Policy studies in Cameroon: Courses, research trends and expertise

The overall strategy, which had as purpose to understand the position occupied by policy studies within political science programmes in Cameroon and their impact on the delivery of research and expertise in political science, has provided multiple explanations of the relationship between policy studies and political science in Africa. It appeared that immensely few political scientists teach policy studies and which others quote as 'specialists'.[20] Their number varies according to the intensity of political science's programme in each public university. The role of policy studies within public universities takes account of the power of political science's programmes and universities' activities. In terms of the number of years, the robustness of the programme, the number of political scientists, international collaboration with other political scientists, and lecturers' background to the study of politics[21] define the

---

[19] The summer school welcomed twenty-two participants among which fifteen participants came from Cameroon, two from France, one from Canada, one from Nigeria and one registered from Ghana though cancelled his participation at the last minute.

[20] This is the qualification often attributed to researchers or scholars to refer them to a particular domain of knowledge, especially in French academic public sphere.

[21] In the University of Buea for instance, the department of political science has been divided into two departments, which are the department of Conflict Resolution and International relations and the Department of Public administration. There are courses on public policy but political scientists who teach such courses do not have the background. In the University of Maroua, political scientists also teach the course of public policy but do not have the background.

intensity of policy studies in each university. In some public universities, there is a significant French culture approach to policy studies which borrows from concepts and methods of political sociology and political anthropology.[22] In others such as Buea and Bamenda's universities, policy studies rely on administrative science and law.[23] In other words, five of the seven public universities share the same orientation in political science and policy studies.

The universities of Yaoundé II, Douala and Buea conduct much more activities in the subfield. Bamenda and Maroua are behind with the smallest numbers of political scientists and lecturers in policy studies. While the previous ones are among the oldest universities in the country, the Universities of Bamenda and Maroua are the newest public universities.[24] Out of the fifteen political scientists in the University of Maroua, only two lecturers teach public policy. In the University of Bamenda, 'two to three political scientists share the courses on policy studies' as said by a political scientist working in that university.

The programmes in political science and the course's orientation in policy studies rely on professional backgrounds, individual curricula and the research collaboration's experience. While in some public universities, there is a significant French culture approach to policy studies that borrows from concepts and methods of political sociology and political anthropology, such as the universities of Buea and Bamenda, policy studies draw from administrative science and law.

> In multicultural societies such as Cameroon, in which chieftaincy play major roles in the governance of society, it is always interesting to take a look at their perception of State's policies.
>
> (Source: Interview. A mention by a political anthropologist
> at the University of Yaoundé II)

Not all political scientists that teach public policies in public universities in Cameroon have a background in policy studies. Compared to the newest public universities, the universities of Yaoundé II, Douala and Dschang are still leading regarding this aspect. In Maroua, for instance, none of the three political scientists specialized in policy studies.[25] Though there was research in the domain, none of the universities had specified the degree in policy studies before 2010.[26] Compared to the other six (6) universities, policy studies at the University of Buea is enclosed in public administration (Interview with the head of Department of Public Administration at

---

[22] See the University of Yaoundé II, the University of Douala, the University of Ngaoundéré, the University of Maroua.

[23] Lecturers in these Universities have a background in these disciplines.

[24] It stands beside the University of Maroua which was also created in 2008.

[25] In the University of Maroua, policy studies remained taught in the department of law and political science until June 2020. It is after the Ministerial decree of 8 June 2020 by the Ministry of Higher Education in Cameroon that the programme of law and political science have been separated. In other words, it is the decree that put in place a department of political science within the Faculty of Law.

[26] Qualifications and PhD domains were very important variables to identify and distinguish the areas of specialisation of each political scientist as well as to interpret the defence's reports.

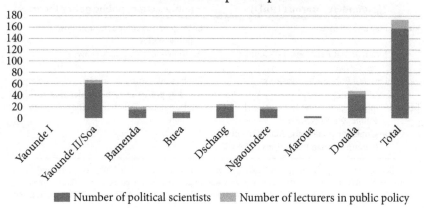

Policy studies within state-run universities
through the teaching of the course and presence
of lecturers in public policies

■ Number of political scientists   ▨ Number of lecturers in public policy

Figure 8.1 The relationship between policy studies and political science within public universities through teaching and programmes. *Source*: Field research's results.

the University of Buea). The following graphic reports the number of public policy lecturers per university out of the total number of political scientists per public university across Cameroon. The Figure 8.1 summarizes the relationship between the intensity of political science programmes and policy studies in Cameroon. It appeared that out of 156 political scientists in public universities in Cameroon, only 15 taught a course on public policy. The larger numbers of PhD theses in Yaoundé II and Douala's universities[27] and the larger number of PhD theses professors in policy studies supervise.[28]

Faculties that hold political science programmes, Law, Social and Management Sciences consist of many political scientists with different backgrounds in teaching policy studies and researching in public policies.[29] They base their perspectives in policy studies on various reasons: 'administrative request in the university'; 'curricula, academic background', 'curiosity'; 'scientific interest'; 'It is the best tool through which to question the state's actions'.[30]

---

[27] We considered the period after 2005.

[28] At the moment of our research, there were only four professors recognized as such, regarding their qualifications held in the domain from the CAMES.

[29] See for instance the University of Buea and the University of Bamenda in which lecturers teaching the course have backgrounds in law and other sub-disciplines in law in political science.

[30] Out of the dozen of the lecturers in public policy that we interviewed, two are teaching the course as a result of a request from university, two do research on state's action and has developed a professional interest and the rest specialize in policy studies and are professors and assistant-professors in the field.

Table 8.1 Common Courses in Policy Studies in Cameroon Public Universities

Universities of Douala, Dschang, Yaoundé II, Ngaoundéré, Maroua (PhD)		Public administration, public policy, administrative science, sociology of public action, public policy theories
Buea	Political Science	Local government, public administration, public policy
	International Relations and Conflict resolution	Advanced foreign policy analysis
	Law and Public administration	Public policy analysis, foreign public policy, public policy analysis and decision-making
IRIC	Communication and International Public Action (CAPI)	Public policies, Policy Evaluation, Foreign policy
	Regional Integration and Management of Communitarian Institutions (IRMIC)	

Source: Political science programmes in Public Universities in Cameroon since 2008, timetables and testimonies of students' results. Information was also summarized from the content analysis of political science programs in the University of Douala, Yaoundé II, Dschang, Ngaoundéré and Maroua in the given period 2008–2020.

Concerning the course's orientation of policy studies in Cameroon, the content analysis of political science's programme[31] in public universities could account for standard practices and differences. In Table 8.1, we present such details which also account for the various relationships between policy studies and the study of the role of municipalities (local government), administration principles (public administration), international relations (foreign policy) and political sociology (sociology of public action).

Table 8.1 mentions the standard practices and particularities of each university. While public administration, public policy, administrative science, sociology of public action and public policy theories' constitute the core elements of policy studies courses in Cameroon, every university develops a specificity. For instance, 'local government' which occupies a significant position within the political science programme of the University of Buea also plays a vital role in the delivery of policy studies' courses. There is a substantial focus on policy evaluation in the University of Yaoundé II Schools such as the Institute of International relations of Cameroon (IRIC) due to its relationship with international policy programmes.

However, course orientations do not only rely on public universities' global programmes and institutional agenda. Lecturers and researchers of public universities in Cameroon also frame the course designs according to their knowledge's background and areas of research interests. The following graphic shows different groups according to the number of years in the subfield of policy studies (Figure 8.2).

---

[31] Though this is not a representation of detailed programs, the major orientation gives an idea on the content of knowledge of trained human resources and academic profiles of lecturers of public policies in public universities of Cameroon. Moreover, the academic programme of public institutions such as the University of Buea, ends up at the master's degree.

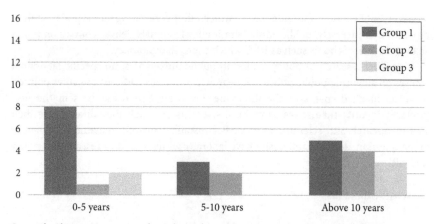

Groups of academics were reconstructed according to their career trajectory at the public university (lecturers, associate professors, 'professor agrégé CAMES') and years of experience in teaching and/or supervising students' research on public policies. While 'lecturer', 'associate professor' and 'full professor' are normal professional trajectories at the university, the 'professor agrégé CAMES' is a distinction obtained through presenting the 'Concours d'agrégation CAMES', a French cultural heritage that distinguishes 'professors' among themselves in French culture public universities in Sub-Saharan Africa.

Figure 8.2 Years of university teaching experience, by different groups of academics within policy studies in public universities in Cameroon.

The lecturers' background to the study of politics[32] and policy studies in Cameroon also gave way to identify three categories of political scientists doing policy studies. The first is that of political scientists who defended a PhD thesis in policy studies named Group 1. The second is that of those who defended a PhD in another area of political science but research, teach, and consultancies in public policies.[33] We named the category Group 2. Compared to Groups 1 and 2, the third category is very exclusive. It includes only associate professors in political science whose specialization in policy studies emerged from their research domain in the PhD and the qualification they obtained from CAMES. Some of the political scientists in that category studied in France and defended a PhD thesis in policy studies. We named this category Group 3.[34] Group 1 encompassed the larger number of political scientists although most of them had less than five years of teaching experience in public universities. Group 2 counted many political scientists with a background in other political science sub-branches such as political sociology, comparative politics and international relations. Group 3 included five political scientists out of the fifteen political scientists we interviewed.

Political scientists also deliver seminars on policy studies in State-run schools such as the National School for Administration and Magistracy (ENAM) and the Public

---

[32] This background has been considered from the date of obtention of the master's in political science (minus 2 years) as level of study.

[33] What we realized is that many political scientists in this group did not read any course on public policy during their academic training in political science. However, they have researched public policy inside professional groups such as the GRAPS. Such political scientists became postgraduate in Cameroon before 2008; that is, they defended [a 'Diplome d'etudes approfondies' (DEA)] before the introduction of the LMD system of education. Remember that, before that year, there was no formal course on public policy in public universities in Cameroon.

[34] The group consisted of one full professor and one lecturer. Both teach at the University of Yaoundé II.

Management School of Yaoundé (PMS), which offers continuing public policy analysis programmes. Inversely, public administration professionals deliver courses on policy analysis in some Schools such as IRIC which trains in diplomacy.

Regarding research in policy studies in public universities, no specific laboratory focuses on analysing public policies. Research laboratories and centres gather political scientists in all domains of the discipline. Lecturers and researchers in the field primarily identify themselves as political scientists although they differentiate their area of research and scientific interest. For instance, answers remained ambiguous to the question 'does the university have laboratories dedicated to research on policy studies?'.

'What? Laboratory?'

Some political scientists were surprised by the question, and when we had answers, there was a lot of hesitation.

'Anyway, the Research centre is called the Center of research on Africa and Contemporary Stakes'.

'The laboratory is named Political Studies, and all lecturers of political science are members'.

(Source: Two interviewees from the University of Douala)

Research production is diversified. Out of sixteen PhD theses in policy studies we analysed for the period 2000–2019, seven focused on the policies of environment and the management of natural resources, nine studied the politics of human rights, elections, migrations, security, the politics of poverty reduction and the role and actions of civil societies. Policy evaluation, political sociology and political anthropology are prominent in research production. Political scientists at the University of Yaoundé II argue:

'Public policy falls within political sociology and that, local objects link them either to the study of power relationships within the State (political sociology)'

and that

'communities' behaviour towards state's actions and public policies (political anthropology)'.

(Source: Interviews with one assistant professor in policy studies and a full professor in political anthropology, both lecturers at the University of Yaoundé II)

Regarding the relationship between political sociology and policy studies, political scientists regularly question public policies' legitimacy, struggle between actors in the implementation process, and mobilization against policies. In this particular case, sociological concepts such as governmentality serve to describe and explain policy problems. Besides, political anthropologists advocate the need to interrogate the relationship between policies and local cultures. Political scientists from universities with French traditions in Cameroon often use public action to raise the links between policy studies, political sociology and political anthropology. Their approaches differ from the ones at English-speaking universities in which public administration maps at best policy studies. However, political scientists in Cameroon do not limit their expertise to the university. Policy studies is a footbridge between public administration, private organizations and think tanks.

Many political scientists that we referred to earlier in Group 3 and Group 2 hold administrative functions at the university.[35] They also have positions inside the government in which they contribute to policy implementation[36] and policymaking as counsellors. They work as special counsellors in higher institutions such as the Presidency[37] and most of them deliver expertise to international organizations such as the United Nations Development Programs (NUDP), non-governmental organizations (NGOs) and think tanks such as the World Wildlife Fund (WWF) to achieve policy evaluation tasks. In periods of social crisis such as the Anglophone crisis in Cameroon, political scientists also advise the government's policies and strategies.[38]

Impact of policy studies on the role of political science within the Cameroonian society

Policy studies amplify the role of political science within society in various manners. Other sub-disciplines of political science such as political anthropology and political sociology are reluctant to normative approaches. They primarily focus on description and explanation, while policy studies highlight the role of expertise within the political community.

Expertise in policy studies solidifies political science as a practical tool[39] and establishes it as an essential resource for transforming society. Regarding such an

---

[35] Regarding this, four of the five political scientists from Group 3 hold administrative positions inside the University and at the level of government. Among them are: one associate professor from the University of Yaoundé II, another one from the University of Dschang, one full professor from the University of Yaoundé II and one lecturer from IRIC.

[36] From the previous category, there are two political scientists who work inside the government: one in the National Council of Communication and the other one, at the Supreme State Audit.

[37] It is the case of one full professor in political science, who is a former head of the department of political science at the University of Yaoundé II, founder of the research group which we referred to in the text as the GRAPS, the professor has a background in political sociology and international relations.

[38] The Anglophone crisis in Cameroon for example in which political scientists were called upon by the government and some decision-makers to advise solutions and evaluate the responses and outcomes of the governmental strategies.

[39] After the introduction of the LMD system in Cameroon and specialisations within political science, the number of students and degrees in the field increased and most of them choose policy studies as a domain of study by saying that 'it is more practical . . . they are not studying public policies to necessarily work at University'. See also the increased number of policy studies experts in the total number of political scientists that the Government recruited between 2019 and 2020.

aspect, students of political science with a master degree in policy studies demonstrate their professional utility inside various organizations.[40]

Policy studies are the critical lens through which lecturers and students in political science evaluate and analyse public policies' quality and governmental action efficiency. Lecturers of political science in public universities carry out multiple actions that contribute to developing policy studies. Although there is still a low volume of scientific production and relatively few policy studies experts in public universities, they contribute to the international scientific debate through their publications and actions.[41] There is a low volume of scientific production in policy studies and a few policy studies experts in public universities. Nevertheless, lecturers of political science in public universities carry out other multiple actions. Their vital positions inside the administration of public universities help to improve programmes. Policy studies is a footbridge between university and society. It contributes to society-making in various ways while giving evidence of political scientists' role in democracy-making through public debates in the media and public sphere, on policies and governmental actions.

Conclusion

Policy studies gave more visibility to political science's activities in Cameroon and Africa. It has also shown evidence of the role political scientists have to play within democracies. The intensification of policy studies since 2008 within public universities in Cameroon has contributed to expanding the numbers of political experts. However, the media has appeared to be the most visible place to discuss public policies and government actions. The limited number of laboratories in public universities, and the absence of a specific research laboratory in policy studies, limits productivity in policy analysis. Consequently, there is nothing as policy briefs that regularly come out from the public universities. Policy studies belong to a broad political science's research programme within universities' laboratories. Moreover, the 'in-between' role of some political scientists, between academies and governmental institutions, may curb policy analysis's efficiency and limit the positive effect on public policies' democratic transformation.

Policy studies constitute a scientific tool through which political scientists can bring knowledge to the decision-making process (Fischer 2003). Still, the absence of a systematic relationship between political scientists, academic production and the solving of social problems limit such professional impact.

Regardless of such limits and constraints in the Cameroonian academic sphere, policy studies appeared to be a pertinent instrument that positively transformed research and teaching in political science.

---

[40] After obtaining a master's degree in political science and during the preparation of their PhD thesis, many political scientists engage in small works consultancy and create cabinets. Out of the sixteen PhD candidates we interviewed, ten were engaged in small consultancies and five held and worked in cabinets and think tanks.

[41] There are many articles and already two books published in the domain by Cameroonian political scientists. Political scientists also chair panels in international conferences on public policies.

9

Beyond disciplinary polemics?

The challenge of informal structures in the study of local political institutions in Africa

Matthew Sabbi

Introduction

On 11 October 2018, research fellows of the Fritz Thyssen Stiftung, which funded my postdoctoral research, gathered in Cologne, Germany, for the foundation's bi-annual autumn *Herbstfest* meeting. When my name tag displayed the label anthropologist, I was surprised not least because all my degrees are in sociology; other fellows had been (rightly) recognized as sociologists. Also, the anthropologists present were curious about my speciality in this field. Contrastingly, my research respondents in the field identified me as neither of the two. A few weeks prior to the Cologne meeting, my interlocutors namely elected councillors and local administrators incessantly labelled me a political scientist – by virtue of my research in local politics – plain and simple. My reflections on those experiences, out of many others, bring out two related – but seemingly divergent – observations. The first regards my apparent unyielding search to be part of an 'epistemic core' in sociology despite the interdisciplinary focus of my research. Second, this search is partly emblematic of the disciplinary paradoxes in the social sciences. The contents of research and teaching of local politics in Ghana and Africa illustrate this point well. I contend that the two scenarios derive from the very conception of informal political structures. In the social science debate on informal institutions, neopatrimonialism in particular stirs controversy by juxtaposing neo-traditional structures[1] with democratic institutions. And traditional political structures are often taken sceptically as problems of state-building; they act as quasi-states and impede economic performance (Acemoglu, Reed and Robinson 2014; Englebert 2002; cf. Neubert 2009: 43–4; Mkandawire 2015).

---

[1] I understand neo-traditional structures as pre colonial institutions, which were integrated into state administration e.g. chieftaincy structures. Their ongoing legitimation and the inherent reinvention of these traditions as times change are interesting topics for research (see Sabbi, Doumbia and Neubert 2020).

Nonetheless, other social scientists seem fascinated by these structures and present them as replicas of accountable institutions particularly for local politics (Ray 2003; Kelsall 2011). My argument in this chapter builds on empirical-derived knowledge that the duality of traditional structures and formal institutions facilitates and co-produces public authority (Karlström 1996; Lund 2006; Neubert 2009; Holzinger, Kern and Kromrey 2016; Myers and Fridy 2017). The burning aim is two-fold: first, to unearth how this duality shapes practical norms of local administration, which often has a weak bureaucracy. Second and as a corollary of the above, to enhance our understanding of how the duality and practical norm shape research and teaching of political science from a continental African standpoint. In the following sections, I draw on the current epistemic claims and practices as well as historical legacies that undergird the founding of social science disciplines in Africa in order to explicate how they frame current scenarios in teaching and research on local politics. Next, I present excerpts of experiences from the field to highlight gains from traditional political structures for political science education and research local in local arenas – once demystified and presented in a non-normative framework. Ghana is used herein for emphasis. However, the country's pioneering experience in the struggle to establish, teach and research African politics (Ayee and Gyekye-Jandoh 2014: 161–5) makes it a compelling case that might reflect the situation elsewhere.

The disciplinary polemics: The gap and local political realities

Sources of the polemics in sociopolitical studies

The debate on interdisciplinarity highlights disciplines' penchant for maintaining their *core* ideas and epistemic claims despite pressures to integrate their knowledge and problem-solving techniques (Clark and Wallace 2015: 4; Ng and Litzenberg 2019: 2). Methodological and theoretical problems, incompatible research styles and techniques, and fears that interdisciplinarity could become a convenient way for some disciplines to dominate others have all been cited for non-integration (Faber and Scheper 1997; Jacobs and Frickel 2009; Burawoy 2013: 14). The justification allows them to remain 'disconnected silos' largely restricted to their core domains of knowledge (Jacobs and Frickel 2009: 48). In the Global South, however, the challenge is even broader: interdisciplinary dialogue (or a lack of thereof) is shaped by disciplinary history, culture and politics. This would at first seem surprising because interdisciplinarity is much cherished and emphasized at least in the fields Area and African studies. Even so, African studies are disparagingly viewed as largely 'an umbrella for the practice of discrete, individual disciplines' (Bryceson 2012: 298).[2] This view squares well with ongoing critiques of the ethical basis for studying Africa altogether (see Mama 2007). This also affects how core disciplines of the social science[3] including political science,

---

[2]   Although a vibrant interdisciplinary future for the field is much hoped for (see Ambler 2011).
[3]   I am aware of the unsettled debate on the core disciplines (see Salter and Hearn 1996: 175–8). I use the idea in a less rigid way bearing in mind the disciplinary changes and splits in several fields of study.

sociology, and anthropology dialogue in a comprehensive way for the study and research of local political action and political legitimacy in Africa, more broadly.

Historically, anthropology's closeness with colonial governments gradually ebbed its popularity within newly independent countries in the Global South (see Hooker 1963). Several African intellectuals derided anthropology's legacy as a 'bourgeois enterprise in the colonies as other social sciences' did in colonizing countries (Mafeje 1976: 317), or being sponsored as information-gatherers to aid imperialist exploitation of the Global South (Magubane and Faris 1985: 91). These views persist, even if subtly, to this day. In Ghana, for instance, perhaps due to sociologists' plain criticisms of anthropology's colonial legacy (Darkwah, Tonah and Assimeng 2014: 102), only one university currently offers a degree programme in anthropology.[4] Darkwah, Tonah and Assimeng (2014: 110) somehow infer that anthropology's focus on pre-modern societies still binds it to the colonial project hence its unpopularity. One instance may be political ethnographers' fascination with traditional political structures but also strongly arguing we preserve and integrate them into local politics (Neubert 2009: 43f; see also Ray 2003; Kelsall 2011). Unsurprisingly in Ghana after independence, sociology prevailed in anthropology's stead for a long time. But sociology as a discipline was reluctant to adjust to and reflect the cultures and worldviews of non-industrialized societies (Smith 1990: 152). In the Global South, sociology's subfields of rural sociology and development sociology offered exciting promise to analyse processes of societal change, although they too could not live up to the hype (see Rose 1966: 181–2; Long 2001; Neubert 2020: 26–7). Particularly in Africa, sociology's contextual challenge is well noted. The tendency to present Western perspectives as cultural universals in university curricula (Wagner 2016: 92) has compelled African sociologists to call for an 'epistemic intervention' and a clear preference for 'indigenous Sociology' for students in Africa, and the Global South broadly (Adésínà 2006: 243).

Political science, on its part, was also hesitant at first to attend to political developments in the Global South, at least in Africa (see Barkan 2009), and underlined by the late start of the discipline in Ghana (Ayee and Gyekye-Jandoh 2014: 161–5). And despite pioneering multidisciplinary studies in processes of democratization and political mobilization in its emerging democratic institutions,[5] political science still gives a great deal of attention to the 'epistemic community' of the discipline in current teaching and research. Despite efforts to transform the curricula since the 1950s, to reflect local context and contents (Ayee and Gyekye-Jandoh 2014: 161–5), the subject in Ghana largely reflects disciplinary core; a scenario which restricts a fruitful dialogue with its neighbouring disciplines.[6] This is perhaps due to conventional political science's sceptical views on informal structures;[7] viewing them as illustrative of state-building challenges and even detrimental to democratic legitimacy (Englebert 2002;

---

[4] This happened through the forceful effort of the American anthropologist Nancy Lundgren during her tenure as head of the sociology department.
[5] See, for example, Apter (2009) and Dunn and Robertson (1973).
[6] I do not in any way dispute extant multi-disciplinary political studies by Ghanaian scholars (see Bob-Milliar 2009).
[7] Even formal political institutions equally suffer the same normative 'no-institution' view (Cheeseman 2018).

Table 9.1 Selected Local-Focus Courses in Ghana's Political Science Departments, 2015–2019

University	Course Code and Title	Remarks on Content Diversity
Kwame Nkrumah Univ. of Sci.	POL 357: Public Administration	Disciplinary core with largely external readings
and Tech., Kumasi	POL 353/4: Comparative Politics	Disciplinary core with largely external readings
University of Education, Winneba	POLI 242: Intro to Development Studies	Disciplinary core with largely external readings
	POLI 361: Decentralization and Local Government	Disciplinary core with largely local readings
University of Ghana, Legon, Accra	POL 211: Intro to Development Studies	Disciplinary core with largely external readings
	POL 213: Intro to Public Administration	Disciplinary core with largely external readings
	POL 362: Development Administration	Disciplinary core with largely external readings
	POL 459: Decentralization and Local Government	Disciplinary core with largely very regional readings

Sources: Author's rendition based on the departments' teaching resources.

Budd 2004; cf. van de Walle 2003; Neubert 2009; Baldwin 2013). Others suggest by restricting the space for civil society, these neo-traditional structures act as quasi-states as they clash with the declining post-colonial state, and ultimately account for poor economic performance (Englebert 2002; Acemoglu, Reed and Robinson 2014; cf. Mkandawire 2015).

The polemic discourages requisite interdisciplinary content in political science education. We get a glimpse of this gap when we consider courses that primarily relate to local-level politics and policy via three public universities in Ghana that currently offer teaching and research in political science namely the University of Ghana in Accra; the Kwame Nkrumah University of Science and Technology (KNUST) in Kumasi; and the University of Education in Winneba (UEW). In Table 9.1, I give a cursory view of the reading materials for a selection of communal-focus courses.[8] Clearly, we find an interesting collection of courses on local, sub-national politics and administration. Yet, there are two striking observations we can make.

First, most of the courses overly rely on the core texts of political science and skew in favour of Euro-American authors. Hence, a near-absence of Africa-based (regional and local) sources. Second and most important, course contents could be more interdisciplinary. Indeed, despite dealing primarily with sub-national and local-level politics that involve multiple actors and institutions – and require a more nuanced perspective on interdisciplinary dialogue – very few ethno-sociological and historical sources emerge from the course materials. Also striking is the minimal variation

---

[8]   This selection of courses is in no way representative of the different course models offered in the three departments. Its illustrative value refers only to courses relevant to local politics and administration.

in the courses offered for local politics.[9] This arises partly from the pre-determined departmental course contents – rather than those derived by instructors. There is limited flexibility to introduce courses on one's own accord. However, the direction of the course and contents actually delivered depend largely on the instructors' discretion.[10] Ayee and Gyekye-Jandoh (2014: 160) suggest this might result from the fact that most faculties in the other institutions originally trained in the University of Ghana, Accra.

Hence, we can safely infer that the attraction to specific political science departments may not depend so much on programme contents. Other factors mediate students' choices. Regarding the contents of the courses, most of them inwardly focus on formal political structures. At the same time, their primary texts rely so much on external readings of the so-called disciplinary core. Overall, we miss a clear dialogue between the readings in those courses and contents from other social sciences that deal with similar topics.

Bridging the gap: A plea for more dialogue between formal and informal structures

Among the well-known challenges presented by the lack of dialogue between the social sciences in Ghana (and Africa broadly) is the prioritization of the Western disciplinary lens and bias towards perceiving African realities. This includes adopting theoretical models that hardly fit the African case (Bryceson 2012: 299–300). Continental African criticism of this misperception – arising from sloppiness and anecdotes – has been rebuffed for politicizing knowledge creation (see Chege 1997; Mkandawire 1997). Even when academic cooperation steps in to mediate, the different expectations to fulfil in the cooperation bring their own inbuilt paradoxes of partnership and changing research interests (Neubert 2008; Cheeseman, Death and Whitfield 2017). Hence, external partners tend to dominate successful cooperation and limit the ability of their local partners to shape the course of projects and the contents of knowledge produced.[11] Against this backdrop, an interdisciplinary approach to studying and researching sociocultural phenomena offers the best bridge for continental African academics to influence knowledge contents, correct empirical and analytical misperceptions and nuance the contents they teach their students.

This effort will require the social science disciplines to jettison their polemical posturing. Going back to teaching and research on how formal and informal interactions play out in practice in the local political arena, only a middle-ground view

---

[9] The UEW programme has a teaching focus while the KNUST programme runs concurrently with history. Apart from that, the contents of the political science degree programme look similar across the three departments.

[10] A department chair can use their discretion to allow individually-designed courses. I owe this clarification to Dr. Seidu M. Alidu.

[11] The need to include African collaborators in project applications while ignoring their conditions of work, restricts their international competitiveness (Neubert 2008: 101). And current funding in Africa studies prioritizes methodological innovations (Cheeseman, Death and Whitfield 2017) over local partnerships.

that brings together varying perspectives seems helpful. While approaches in political and administration sociology promise useful prospects, the current state of research and teaching of local politics in Ghana reveals that it has yet to succeed. For example, a burgeoning sociological interest views programmes of decentralization as based on internationally derived concepts. Studying their implementation in local arenas requires us to adopt a non-normative understanding of how tradition and modernity come together to shape their political legitimacy when viewed from wider societal transformation processes (see Elias 1978). Likewise, the anthropology of public bureaucracies points out daily strategies for performing state functions and unearths inherent informality and practical norms on which formal structures thrive (Blundo 2015; Olivier de Sardan 2015; Bierschenk and Olivier de Sardan 2019: 248).

Additionally, ethno-sociological analysis offers productive insights into state structures with a view of the state as a continuum (or so-called *heterarchy*), which comprises formal and informal structures in a mutually constitutive and interdependent fashion (Bellagamba and Klute 2008). Equally, in political studies, these views are not new per se. Prior studies have foregrounded the sociocultural underpinnings of adaptation and resistance of political institutions (see Dunn and Robertson 1973; Apter 2009: 186). But many contemporary approaches do not follow that through. Thus, the newer challenge is for political studies and research to acknowledge and emphasize this strongly. The challenge is somehow apparent. The discussion on local politics and democracy tends to juxtapose neo-traditional and neo-patrimonial frameworks with state institutions.

But even here, the problem comes from how we define institutions. Sociologically, institutions are conceived as forms of cognitive structures based on societal consensus whose production does not depend on command structures or third-party enforcement agencies (Luhmann 1986; Habermas 1989). This open, consensual approach would suggest an ongoing dialogue between state-sanctioned rules and neo-patrimonial structures in sociopolitical life. However, other perspectives less favourably view informal political structures as competitors of the state's authority and official decision-making (see Lauth 2000: 25; Helmke and Levitsky 2004: 725). This latter perspective promotes the strong focus on formal institutions despite their joint interaction in fulfilling local public authority, especially in contexts with limited state penetration (Lund 2006; Neubert 2009; Börzel and Risse 2016; Brinkerhoff, Wetterberg and Wibbels 2018). This scenario frames the lack of crucial interaction between the core social science disciplines in the teaching and research of political science.

Analysis of Ghana's decentralization programme – in no way indigenous – benefits from a non-normative view of neopatrimonialism; by capturing how the politico-administrative system integrates tradition in its action structure (Pitcher, Moran and Johnston 2009: 126; Mkandawire 2015: 565).[12] As an internationally-sanctioned concept, decentralization helps us shine an important light on how formal state institutions adapt to neo-traditional and informal structures in local political arenas.

---

[12] This is often normatively deployed to mean the privatization of a public office. In contrast, patrimonial analysis examines the agency that comes from a fusion of traditional and modern political structures. This latter view facilitates the understanding of societal mobilization and the transformation of both structures (Elias 1978; Mkandawire 2011: 21, 2015: 565).

In the section that follows, I offer two examples namely neo-traditional structures and patronage-client networks to demonstrate how formal local administrations and neo-traditional and patrimonial structures interact to deliver public authority, in areas with limited state presence. They also bring out the analytical benefits when local political action is nuanced with an ethno-sociological lens.

'Informality' and daily interaction in local administration: Two examples

Informal interactions inside the village administration

Chieftaincy represents one of those structures that can typically be presented as a problem of state-building given chieftaincy's overbearing influence on informal local councils right from the outset (Dunn and Robertson 1973: 294). However, a nuanced assessment emerges when we consider the fact that much of Ghana's rural administrations heavily depends on chiefs and local councillors. They not only provide physical structures but also commit funds to the daily operations of the administration.[13] The district administration depends as much on councillors and chiefs to generate local government revenue. Given the often limited state presence (Neubert 2009; Börzel and Risse 2016; Brinkerhoff, Wetterberg and Wibbels 2018), chiefs and elected councillors remain the only credible actors to convince residents to pay local taxes,[14] even when they receive relatively little municipal services in return.[15] Additionally, residents view efforts by their councillors and chiefs more positively than other formal actors. In particular, chieftaincy agents acting as gatekeepers broker crucial deals to procure and deliver public services while maintaining security and community problems more effectively than district officials (Fridy and Myers 2019: 87–8; Tieleman and Uitermark 2019: 718–19).

Local council activities including town hall meetings, public budget hearings, and accountability forums gain enormous legitimacy when chiefs intervene. They help bring the local population in contact with the formal administration. My experience in the field since 2013 reveals that councillors and chiefs lead this mobilization, encourage participation or even select specific community members as their representatives. Elsewhere, such public forums have adapted pre-colonial conceptions of public participation and accountability in garnering political legitimacy. Among others *'Barazas'* in Uganda, *'Umuganda'* and *'Imihigo'* in Rwanda, and *Kgotla* in Botswana have all become central forums for local political decision-making and mobilization. This strong link between formal institutions and precolonial conceptions may sometimes be reinvented. Nonetheless, they tend to enhance positive attitudes towards

---

[13] This is in addition to their statutorily-sanctioned functions of dispute settlement, codification of customary law, and custody of stool lands (Kleist 2011: 634). Chiefs help build and resource the local school, health and recreational facilities with furniture and staff.

[14] As elsewhere in Africa including Malawi and Mozambique, the state appoints chiefs to realize both only customary law functions and formal state obligations such as tax collection and general administration (see Buur and Kyed 2006: 848; Eggen 2011: 328).

[15] This is remarkable since urban local administrators frequently complain of their inability to collect local taxes in urban Ghana (Sabbi and Mensah 2016: 71).

state institutions (Dipholo, Mafema and Tshishonga 2014: 19; Sabbi, Doumbia and Neubert 2020: 80). This underpins calls for chiefs to take even more active roles in local councils (Ray 2003; Kelsall 2011).

On the flip side, chiefs have been described as anachronistic and too despotic for modern politics (see Mamdani 1996). Critics perceive chiefs to use their influence to pursue private ends – or favouritism more broadly. Given the hereditary mode of appointment, chiefs and their selectors use ever-shifting allegiance to reward and punish, especially in struggles with feuding paramountcies and minor chiefs over land management (see Kirst 2020). And when chiefs felt their position and material interests were threatened, they even tried to re-centralize authority (Grischow 2008: 87–9). This instrumentalization of chieftaincy to strengthen power, discretion and privileges underpin criticism of chiefs as being accountable to a select group of elites. Chiefs' privileged role in local council decisions helps consolidate their interests in local politics. In Kumasi, where the city authority has six council seats for chiefs, the *Asantehene* and the chieftaincy in general enjoy a revered status and could submit the local bureaucracy to their preferences (see Ubink 2007: 145). Chiefs' privileged status chiefs enabled them to decide those who ran for municipal office. At the same time, incumbents warily served knowing 'a collective decision by the chiefs and opinion leaders' could send them packing instantly (Sabbi 2018: 20). In addition, in municipalities with rival chieftaincies, chiefs try to promote their preferred councillors in anticipation of political advantage on the municipal council.

Chieftaincy actors equally react to government policy on municipalities, particularly where district capitals must be situated. While the official argument for district capitals follows economic robustness to generate their own local funds, chiefs often base their incessant demands on culturally relevant locations without recourse to economic viability (Table 9.2). Chiefs' interventions are sometimes far-reaching, going beyond the general struggle for local political resources, to broader definitions of who can access those resources. Indeed, chiefs are known to stoke up tensions over citizenship rights and obligations (Lentz 2006). It has become commonplace

Table 9.2 Selected Interventions in District Councils Affair by Chiefs

Date	Subject	Chiefs' Action	District	Region	State Response
14.03.2008	Capital	Reject	Gomoa East	Central	Capital maintained
09.06.2008	Mayor	Endorse	Nabdam	Upper East	Nominee confirmed
14.04.2009	Mayor	Reject	Agona West	Central	Nominee withdrawn
21.04.2009	Mayor	Reject	Kadjebi	Volta	Nominee confirmed
12.07.2013	Mayor	Reject	Kwabere East	Ashanti	Nominee rejected
09.10.2013	Mayor	Reject	Dormaa East	Brong Ahafo	Different nominee
25.11.2013	Mayor	Reject	Kadjebi	Volta	Nominee confirmed
07.01.2016	Mayor	Reinstate	Ada West	Gt. Accra	Different nominee
27.04.2017	Mayor	Reject	Tolon	Northern	Nominee withdrawn
08.05.2017	Mayor	Endorse	Shama	Western	Nominee confirmed

Source: Author's compilation based on relevant media sources: Daily Guide 14.03.2008; Ghanaian Chronicle 09.06.2008; Ghana News Agency 14.04.2009; Ghanaian Chronicle 21.04.2009; Ghanaian Chronicle 12.07.2013; Daily Guide 09.10.2013; Daily Graphic 25.11.2013; Daily Guide 07.01.2016; Citifm Online 27.04.2017; Daily Guide 08.05.2017.

for chiefs to endorse or reject regime-appointed nominees as council chair on some vague definition of citizenship that follows a *settler-indigene* norm, even when such individuals were born, raised, and call these areas their home (Sabbi 2018: 21–4). The chiefs' action reflects their anxiety that without their preferred candidates, patronage benefits would not trickle down to them. The national government often gave in to such demands or compensated those chiefs with other development projects in their respective communities.

Apart from helping to select municipal leaders, chiefs cajole municipal leaders to listen to them or face their wrath. This was the case in 2016 when the Kumasi mayor was removed following 'enormous pressure by the Kumasi chiefs' just for what they described as 'acts of disrespect towards the chiefs' (Sabbi 2018: 24). Apparently, the mayor fell out of favour for questioning rumoured extortions of marketeers by one of the chiefs who attended the municipal council. But chiefly associates reacted to the backlash with no clear explanation save the oft-mentioned rhetoric that 'Kumasi belongs to the [king]' and not 'the council' (Sabbi 2018: 24). Moreover, chiefs sometimes create parallel institutions in the communities where they exercise chieftaincy responsibilities such as setting up their own local development committees that duplicate or run counter to activities of elected councillors and unit representatives (Sabbi 2018: 24). These actions typically point to competing claims for authority and legitimacy between local institutions and informal structures. However, an interdisciplinary view suggests the chiefs might be responding to claims and obligations inherent in the ongoing negotiations of broader societal transformation processes.

Patron-client networks

Another analytically relevant neo-patrimonial variable is patron-client relationship, which marks a long-standing debate on sociopolitical life in Africa. Typically, democratization studies tend to see clientelism as symbolizing state capture (see Englebert 2002; Budd 2004; cf. Pitcher, Moran and Johnston 2009) since the ruling elite and politicians craftily keep networks of clients to gain and maintain political support. But the political sociology literature pursues a pragmatic question: in the absence of well-functioning state bureaucracies even in multiparty democracies, what are the alternatives to fulfil public authority?[16] Against the backdrop of limited access to public resources, actors who control access naturally gain prominence. They become patrons while their clients promise loyalty in exchange for access to resources (see Eisenstadt and Roniger 1984; Neubert 1999, 2004; Korff, Korff and Manakit 2006). The generally voluntary but asymmetrical relationship[17] allows patrons to keep several clients in a pyramidal relations hip: one patron with many clients at the bottom. However, the level of reciprocity implies efficiency to the extent that the relationship exists. Clients can withdraw loyalty if the patron refuses to honour their promise and vice versa. Implicitly,

---

[16] The anthropology of bureaucracies suggests patron-client arrangements are embedded in the practical norms of administration in contexts with weak state bureaucracies (see Blundo 2015; Olivier de Sardan 2015; Bierschenk and Olivier de Sardan 2019).

[17] Patrons have access to information and material resources (including money, goods, political power and prestige) that the clients need more.

there is an inbuilt accountability mechanism to the extent that patrons provide protection and benefits to the clients while patrons can count on their clients' promise of loyalty.

Coming back to our Ghana discussion, the democratic transition, as elsewhere in Africa, did not cause patron-client relations to disappear but instead transformed into competitive multiparty clientelist networks (Neubert 2004: 212–13; Hicken 2011: 296–8). Consequently, patron-client arrangements shape both local and national politics. Clientelist networks bridge the distance between the centre and periphery allowing hitherto distanced elites a channel to integrate into the national political process informally. And by supporting patrons at the national level, local elites become significant nationally (Korff, Korff and Manakit 2006: 77). Local democracy studies criticize district mayors' role in the state-elite capture of local arenas, as mayors use their office to create a local base for national politicians (see Crook 2003; Crawford 2009). But the relationship between district mayors and national elites is only one part of a broader picture. Locally, mayors create and maintain a clientele with exclusive access to municipal resources and services. Through this arrangement, the clients see themselves as participating in the democratic process (Neubert 1999: 268–9; Korff, Korff and Manakit 2006: 77–8). In exchange, mayors become politically relevant in peripheral and national political circles. Thus, there is an inherent social mobility for peripheral politician elites and local notables.

Remarkably, in what we may term inverse patronage relations, we observe how some elected councillors – who ordinarily apply checks on district mayors – rather chase mayors for access to petty patronage resources sometimes at a hefty financial and material expense. Effectively, councillors become clients of the mayors with the implication that they can hardly apply checks and oversight on mayors and municipal executives. Given councillors' poor remuneration, however, this inverse patron-client relation certainly supports them to remain relevant in the local political arena. Furthermore, competitive clientelism at the national level creates further competition among elites who must find access to state resources that they would distribute to local clients.[18] An implicit political accountability reflects efforts by said politicians to struggle and maintain trustworthy clients.

Despite the potential bias to favour intra-elite interests, national patrons are more likely to present their patronage as community goods vis-a-vis private goods to procure community votes (van de Walle 2003: 312–13).[19]

Conclusion

This chapter has highlighted the apparent need for interdisciplinary dialogue in social scientific studies of local political arenas. The historical and sociopolitical background of the disciplines certainly account for their being kept apart even to this

---

[18] Local citizens who get school support and health insurance coverage generally believe they are participating in the democratic process.
[19] We must bear in mind that with repeated competitive elections, clients tend to extract patronage benefits while voting on economic factors (see Lindberg and Morrison 3492008; Lindberg 2013).

day. But definitional differences, the narrow conception of informality and traditional structures, and polemics towards informality and patrimonialism are key reasons that undergird as much this lack of interdisciplinary engagement in studies in local political structures in Africa. Consequently, research and teaching of local politics follow a core discipline standpoint. The persistent lack of dialogue affects not only nuanced contributions to knowledge but also the contents taught to students of African politics. But the polemic that keeps disciplines apart seems misplaced. Even if we distinguish formal and traditional structures for analytical purposes only (Bratton 2007: 98), they cannot be kept apart since both institutions interpenetrate each other particularly in local arenas. Indeed, as happens elsewhere, the marriage between formal institutions and traditional structures is crucial, as they are inextricably bound up within broader societal transformation processes. Their apparent tensions reflect ongoing negotiations to secure claims, functions and privileges in the emergent social order (Elias 1978).

Thus, the view that traditional structures clash with state institutions – which leads to the essentialization of traditional political institutions – is an anomaly and only works to undermine the public authority contributions of non-state institutions. Indeed, Meyer Fortes has already urged Africanist scholars to understand African traditional political institutions not as unique but as 'local forms of types of institutions and customs found all over the world' (in Ayisi 1979: viii). To elaborate further, students of African politics, especially local politics, must learn to analyse neo-traditional and informal structures impartially. This is best realized from an interdisciplinary approach that embraces sociological and anthropological perspectives. And it should systematically show informal structures neither contradict nor replace the local state administration state. They help fulfil public authority in settings with limited state presence while enhancing the democratic legitimacy of state institutions.

10

Ethnicity and democracy in Africa

A comparative study of Ghana and Nigeria

Maame Adwoa A. Gyekye-Jandoh

Introduction

Two countervailing themes have dominated African political science research over the past three decades: the continuing spread of democratic government and the explosion of inter-communal ethnic violence (Udogu 1999, 2018). In many cases, the rising levels of ethnic conflict have accompanied transitions from authoritarian rule to democracy. Thus the prevailing view among mainstream political science is that ethnic diversity and politicization of ethnicity are barriers to stable democracy (Chazan 1983; Beissinger 2008: 85; Young 2012). Empirical evidence such as conflicts in Rwanda, Bosnia, Kosovo and Sierra Leone buttress this. It must be stressed right from the start that the theme of ethnicity and democracy, and the effects of the former on the sustainability of the latter in African countries, is a major point of discussion in African political science classrooms especially in the universities, and the cases of Ghana and Nigeria in this chapter will be illustrative of this.

Ethnic diversity is often associated with competition for scarce resources especially in nation-states where the degree of inequality is rife as is the case in Africa. This competition among the ethnic groups results in conflict because no ethnic grouping wants to be consigned to the bottom of the resource ladder (Anugwom 2000: 67). The conflict is exacerbated in democratic regimes because the choice is the guiding principle in the determination of the authoritative allocation of state resources. As a result, getting represented in strategic positions in order to get their fair share (if not more than) of the national cake becomes existential to ethnic groups. This situation has negatively impacted democratic development.

With the 'third wave' of global democratization, there has been a surge in studies on ethnic conflict in Africa, however, most of these studies have focused on inter-ethnic conflict (Anugwom 2000; Pul 2003), the causes and cost of ethnic conflicts (Debrah, Alidu and Owusu-Mensah 2016), managing and mitigating ethnic conflicts (Jinadu 2004; MacLean 2004) actors in ethnic conflict (Osaghae 1994), ethnicity and the economy (Petchenkine 1992; Debrah 2009), and ethnicity and electoral politics

(Frempong 2014). Globally, scholars such as Beissinger (2008), Nevers (1993), Reilly (2001), Vorrath and Krebs (2009) among others have discussed extensively the relationship between ethnicity and democracy and found that the two reinforce each other based on the existence of some conditions. Though the issue of ethnicity and democracy has received sufficient attention, there is a lacuna in the comparative study among African countries. This lacuna also affects the approaches to democracy in African Political Science and gives currency to this study which sought to comparatively examine the dynamics that shaped ethnicity and democracy in Ghana and Nigeria using four indicators, namely: ethnic grouping, religion, legal framework and party politics.

The chapter is structured into five sections. The first section examines the state-of-the-art literature on ethnicity and democracy, the second section looks at the justification for selecting the two countries, the third section outlines the methodology employed, the fourth section comparatively analyses ethnicity and democracy in the two countries and the fifth section highlights the lessons learned with recommendations for political science teaching and research in Africa.

State-of-the-art literature on ethnic conflict and democracy in Africa

Much study has been done on ethnicity, ethnic conflict and democracy across the globe. To put the study in context, the chapter will attempt to define terminologies such as ethnicity, ethnic grouping, ethnic conflict and democracy before zooming in on issues such as the causes of ethnic conflict, the implications of ethnic conflict on society, how ethnic conflicts spread and the relationship between ethnicity and democracy.

Ethnicity is defined as a large social group of people who share similar and distinctive cultural, racial, religious, language and national origins or traditions. From ethnicity emanates ethnic grouping which has been defined variously.

Lijphart (1977) for instance elaborately defined ethnic group as people who see themselves as a distinct cultural community, often sharing a common language, religion, kinship and/or physical characteristics such as skin, colour and who tend to harbour negative and hostile feelings towards members of other groups. Esman (1994) on the other hand narrowly defined the concept as denoting a community that claims common origins and possesses distinctive and valued cultural markers such as customs, dress and especially language and that expects to share a common destiny. Ethnic groups are defined as groups formed based on cultural, religious, linguistic or biological characteristics perceived to be shared by their members (Vorrath and Krebs 2009: 1). Ethnic groups are also divided and dispersed across international boundaries, among states and territorially concentrated. It is imperative to note that apart from the similarity among members of one ethnic group and their spread, their united hostility towards other ethnic groups is the linchpin for the occurrence of ethnic conflict and the ramification, manifestation and consequence is dependent on the spread of ethnic groups and the capacity of the political system to manage (Reilly 2001: 163).

Ethnic conflict is defined as conflicts arising from situations in which people from varying ethnic groups decide to employ their differences in the pursuit of competing interests (Osaghae 1994). Ethnic conflicts exist in a continuum, in which minimal ethnic rivalry may be considered healthy for the development of society. From this, ethnic rivalry could be seen as prevalent throughout the sociopolitical history of even the most developed nations of the world. But when this conflict goes beyond the minimal level, it becomes a threat to the survival of the social entity concerned. The ethnic conflicts ravaging most African countries can appropriately be situated at the extreme of the continuum (Anugwom 2000: 69). Ethnic conflict is shaped by dynamics such as the number of groups, the level of uneven development among them, the level of development of the elite and the ethnic vanguard (Osaghae 1994: 17). On the causes of ethnic conflicts, scholars have adduced several reasons, some of these are discussed below.

Nevers (1993: 32) intimated that the occurrence of ethnic conflict is linked to the existence of the state and that the fundamental causes of ethnic conflicts are universal because there is no mono-ethnic state. He espoused that ethnic conflicts occur due to the existence of mixed ethnic communities within a state who struggle for political power and status over the allocation of state resources. Ethnic conflict requires a situation in which at least one group feels aggrieved about the distribution of power among the ethnic groups or the feeling that it is being discriminated against and that it is impossible to resolve their grievance through political or legal channels (Nevers 1993: 32).

Rabushka and Shepsle (1972) argued that ethnic conflict occurs because of the rewards that 'ethnic entrepreneurs' derive from 'outbidding' on ethnic issues. The existence of ethnic diversity provides incentives for ethnic entrepreneurs to harness ethnic diversity as a political force for voter mobilization. This leads to divisiveness and conflict because the demands of one group generally come at the expense of the others (Reilly 2001: 164). Ancient ethnic hatreds created by communal cleavages and ethnic heterogeneity have been identified as the chief causes of ethnic conflict (Kaplan 1993; Collier 1998; Vanhanen 1999). The imposition of representative governments via competitive national elections. Material reasons have also been identified as a cause of ethnic conflict. This happens both at the leadership and foot soldier levels. Here, ethnicity is seen as a tool used by the political elite to manipulate the masses into supporting them in the pursuit of their personal material goals (Collier and Hoeffler 2004). Debrah, Alidu and Owusu-Mensah (2016) identified chieftaincy power struggle, competing claims to land titles, and marginalization and religious differences as the causes of the Nawuri-Gonja conflicts in the Northern Region of Ghana.

Democracy according to Schumpeter (1950) is an institutional arrangement for arriving at political decisions, in which individuals acquire the power to decide, by means of a competitive struggle for the peoples' vote. This definition augurs well for this chapter because ethnic conflict is partly about developing hostility towards other ethnic groups in order to assume political power to decide the authoritative allocation of state resources.

There exist age-old debates on the relationship between ethnic pluralism to an extent ethnic conflict and democracy. Some scholars argued that ethnic pluralism (ethnic conflict) hinders democracy while others also argued the opposite and vice versa. To this debate, the chapter focuses attention.

First, is the argument that ethnic pluralism, which results in ethnic conflict, lowers the prospect for democracy. Great political scientists, philosophers and thinkers such as J. S. Mill (1958 [1861]), Almond (1956) and Dahl (1971) all belong to this school of thought. To them, democracy will find it difficult to thrive in multi-ethnic societies for varied reasons. Mill, for instance, posits that free institutions are next to impossible in a country made up of different nationalities or identities. Dahl on his part postulates that pluralism often places a dangerous strain on the tolerance and mutual security required for a system of public contestation and hence a competitive political system is less likely in countries with a considerable measure of subcultural pluralism. Almond advanced the point that in ethnically fragmented societies, conflict rises very high while democracy becomes very difficult. Lijphart (1977) in his famous work consociational democracy averred that the optimal number of groups for peaceful ethnic conflict management is three or four, with conditions becoming progressively less favourable as numbers increase because cooperation among groups becomes more difficult as the number participating in negotiation increases. The injection of open political competition into an ethnically plural society inevitably unleashes a tendency towards 'ethnic outbidding' by politicians vying to maximize support from voters within their respective ethnic in-groups. The result is a slide towards democratic breakdown and violence, whether because elites try to manipulate electoral processes or because minorities reject majority decisions in which the minorities feel they have had no voice.

Democracy exacerbates ethnic conflicts. Two key broad causes have been identified. These are; the interests of authoritarian rulers and how they manipulate ethnicity in order to gain and keep power for themselves. This view is supported by Snyder (2000) who argued that politicians play the ethnic card to avoid challenges and consolidate their rule to perpetuate themselves in power.

The second cause is that democracy is a game of numbers. Majorities rule. Minorities are potentially threatened. In this sense, democratization in culturally or ethnically plural societies typically faces a 'minority problem' that must be dealt with in order to forestall strife or instability. Ethnic minorities are potentially among the biggest losers in any democratization process that empowers ethnic majorities, so the dilemma facing democratization in a multicultural society is how to marginalize destabilizing forms of mobilization and to integrate the interests of minorities in a revised system of power whose legitimacy critically depends on majority rule (Beissinger 2008: 91).

The link between ethnic conflict and democracy is especially crucial in view of the popular assumption that democracy engenders development. However, development has not been possible where there are marked divisions or intense conflicts between groups in a given society. In this vein, ethnic conflicts negate the developmental function of democracy and ultimately attack the root of democracy in society (Anugwom 2000: 69).

Other scholars have also argued that ethnic pluralism has the opportunity to boost the chances of democratization. Scholars such as Horowitz (1985) have argued that in areas where there are many small geographically concentrated groups, it may make little sense for them to devote energy to political activity much beyond their locality, thus from the standpoint of ethnic conflict, much of the attention is off the centre.

Hardgrave (1994) has also argued that where there is ethnic pluralism, it becomes very difficult for a single ethnic group to dominate. Crouch (1993) and other scholars have also made similar arguments that where the ethnic composition makes it difficult for any single ethnic group to predominate, the formation of multi-ethnic alliances is encouraged, thereby boosting the chances of democracy.

Ali Mazrui (1970: 54–5) echoed that while African countries such as Nigeria, Congo Kenya and Uganda had troubles because of big tribes competing with each other, this may serve as an asset in Papua New Guinea because of the small fragmentation of its tribes. This is because the small ethnic groups' conflicts may remain local thereby not shaking the foundation of the nation. The outbreak of ethnic conflicts is less likely in democracies. This is because citizens are consulted on a regular basis and institutionalized checks and balances are in place (Vorrath and Krebs 2009). The existence of minimal conflict may be regarded as dynamic forces which help to propel the development of a society. Minimal ethnic conflicts are seen as one of the principal variables that explain social change in society (Dahrendorf 1976). On the other hand, when ethnic conflicts are extreme, either as a factor for impeding democracy as in Nigeria, or as the basis for senseless violence in Rwanda, Burundi, Zaire (now the Democratic Republic of Congo) and so forth, it becomes a major disintegrating force in society (Anugwom 2000: 69).

Reilly (2001: 169) rejected the two assertions by counselling that the two schools of thought or theories or wisdom require revision and advanced the following three arguments: First, a high degree of ethnic pluralism may actually help prospects for democracy if the ethnic structure is such that no group can act as a national hegemon and control power alone. Second, there is a need to move away from the generic concept of ethnic groups and look more at the different types of ethnic divisions, particularly ethnic group size, demography and the crucial question of whether ethnic conflicts take place at the national, regional or local level. Third, better data sources and a more sophisticated way of measuring ethnic differences is needed to understand the true relationship between democracy, ethnic fragmentation and internal conflicts.

In spite of these counterclaims for ethnic conflicts and democracy, it has equally been established that democracy's ability to mitigate ethnic conflict is based on the following conditions (Nevers 1993: 38–41):

(a) if the negotiating process associated with democratization can establish a workable distribution of power among ethnic groups so as to preclude the development of severe tension,

(b) if ethnic issues are resolved early in the transition process,

(c) if ethnic tension is low to begin with, democratization is less likely to unleash ethnic conflict,

(d) if ethnic groups are relatively equal in size and power. This is dependent on the development of an electoral system that promotes intra-ethnic voting,

(e) if the previous authoritarian regime was not dominated by an ethnic minority,

(f) if the main ethnic groups in the state were united in opposition to the previous regime, either in one movement or a coalition,

(g) if the leaders of large ethnic groups are moderates, rather than extremists. Moderation in this context means avoidance of extremism and hostility in developing positions vis-a-vis other ethnic groups,

(h) if external allies are not present, and

(i) if the army is loyal to the state, rather than to a particular ethnic group, democratization is less likely to lead to ethnic conflict.

In the words of Nevers (1993: 41–3), democracy exacerbates ethnic conflict through the following nine mechanisms:

> First, the existence of historical grievances and the presence of strong ethnic stereotypes may not exacerbate ethnic conflict, but they will certainly make bargaining among different groups more difficult,

> Second, the previous regime's identification with a specific ethnic group, in particular one that was a minority in the state, is likely to hamper efforts to avoid ethnic conflict,

> Third, if the previous regime manipulated the ethnic mix in parts of the country, there is a greater likelihood that ethnic tension will emerge,

> Fourth, if oppositions to the authoritarian regime were dominated by a single ethnic group or fragmented along ethnic lines, the process of negotiating new political structures would be complicated,

> Fifth, if some ethnic leaders embrace extreme positions with regard to ethnic rights, the ability of the democratization process to lessen ethnic tension would be weakened,

> Sixth, the mitigation of ethnic conflict will be more complicated if ethnic groups are of greatly uneven sizes,

> Seventh, if one or more groups in a given state are members of an ethnic group that governs a neighbouring state, democratization could face additional challenges,

> Eighth, if the military is loyal to one ethnic group, it can cause severe problems for the democratization process and the search for solutions to the ethnic conflicts, and

> Ninth, if the ethnic issues are ignored in the early stages of constitution-building, democratization may do more to exacerbate than mitigate ethnic tension.

Reynal-Querol (2002) and Beissinger (2008: 87) intimated that the existence of democracy alone does not suffice for the absence of ethnic conflict. Other factors such as the type of political system, the level of representation of the population (inclusiveness and participation) economic growth, the prevalence of Islam, oil-based economies and prior colonial experience are all important. Reynal-Querol (2002) further recommended consociational systems in divided societies, because they provide adequate procedures for channelling participation.

Studies on ethnic conflict and democracy have also focused on the spread of ethnic conflict. Weiner (1996), Muggah (2006) and Lambach (2007), for instance, identified the following as factors that cause the spread of ethnic conflict: the existence of transnational ethnic groups with their associated refugee flows and the phenomenon of 'refugee warriors'; transnational arms trafficking; state weakness; regional alliances and porous boundaries.

Diffusion and escalation were identified as the dynamics that bring about the spread of ethnic conflicts (Lake and Rothchild 1998). Diffusion here refers to conflict in one area altering the likelihood of conflict elsewhere, and escalation means the spread of conflict through the involvement of new actors-usually foreign participants entering an otherwise internal conflict. Escalation means intra-state conflicts developing into inter-state conflict.

Debrah, Alidu and Owusu-Mensah (2016) have also examined ethnic conflicts in Ghana and came up with both monetary and non-monetary costs of conflict. In terms of the former, the conflict resulted in the loss of GH¢ 600,000, which was US$ 300,000 at the time, and loss of daily income. In terms of non-monetary, personal properties such as houses were destroyed in arson. People faced starvation due to loss of income, and there was a complete halt in agricultural activities in the areas of the conflict. Infrastructure such as roads, school buildings, health centres and private homes, and market centres were all destroyed during the conflict. The conflict in its wake also brought about an outbreak of cholera, infant and childhood mortality, nutritional deficiencies, food insecurity, high rate of school dropouts, teenage pregnancy and forced marriage as spillover effects as well as internal displacement.

Anugwom (2000) examined ethnic conflicts and their implications for democracy in Nigeria. He identified ethnic conflict and distrust as the bane of previous attempts at democracy in Nigeria. Marginalization and agitations by ethnic minorities were identified as disturbing new dimensions of ethnicity in Nigeria. In his view, marginalization breeds suspicion, distrust, heightens ethnic tension and may eventually result in conflict over the allocation of resources and state power. This has dire consequences because the marginalized have the potential for disrupting the drive to democratization.

Debrah (2009) postulated that political transitions in Ghana since independence were shaped by events on the economic front more than the popularized issues of ethnicity, regionalism and personal ambitions.

Frempong (2014: 87) intimated that democracy does not automatically and necessarily lead to more or fewer ethnic conflicts. But ethnicity is a reality that can be mobilized for electoral purposes and Ghanaian politicians remain vulnerable to elite manipulation along ethnic lines largely because elites play upon the latent fears ethnic groups hold about their group's social and economic security. In his view, there is the need for sensitivity towards the interests and demands of various ethnic groups as well as equity and justice in the manner in which ethnic demands are addressed. He, like other scholars, identified the speed with which ethnic issues are acknowledged and addressed with justice to all as preconditions for the success of democratic governance in defusing ethnic conflicts in Ghana.

Agbu (2011) examined the interplay between ethnicity and democratization in post–Cold War Africa and their implications for politics and development in Africa.

He opined that even though ethnicity complicates issues, degenerates into conflict and a serious threat to democracy, it cannot be swept under the carpet because of its relevance to the democratization process in Africa. Agbu (2011) further asserted that ethnicity is significant in comprehending the politics of civil society and the struggles that accompany nation-building. To derive dividends from ethnicity, Agbu (2011) espoused the management of ethnic cleavages and diversities that is anchored on harmonizing ethnicity and citizenship for inclusive democratization.

Ugbem (2019) traced the background of ethnicity in Nigeria and asserted that ethnicity was a colonial creation, which has been reconstructed over time to reflect changing perceptions, aspirations and contentions and needs. Over the years, ethnicity has been mobilized to contest inclusion/exclusion, issues in the Nigerian political process and structure thereby undermining the democratization process. The fall out of the social reality of ethnicity and democracy in Nigeria has culminated into majority and minority groups locked up in protracted competitions for the control of state power, larger access to scarce resources at the expense of others as well as inter-ethnic showdown by deprived ethnicities. This has had ramifications on the development of Nigeria.

From the aforementioned reviews, it can be deduced that extensive studies have been done on the subject matters of ethnicity, ethnic conflict and democracy, however, one issue that has not received sufficient scholarly attention is the comparative analysis of ethnicity and democracy in Ghana and Nigeria.

Justification for selecting Ghana and Nigeria for the study

Both Ghana and Nigeria are nation-states within West Africa. They were both colonized by the British and used English as the official language. They gained independence in 1957 and 1960, respectively. The two states have experienced democratic interruptions on several occasions and are all in their fourth republics. They both practice multiparty democracy – an elected president has a four-year term and can be president for two terms only. Since both countries returned to democratic rule, political power has been won by two main political parties namely the National Democratic Congress (NDC) and New Patriotic Party (NPP) in Ghana and the Peoples' Democratic Party (PDP) and All Peoples' Congress (APC) in the case of Nigeria. In terms of the system of governance, Ghana practices the unitary system with a unicameral parliament while Nigeria practices the federal system of governance with a bicameral parliamentary system. Nigeria has more ethnic groupings than Ghana due to the latter's large geographical coverage of land. These vast similarities espoused earlier have rendered the two countries for a comparative study.

Methodology of the study

The chapter is a desktop study that relied on secondary data from articles in journals, chapters in books as well as conference papers and seminal works by authorities in the field of ethnicity and democracy. The studies by the various scholars on the two countries were collated, similarities were drawn and a comparative analysis was done to deduce whether ethnicity hindered or promoted the democratization process in the two nation-states used as the unit of analysis. The comparative analysis was done using the following variables or indicators: (a) ethnic grouping, (b) religion, (c) legal frameworks and (d) party politics.

The study used the multiple case study approach to overcome the challenges of lack of rigour associated with single case studies.

Findings and discussions

The findings of the chapter are comparatively analysed along with four-fold thematic areas. These are: first, ethnic grouping and its effects on ethnic conflicts and democracy, second, religious influence on ethnicity and the dynamics it brought on the democratization process, third, the legal framework vis-a-vis ethnicity and the degree to which it deepened democracy, and fourth, party politics and ethnicity and the dynamics of democratization.

Ethnic grouping and its effects on democracy in Ghana and Nigeria

According to Diamond (1988: 21), 'Nothing can be understood about Nigeria until its pattern of ethnic diversity is delineated'. Nigeria has a large number of ethnic groups, with inequalities among them in size, resource endowment, education and access to state power and resources, and a highly developed and factionalized indigenous bourgeoisie, which makes Nigeria's ethnic situation perhaps the most complicated in Africa (Osaghae 1994: 29). Nigeria, in addition, has a historically serious minorities' problem, and at some stage in the transition to democracy under Babangida, the 'national question' became a critical political matter (Osaghae 1994: 30). Nigeria, having had its boundaries drawn by the British in 1914, has within it a staggering number of ethnic groups, exemplified by the presence of some 248 distinct languages (Coleman 1958: 15). In spite of this fact, only three groups comprise roughly two-thirds of the population, rendering Nigeria (in Horowitz's terms), as having a relatively 'centralized' ethnic structure. These are the Hausa-Fulani, the Yoruba and the Igbo (Diamond 1988: 21). The Hausa and Fulani are grouped together because the Fulani adopted the Hausa language and culture as they conquered the Hausa, and intermarried with them to such an extent that the two groups have become difficult to distinguish (Coleman 1958: 21; Paden 1971: 22–3; Diamond 1988: 21). Closely related to the Hausa-Fulani are the Nupe and the Kanuri. Both groups shared with the Hausa-Fulani the two cultural elements that most sharply distinguished them from the Igbo and to a lesser extent from the Yoruba; a deep and diffuse faith in Islam, and a tradition of large-scale rule through centralized authoritarian states (Diamond 1988: 21).

In contrast to Nigeria, Ghana does not have as many ethnic groups and as much regional rivalry, although it does have quite a number of ethnic groups. It is estimated that there are about ninety ethnic groups in Ghana, but these are often reduced to a few large groups: Akan, Mole Dagbani, Ewe, Ga-Adangbe, Guan and Gurma among others (Frempong 2014: 73–4). The ethnic grouping is also divided along geographic locations, namely: northern and southern with the former comprising Mole Dagbani, Gurma and Grusi and the south made up of Kwa which includes Akan, Ewe, Ga-Adangbe and Guan. There exist subdivisions among these groups based on culture, language and other characteristics (Petchenkine 1992: 178).

The ethnic grouping had repercussions for democracy. For instance in Nigeria, the dominance of the three major ethnic groups is solidified by their regional concentration in the country – the Hausa-Fulani in the North, the Igbo in the East and the Yoruba in the West. Significantly, this regional structure gave the three major ethnic groups (and their political cultures and aspirations) dominant political roles in each of their regions, exaggerating substantially the centralized character of the ethnic structure (Diamond 1988: 23). To make matters worse, the regional distribution of the population itself became 'an important dimension of the ethnic balance of power, and this distribution was much more skewed. While the Eastern and Western regions were roughly equal in size . . . the Northern Region contained an absolute majority of the nation's population . . . and more than three-quarters of its physical territory' (Diamond 1988: 23–24). In addition, each region consisted of important ethnic minorities, who feared and resented the dominance of the ethnic majorities in the region and therefore demanded greater autonomy. The ethnic structure in Nigeria was therefore not completely centralized. While each minority group was relatively small, together they made up more than a third of the Nigerian population, and while they were politically fragmented, they formed a 'strategic political constituency' in each region. Thus, the demographic balance of ethnic groups within each region became an important factor in Nigerian politics (Diamond 1988: 24). The Yoruba and Igbo, however, each comprised a little more than two-thirds of their regional populations and the Hausa-Fulani about half of the Northern population (Coleman 1958: 15). Although this numerical advantage ensured enough political dominance of the majority ethnic groups within the regions, it could not preclude determined separatist movements by minority groups such as the Ibibio and Efik in the Southeast, the Ijaw in the Niger River Delta of the East and the Mid-West, the Edo (or Bini) and Urhobo of the Mid-West, the Kanuri in the Northeast, and the many ethnic groups of the lower North, or 'Middle Belt', especially the Tiv (Diamond 1988: 24). In addition to the Igbirra, Idoma, Igala and Birom, these people shared a common heritage of resistance to the Muslim religion and authoritarian state structure, as well as the slave raids of the Fulani (Post 1963: 78).

In Ghana, each of the ethnic groups has its traditional home (regions). The Akans spread across five regions –Western, Central, Eastern, Ashanti and Brong Ahafo; the Mole Dagbani cut across the Northern, Upper East and Upper West regions, the Ewes are in southern Volta Region, the Ga-Adangbe are in the Greater Accra and Eastern regions and the Guan speaking groups are dotted in Northern, Central, Eastern and Volta regions. Spatial mobility, economic factors have altered the ethnic homogeneity of the regions and its associated ramifications for electoral politics (Frempong 2014: 74).

In comparative terms, the two countries share some similarities in terms of ethnic grouping culminating into regionalization; ethnicity was very sharp in Nigeria due to the existence of multiple minority groups as compared to Ghana where the minority groups are less.

Religion and its impact on ethnicity and democracy

Religion is also another factor of division among the Nigerian peoples, but this cleavage was generally less significant than ethnicity and region. According to Diamond (1988: 25), 'where religion was a factor in social and political conflict, it typically reflected broader cultural conflict, as in the Middle Belt, which contained "vigorous concentrations of Christianity among groups of resolute animists"' (Kirk-Greene 1967: 6). Among the Igbos in the East, the majority were Christians, while Islam was virtually absent. In the West, 'where religion might have functioned to crosscut ethnicity, among the Yoruba – who were fairly evenly split between Christianity and Islam – it failed to do so because Islam took a different, less encompassing form in the South. As a result, "Hausa and Yoruba [prayed] at different mosques, and Islam does not function as a crosscutting interethnic solidarity structure" (Young 1976: 280)' (Diamond 1988: 25).

It must be noted, however, that in recent times, religion has become even more of a salient issue (although it has always been) in Nigerian politics and society, with clashes between Muslim and Christian groups in the North and even in some parts of the South; there have also been debates as to whether Nigeria should join the Organization of Islamic Countries (OIC), an action which has been opposed by many Christians. The North has always been wary of any attempt at Christian infiltration of its peoples, as has the South, and leaders of both the North and the South are watchful that the government does not take on the identity of, or side with one religious group over the other.

Although religion has not been a major contentious issue in Ghana as it has been in Nigeria, religion is still a factor of political pressure in Ghana, especially by way of the political activity of church leadership. The three main religious groups in Ghana are Muslims (30 per cent), Protestants (29 per cent) and Catholics (14 per cent). These groups are not evenly spread geographically. Muslims are the largest populations within the northern regions, whereas Christians live mostly in the South (Petchenkine 1992: 218). Interestingly, the activities and political influence of the religious communities do not correspond to their proportion of the population. Due to the fragmentation of the Muslim community, until recently, Muslims have had quite limited opportunities to influence political decision-making in Ghana. The Protestant community is also very fragmented with uncountable denominations springing up as the days go by. In spite of the fragmentation, the religious groupings through their national leaders such as the Catholic Bishops Conference, the Christian Council, the Ghana Pentecostal and Charismatic Council, the Office of the National Chief Imam and the head of the Ahmadiyya Mission in Ghana work hand in hand in deepening democracy in Ghana as compared to Nigeria where the religious bodies are suspicious of each other's activities. It is also instructive to note that in Ghana, there is the National Peace Council and National House of Chiefs with the former composed of various religious and ethnic groups and the latter made of chiefs from ten (now sixteen) administrative regions. These two institutional frameworks have aided in watering down the exacerbation of both religious and ethnic conflicts thereby boosting democracy.

Regionalism and its effect on ethnic conflict and democracy

Regionalization also produced seeds of disunity and a possible breakup of the Nigerian nation. This is because, with each region being large enough at least in comparison with many states in Africa, making the regions into independent states was considered by some ambitious regional leaders. After the breakdown of Ironsi's regime in 1966, regional memoranda were presented at the ad-hoc constitutional conference by regional delegates who, except the Midwest, advocated a confederation of four regions with each region having the right to secede completely and unilaterally whenever it so desired. Although there were rumours of secession, 'between September 1966 and March 1967, Nigeria faced political uncertainty, followed by an indefinite adjournment of that (ad-hoc) constitutional conference' (Umoren 1996: 104). The historic creation of the Republic of Biafra by Ojukwu on 30 May 1967 seemed to support the feasibility of secession. However, Gowon's administration remained steadfast in its goal of keeping Nigeria one. Many scholars perceived the civil war that ensued as predominantly a struggle to maintain control of natural resources, especially 'eastern crude oil', perpetrated by tribalism (Umoren 1996: 106). In fact, Umoren (1996) argues that the creation of states in Nigeria in 1967 and thereafter, like the regionalization policy, had similar political and economic goals for ethnic economies (Umoren 1996: 105). However, regionalization, provincialization and even the creation of additional new states, though a welcomed development, are equally frail and short of meeting Nigeria's political goals for unity (Umoren 1996: 106).

Ghana also comprises ten (now divided into sixteen) regions, which have some measure of local autonomy, through decentralization mechanisms such as the Metropolitan, Municipal and District Assemblies but which are mainly subordinated to the centre. The regions are the Upper East, Upper West and Northern regions, comprising mainly the northern group; the Brong Ahafo, Ashanti, Eastern, Western and Central regions, comprising mainly the majority subgroup, the Akan with the Ashantis, Fantes, Akims, Akuapems, Bono and so on comprising tribes within this subgroup; the Greater Accra Region comprising mainly the Ga and Ga-Adangbe subgroup, because the capital city Accra is located within this region, it also comprises increasing numbers of migrants from all parts of Ghana including the Akan, Ewe, Northerners, and others; and finally the Volta region, which comprises the Ewe and Central-Togolese.

In comparative terms, the Nigerians had a sharp north-south rivalry which also fed into the religious grouping hence ethnic conflict was rife. Ghana, on the other hand, experienced the Akan-Non-Akan rivalry and later narrowed to Ashanti-Ewe rivalry as far back as the 1969 election and the reign of Provisional National Defense Council (PNDC) and perpetuating itself into the Fourth Republic (Frempong 2014: 74–5).

Legal frameworks and their contribution to ethnic conflict and democracy

Nmoma (1995: 314) asserts that 'as in most African countries, the salience of ethnic conflict in Nigerian politics owes much of its genesis to the pre-independence constitutions'. The South held the advantage temporarily under the 1922 Clifford Constitution until 1939, when separate regions and legislatures were created under the 1946 Richards Constitution, so that Northern Nigeria was no longer excluded from participation in the legislative council. This political advantage by the South was short-lived and quickly shifted to the North, due to the North's numerical strength and its voting behaviour based on ethnicity and ethnic politics (Nmoma 1995: 316). Opportunities for national integration and a more united democratic country were frustrated by a preponderance of the North's monopoly of the presidency since independence. The two exceptions were the military regimes under Major Generals Aguiyi Ironsi and Olusegun Obasanjo, both Southerners.

The South's fear of Northern domination is very deep, 'because control of political power has enabled the North to pursue policies designed to reduce Southern control of the economy and advance the interests of Northerners in the bureaucracy' (Suberu 1990: 153). Economic development of the North has been pursued by Northern-dominated governments to the neglect of eastern and western (Southern) regions. Such unequal development led to the breakdown of consensus and the first military coup in 1966 (Smith 1981: 355–78). It should be noted that the 1951 MacPherson Constitution exacerbated Nigerian ethnic politics by granting the North 50 per cent of the seats in the central legislature (Nmoma 1995: 316). Thus, the Nigerian constitutions have had the effect of reinforcing the regional, communal and ethnic cleavages in the society.

Just as in Nigeria, ethnic tensions were high in Ghana in the run-up to independence because of the emergence of ethnic and regional-based parties to challenge Kwame Nkrumah's Convention Peoples' Party (CPP) (Frempong 2001: 145). However, legal regimes such as the passage of the Avoidance of Discrimination Act were enacted by Nkrumah immediately after independence to forestall the formation of political parties along ethnic, regional and religious lines. This attempt could not last, ethnicity became a major issue in the 1969 elections more than the case in the 1950s (Frempong 2014: 74). The return to constitutional rule in 1992 brought a sigh of relief to the perpetuation of ethnicity in the body politics of Ghana. The 1992 Republican Constitution in Article 55(1) guaranteed the right to the formation of political parties and a political party is free to participate in shaping the political will of the people, to disseminate information on political ideas, social and economic programmes of a national character (Republic of Ghana 1992). In Section 4 of Article 55, the Constitution espoused that 'every political party shall have a national character, and membership shall not be based on ethnic, religious, regional or other sectional divisions'. Further in Section 7(c), the Constitution provides that 'the party's name, emblem, colour, motto or any other symbol has no ethnic, regional, religious or other sectional connotation or gives the appearance that its activities are confined only to a part of Ghana'. In Article 55(11), the Constitution provides that 'the state shall provide fair opportunity to all political parties to present their programmes to the public by ensuring equal access to the state-owned media'. Finally in Article 56, the Constitution intimates that 'parliament shall have no power to enact a law to establish or authorize the establishment of a body or movement with the right or power to impose on the people of Ghana a common programme or set of objectives of a religious or political nature'. In Article 89(c), the

Constitution provides for representation of each of the administrative regions on the Council of State.

Comparatively, it can be deduced that the Nigerian legal regimes to a large extent championed ethnicity through their provisions, while that of Ghana sought to water down ethnicity in order to bolster the prospects of democracy.

The role of ethnicity (ethnic conflict) in democratic regimes – an analysis

Both Ghana and Nigeria since independence in 1957 and 1960, respectively, have failed in entrenching democracy on three counts. Both countries are now in their fourth republics starting 1992 and 1999, respectively. This subsection examines the role of ethnicity in the democratization process in both countries.

The first five years of Nigeria's post-independence were chaotic and bloody due to bitterness and infighting. The bitterness and infighting could be traced to the existence of ethnic rivalries between the three large regions namely; Hausa-Fulani (Northern Nigeria), the Yoruba (Western Nigeria) and Igbo (Eastern Nigeria). The democratic experience of the 1960s was not only derailed by the military, there were severe ethnic rivalries due to competition for power and national resources as well as the partitioning of Nigeria along ethnic lines by the British colonial masters. During the colonial era, linguistic groups were categorized as tribes and differences between them were emphasized, this culminated into a strong sense of ethnic consciousness, resulting often in unhealthy competition before the 1960s (Anugwom 2000: 70). This division heightened and intensified the politicization of ethnicity in Nigeria immediately after independence. The case of Ghana was not different, because activities leading to independence were also characterized by ethnicity where political parties were formed along ethnic lines. The only variation was that Ghana's case did not result in bloodshed as was in Nigeria.

Regime analysis

The first republic was characterized by ethnic sentiments and sectionalism. The republic was based mainly on ethnic considerations. The three main political parties: Nigeria Peoples' Congress (NPC), National Council of Nigeria Citizens (NCNC) and the Action Group (AG) were all ethnically based as were their leaders. No single political party was broadly based or cut across ethnic lines. This made all political and governance policies and actions be seen through an ethnic prism and its concomitant events of 1966 and 1967. On the contrary, Ghana's First Republic witnessed the passage of the Avoidance of Discrimination Act which abhorred the formation of political parties on ethnic, regional and religious line. This Act compelled the sectarian groups to merge into the United Party (UP). By February 1966 when Kwame Nkrumah was overthrown, he had succeeded in reducing ethnic politics to the barest minimum (Frempong 2014: 74).

Nigeria's second republic was also associated with ethno-regional conflict where the three major political parties: National Party of Nigeria (NPN), Unity Party of Nigeria

(UPN) and Nigeria Peoples' Party (NPP) were all ethnic and regional in outlook and nature rather than central or national political parties. Ethnicity contributed to the demise of both the first and second republics, however, the second republic could not stand the test of time due to additional factors such as the immaturity of its politicians and the absurdity of their politics, corruption, economic mismanagement and worsening social infrastructure, among others. In spite of these, the ethnic factor and its twin evil of 'do or die politics' served as the main factors to the breakdown of the regime and the basis for the other negative elements (Anugwom 2000: 71).

Ghana's second republic experience is similar to the Nigerian case. According to Frempong (2014: 74), the 1969 election which ushered in the second republic was characterized by ethnicity. The ruling National Liberation Council had a leadership crisis where Chairman Afrifa supported the Akan based Progress Party and his vice Harlley and Deku supported the Ewe based National Alliance of Liberals (Frempong 2017: 91). In the words of Twumasi (2014), the 1969 election results reinforced the Akan-Ewe ethnic divide and deepened further with Victor Owusu's ethnocentric description of Ewe's as 'inward-looking' in a parliamentary debate during the Busia regime. This Akan-Ewe rivalry has lingered on into the Fourth Republic. In comparative terms, both republics saw ethnicity playing a pivotal role, however, corruption, greed and economic mismanagement brought the second republic in both countries to an unexpected end through military coup d'états.

In Nigeria, the third republic's breakdown was preceded by the annulment of the official results by the military ruler Ibrahim Babangida (a northern Hausa-Fulani) in which Moshood Abiola (a Southerner) was leading, though the 1993 election was described as a free, fair and transparent one. The annulment was seen by many as nothing but an attempt to perpetuate the Hausa-Fulani hegemony in power hence ethnically motivated (Anugwom 2000: 72). Ghana's third republic saw both religious and ethnic balance in the permutation for presidential and vice-presidential candidates hence watered down the effect of ethnicity on democracy (Frempong 2017: 111–12) unlike Nigeria which was neck deep into ethnic politics and its resultant conflict. Again, both republics came to an end through the barrel of the gun with economic mismanagement and lack of political will to fight corruption being the culprit in Ghana and ethnicity being the nerve centre in the case of Nigeria.

The fourth republics of both Ghana and Nigeria are currently underway. Anugwom (2000: 72) has argued that ethnicity has assumed a different dimension through the concept of marginalization of ethnic groups. This is a threat to democracy because once ethnic orientation determines one's access to state resources and power, other ethnic groups will have grievances that they always perceive cannot be solved by the political and legal system. Ethnicity has also reared its ugly head in Ghana's fourth republic through a series of inter and intra-ethnic conflicts not for state power and resources but local dominance. The age-old Akan-Non-Akan rivalry is also at play through the mobilization of ethnic groups for political fortune by ethnic entrepreneurs and political elites. Both countries in the fourth republic have had elections that have been described by observers as free, fair and transparent with alternation of power from the ruling governments to the oppositions. And the 'ethnic card' is now played positively to advance democracy: thus presidential candidates in both countries now do not choose their tribesmen as their vice-presidential candidates but they look for running mates from other tribes and in some cases from other religions. This has to a large extent brought about some ethnic balance in the politics of the two countries. For instance, currently in Ghana, a Christian who is a southerner is the president with the vice-president being a Moslem and a northerner while in Nigeria the president is a Moslem from the north with a Christian southerner as the vice-president. These permutations tend to suggest that at every point in time, all ethnic and religious groups are actively represented at the helm of affairs; hence, the perception of ethnic and religious exclusion is minimized.

Conclusion and recommendations for ethnicity and democratization prospects in Ghana, Nigeria and Africa as a whole

In conclusion, the study found that the four variables: ethnic grouping, religion, regionalism and legal regimes did shape the relationship between ethnicity and democracy in both countries. In addition, it found that factors such as corruption, greed and economic mismanagement also assisted ethnicity in contributing to democratic breakdown in both countries. It is pertinent to note that ethnicity derailed the democratization process in Nigeria but not in Ghana.

Despite these findings, there is a glimmer of hope for democracy and ethnicity to catapult each other as espoused by other scholars. This is because both countries now have unofficial ethnic and religious arrangements where political parties choose their presidential and vice-presidential candidates from different ethnic, regional and religious groups. If this arrangement is sustained, democracy in both countries will be sustained for a long time. This sustainability will be achieved and especially enhanced if political science teaching, research, and scholarship in Ghana, Nigeria and Africa as a whole make it a point to focus their energies on understanding and solving the phenomena and pitfalls of corruption, economic mismanagement and ethnic conflicts, and especially their potentially fatal effects on democracy, democratic consolidation and socio-economic development on the African continent. Thus, such education must begin right from the cradle to the grave, and primary, secondary, and tertiary educational institutions will have consequential roles to play, teaching the history of the continent while at the same time striving to decolonize mainstream political science, civics and history subjects that are taught.

11

Research on gender, women and politics in Africa

Contributions and innovations

Aili Mari Tripp and Olajumoke Yacob-Haliso

Introduction

Research on women and gender and politics in Africa has grown rapidly since the 1990s and has made important contributions to scholarship on African politics and the study of gender and politics broadly defined. This chapter looks at the interdisciplinary roots of the subfield and the methods employed. It examines some of the particular characteristics of this subfield as it has evolved in Africa and some of the factors that have shaped it.

Much of the early scholarship, starting in the 1970s, documented women's involvement in independence movements, the impact of the spread of Islam and Christianity on women's political leadership, women's local and national mobilization during the early one-party states, and their involvement in state- and party-controlled women's organizations. This was evident, for example, in Nina Mba's 1982 study of women's political activity in Nigeria, Filomena Steady's 1975 study of the National Congress of Sierra Leone and the work of Maria Nzomo on local women's mobilization in Kenya in 1987.

New research has examined the politics of naked protest carried out by women in a variety of contexts, African feminism(s), the new interest in LGBTQ+ activism, motherhood and politics, public opinion, digital democracy and decolonizing knowledge about women and politics. Political memoirs of early women leaders have emerged as a new genre of writing in many African countries and serve as an important resource for understanding women's role as presidents, ministers and in parties, conflict, constitution making and many other aspects of politics. While much of this literature has been produced by women, it has increasingly been an area of concern for men as well, particularly given that women make up a large proportion of the electorate and increasingly a greater proportion of the legislature and other political institutions. Much of this scholarship has also been written by women who have bridged academia and the women's movements in their countries, giving added salience to their work.

This chapter starts with the evolution of institutional contexts for the emergence of scholarship on women and politics: women's studies programmes, centres and departments; academic networks; and publishing venues. It then discusses some of the characteristics of the study of women and politics and how they evolved. In particular, the chapter looks at the relationship of women academics to and their role in politics, in pro-democracy movements and in women's movements. It examines the interdisciplinary nature of the research in this area and the distinctive African contributions and experiences. It explores contemporary debates, and some of the particular challenges confronting research and publishing in this area arising out of global inequalities in access to research resources.

Evolution of women's studies in Africa

The number of scholars publishing widely on women and politics within political science departments in Africa are few and far between. There are some established scholars like Josephine Ahikire (Uganda), Maria Nzomo (Kenya), Amanda Gouws and Shireen Hassim (South Africa), and Fatima Harrak (Morocco). However, most of the scholarship on women and politics has been carried out by scholars doing work in women and gender studies, history, communications, sociology, literary studies and other related disciplines.

Women's studies scholars formed interdisciplinary women and gender studies programmes, centres and departments starting in the early 1980s, in part because their work was not valued or given sufficient visibility in the disciplines. The Women's Research and Documentation Project was started as early as 1980 at the University of Dar es Salaam, Tanzania. It served as a forum for networking scholars in the field of women's studies and as a documentation centre (Meena and Mbilinyi 1991). Other such centres soon formed. Nina Mba, for example, was a founding member of the Women's Research and Documentation Center at the University of Ibadan, formed in 1987. A women's studies teaching programme was started at Eduardo Mondlane University in Mozambique in 1988, at Ahfad University in Sudan in 1989, and others soon emerged at universities in Ghana, South Africa, Kenya and elsewhere.

One of the main goals of these programmes was to bring African women's knowledge, perspectives and experiences to the fore and bring them into academic and policy debates and other national, regional and international fora. It was significant that the feminist approaches that emerged were rooted in African women's experiences rather than Western feminist epistemologies and theories (Rodriguez, Tsikata and Ampofo 2015).

The issue of relevance is central to the study of gender and politics and was a key impetus in the creation of various gender studies programmes. They were seen as a locus of policy development, advocacy, training, and in service of key constituencies such as the legislature, judiciary and ministries, for example. Thus, research and teaching have focused on political, economic, and social concerns, such as maternal mortality, land ownership, property and inheritance rights, women's health, poverty, water, women's education, children and other issues that weigh heavily on women and their communities.

The Addis Ababa University Center for Research Training and Information for Women in Development (CERTWID) was formed by the Ethiopian government and the United Nations Population Fund (UNFPA) to carry out research, teaching, and engage in documentation as its main activities. It trained parliamentarians and assisted the former Women's Affairs Bureau in the prime minister's office. Its members also participated in various women's non-governmental organizations (NGOs). Similarly, a Department of Women's and Gender Studies (WGS) established at the University of Buea in Cameroon in 1993 was also intended to train gender experts to work in various governmental ministries, departments, and units as well as NGOs. Makerere University's School of Women and Gender Studies was also created to become a catalyst for integrating gender concerns in policymaking in government and NGOs and promote gender mainstreaming (Tripp et al. 2009). Makerere's leadership in promoting women's studies gained international recognition in the field of gender studies when it hosted the 2002 Women's World Congress, one of the first major international academic conferences to be held in Uganda. Today, there are approximately nineteen gender studies degree programmes being offered at universities across the continent. Five universities have a full-fledged department, while one, Makerere's School of Women and Gender Studies, offers several programmes. At least sixteen other universities have gender units, institutes, or centres.

The Africa Gender Institute at the University of Cape Town emerged as an especially important regional node for research and training in women's studies. Formed in 1996, it was established with a mandate to foster gender research throughout the continent. It launched *Feminist Africa*, the leading online journal on African feminist scholarship. Influential feminist scholars like Sylvia Tamale from Uganda, Takyiwaa Manuh, and Akosua Adomako Ampofo from Ghana; Charmaine Pereira and Amina Mama from Nigeria; and Elaine Salo, Sisonke Msimang, Jane Bennett, Yaliwe Clarke and Amanda Gouws from South Africa have all been associated with the Institute at one time or another. The institute faced multiple challenges of critiquing the scholarship of African male colleagues for its gender blindness, while at the same time sharing concerns with them of the imperialist, colonialist and racist constructions of Africa in mainstream Western literature. They were often accused of being overly Western when they argued that African culture and traditions were contested (Pereira 2002).

Networks of women's studies scholars

The study of women in the social sciences was supported by a variety of networks of women researchers, including the Association of African Women for Research and Development (AAWORD), which was formed in 1977 in Dakar, Senegal, to advance feminism in Africa through research and activism. It held workshops on methodology, women and rural development, reproduction, the mass media, and development assistance (Mama 1995). Among the attendees at the founding conference were

Fatima Mernissi, Fatou Sow (Senegal), Marieme Hélie-Lucas (Algeria), Ayesha Imam (Nigeria), Achola Pala (Kenya), Filomina Steady (Sierra Leone) and Marie-Angélique Savané (Senegal).

The Council for the Development of Social Science Research in Africa (CODESRIA) has also been a key influence on feminist work in Africa. A 1991 workshop in Dakar on 'Gender Analysis and African Social Science' was CODESRIA's first major institutional initiative focusing on gender. The workshop resulted in the publication of *Engendering African Social Sciences*, which was a major review of feminist scholarship in the 1990s, edited by Ayesha Imam, Amina Mama and Fatou Sow in 1997. In 1994, these same three scholars set up the Gender Institute at CODESRIA, which has met on an annual basis since that time.

The cross-fertilization of academic networks and women's movements was evident in the debates that emerged in various AAWORD meetings. One of the earliest debates, for example, focused on women's organizational independence from political parties, which occurred at a 21–25 June 1982 meeting of AAWORD held in Dakar, Senegal. There, participants questioned whether it would be better to give priority to women's issues through autonomous women's associations or whether they should be integrated into the existing political parties and their structures.

Another influential network was formed in Harare by the Southern African Regional Institute for Policy Studies (SARIPS). SARIPS benefitted from the feminist leadership of Swazi sociologist Patricia McFadden, Zimbabwean sociologist Rudo Gaidzanwa, Tanzanian political scientist Ruth Meena and South African scholar Desiree Lewis. Their work on gender provided a new deeper understanding of postcolonial nationalism. The Forum of African Women Higher Educationalists (FAWE) was another network formed in 1993 that was made up of women ministers of education and vice-chancellors among others. Other influential networks that included scholars emerged such as Réseau de recherche sur la santé de la reproduction en Afrique francophone (RESAR), the Development Alternatives with Women for a New Era (DAWN), Africa Feminist Forum (AFF), and Women Living under Muslim Laws (WLUML).

Characteristics of the subfield in Africa

Much of the subsequent writing on women and politics emerged out of the experiences of women academics who also were women's rights activists and politicians. In Nigeria, for example, Bolanle Awe, Zaynab Alkali, Remi Sonaiya, Dora Nkem Akunyili, and Bene E. Madunagu were political actors and activists who translated their scholarship into policy through their work in government and wrote about their own experiences in politics (Omotoso and Faniyi 2020). Victoria Mwaka in Uganda was the founding chair of the Department of Women's Studies at Makerere University and also served as the vice chair of the constituent assembly that debated the 1995 constitution. She later held a position in parliament representing Luweero District.

Another characteristic of women's studies was the close ties between scholarship and the women's movement, which is evident in most countries in Africa to this day. Leaders in the study of women were often referred to as the 'academic arm' of the women's movement and regarded the connections to the women's movement as critical to their existence. In Uganda, for example, there have been close relationships between women activists and scholars of women's studies, and many scholars were leading activists in the women's movement in their respective countries. Joy Kwesiga, who was one time dean of the Faculty of Social Sciences at Makerere University and head of the Department of Women and Gender Studies, was head of a women's rights organization, Action for Development (ACFODE), and a leader in nationwide debates regarding women's rights. Kwesiga later became vice-chancellor of Kabale University.

Some of the most inspired research came out of women's own experiences in pro-democracy movements. For example, Wanjiku Mukabi Kabira wrote about her role and those of other women's rights activists in the constitution-making process in Kenya in *Time for Harvest: Women and Constitution Making in Kenya* (2012). Virtually all African countries adopted new constitutions after 1990 and the efforts by women to influence these processes and introduce key affirmative action provisions are documented in accounts from Kenya (Kibwana 2001) to Nigeria (Pereira 2001) and Uganda (Tamale 2001; Matembe and Dorsey 2002). Scholars have documented the role African women have played in struggles for democracy, from the Greenbelt Movement in Kenya (Ndegwa 1996) to the efforts of Sudanese women to confront authoritarian repression (Ibrahim 2000), and the efforts to increase representation of women in parliament, cabinet and local government throughout Southern Africa (Lowe Morna 2004).

New genres blending personal experiences with analysis have emerged, such as the wonderfully creative collection of essays from South Africa, *Nasty Women Talk Back* (Watson and Gouws 2019). The book is a collection of beautifully written personal narratives by a group of friends and academics who had participated in feminist activism of various kinds and found themselves talking back to patriarchy. It includes such essays as 'Pussies Are Not for Grabbing' (Joy Watson), 'My Arms Are Tired of Holding This Sign' (Amanda Gouws), 'Oh, No You Can't Go to Heaven in a Broke Down Car' (Anastasia Slamat), 'I'm with Her' (Zama Khanyile), 'Womb with a (very strong) View' (Helen Moffet) and 'Diary of an Indian woman' (Aarti Narse).

Other research came out of the experiences of movements focused on women's rights, particularly around quota laws, land rights, the impact of customary law on women's status, and violence against women (Coleman 2009). Albertyn (2005), for example, examines how the Constitutional Court and the Supreme Court of Appeal in South Africa have been a source of gender reform. Fareda Banda (2005) has written an expansive comparative book-length study that looks at the ways in which law shapes gender relations within African societies, while obscuring the unequal treatment of women within the household. In many countries, courts have become an important avenue for reform, in the face of legislative intransigence, particularly when it comes to controversial issues like LGBTQ rights and abortion.

Another characteristic of the study of gender and politics and gender studies more generally in Africa has been the effort to highlight particular contributions of African scholarship and to show how they emerged from experiences in Africa.

One of the earliest challenges African feminists faced was the domination of women's studies, including women and politics, by Western scholars and the downplaying of contributions of lower income women who made up the majority of women in these countries. These tensions came to the fore at a conference funded by major US foundations at the Center for Research on Women at Wellesley College on Women and Development in 1976. One-third of all the papers were presented by women from developing countries. At this conference, Moroccan sociologist and a founder of AAWORD, Fatima Mernissi, together with Egyptian novelist and physician, Nawal Al-Saadawi and Thai United Nations civil servant, Mallica Vajrathon, met in the hallway with other participants from developing countries and shared sentiments of exclusion. They resented the way in which women were presented through the prism of a Western middle class perspective.

Already such sentiments had been brewing at other UN conferences but they came to a head at the Wellesley conference. As a result of these experiences, Mernissi, El Saadawi and Vajrathon wrote an article in the journal *Quest* (1978) that addressed the way the feminist agenda was emerging globally in a way that replicated rather than challenged global power relations. They identified differences in the way that women in the Global North and Global South prioritized issues and highlighted how the Wellesley conference offered only a limited understanding of feminism that sidestepped global inequalities, and how multinational corporations and trade relations impacted gender relations. They challenged the false sense of an international sisterhood of women that could gloss over unequal power distributions globally and the naïveté that women were not political beings. Many women at the conference expressed the need for more research by local scholars who would have better insights into problems and areas that needed the most attention (Awe 1977). The article and the debate it stirred up had a tangible impact on development agencies like the United States Agency for International Development (USAID) and various UN agencies and created an awareness that it mattered who was involved in planning and setting the development agenda. It would seem that this remains an unfinished project as the lack of such awareness persists to this day (Tripp, forthcoming).

The experiences at Wellesley and other conferences gave impetus to African scholars to form the Association of African Women for Research and Development, also known as the *Association des Femmes Africaines pour la Recherche et le Développement* (AAWORD/AFARD) to decolonize African social science research from 'subjective Western analysis, which was not reflecting women's status and commitment in the development process of the continent'[1] (Tripp forthcoming).

These debates have continued to feature in discussions of feminist studies in Africa. Feminism is no longer a 'dirty word' for a new generation of scholars and activists for whom it no longer carries Western feminist connotations as was once prevalent when the field of women's studies first emerged in Africa in the 1970s and 1980s. Today, feminism in Africa is being defined on African terms and as originating in African experiences and sources of activism. One example of this can be found in the work of Sylvia Tamale (2020), who in her 2020 book *Decolonization and Afro-Feminism*

---

[1]   https://www.senegel.org/en/senegal/organizations/details/25/114

critiques the literature on decolonization for not incorporating African feminist perspectives and epistemologies in the study of customary law, traditional practices, or Pan-Africanism or anti-imperial struggles, for example.

Gabeba Baderoon and Desiree Lewis in their book *Surfacing: On being black and feminist in South Africa* (2021) similarly ask new questions having to do with changing African feminist traditions, the cultural logics outside of the centres of power, the relationship between spirituality and feminism, the experiences of queer Africans, and imaginative forms of feminism in Africa. They discuss how South African feminism today is the product of a variety of influences, such as scholars like Yvette Abrahams, Elaine Salo, Pumla Gqola and Zimitri Erasmos. It is also influenced by African American feminism with respect to intersectionality and literary influences of fiction writers Bessie Head, Yvonne Vera and Zoe Wicomb, among others, who have grappled with their positionality relative to white-centric academia and masculinism (Jacobs 2022).

Some feminist scholars in Africa go so far as to say that African political realities cannot be understood through Western theories. Thus, for example, in a study of women and political communication in Africa, Omotoso and Faniyi (2020) argue that one needs to adopt an 'Afropolicom stew approach' that was proposed by Eweka et al. (2020), which is an intersectional tool for examining political communication by using the analogy of a stew that encompasses African history, philosophy, culture and values. These ingredients are combined like food into a stew that identifies a dominant continental logic which engages with the colonial, class, ethnic, national and racial dynamics through a feminist lens, looking at political gestures, campaign emphasis, strategies and leadership styles of female political leaders. This includes the media erasure of women from the discussion of the 2012 Marikana massacre of thirty-four miners by the South African police force during a wildcat strike (Mokoena 2020); the media trivialization of political women by focusing on their handbags, clothes and beauty and less on their political agendas (Tshuma 2020); the role of women in social media in Zambia (Phiri 2020); and Liberian President Ellen Johnson Sirleaf's political communication strategies (Elebute and Ocheni 2020).

New research agendas

This effort to break out of more traditional moulds in scholarship, particularly Western-inspired scholarship on politics, has produced some novel and exciting research, pushing the boundaries of social science in new and imaginative ways. A few examples are illustrative of these new approaches. Nwando Achebe (2020) in her book *Female Monarchs and Merchant Queens in Africa* offers an Africa-centred narrative based on African sources to open up new ways of thinking about female power, connecting the physical world of human leaders with the spiritual realm of gods. She provides an overview of women political and spiritual leaders as well as business women throughout history, showing how the physical world of humans and the invisible realm of spiritual gods and forces are interconnected and inseparable. One cannot understand the physical realm without understanding the spiritual realm. She therefore is interested in power broadly defined from gods and goddesses like Hathor and Nut of ancient Egypt, to spirit mediums of the Nyamwezi in present-day Tanzania, to diviners, healers, priestesses, prophetesses, and Lovedu Rain Queens among the Sotho of southern Africa. She writes about the Meroe royalty, the empresses of Ethiopia, and paramount queen mothers (ahemaa) and paramount chiefs (amanahene) of the Asante in Ghana, the warrior queens like Al-Kahina in North Africa, the Nigerian queens prior to colonialism, and the Queen mothers of Buganda in Uganda. Achebe explores the fluid nature of queer identities in African history. She shows how biological men can become female, and biological women can become males in an interconnected universe in which biological sex and gender do not necessarily align. This fluidity allows for such phenomena as female husbands, male priestesses, female kings, and female pharaohs. This allowed women such as Nzinga, Wangu wa Makeri and Ahebi Ugbabe to take on identities as gendered men and rule as headmen, paramount kings, and chiefs.

Naminata Diabate's 2020 book, *Naked Agency: Genital Cursing and Biopolitics in Africa*, is another example of how African feminist scholars are introducing new approaches to the study of gender. Diabate puts the spotlight on the variety of contexts in which women have disrobed to express their most vehement opposition to authority, from struggles against pollution in Nigeria and Cote d'Ivoire to protest against rebel groups like Boko Haram in Nigeria and the demolition of houses in South Africa. She uses various examples to show that the practice of disrobing has many different meanings depending on the context. Through her approach, she values the symbolic and performative aspects of protest, which is often absent from much of the social movements literature in political science and sociology. She highlights the ambiguity of this type of agency, which is at the same time an act of resistance, and a last resort, and an act of desperation. Exposing mature women's bodies and women's body parts in some contexts is a curse. It is the ultimate expression of the power of women, who give life but who, through a curse like can take it away through social annihilation.

There is a rich discussion of the fluidity between women's private and public roles in many African contexts historically, allowing women to enter the public sphere with relative ease. This is evident in the large literature that has emerged, particularly from Nigeria, that has sought to describe this fluidity through concepts like dual sex political systems in which representatives of each gender (male and female) govern their own members' political, economic, cultural, and social lives. This is particularly evident in Igbo and Yoruba Nigerian communities (Nzegwu 1995), in which the male and female spheres of authority are separate and do not seek to usurp each other (Chuku 2009; Okonjo 1976; Sofola 1998). This general notion of complementarity encompasses variants on the notion of the duality of male and female spheres, in which each sex governs separate spheres of activity and life. It is described differently by various scholars: Ogundipe-Leslie (1994) has developed a notion of *stiwanism*, Nnaemeka (2004) calls it *nego-feminism*, Catherine Acholonu (1995) talks about *motherism*, Rose Acholonu (1995) describes *negative and positive feminism*, Chioma Opara (1999) develops a notion of *femalism*, and Marie Pauline Eboh (1999) refers to *gynism*. Complementarity in marriages and partnerships is also evident in the fictional work of Nigerian feminists Flora Nwapa as well as Ifeoma Okoye and

Akachi Adimora-Ezeigbo (Arndt 2002). Political motherhood, thus, becomes a basis for political power and allows for the expansion of women's roles rather than circumscribing them, as has often been the case in contexts where a liberal ideology prevails. Thus, motherhood is drawn on in figurative ways and as an archetype to symbolize the values and goals of women in fighting for justice, peace, or equality (Tripp 2016).

Another area of scholarship that has emerged in the African context that is somewhat unique is the study of the ambiguous and sometimes not-so-ambiguous role of first ladies in African countries. At times they have been key power brokers in their own right, especially in authoritarian contexts. This is evident in the work of Jibrin Ibrahim (2004) on Ghana and Nigeria, Amina Mama's work on Mariam Babangida (1995), and more comparative work by Van Wyk (2017) and Nyere, Van Wyk and Muresan (2020). Hassim (2014b) brilliantly complicates the role of leaders like Winne Madikizela-Mandela by showing the many sides of her career as the wife of Mandela who played a pivotal role in leading the country out of white minority rule to democracy. At the same time, she did not fit the master-narrative of women and nationalism, simultaneously carrying out acts of violence with political intent and acts of violence that could be considered criminal. Similar work has been done to describe the complicated role of Grace Mugabe, wife of the late former president of Zimbabwe, Robert Mugabe (Nyarota 2018; Tendi 2020).

One of the most interesting trends in the literature on women and politics has been the explosion of memoirs by women politicians. While these are perhaps better regarded as primary sources, they provide a wealth of information about the role of women politicians in Africa that has yet to be tapped. In Uganda, for example, the first generation of women politicians, like Sarah Ntiro, Rhoda Kalema and Princess Elizabeth of Toro, have written about their experiences through memoir, but increasingly those who took up leadership posts after Yoweri Museveni came to power in 1986, have also put pen to paper to describe their experiences in constitution making (Miria Matembe), in the women's movement (Judy Kamanyi), in ministerial positions (Joyce Mpanga, Victoria Sekitoleko, Janet Museveni) and in the opposition (Olive Kobusingye). Another genre of women's memoir delves into women's engagement in conflict (China Keitetsi, Grace Akallo) and in climate activism (Vanesa Nakate) and other forms of public engagement.

Women politicians who were Nobel Peace Prize winners have also written about their experiences. Leymah Gbowee wrote a memoir about her involvement in the peace movement in Liberia; Ellen Johnson Sirleaf about her rise to power as she claimed the presidency in Liberia; and Wangari Maathai about her involvement in the environmental movement in Kenya.

One finds wide-ranging research today on a myriad of more conventional topics ranging from women's involvement in constitution-making exercises and legal reform around women's rights; in democracy movements; in women's movements at the national and local levels; and within traditional governance arrangements. Much of the impetus for such research came with the opening up of countries to multipartism and the increase in freedom of association and freedom of speech after the 1990s. As a result, the research was influenced by struggles both for democratization and against neoliberal economic reforms (Akpofo, Beoku-Betts, Njambi and Osirim 2004). The research was also influenced by the growing women's movements as well as international women's movements. With the increase of women's participation in politics after the 1990s, studies have also examined women's roles in elections, parties, gender quotas, legislatures, the judiciary, the executive and other institutions, as well as women's relationship to patronage politics, conflict and peacebuilding, migration, the politicization of ethnicity and religion, and a broad range of topics.

African scholars have examined the presence of women in local government, often as a result of the use of quotas (Ahikire 2007), while others have focused on the absence of government attention to this arena (Gwagwa 1991; Lowe Morna and Tolmay 2007; Todes, Sithole and Williamson 2007). While there has been some attention given to gender quotas in legislatures (Abbas 2010), one area of institutional reform that has received considerable recent attention from African scholars has been the role of women in the judiciary as the numbers of women in the judiciary increased after the 1990s, changing the face of African judiciaries (Dawuni and Kang 2015; Dawuni and Bauer 2016). Others focused on women and political parties such as the Ghanian Convention People's Party during the time of the founding president, Kwame Nkrumah and the African National Congress in South Africa (Hassim 2014a).

The state itself has attracted considerable attention, particularly with respect to the formation of national machineries in the form of ministries, commissions, bureaus, and national councils to manage 'women's affairs', as they were often referred to (Kwesiga 2003; Tsikata 2000). The notion of gender mainstreaming also became popular as the United Nations encouraged ministries and gender 'focal points' within ministries to focus on the gender implications of their policies and funding. The idea of gender budgeting also became a concern as governments, under pressure from women's movements, sought to look at the gender implications of national budgets.

Challenges in research on women and politics in Africa

It is notable that there is still relatively little research on women/gender and politics especially compared to other subfields. There are several factors, historical and contemporary, that account for these patterns. To begin with, studies of African women were initially scarce as colonial education was discriminatory and neglected the education of women (Falola 2021; Idahosa 2021). Funmilayo Ransome-Kuti, the Nigerian woman nationalist and educator, notes that as of 1947, less than 1 per cent of Nigerian women could read and write, with only four girls' schools in the entire territory (Ransome-Kuti 1947/2011). Additionally, the vocations chosen were gendered according to societal expectations. While boys were encouraged to train for the professions such as law, engineering and medicine, girls were expected to train for jobs that approximated domesticity such as teaching, nursing, and clerking. Such structural issues in colonial education left many parts of the continent with far fewer qualified females in higher education to advance gender and feminist research (Pereira 2002). And, as in many other parts of the world, political science developed as an essentially masculine discipline, with many politics departments lacking female faculty for decades after their founding, relative to the other social sciences. For example, the Department of Political Science at Nigeria's oldest university, the University of Ibadan, did not have a single tenured female professor from its founding in October 1960 until 1999, nor were there any gender and politics courses in the entire curriculum until the 2010s.

The economic crisis and structural adjustment programmes imposed by the Bretton Woods institutions across the continent from the 1980s onwards further had a deleterious impact on African education (Mkandawire and Soludo 1999). African governments massively divested from public education, lowering the quality of education at all levels which limited access to tertiary education for the poorer segments of society, impacting mostly women and girls. African academics also had to supplement their meagre incomes with all kinds of other paid work, significantly reducing the commitment to research and academic productivity. Many of the research agendas were also driven by donors and the consultancy culture. This meant that many scholars vested considerable time and energy producing reports to serve donor agendas and interests and, as a consequence, they sometimes jumped from one subject to another in their research output, resulting in extremely broad research agendas, sometimes without developing adequate deep expertise. The types of publications that emerged from this type of research were often not publishable in international journals that would have given them greater visibility. The consultancy culture seeped into the style of writing, as one would often find policy recommendations at the end of many articles even where it was not appropriate (cf. Beoku-Betts 2021; Arnfred and Adomako Ampofo 2009).

Researchers faced other related challenges. A lack of minimal funding for basic research, limited publication outlets, heavy teaching loads and demanding administrative responsibilities all made it difficult to maintain a consistent research agenda. Moreover, university administrations have increasingly demanded research that serves instrumental purposes, making it more challenging to conduct basic research and promote creativity. There are a lot of locally published articles and books which are not broadly distributed outside individual countries, making it difficult for African and international scholars to read widely across the continent to develop comparative perspectives. Language constraints also pose challenges to scholars trained primarily in one language tradition be it English, French, Portuguese, Arabic, Swahili, or another major language used in research.

One disturbing trend is found in international publishing. The proportion of articles by Africa-based scholars have decreased over the past few decades in international area studies journals like *African Affairs* and the *Journal of Modern African Studies*, even as submissions from the continent have increased (Briggs and Weathers 2016). There is a virtual absence of African scholarship in international gender and politics journals, comparative politics and international relations journals, not to mention general interest political science journals (Medie and Kang 2018). Moreover, citations of scholars based on the continent have also decreased in the area studies journals.

These trends in international publishing, including the politics of citation, are rooted in global political economies of knowledge production. This set of limitations faced by African scholars are products of structural conditions imposed by a global knowledge system that was created in the West to serve its own interests and which continues the colonial marginalization of African and indigenous knowledges (Mama 2007). With the rapid neoliberalization of higher education the world over, and the rise of a market model of academia or 'academic capitalism', only the strongest academic institutions can survive while weaker academic systems, mainly to be found in developing parts of the world including most of Africa, vegetate and struggle to maintain their mission. This affects the survival of programmes and departments, as well as of academic journals, and access to other scholarly resources (Olufadewa, Adesina and Ayorinde 2020).

To take the argument further, African scholars cannot publish in journals that they have not read or which their institution cannot access. Most of the top politics, area studies and gender studies, journals are published by leading presses, themselves major commercial entities: Cambridge, Oxford, Sage, Taylor and Francis and Wiley, and they have the latest developments in the field locked behind high and expensive paywalls that African institutions and academics can barely afford. Thus, much of the research on women and gender by African scholars are published locally or nationally and do not enjoy the circulation, visibility, and citation counts of articles by their counterparts based at institutions in the rich countries of the Global North.

But beyond the commercialization of knowledge production, there is also the politics of citation which brings to relief issues relating to hegemonic knowledge, the persistence of the colonial library, and issues of representation (Yacob-Haliso and Falola 2021b). These are issues that have not abated since they were called out at the infamous Wellesley Conference of 1976. To date, African epistemologies and methodologies are sidelined both in academia and policy in favor of Western-originated theories, methods, sources, knowledges, and canons. There is a prevalent perception in the Western academy and publishing world that 'expertise' about politics or gender or society resides in Western academics (Beoku-Betts and Njambi 2005; Kwachou 2022), and all others are judged by their deference to these Western academic authorities in citation and theorization. But there is no converse requirement that Western academics, even when they write about Africa or African women, should acknowledge, cite, or privilege Africa-originated or Africa-derived research and scholarship (Awe 1977). Many edited books about African women and politics authored by Western academics and published in prestigious presses do not include a single African scholar or include a token one or two among a dozen other authors, with few exceptions (Beoku-Betts and Njambi 2005).

As for citation, since African scholars are often not deemed to have the right 'expertise' and they often cannot access the latest literature, many African gender scholars based in Africa have very low citation counts relative to their counterparts elsewhere who recycle the colonial library and its ideologies, pay respect to one another in citations, and largely ignore the wealth of knowledge and theorizing about African women on the continent. The continental exceptions may be for the gender studies scholars in the large academic centres represented by the universities in South Africa, Egypt, Uganda, Nigeria and Ghana.

Further, it may be that articles that generalize to the entire continent are more likely to be cited, while Africa-based scholars focus more on a small number of larger and wealthier countries in Africa (Briggs and Weathers 2016). These are not new trends, thus this explanation does not entirely account for the changes we are seeing in international publishing. One of the main critiques of Western feminism by Black and African feminists is its tendency to homogenize and generalize whereas African women's studies is founded on a theory of difference that emphasizes historical specificity and contextual fidelity (Lewis 2002; Oyewumi 1997; cf. Mohanty 1991). Studies by Tamale (2011) and Ahikire (2007) exemplify the enduring value of case study, small-N research on women and politics in Africa. Another explanation for the lack of citation of African scholars might have to do with the divergence in methodologies, as political science in the United States and Europe has become more quantitative, whereas the majority of political science departments on the continent and interdisciplinary studies of women and politics are only marginally oriented towards quantitative techniques. This ordinarily should create a corpus of knowledge between both sides of the Atlantic that would be complementary. The fact that this has not been so and one side remains marginalized suggests that the issues of Western dominance and assumed superiority may be more salient explanations.

Relatedly, differences in presentation and style have been noted. Much of the writing about women and politics in Africa has involved efforts to document women's roles in African politics: in Nigerian politics 1986-1993 (Osinulu and Mba 1996; Agbalajobi 2021), in constitution making in Kenya (Kabira 2012), in associational life in Sierra Leone (Steady 2006), in struggles for democracy (Hassim 2006), in the Biafran war in Nigeria (Uchendu 2007), and in other conflicts (Olonisakin and Okech 2011). Much of the work is descriptive and deeply rooted in the contexts of particular countries. Use of the comparative method is found only on occasion in work on gender and politics (e.g., see Charrad 2001). When comparisons are made, they are generally additive rather than based on systematic analyses using the comparative method or statistical methods that would allow for greater generalization. One reason for the single country focus is that many of those working on gender and politics are activists and they are addressing issues of direct concern to the women's movement (Sadiqi 2008; Arnfred and Adomako Ampofo 2009; Bouilly et al. 2016; Mama 2019). Lack of research funds and institutional support also hamper ambitious comparative research agendas. Nevertheless, these country studies are necessary building blocks for comparative work. Moreover, the approaches and the themes point to some creative and new ways of thinking about politics beyond the case studies.

While there are efforts by international journal editors and associations to address these gaps, they are only making a small dent in the overall patterns. But what is clear is that the lack of articles by African scholars in international venues impoverishes the field overall and weakens the quality of comparative scholarship more generally. This is not to say that there aren't venues for publication of work on gender and politics in Africa, but they are limited. *Agenda: Empowering Women for Gender Equity, Feminist Africa*, JENdA: *A Journal of Culture and African Women Studies* and the *African Journal of Gender and Women's Studies* are all excellent sources of scholarship by African gender scholars. There are important edited volumes that feature scholarship on gender and politics by African scholars (e.g., Kwesiga and Tripp 2002; Achebe and Robertson 2015; Rodriguez, Tsikata and Ampofo 2015; Badri and Tripp 2017; Tamale 2019;

Yacob-Haliso and Falola 2021; Beoku-Betts and M'Cormack-Hale 2022). Nevertheless, the danger here is not just the further marginalization of African scholarship but the impoverishment of international scholarship because of lack of access to the work of African scholars.

Conclusion

This chapter has contributed an overview of the growth and impact of gender and women's studies on the development of political science and the broader field of African studies. While the formal inclusion of gender studies in political science curricula and of women's studies scholars in political science departments has been low, the scope of research on women, gender, and politics in Africa has been broad and wide-ranging. The interdisciplinary field has been propelled by the activism, scholarship, networks and publications of African women mostly, along with some men.

By participating in anti-colonial/nationalist movements, rewriting African political histories, documenting development challenges affecting women and other marginalized persons, advocating for democratization and democratic dividends, writing the stories of their own roles in politics, creating activist-intellectual networks and linkages, and building feminist academic institutions, African women's and gender studies has been indispensable to the development of political science in Africa. The innovation, commitment, and drive that have produced the current body of work on African women and politics are outsized compared to the relatively small number of political scientists who participate in this work.

The challenges that remain for the expansion and integration of studies of women, gender and politics in Africa are indicative of institutional weaknesses, complex social systems of exclusion, discrimination, and oppression of women, weak or inequal North-South collaboration and linkages, constraints of global political economy, and unequal knowledge production infrastructures. Interestingly, these issues themselves have been the subject of considerable writing and theorizing within the field of political science itself. As such, the remedies are known. A good place to begin a more thoroughgoing integration of women and politics studies with the broader politics literature is in more gender-focused and less gender-blind curricula and pedagogy, specialized graduate programmes, and other training in feminism and politics. As institutions have often been reluctant to create the space and resources for these strategies, a rekindling of pan-African, intracontinental and equitable intercontinental feminist collaborations to achieve these specific aims could be transformative. As the world witnesses ever-burgeoning demands for de-centring hegemonic knowledge and the democratization of the means of access to wealth, opportunities and academic productivity, an added impetus is the vast benefits that this can bring not only to studies of women and gender in Africa but also to the global study of political science broadly defined.

12

The impact of political science research on teaching political science in Southern Africa

Njekwa Mate

Introduction

This chapter discusses the impact of the production of political science research data in teaching political science in Southern Africa. Some political science research data sets produced by researchers cover a period of about 100 years in almost all the 195 countries of the world. The use of survey data is particularly interesting (Le Roy 2013). This chapter outlines the methodology used to gather data from political scientists in Southern Africa. Second, a detailed description of some of the prominent databases on political science research is presented. Third, a discussion on the use of political science in teaching political science at various universities in Southern Africa is given. This is followed by a section discussing the use of databases by students. Fifth, the impact and/or contributions of the political science databases on teaching political science is presented. Following this is a discussion on the availability of infrastructure and capacities at the various universities in Southern Africa to make use of the databases. The last two sections provide the conclusion and recommendations, respectively.

Methodology and political science research databases

First, a document analysis was conducted to uncover the views of political science scholars on the impact of research data on teaching political science in Southern Africa. Second, a self-administered questionnaire (SAQ) was emailed to political science faculty members in Southern Africa. Lastly, Key Informant Interviews (KIIs) were carried out with a selected few political scientists in Southern Africa. The purpose of KIIs was to collect information from a wide range of political scientists who possess the knowledge and experience in teaching, researching and publishing in political science at Southern African universities.

The political science research databases that have been produced by researchers around the world focus on aspects such as governance and democracy. The most important ones are shown in Table 12.1: Polity V (from 1800 to date) – 195 countries; Adam Przeworski et al. (between 1950, or the year of independence, and 1990) – 141 countries; Freedom House (1973 to date) – 195 countries; Vanhanen Index of Democratisation (1810–2000) – 187 countries; José Cheibub Type of Regime – Presidentalism, Parliamentarism, Democracy (1945–2002); Economics Intelligence Unit (EIU) Democracy Index – 167 countries since 2006; Ibrahim Index of Africa Governance (IIAG) – 54 countries from 2007; Afrobarometer – 37 countries in Africa from 1999; Varieties of Democracy (V-Dem) – 1900 to date (202 countries); Global Integrity (GI) 54 countries since 2013; Quality of Government (QoG) from 1946 to present; Transparency International (TI) from 1993 to date; and World Bank Governance Indicators – 200 countries from 1996 to date.

Polity IV focuses on Political Regime Characteristics and Transitions in 195 countries from 1800 to 2018. Polity IV contains information on and access to the most recent update of the well-known and highly respected Polity data series, originally designed by Ted Robert Gurr, containing coded annual information on regime and authority characteristics for all independent states (with greater than 500,000 total population) in the global state system (Marshall, Gurr and Jaggers 2019).

Freedom House, a US-based government-funded, non-profit, non-governmental organization, conducts research and advocacy on democracy, political freedom and human rights. Freedom House was founded in October 1941 to measure the degree of civil liberties and political rights in every nation and significantly related and disputed territories around the world. Freedom House has been doing this from 1973 to date, and currently covers 195 countries (Freedom House 2021).

Przeworski, Stokes and Manin (1999) present a classification of political regimes as democracies and dictatorships for a set of 141 countries between 1950 or the year of independence and 1990. It improves the existing classifications by providing a better grounding in political theory, exclusive reliance on observable rather than on subjective judgements, an explicit distinction between systematic and random errors, and more extensive coverage (also see Przeworski et al. 2000).

Tatu Vanhanen, an emeritus professor at the University of Tampere, compiled The Polyarchy dataset covering 187 countries over the period 1810 to 2000. The release of Version 1.0 accompanied an article in the *Journal of Peace Research* (37-2, March 2000). The current version of the dataset is Version 2.0. Both the index and the complete dataset are available for download. There are four previous versions of the Vanhanen Index of Democracy, based in part on manual calculations. These are still available, but can only be used for replication of previous works based on these versions. This especially applies to the 1.1 revisions. Version 2.0 is a major update to the format adopted in Version 1.2, in addition to new and updated data for the years 1998–2000. For any new studies using Version 2.0 data is recommended (Vanhanen 2000).

José Cheibub compiled a dataset known as Type of Regime – Presidentalism, Parliamentarism and Democracy – covering the period 1945 to date. Cheibub contends that the well-known empirical correlation between presidential executives and democratic breakdown is spurious. For Cheibub, the real political risk factor for democratic governments is the presence of a 'military legacy'. Thus, Cheibub explains the fact pattern in the following way: (a) presidential democracies tend to be born

Table 12.1 Political Science Research Databases

Database	Description
Polity IV: Political Regime Characteristics and Transitions, 1800-2018, 195 countries	Polity IV contains coded annual information on regime and authority characteristics for all independent states (with greater than 500,000 total population) in the global state system.
Freedom House, 1973 to date, 195 countries	Freedom House measures the degree of civil liberties and political rights in every nation and significant related and disputed territories around the world.
Adam Przeworski *et al.*	Adam Przeworski *et al.* present a classification of political regimes as democracies and dictatorships for a set of 141 countries between 1950 or the year of independence and 1990.
Tatu Vanhanen Index of Democratization	The Polyarchy dataset compiled by Tatu Vanhanen, covers 187 countries over the period 1810 to 2000.
José Antonio Cheibub, Type of Regime – Presidentalism, Parliamentarism, Democracy – 1945–2002	José Antonio Cheibub categorizes democracy as: (a) presidential democracies; (b) parliamentary democracies. Cheibub argues that democracies born from military dictatorships are more prone to lapse into dictatorship, whether they are presidential or parliamentary.
Economist Intelligence Unit (EIU) Democracy Index 167 countries since 2006	The EIU Democracy Index provides a snapshot of the state of world democracy for 165 independent states and two territories. The Democracy Index is based on five categories: electoral process and pluralism; civil liberties; the functioning of government; political participation; and political culture.
Ibrahim Index of Africa Governance (IIAG) 54 countries from 2007	The IIAG provides data measuring the governance performance for all fifty-four African countries from 2008 to date covering the following dimensions: Safety and Rule of Law; Participation and Human Rights; Sustainable Economic Opportunity; Human Development.
Afrobarometer – (37 countries in Africa) 6 surveys from 1999	Afrobarometer is a non-partisan, Pan-African research institution conducting public attitude surveys on democracy, governance, the economy and society in 30+ countries repeated on a regular cycle.
Global Integrity (GI) 54 countries since 2013	GI provides empirically supported information that analyses corruption and governance trends. It also produces the Global Integrity Report that analyses the institutional framework underpinning countries' corruption and accountability systems (ranging from electoral practices and media freedom to budget transparency and conflict-of-interest regulations).
Varieties of Democracy (V-Dem) – 1900–date (202 countries)	V-Dem Institute provides a multidimensional and disaggregated dataset that reflects the complexity of the concept of democracy as a system of rule that goes beyond the simple presence of elections. The V-Dem project distinguishes between five high-level principles of democracy: electoral, liberal, participatory, deliberative, and egalitarian, and collects data to measure these principles
Quality of Government (QoG) 1946–date	The QoG Institute has thirty researchers who conduct and promote research on the causes, consequences and nature of Good Governance and the Quality of Government (QoG) – that is, trustworthy, reliable, impartial, uncorrupted and competent government institutions.

(Continued)

Table 12.1 (Continued)

Database	Description
Transparency International (TI) since 1993 in over 100 countries	TI aims to take action in order to combat global corruption with civil societal anti-corruption measures and to prevent criminal activities arising from corruption. Its most notable research outputs covering over 100 countries include the Global Corruption Barometer and the Corruption Perceptions Index.
Worldwide Governance Indicators (WGI) Indicators – 200 countries from 1996	WGI project reports aggregate and individual governance indicators for over 200 countries and territories over the period 1996–2018 on six dimensions of governance: Voice and Accountability; Political Stability and Absence of Violence; Government Effectiveness; Regulatory Quality; Rule of Law; Control of Corruption.

Source: Compiled from the listed Political Science Research Database websites.

more often from military dictatorships than are parliamentary democracies; and (b) democracies born from military dictatorships are more prone to lapse into dictatorship, whether they are presidential or parliamentary (Cheibub 2007). It is worth noting that Cheibub does not argue that there is a causal relationship between military legacies and presidential executives. On the contrary, according to Cheibub, the fact that presidencies have disproportionately followed military dictatorships reflects Latin American dictators' historical predilection for presidential regimes rather than a more general systematic tendency of military dictatorships to prefer presidentialism.

The Economist Intelligence Unit (EIU) Democracy Index gathers information from 167 countries since 2006. The EIU Democracy Index provides a snapshot of the state of world democracy for 165 independent states and two territories. The Democracy Index is based on five categories: electoral process and pluralism, civil liberties, the functioning of government, political participation, and political culture. Based on their scores on sixty indicators within these categories, each country is then itself classified as one of four types of regime: full democracy, flawed democracy, hybrid regime and authoritarian regime (EIU 2020).

The Ibrahim Index of African Governance (IIAG) gathers information from fifty-four countries in Africa from 2008 to date. The IIAG covers over ten years' worth of data (2008–2019) for all fifty-four African countries on the following dimensions: safety and rule of law, participation and human rights, sustainable economic opportunity and human development. The construction method provides vast amounts of data. To construct the 2019 IIAG, the Foundation's Research Team collected 191 variables that measure governance concepts from thirty-five sources. These were combined to form 102 indicators, then organized under the IIAG's key governance dimensions; the fourteen sub-categories and four categories that make up the Overall Governance score. Including all the data collected from the source and the calculations made expressly for the IIAG, there are a total of 273 different measures of governance for any given country or group in any given year across ten years. These are made up of indicators that measure specific issues such as the independence of the judiciary, which is one indicator of the broader subcategory 'Rule of Law', which is in turn part of the overarching category 'Safety & Rule of Law'. In total, there are almost 150,000 data points in the 2019

IIAG. The Index provides data measuring the governance performance across all the dimensions described above for all fifty-four African countries for the years from 2008–2019. In order to provide a broad, documented and impartial picture of governance performance in every African country, the 102 indicators used to measure governance in Africa are collected from thirty-five independent sources. It should be noted here that for this index updates are usually done every year (Mo Ibrahim Foundation 2019).

Afrobarometer gathers information from thirty-seven countries in Africa and since 1999 Afrobarometer has conducted six surveys. Afrobarometer is a non-partisan, Pan-African research institution conducting public attitude surveys on democracy, governance, the economy and society in over thirty countries repeated on a regular cycle. It is the world's leading source of high-quality data on what Africans are thinking about democracy, governance, the economy and society in their countries (Afrobarometer 2017).

Global Integrity (GI) provides empirically supported information that analyses corruption and governance trends. Among other work, it produces the Global Integrity Report: an annual collection of original, in-depth national assessments combining journalistic reporting with nearly 300 'Integrity Indicators' analysing the institutional framework underpinning countries' corruption and accountability systems (ranging from electoral practices and media freedom to budget transparency and conflict-of-interest regulations). Global Integrity's analytical method is based on the concept of measuring the 'opposite of corruption' – that is, the access that citizens and businesses have to a country's government, their ability to monitor its behaviour, and their ability to seek redress and advocate for improved governance. The resulting data allows policymakers, private industry, non-governmental organizations and the general public to identify specific strengths and weaknesses in various countries' governmental institutions (Global Integrity 2019).

Varieties of Democracy (V-DEM) gathers information from 1900 to date focusing on 202 countries in the world. Since 2015 V-Dem has released ten data sets. V-Dem is a new approach to conceptualizing and measuring democracy providing a multidimensional and disaggregated dataset that reflects the complexity of the concept of democracy as a system of rule that goes beyond the simple presence of elections. The V-Dem project distinguishes between five high-level principles of democracy: electoral, liberal, participatory, deliberative and egalitarian, and collects data to measure these principles. The Version 10 data was released in the first quarter of 2020. V-Dem draws on theoretical and methodological expertise from its worldwide team to produce data in the most objective and reliable way possible. Approximately half of the indicators in the V-Dem dataset are based on factual information obtained from official documents such as constitutions and government records. The other half consists of more subjective assessments on topics like political practices and compliance with de jure rules. On such issues, typically five experts provide ratings. The V-Dem Institute, based in the Department of Political Science at the University of Gothenburg in Sweden, works closely with leading social science research methodologists and has developed a state-of-the-art measurement model that, to the extent possible, minimizes coder error and addresses issues of comparability across countries and over time. V-Dem also draws on the team's academic expertise to develop theoretically informed techniques for aggregating indicators into mid-level and high-level indices. In this sense, V-Dem is at the cutting edge of developing new and improved methods of social science measurement (Coppedge et al. 2020).

The Quality of Government (QoG) Institute was founded in 2004 by Professor Bo Rothstein and Professor Sören Holmberg. It is an independent research institute within the Department of Political Science at the University of Gothenburg. The QoG Institute has thirty researchers who conduct and promote research on the causes, consequences and nature of Good Governance and the Quality of Government (QoG) – that is, trustworthy, reliable, impartial, uncorrupted and competent government institutions. QoG gathers data from 1946 to date (QoG 2021). In fact, the American Political Science Association (APSA) has classified the Quality of Government Index as one of the best. The QoG Expert Survey is a dataset based on the survey of experts on public administration around the world, available in an individual dataset and an aggregated dataset covering 107 countries. The QoG Organisation for Economic Co-operation and Development is a newly available dataset published by the QoG Institute. It covers countries that are members of the Economic Co-operation and Development (OECD). The dataset is further distinguished due to its high data coverage in terms of geography and time. The EU Regional Data consists of approximately 450 variables from Eurostat and other sources, covering three levels of European regions – country, major socio-economic regions and basic regions for the application of regional policies. In addition to these datasets, the QoG EQI Dataset contains data on sub-national governance in Europe from three rounds of a large, pan-European survey on citizen perceptions and experiences with public services. Both micro and sub-national data are provided.

Transparency International (TI) is a global movement working in over 100 countries to end the injustice of corruption. TI focuses on issues with the greatest impact on people's lives and holds governments to account for the common good. Through advocacy, campaigns and research, TI exposes government systems and networks that enable corruption to thrive and demands greater transparency and integrity in all areas of public life with a mission to stop corruption and promote transparency, accountability and integrity at all levels and across all sectors of society. TI is a German non-governmental organization founded in 1993. Based in Berlin, its non-profit purpose is to take action to combat global corruption with civil societal anti-corruption measures and to prevent criminal activities arising from corruption. Its most notable publications include the Global Corruption Barometer and the Corruption Perceptions Index (Lambsdorff 2006).

The Worldwide Governance Indicators (WGI) project by the World Bank, provides aggregate and individual governance indicators for over 200 countries and territories over the period 1996 to date on the following six dimensions of governance: voice and accountability, political stability and absence of violence, government effectiveness, regulatory quality, rule of law and control of corruption. These aggregate indicators combine the views of a large number of enterprise, citizen and expert survey respondents in industrial and developing countries. They are based on over thirty individual data sources produced by a variety of survey institutes, think tanks, non-governmental organizations, international organizations and private sector firms (Kaufmann, Kraay and Mastruzzi 2010).

Use of databases in teaching

Political science research databases aid the delivery of courses such as research methods in political science, comparative politics, democracy, democratization and governance. Instead of relying on textbooks and articles alone, students are taught how to work with different datasets available in political science to develop hands-on practical skills enabling them to use different data for evidence-based analyses of various political developments in their own country or region of origin. Databases make it easy to carry out comparisons regarding developments in other countries or regions. However, most course outlines or modules at Southern African universities do not include topics on how to work with various datasets with statistical software. Sources of cutting-edge research information are somewhat limited due to limited expertise, publication and resources.

In addition, there are few lecturers interested in the use of quantitative datasets, perhaps due to the fact that most curricula and approaches to teaching and researching in the social sciences from the 1960s to the 1990s emphasized the use of the qualitative approach. Consequently, teaching students the skills to use large datasets, and analyse and interpret quantitative data, has not been at the centre of teaching and learning. Currently, only a few faculty staff at universities in Southern Africa claim to have sufficient competence in this area. However, this trend is likely to change as a result of the increase in the number of research institutes that are producing and using quantitative empirical data in publication and advocacy work. There is also a notable rise in the number of young academics, most of whom are millennials, that are being or have been trained in quantitative research methods at master's and PhD level.

The availability of political science research databases presents an opportunity to teach, research and publish using empirical data with practical examples. Databases make it possible to get supplementary teaching and research information that can be used in class discussions, and in writing research and conference papers, dissertations and theses (see Mate 2009, 2014). For example, the latest research information that is regularly shared by V-Dem provides up-to-date data on various aspects or facets of democracy. Afrobarometer and Mo Ibrahim Foundation also provide useful regular updates about peoples' views and attitudes towards democracy and the nature of governance in African countries, respectively. Teaching would be more theoretical in the absence of such databases. Databases also enable students to learn and develop hands-on skills and experience in research courses. For instance, in terms of understanding political developments, students have a better grasp of political science when they are given tasks to analyse democracy and governance indicators instead of just reading textbooks, journals, dissertations, theses and reports.

Some critics have however argued that such databases frame African scholars to have a standard way of conceptualization of political issues framed from the West which may be not applicable in Africa (Zeleza 2002, 2003, 2005c; Cheibub, Gandhi and Vreeland 2010; Sueyoshi 2018; Bjørnskov and Rode 2020). However, Afrobarometer, V-Dem & IIAG use local knowledge or experts to gather data (Dr Carlors Shenga, Joaquim Chissano University, personal communication, 17 September 2019). Political science databases not only make it possible to make cross-national and longitudinal comparisons but also make scholars grasp local particularities not captured by questions from the databases.

Use of databases by students

Some students at undergraduate and postgraduate levels have used databases in courses such as research methods and comparative politics. Working with datasets downloaded from databases makes students understand and apply current empirical data better, thereby enriching their discussions in class and tutorials (Mr Joseph Chunga, University of Malawi, personal communication, 27 September 2019). The most widely used database in Southern Africa is provided by Afrobarometer. However, the usage of datasets is still low given the limited number of student research reports, dissertations and theses that have analysed data obtained from the available datasets. Many students have deficient skills or lack the necessary grounding in data analysis and interpretation. Responses from the region and analysis of library repositories indicate that undergraduate students rarely use political science research databases. The need for using these databases calls students to use the internet, as a source of information, as opposed to the previous reliance on hard copy textbooks. This is a challenge because of the limited capacity in the majority of universities in Southern Africa to provide adequate or sufficient computer laboratories, computers and internet connectivity for students.

Impact of databases

The availability of political science research databases has opened up new possibilities for specific and multi or cross-country/regional analyses of various political phenomena. Research institutes, such as Afrobarometer and V-Dem, have created networks that use empirical and evidence-based data to produce policy briefs that are aimed at influencing policymaking in targeted policy areas. According to Perkin and Court (2005: v; also see Pollard and Court 2005), 'there is a considerable body of evidence suggesting that networks can help improve policy processes through better information use. They may, for example, help marshal evidence and increase the influence of good-quality evidence in the policy process'. In turn, they can foster links between researchers and policymakers, bypass formal barriers to consensus, bring resources and expertise into the policymaking arena and broaden the pro-poor, pro-democracy and pro-good governance impact of a policy. Sometimes politicians and bureaucratic technocrats react to research findings (i.e. positively or negatively) and they cite such findings to support or reject a proposed policy measure.

Thus, the increasing use of empirical and evidence-based data provided by the various databases on political science research can be used as a proxy for measuring the impact of the databases. This impact is in fact increasing. In addition, databases that are generated through public surveys, such as the Afrobarometer survey series, can be assumed to indirectly shape the decisions of political leaders in Africa as they worry about votes in the next elections. Another proxy for gauging the impact of databases on political science research include the following: counting the number of internet downloads of datasets from the databases, the number of dissertations and theses produced by students that have used the datasets on political science and have been deposited on university library repositories, the number of journal articles and book chapters written by scholars from Southern Africa that have analysed and discussed data obtained from the databases and the number of evidence-based policy briefs that have been produced. These numbers, though low, are steadily increasing in Southern Africa as can be seen from the number of database downloads, especially from the Afrobarometer, V-Dem and IIAG databases. As Dr Alex Ng'oma, a lecturer from the University of Zambia observes, politics and political developments in Africa are, understandably, not static. What political science databases do, and do very well, is to tell the story of the political phenomena as they evolve. In that way, those who use political science databases are kept abreast of their development or evolution (Dr Alex Ng'oma, personal communication, 1 October 2019).

Availability of infrastructure, resources and capacity

The availability of adequate infrastructure, resources and the required capacity remains a challenge in the majority of universities in Southern Africa. There could be many reasons for this. First, Southern Africa has seen a reduction in funding for higher education over the last decade. This is mainly due to the shifting logic from government funding towards self-financing models because most governments in Africa have limited resources, as a result of poor economic performance, to be shared among all the sectors (Napier and Labuschagne 2018; Masaiti and Shen 2013). Thus, it is not uncommon, especially in country like Zambia, to hear government officials and ruling party functionaries echoing the need for public universities to fund themselves and emulate private universities. Private universities are self-financed and their students are mainly self-sponsored. This shifting logic has led to the 'massification' of higher education whereby lecturers are spending more time teaching, marking scripts and making assessments for large classes with little time left for research and publishing (see Mohamedbhai 2008). Coupled with this, reduced funding to universities has made it very difficult to implement capacity training programmes for academics, conduct research, invest in infrastructure (i.e. offices, lecture theatres, tutorial rooms, computer laboratories and software) and sponsor students through scholarships, bursaries or loans schemes. Further, limited collaboration and cooperation among political science departments and political science associations in Africa has made it very difficult to improve the capacity of political science academics in teaching, research and publication (see World Bank 2010; Masaiti 2015; Oketch 2016; Amin and Ntembe 2021).

As earlier noted, there is inadequate computer and internet infrastructure in the majority of the universities in Southern Africa, with the exception of South Africa. There is also a lack of sufficient statistical software (e.g. SPSS, STATA, NVivo and ATLAS.ti) installed on computers for staff and computer laboratories being used by students. At the University of Zambia, for instance, lecturers sometimes have to purchase their own computers, software and internet bundles in order to execute their duties effectively and efficiently. Thus, the Information and Communications Technology (ICT) allowance was introduced in 2022 to help mitigate the challenges faced. Statistical software packages have proved to be very expensive for most research institutes and universities in Southern Africa, though others such as 'R' and 'Python' are free and can be easily downloaded and used for statistical computing, graphics, data visualization and reporting. The outbreak of the novel coronavirus (Covid-19) has further exposed the capacity challenges at most Southern African universities as it is now inevitable to adopt the use of virtual classes and meetings which require investments in technology.

Conclusion

There are many political science databases now available for use by political scientists and researchers the world over. These include databases produced by Polity V, Adam Przeworski et al., Freedom House, Vanhanen, José Cheibub, EIU, IIAG, Afrobarometer, V-Dem, GI, QoG, TI and the World Bank. In spite of these databases being available, the majority of the scholars and researchers in Southern African universities do not use them mainly due to a lack of skills and capacity to work with quantitative and/or statistical datasets. Usage by students, especially undergraduates, is very low. Notably, the Afrobarometer survey datasets are the most widely used datasets by political scientists and students in Southern Africa.

It is important to also note that political science research databases have made it possible to conduct specific and multi or cross-country/regional analyses of various political phenomena. The databases are also evidence-based and through networks, political scientists and researchers can influence the policy process by producing policy briefs and engaging in advocacy in collaboration with the relevant civil society organizations. The majority of the universities in Southern Africa have inadequate infrastructure, resources and capacity to carry out research and work with the different types of datasets that are available. Lack of collaboration and cooperation among political science departments and political science associations in Africa has contributed to this.

Governments and universities in Southern Africa should rethink their funding logic for higher education and release more funds for staff development, capacity-building training and infrastructure development and improvement. In addition, international, continental, regional and national political science associations should contribute towards developing the capacity of political scientists through training workshops and fellowship programmes. There is a need for training more scholars at master's and PhD levels in political science. Furthermore, Research institutes need to run summer or winter schools on research methods in political science, perhaps following the Afrobarometer and Council for the Development of Social Science Research in Africa (CODESRIA) models. All in all, political science departments and associations in Africa need to collaborate more and provide training for students and academia in political science since the number of political scientists in the region is still low.

13

Use of empirical data in research and teaching of political science in Africa

Olugbemiga Samuel Afolabi

Introduction

To what extent do political science departments use empirical data in research and teaching? Has the use of empirical data in research and teaching increased knowledge that has positively affected political institutions in Africa? Are there similarities and differences in the trajectory of the political science departments selected for this study in the application of empirical data in its research and teaching? While political science is the study of governments and politics at different levels, it is also supposed to be the name of a method: the science or scientific approach in knowing and explaining politics. At the descriptive stage, it was initially a branch of philosophy, but as a discipline in the social sciences, it acquires and uses social sciences methodology to investigate and predict human behaviour. Its twin status as an art and science have often raised the paradoxical question: How scientific is political science? To what degree are works and research outputs in political science scientific? Given these questions, this study will strive to provide answers within the African context.

First, African universities have a high number of departments that offer political science as a course of the programme. As a body of knowledge, the discipline, which took off with the establishment of universities during colonial administration, has transited from its colonial heritage to reflect changes that have been wrought in politics and society, especially in the fights for independence and in post-independent Africa, given the poor state of society, democracy and development in the continent. More importantly, questions remained as to the level and extent of the use of empirrical data in research and teaching of political science in Africa.

With advances in human progress and society, the use of data that is derived from research is often used to explain and teach social realities. This has led researchers generally to emphasize the mastery and use of quantitative 'scientific tools', relying on what has been categorized as dependence on causality (Box-Steffensmeier, Brady and Collier 2008). Since the time of behavioural revolution in the social sciences, particularly in political science, the dependence on empirical data that is mostly based on quantification has held sway. The argument is that empirical data is more reliable, evidence-based and more accurately explains political and social realities. While the use of data in research and teaching may be more hyped in Western universities than in Africa (Schedler and Mudde 2008), the use of empirical data in research and teaching of political science in Africa still presents a picture that calls for an investigation.

The need for an investigation is predicated on the realization that the development and growth of political science discipline in Africa did not follow a uniformed and unidirectional path. At the level of uniformity, the discipline has witnessed changes that reflect each state's socio-economic and political dynamics. For instance, in South Africa, the changes in political science as a discipline were a reflection of political transition that ensued from 1994 post-apartheid South Africa state and society as well as the clamour for the decolonization of knowledge production, especially in curriculum and pedagogy in South African universities (Booysen and van Nieuwkerk 1998; Afolabi 2020). All these happenings affected the use of empirical data in research and teaching of political science. Still in South Africa as an example, it has remained in a near-permanent state of reformation, given the continuing debate about coloniality and decoloniality of knowledge production, which encapsulates political science knowledge at that time. However, more attention is being paid to the use of empirical data after independence in 1994.

In the same vein, changes in political science in Nigeria as a tool of change and body of knowledge underwent significant changes that first supported the struggle for independence and late, in the fight against military rule. Even though the period of change in Nigeria differs from South Africa, it is nonetheless obvious that there were changes in the discipline and its delivery, being traditionally reliant on descriptive method, instead of empirical data, in research and teaching of political science. The reliance on the descriptive method was necessitated by the uncertainties and turmoil that characterized pre- and post-independent Nigeria. This turmoil manifested in form of political crisis, coups and counter-coups. Most political science research and teaching were directed to describing political happenings (Wilmot, 2005). Such was the case in political science discipline in other universities across Africa, especially in older ones like University College, Ibadan (now the University of Ibadan), Makerere University, Uganda, and University of Zambia (UNZA).

In terms of direction, the changes witnessed in the use of empirical data in research and teaching have not been towards the same objectives as different historical and political imperatives dictated political science discipline direction in each country. For instance, in Nigeria, the changes were mainly towards independence and democracy. In South Africa, the direction was mainly towards decolonization and now, decoloniality of knowledge. At UNZA, the discipline faced the challenge of training a new set of bureaucrats and its focus and direction has majorly remained the same. In a nutshell, the direction of the discipline has not moved in a unidirectional format in the adoption and use of empirical data in the research and teaching of political science in the continent. Rather, it has resulted in the democratization of political science knowledge, but of many shades and of different stages of change.

For wholesale changes, the discipline use of empirical data has moved in fits and bits reflective of socio-economic and political happenings in each African state. It is arguable that South Africa reflects the most wholesale change in the discipline in terms of the use of empirical data in political science research and teaching (Gouws, Kotze and Van Wyk 2013). As said, empirical data usage, cursorily, could be argued to be largely present and widespread in South Africa, but not as deep in other universities sampled in this write-up. It means therefore that there is the need to engage in more interrogation of the nature and depth of the usage of empirical data in research and teaching as well as its use as the basis of political science knowledge and its utility within the African society. This forms the central objective of this chapter. Thus, the chapter concerns itself with what is the state, level and depth of the use of empirical data as a source of knowledge of political science in Africa, namely, research, teaching and usage by academic and non-academic actors.

It is noteworthy that the debate among political scientists and policy analysts in Africa often centre on the balance between teaching and research, use of datasets to drive research outputs, research relevance to policymakers, academic-industry partnership, the relevance of the discipline, quality of teaching and graduates of the discipline, and between disciplinary autonomy, state interference and mass literacy/career-oriented interdisciplinary programmes (Napier and Mtimkulu 2013). Frequent questions among faculty include: Are the discipline research outputs empirical and data-driven? Is teaching informed by research data? Is the discipline equipped to deliver academically credible, high-quality political science knowledge to students in teaching and to the public through research? What is the state of the use of empirical data in the research and teaching of political science in Africa? And to what extent are these research outputs and political science datasets used?

Profound and all-consuming as these questions are, the basic challenge is how political science knowledge is conceived and appreciated in society and governance. The nuances of such conception and appreciation are likely to inform of the usefulness of the discipline in driving and impacting political institutions while forming the basis for data usage by practitioners (academics and policymakers). The reverse is likely to be the case when conceptualization of the discipline is muddled up and the disciplinary knowledge benefits it could offer is underappreciated or in some cases, unappreciated. Therefore, for the discipline in Africa, the conception/misconception dichotomy dilemma is real and this arguably could be traced to the nature of the colonial knowledge system that obfuscates rather than enlightens, given the wholesale condemnation of the indigenous knowledge epistemic and pedagogy platforms.

It is within this overarching context, particularly on the state, level and depth of the empirical use of data in research and teaching of political science in Africa, that this study attempts to provide an explanation of the state of knowledge of the discipline in Africa, using three universities in three different countries (South Africa, Nigeria and Zambia) as case studies. This is done through the examination of the level of application of empirical data in teaching and research of the discipline, appraise the frequency of the use of the empirical data in teaching and research, undertake a situational comparative analysis of the extent of the use of empirical data on teaching and research in selected universities. This is with a view to determining the impact of political science knowledge on the quality of political institutions in the continent.

Following this introduction, the next section provides an understanding of the political science in Africa, followed by histories of the three universities selected

(Universities of Johannesburg, South Africa; Obafemi Awolowo University [OAU], Nigeria, and University of Zambia [UNZA]) as case studies. The third section examines the dilemma of the political science discipline in Africa, while section four looks at the research design of the work. The next section after this surveyed the field in terms of the usage and non-usage of empirical data, followed by an examination of quantification and the challenges of political science. The last section, which is the conclusion, discusses the research findings and the future of political science in Africa.

Understanding political science in Africa: Political science departments in South Africa, Nigeria and Zambia in focus

The study of political science as a course of study started in Africa with the need for the discipline to train needed manpower for the colonial administration and the post-independent administration. While the discipline was established much earlier in South Africa, other African countries offered the course just before independence. The influence of the struggles for independence and the fate of new states were part of the curriculum and pedagogy. The consensus at the time of the establishment of the universities was the view that economics, sociology and political science as separate programmes/departments should be established, and the courses taught to provide skilled labour and influence various aspects of public policy in South Africa, Nigeria and Zambia (Jinadu 1987), the three countries selected for this research work. With this background in mind, it is important to situate and examine the histories of the selected African political science departments and their universities.

Histories of three universities and their political science department structures

University of Johannesburg

The University of Johannesburg (UJ) came into existence on 1 January 2005, as a result of the synthesis between the Rand Afrikaans University (RAU), the Technikon Witwatersrand (TWR) and the Soweto and East Rand campuses of Vista University. Historically, the Witwatersrand Technical Institute was founded in 1903 and later renamed in 1979 as the Technikon Witwatersrand. It came into light with the primary aim of producing technicians that are capable of mining gold in the country. In a similar vein, the Rand Afrikaans University (RAU) was established in 1966 and was the second university to be established in Johannesburg. It should be clearly stated that UJ was a product of union given the number of universities that came together to birth the modern university. More importantly, the Department of Politics and International Relations are synthesized together under the Faculty of Humanities. It offers courses at undergraduate and postgraduate levels. While the undergraduate includes BA in politics, BA in politics, philosophy and economics (PPE), and BA in international studies; the postgraduate level includes honours, master's and doctoral levels. Next is the staff structure of the department. The structure consisst of academic, administrative and student bodies, each with its defined roles, responsibilities and duties.

Obafemi Awolowo University

Obafemi Awolowo University, OAU is an ivy league and one of the first-generation institutions in Nigeria. It was founded in 1961 and commenced operation in October 1962 under the name University of Ife, before it was later renamed as Obafemi Awolowo University on 12 May 1987 in commemoration of the giant strides of late Chief Obafemi Awolowo, the first Premier of the old Western Region of Nigeria. The Nigerian federal university temporarily began operation at the previous college of arts and sciences, Ibadan, Oyo state before relocating to its permanent site of 5,000 acres of land in Ile-Ife, Osun State, Nigeria, in January 1967. It should be noted that the emergence of OAU is inextricably linked to the commission created during the last years of the British colonialists in Nigeria. The commission, headed by Sir Eric Ashby, was charged with the responsibility of researching the country's future manpower needs of university graduates. While the commission maintained that the University of Ibadan was sufficient enough, the Western regional government went forth with the creation of OAU. This was a position instigated by the Action Group Party in protest against Ashby's report.

It is important to state that Professor Oladele Ajose was the first vice-chancellor of the university, and the university began with five faculties: Agriculture, Arts, Economics and Social Studies, Law and Science. Five years after academic operations, the Department of Political Science came into existence in the 1967/1968 academic session. Prior to then, courses related to political science discipline were taught under Economics and Social Studies. As is the case with UJ, the department offers courses at undergraduate and postgraduate levels. It runs two undergraduates' courses: BSc in political science and BSc in PPE. It runs postgraduate programmes which include professional/specialized master's, academic master's and doctoral studies.

The staff strength and structure are evenly distributed and balanced. This is shown for each university discussed here in Tables 13.1, 13.2 and 13.3, respectively.

University of Zambia

University of Zambia (UNZA) is a national institution that was established in 1965 and commenced operation on 12 July 1966. The varsity is located in Lusaka, Zambia. It should be noted that it is the largest and oldest institution in the country. The movement towards the creation of UNZA was initiated by the colonialists. While there was contention in using the project to compensate Northern Rhodesia, it was eventually established at the capital of the country, Lusaka, on the basis of autonomy, academic excellence and non-alignment. President Kenneth David Kauda was appointed as the first Chancellor of the institution on 12 July 1966. It is instructive to note that the Department of Political and Administrative Studies is under the Faculty of Humanities. The Department offers academic programmes in Public Administration and Political Science at both undergraduate and postgraduate levels.

It is interesting to note that all the departments surveyed and described earlier are largely staffed by qualified academic personnel, most of which have doctoral degrees. This assumes that most (over 80 per cent) of the staff have received training and experience in the use of empirical data. The distribution is evenly spread among the different staff categories such that there is room for mentorship and guidance in the use of empirical data. It is equally important to note that there are more professors at UJ (South Africa) than at either OAU (Nigeria) or UNZA. As mentioned in the preceding section, this may be due to the early establishment of the discipline in South Africa than in the rest of Africa.

As can be seen from the earlier descriptions, these departments were purposely selected to provide context for the study and justification to make claims about the state of political science use of empirical data in research and teaching in Africa. The universities selected were because they are among the first set of universities, inclusive of the political science departments, that were established in their respective country. While UJ, as presently known, was established in 2005, it has been in operation since 1903; OAU was established in 1961 and commenced operation in 1962 and the department in 1967/1968. UNZA was established in 1966 and the department commenced thereafter. These universities and the political science departments were created to develop and train individuals to man the public service of various countries, with the resultant effect being the introduction and expansion of the discipline in Ibadan, Makerere, Legon and other centres of learning in addition to selected case studies described above (Barongo 1983: 1).

Descriptive or predictive: Political science in dilemma

The establishment of the political science discipline in Africa was accorded a place of honour and influence and to positively transform the society (Jinadu 1987). However, on the one hand, this proposition did not materialize due to two reasons. The first has to do with the misconception that political science as a course of study leads to a career in politics; or in local parlance, it involves training to become a politician. This has led to the mischaracterization of what the discipline as a body of knowledge should and can do in Africa. The second misconception has to do with the training of teachers of the course. With most of the teachers trained to see the discipline in descriptive and normative terms, there is little recourse to quantification, replication and validity of findings. It is debatable that the descriptive nature of the discipline has changed till now except modestly in South Africa.

On the other hand, the debate about the discipline has had to do with whether the discipline should be more descriptive, philosophical and idealistic with less emphasis on empirical data, particularly those that rely on quantification. For those in this category, the discipline being normative reflects the colonial orientation, exposure and post-independence struggle for democracy. In other words, the methodological approach was and still is normative, traditional and historical. It was less concerned with science and quantification, especially with using quantification to explain and predict political happenings. Even though behaviouralism has gained prominence in the discipline, it has not permeated the discipline as expected. Resistance to the quantification and use of data remained fierce because of the continued training received from those that were originally trained in the normative, traditional and descriptive nature of the study of political science. Arguments abound on the shortcomings and inappropriateness of quantification and of the behavioural revolution in political science (Ake 1982).

Arguments against, distrust for and amplification of quantification shortcomings has affected quantified research endeavours in the discipline in Africa and thus, research outputs are largely descriptive, prescriptive and normative, rather than explanatory, replicable and predictive. Disputations over the usefulness and level of usage of quantification in political science in Africa notwithstanding, the reality is that political science teaching and research in the continent cannot be divorced from the larger body of political science knowledge and practice in the world whose emphasis is on quantification of political phenomena to explain political realities (Box-Steffensmeier, Brady and Collier 2008). This is evidenced by the increasing number of top-rated journals that demand empirical data before papers are accepted and published, particularly those in the West. But a word of caution here. The reality is that even in the developed world, the disciplinary reliance on quantification is based on and determined by available data (Schedler and Mudde 2008). This available data is evidently not readily noticeable nor understandable by supposed end users for a variety of reasons including lack of skills and the fluid nature of human behaviour and conduct.

The aforementioned caution notwithstanding, the seeming resistance to quantification (empirical data) and contradiction in political science teaching and research in African universities reflects two streams of thought on what the discipline should be like in the continent. The first stream is based on the argument that the discipline should focus on the description and direct application of political science knowledge. The second stream is based on the arguments that the quantitative method is more appropriate in view of the modern world and therefore usage of empirical data in research and teaching deserves more emphasis than the normative, descriptive approach (Beck 2000; Hay 2002; Sadie 2013). This seeming dichotomy in the discipline in Africa has spurred concerns about the growth of research and teaching of political science in Africa and its utility in the larger African society (Napier and Labuschagne 2018). However, this has been resolved with a descriptive traditional approach remaining dominant. This would be explained in greater details in the discussion section.

Research design

In order to adequately assess the state of political science discipline in Africa, the study used a two-phase survey. The first is an in-depth interview of colleagues, particularly the heads of departments of political science/political studies programmes and two other lecturers in three African countries of South Africa, Nigeria and Zambia. Academic Staff publication outputs in the three departments were examined and assessed to determine the extent of the use or non-use of the datasets generally in their teaching

Table 13.1 Staff Structure of Department of Politics and International Relations, University of Johannesburg

Academic Rank	Number	Qualifications
Professors	9	All with PhDs
Associate Professors	3	All with PhDs
Senior Lecturers	2	All with PhDs
Assistant Lecturers	2	On doctoral training
Office Manager	1	
Total	17	

Source: University of Johannesburg, n.d.

and research works. This provides the quantitative basis of the survey. The responses to both the quantitative and quantitative survey, satisfy the standards of qualitative and quantitative survey research and provide the basis for a credible assessment of the discipline in selected African countries. Each department selected has nothing less than fourteen academic staff of various cadres, from assistant lecturer to professor. Interviews were done on the basis of strict confidentiality and the response rate was more than 80 per cent. The analysis of lecturers teaching and research outputs were also done on the basis of strict confidentiality.

The total number of academic staff in the three political science departments was forty-five at the time of the sample. UJ had sixteen academic staff out of which five were females; OAU with fifteen, out of which four are females and UNZA with fourteen academic staff with only one female as an academic member of staff. Tables 13.1, 13.2 and 13.3 showed the number of professors, senior lecturers and lectures. There were virtually no foreigners in the departments; each department was staffed by its nationals from the country. A word of clarification here. Datasets are quantitative in nature hence they form the major focus of our analysis of quantitative methodology. The major theme running through the question was the level and extent of the use of empirical data in research and teaching. Awareness of the databases, use of datasets to teach, research and publish were part of the questions asked through personal interactions. Qualitative methodology is subsequently tied to the descriptive aspect of the discipline. It is interesting to note that most of the research outputs in the departments are mainly desk reviews with little or no ties to the systemic method. This is shown in Figure 13.1.

Surveying the field

The use of political science knowledge, especially the usage of quantitative tools and data, would arguably give the picture of what sort of knowledge is dispensed to students and the public in the continent. This speaks to the continuing debate in political science, though somewhat muted in modern times, about the pros and cons of qualitative versus quantitative research. From Figure 13.1, most respondents affirmed the knowledge of databases and datasets but with about eighteen staff using it for research and teaching, while unused by about twenty-seven staff.

Table 13.2 Staff Structure of Department of Political Science, Obafemi Awolowo University

Academic Rank	Number	Qualification
Professors	3	All with PhDs
Associate Professor/Reader	3	All with PhDs
Senior lecturers	4	All with PhDs
Lecturers I	4	All with PhDs
Lecturer II	1	On doctoral training
Office Assistants	4	Not applicable
Total	19	

Source: Obafemi Awolowo University, n.d.

Table 13.3 Staff Structure of Department of Public Administration and Political Science, University of Zambia

Academic Rank	Number	Qualifications
Professors	0	
Associate Professor/Reader	1	PhD
Senior lecturers	5	All with PhDs
Lecturers	8	3 with PhDs
Office Assistants	2	Not applicable
Total	16	

Source: University of Zambia, n.d.

Figure 13.1 Academics use of datasets. *Source:* Author survey of staff publications (2020).

From the sample drawn and analysed, most of the lecturers' research outputs were mainly qualitative and largely descriptive. This is seen in the publications of the staff of the three departments. This is evidently so in Nigeria and Zambia where reference to Afrobarometer, V-Dem and Mo Ibrahim datasets were largely known but unused. However, South Africa's knowledge of these databases was much better and its usage more significantly higher than in Nigeria and Namibia. Figure 13.2 gives a composite picture of research outputs by South Africa, Nigeria and Zambia, respectively.

From the figure, there appears a disparity in the usage of databases by academic staff across the three universities. In OAU, Nigeria, about 24 per cent of the academic staff interviewed for this study said that they used databases; about 53 per cent used databases in UJ (South Africa) and 24 per cent used database in UNZA. It would mean that the usage is relatively low in only two cases/universities except in South Africa where it is more than average. But the usage does not correspond to the level of awareness as Figure 13.3 shows. The level of usage is significantly lower than that of awareness.

As seen from the figure, it is observed that the level of awareness of databases seems very high across the universities. The level of awareness in South Africa (34 per cent), Nigeria (34 per cent) and Zambia (32 per cent) remained fairly the same in the three departments/countries. It suggests that the level of awareness of the databases is high compared to its usage (see Figure 13.3). This would therefore mean that some reasons could be adduced for the gap in knowledge (awareness) and usage (see Figure 13.4).

It was evident from interviews on this disparity in knowledge and usage, that many are unskilled in quantitative approach (method) to research and in using datasets to publish. There is high resistance to quantification and its use mostly by older political scientists and from many upcoming ones. The reasons are in lack of knowledge of and training on the uses of datasets. The problem, while not peculiar to Africa, is however more prevalent in the continent (Duermeijer, Amir and Schoombee 2018).

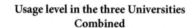

Usage level in the three Universities Combined

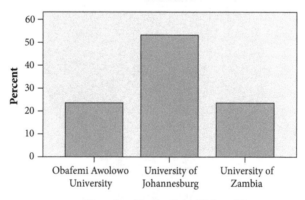

Usage level in the three Universities Combined

Figure 13.2 Analysis of academic staff usage of databases. *Source:* Author analysis of staff publications in Political Science Departments in three Universities of (2020).

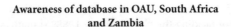

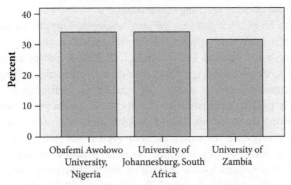

Figure 13.3 Analysis of the level of awareness of databases. *Source:* Author analysis of staff publications in Political Science Departments in three Universities of (2020).

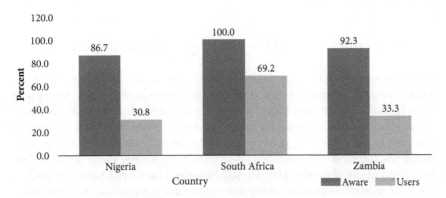

Figure 13.4 Empirical data (datasets) knowledge and usage. *Source:* Author analysis of staff publications in Political Science Departments in three Universities of (2020).

It is also interesting that most senior colleagues who studied outside Africa and who became teachers/lecturers belonged to the normative school. Their research works were largely descriptive, relying on logic and philosophical reasoning to explain political phenomena. Those trained in normative and descriptive political science and are now instructors have largely continued the descriptive lane. The argument for those normative descriptive school has been that political science, whose enterprise is studying fluid human conduct should take into account 'the importance of philosophical inquiry and epistemological validity to political and social enquiry which would lead to grounded theory and an effective political (social) theory building' (Afolabi 2018). On this position, Hughes earlier argued that 'ontological and epistemological questions are not to be answered by empirical enquiry since they are engaged in examining, among other things, the general nature and significance of empirical inquiry (Hughes and

Sharrock 1997: 5–6), yet it is also noteworthy that 'the choices of research questions and of methods of tackling them' (Rosenberg 1988: 5) matters. This has implications on the nature and utility of teaching and research.

It must also be pointed out that various academic support institutions within and outside Africa have recognized this limitation in the use of quantitative data to teach, research and publish. For instance, CODESRIA has for over several years organized research methodology programmes and scholarly writing workshops, though a noticeable trend is a bias for qualitative methodology (CODESRIA 2014). Little is paid to quantification, though that might be to suit humanities candidates among the laureates. Likewise, American Political Science Association has organized yearly until recently, a methodological workshop that largely focuses on quantitative methodology training through practical hands-on experience. The programme is funded by the American Political Science Association within the African continent with the beneficiaries comprising African and US-based participants that are usually selected and funded through a competitive process. The programme is called American Political Science Association's (APSA) Africa Workshop. The intention of such interventions is the recognition of the appalling state of quantitative knowledge/approach in political science research and publication in the continent.

Quantification and the challenges of political science

As discussed in the preceding section, political science, much like the rest of the social sciences, has remained tied to its normative descriptive heritage. Attempts at quantification have not been widely successful given its historical roots in normative training, lack of quantification skills as well as the need to explain political occurrences that were happening at a rapid rate immediately after independence in the countries within the continent. The reliance on descriptive methodology was/is not helped by the subject matter of the discipline investigation, that humans and human conduct in the political arena. Human behaviour and conduct are unpredictable and fluid. Thus, in addition to the issues highlighted above, quantification has remained an issue in the discipline, particularly in Africa. Even in the West, questions persist of the utility of the empirical data in understanding and proffering solutions to political problems and political realities.

If the aforementioned postulations are true and workable in other parts, demonstrated and noted by Schedler and Mudde (2008), then what are the challenges of quantification, either to teach, research or publish in political science in Africa?

From literature and the answers from those interviewed, the reasons though varied, speak to common peculiar challenges across the continent. First is the lack of training. As earlier mentioned, most of those who teach political science are not trained and are, therefore, not particularly proficient in mathematics and statistics. This is the number one drawback. This is in relation to the challenge of training as some of those given the opportunity to become equipped with quantification skills are unable to master the techniques. This is because, for some, their research approach/analysis is not based on quantification, while for some others, they are simply not interested or adept at quantification.

Thus, the stress, efforts and time required to become skilled in the use of empirical data are some of the noted reasons for the lack of interest. Added to this is the dearth of skilled quantitative methodologists in the discipline to teach others, guide and mentor others. Interestingly, as earlier noted, the problem, it can be argued, starts from the type of students admitted. In some universities across Africa, a credit pass in mathematics is not required to study political science. Yet, it is from these groups that lecturers are recruited. In Zambia for instance, statistics or basic mathematics is optional. In many departments across the continent, apart from lack of training, students are not exposed to rigorous quantitative research methodologies and associated research fieldworks from which practical experience can be derived (Moahi 2010). Emphasis is often on descriptive surveys, though changes are beginning to occur as more postgraduate political science programmes take empirical research more seriously and research at an advanced level. Some of these issues and criticisms have been noted elsewhere (Adetula 2011).

The second challenge has to do with the dwindling academic staff meant to cope with the burgeoning number of students in political science departments. For instance, in South Africa, since the post-independence in 1994, the number of students has more than tripled, while staff strength has only marginally increased (Booysen and van Nieuwkerk 1998; Sadie 2013). The same is true of Nigeria, Zambia, Tanzania, Kenya and other African countries, even with the establishment of private universities. This should be understood against the background of independence, the democratization of several states and youth unemployment. As more students enrol for the course, the teaching load increases, while lesser time is devoted to skill acquisition and re-training, particularly on quantitative research methodology. The teaching load is particularly heavy such that 'junior' academics (those in training positions) are now compelled to teach (Afolabi 2019). This is noticeable in the three universities used as case studies in this paper. In several African universities, the emphasis is on teaching rather than on research outputs, with the possible exception of South African universities. This emphasis is a misconception of what a discipline or university should focus on as research should inform teaching (Booysen and van Nieuwkerk 1998; Sadie 2013; Adeyemi 2017).

The third challenge relates to funding. Several African universities are pressed for funding, including funds to train and retrain academic staff on requisite knowledge and skill acquisition. While this is a global trend, the funding situation in Africa has never been particularly outstanding nor encouraging. In many universities, self-sponsorship is common, while institutional sponsorship is low. What has helped is the funding provided by some institutions like CODESRIA, DAAD, Humboldt, SSRC, ACLS, NAI, APSA, NRF, TETFUND and so forth to boost research and skill acquisition. In several African states where salaries are low, delayed and/or not paid for months, quantitative methodology skill acquisition would be a non-starter. In some ways, lack of quantitative skills has affected research outputs, level acceptance at high-impact journals and academic quality management (Afolabi and Idowu 2020).

Political science knowledge and quality of political institutions in Africa

Given the disciplinary components, there are bound to be differences in methodological preferences. But to be dominated by a seemingly uniform descriptive methodological approach in political science in Africa would be a great disservice to the discipline in the continent. The reason for such a conclusion is not far-fetched. The reason is located in the need for the discipline to explore the usefulness of empirical data in research and teaching and contribute, using this knowledge to improve political institutions in the continent. A balanced approach combining the descriptive with empirical data would result in a more nuanced approach to research and teaching which would make for more clarity in explaining political phenomena. Such an approach would also help to make claims that are backed up by empirical data.

Continued dysfunctional political institutions are reflective of the non-empirical engagement of political scientist with issues, problems and research that can inform their design, reform and function. Except for Afrobarometer, Mo Ibrahim and few others, political scientists in the continent generate little or no datasets that can be used to explain and predict institutions behaviour in Africa. This, expectedly, hinders political scientists' abilities to contribute to functional political institutions. Generating needed data would, even in view of some of the extensive branches of political science, enable us to understand, explain and develop models of political institutions that leverage on existing databases usage while noting the methodology, thematic field and scope/periodization.

It is necessary to address the seeming lack of interest in quantitative methodology and associated criticisms. While some of the criticism and lack of interest have been associated with charges of Western bias, prejudice and contestation about values, it is important to note that there is no methodological approach that is totally value-free. Undertaking empirical research work is consciously determined by subjective choice as there could be many tasks to choose from. Choosing a task from many is a subjective value even when the task is scientific in nature. This is because 'the affirmation of objectivity or value-freedom as desirable features of scientific procedure is itself the expression of a value' (Holub 1991: 25). Political science knowledge issues, especially its political methodology in terms of quantitative methodology, must be paid rigorous attention so as to derive maximum benefits from the prevalent science that is advancing daily. The advent of the Fourth Industrial Revolution has made this more imperative, not less if the discipline does not want to be left behind in Africa.

Renaissance, revolution or reversion? The future of political science in Africa

The task about the future of political science in Africa needs to revolve around the issue of decoloniality, objectivity and rigorous reformulation of the discipline. As can be deduced from our analysis, the major reasons for over-reliance on descriptive methodology rather on empirical data use in research and teaching of political science in the continent seem to be lack of skills and training and resources for that engagement.

But while some of the offered criticisms of quantitative methodology might be valid, the lack of alternatives to counter the dominant normative descriptive narratives have not helped the discipline. Rather, it has resulted in a litany of complaints about the limited usefulness of the discipline in research, teaching and critical knowledge production that addresses African realities. Critical engagement with quantification within the discipline is a necessary condition, while not neglecting the philosophical basis of most of these concepts. Taken a little further, the presence of philosophical inquiry in political science methodology is not an abnormality signifying subjectivity but becomes a well-nuanced approach when combined with empirical research which then produces outputs, which is predicated on observable mathematical results, where applicable, guaranteeing results that are testable, explanatory and replicable. Such research production is what is scientific about political science and what political science in Africa should aim at.

14

Political scientists as public intellectuals in Africa

Perspectives on relevance[*]

Adigun Agbaje

Introduction

This chapter addresses the issue of relevance of political science in Africa through a profile of self-assessment reports of African political scientists who are public intellectuals. To be sure, questions of relevance and irrelevance, as well as those of related issues of freedom and impact, appear in historical perspective to have been easier to decipher and construct in earlier contexts when much of Africa was under rampart military and other forms of dictatorship and minority rule. This is especially so when compared to the present conjuncture in which the continent is experiencing a rash of pseudo-democracies and troubled governance and political regimes. Moreover, as is suggested further, the concept of public intellectual and its relevance occupies a highly contested terrain in the best of circumstances. It raises issues that conduce to opacity rather than clarity such as intellectual integrity, responsibility and accountability, the role, location and constituents of the public, and the universality of the process versus its specificities of context, including time and space, as well as the content. Other issues include the determinants of relevance (to and for whom? Bestowed or achieved? In regard to what task, context and language?) (cf. Jega 1995; Beckman and Jega 1995; Hansen 1969; Hirschman 1981; Nye 2009: 252–4; Rogowski 2013: 216–21; Gerring 2015: 36–49; Hay 2015) and the political economy of the balances of knowledge and power in a period of enhanced commodification of exchanges in society (Amuwo 2002: 93–121).

The chapter explores some of these issues below in the context of its focus on self-reporting of the experiences of African political scientists who are public intellectuals. These include eight Nigerians (two of them based in the diaspora – the United Kingdom and the United States, respectively), one Ghanaian, one Ugandan and three South

[*] I hereby thank Wale Adebanwi, Ebenezer Obadare, Dominica Dipio, Fred Hendricks, Kwame Boafo-Arthur, Bertram Mapunda, all the thirteen public intellectuals interviewed for this work and the editors of the volume for facilitating the writing of this chapter.

Africans. The majority (seven in all) are in the 50–59 age bracket, with one below 40, one between 40 and 49, three between 60 and 69, and one in the 70–79 age bracket. Only two out of the thirteen interviewed are female. The overwhelming majority (eleven) are male. The main careers of the respondents include academic/research (eight out of thirteen), journalism/communication (four), and non-profit (one). Of the eight in academia/research, five are full professors, one an executive director, one a lecturer and one an independent scholar/researcher. The rest comprise one retired top management staff of a media organization, one executive director of a centre (previously a university-based professor), and three journalists. Nine are holders of the PhD degree as their highest qualifications, two the MPhil degree, and the remaining two are MSc/MA degree holders. They were all interviewed by email and WhatsApp in the context of the Covid-19 pandemic. Whenever I consider it necessary, I have protected the identities of the respondents, revealing the same only in regard to matters I consider non-sensitive.

Specific objectives of the study outlined in the pages ahead included to:

- Capture the perspectives of public intellectuals on their relevance, and those of their national and other professional associations, to socio-economic, policy, and political life in regard to the epistemic and practitioner boundaries of the discipline of political science; and
- Examine the public intellectuals' perception of their role in addressing the travails of democracy and development in Africa.

In more detail, the respondents were asked to address the following items:

- Relevance of training as a political scientist to the role as a public intellectual;
- Influence of political science traditions, philosophies and ideologies on the role as a public intellectual over time;
- Role of the regional/national professional associations of political scientists and others that include political scientists;
- The state of democracy and development;
- The extent of engagement with government and others;
- Instances of high and low points in the role as public intellectuals; and
- Divisions among public intellectuals (along ideological, ethnic, religious, gender, regional lines).

The sections that follow detail the respondents' perspectives on these issues against a backdrop of an overview of aspects of the literature on the nature and role of the public intellectual, and matters arising therefrom. The last section concludes the chapter.

The public intellectual across time and space

Public intellectuals, simply put, are individuals who consistently deploy their intellect, discipline, profession and skills through their thoughts, writing and public speaking to seek to identify, address, discuss and influence matters of public interest (Desch 2016). They could have their primary base either in educational institutions such as universities or other organizations such as think tanks, the media and other knowledge/cultural institutions. In itself, all this reflects both the universal, ambiguous and relativist nature of the public intellectual and, in this instance, its intellectual base and subject matter – political science and politics and related public policy matters (on this, cf. an early statement in Coleman and Halisi 1983). At one level, Jean-Paul Sartre (in Adebanwi 2014: 1) notes that 'a critical intellectual's task is to bear witness, analyse, expose and criticize a wide range of social evil'. In the same vein, Easton (1969) sees the role of intellectuals as that of promoting the humane values of civilizations. At a second level is the viewpoint that intellectuals are 'ambiguous characters representing different things in different societies' (Adebanwi 2014: 1); as a result, the meaning of the term, intellectual, 'has shifted over time and across cultures' (Adebanwi 2014: 1 citing Baert and Isaac 2011: 200). This tendency can be stretched to imply that there is neither an 'essentially timeless intellectuality' nor an 'ideal social posture adopted by intellectuals throughout the ages' (Adebanwi 2014: 1). A more useful perspective, in my view, is one that admits of a universal image of the intellectual as the bearer and merchant of ideas described as 'the most migratory things in the world' (Lovejoy 1940: 4; also Armitage 2013), and yet emphasizes the local specificities and varied nature of the practice of the intellectual across time, space and cultures as indicated earlier.

In regard to the subject of this chapter, it is often indicated that perhaps nothing could be more public than politics and its sciences. On the streets of Africa, as in other places, virtually everybody claims expertise in political matters, and the traditional line of separation between arcane expertise on one hand and popular knowledge and passion on the other often appears to disappear when politics is the subject of public discourse. As far back as the dawn of independence for many African countries, Gwendolen Carter, a noted Canadian-American political scientist, narrated her experience in this regard thus:

> The joy of being a political scientist in Africa is that everyone talks my business ....
> It is not necessary to spend long hours, or patient coaxing to persuade almost any
> articulate African or African-based European to expound on how things should be
> done in his country. (Carter 1959: 1)

This level of interest in matters political is itself not a bad thing, and recent literature on the public intellectual in fact seems to suggest the need for a reinvigoration of such a state of affairs, involving bringing 'the general public, particularly from within communal and political organizations' (Wright 2019: 172), into the centre of 'public intellectualism' (Giroux 1995; Kenny et al. 2001; Alcoff 2002; Desch 2016; Peters, Alter and Shaffer 2018; Wright 2019). For the purpose of this chapter, it is enough at this stage to underscore the fact that the general interest in politics makes the work of the political scientist as a public intellectual even more important and strategic to the overall well-being and future of African societies and politics. On the other hand, the fact that 'in any democratic society, you have not one but many publics . . . and so the idea of a broad public is largely a mirage' (Interview with Prof Steve Friedman, 12 August 2020) complicates the role of political scientists as public intellectuals.

As indicated earlier, the larger contexts and intents of this work at the level of the wider society and with reference to changes in the discipline of political science has been shaped by factors and forces across time and space (global, continental, regional, country). Many of these are treated in greater detail in other chapters in this volume. Suffice here to note the varying experiences of colonial and post-colonial rule and interfaces with the global environment and their legacies and import for higher education in general and the development of different traditions of political science and the idea and practice of the public intellectual in particular (Lofchie 1968; Barongo 1983; Jinadu 1987, 2000, 2002; Diouf and Mamdani 1994; Mafeje 1994; Nzongola-Ntalaja 1997; Ibrahim 1998; Nzongola-Ntalaja and Lee 1998; Nyong'o 2002; Aiyede and Udalla 2013: 22–32; Gouws, Kotze and Van Wyk 2013; Adem 2014; Mngomezulu and Hadebe 2018; Napier and Labuschagne 2018; Southall 2019).

The central argument pursued in the rest of this chapter, therefore, is that perceptions of relevance by political scientists operating as public intellectuals in Africa are simultaneously a function of, as well as a factor in, the shaping of the local and international contexts, memories, contents and intents of their locations and situations.

Narratives of the travails of relevance

Against this background, this section of the chapter provides insights from political scientists serving as public intellectuals about their experiences as outlined in the introduction above. It is important at this stage, however, to indicate a few generational, gender and country-specific cross-currents noted in the course of this study. For instance, the two women (one South African, CH, one Nigerian, MO) among the thirteen interviewed prioritize gender in their responses, whereas the remaining eleven respondents do not. The observed differences in gendered priorities along gender lines are an important reflection of experiential differences among male and female political scientists in work and other spaces and underscore the need to address the challenges posed by a dominance of male voices among political scientists involved in public intellectual work on the continent. Interestingly, the two women also state that they deploy interdisciplinary approaches and traditions in their role as scholars and public intellectuals. This helps to provide a more nuanced lens for a deeper comprehension of gender in theory and practice beyond the strictures of disciplinary boundaries. In the words of one of them, MO, although she has been influenced by political science traditions, she is also

> now committed to interdisciplinary traditions, philosophies, and ideologies, because I don't think that Political Science in and of itself is sufficient to facilitate either understanding or explication of the issues, subjects, and phenomena that interest me. (Interview with MO, 3 June 2020)

The views of LS, a radical black South African public intellectual in his early 40s and those of SF, a more elderly white South African liberal public intellectual in his late 60s, also make interesting reading on the issue of the location and experience of public intellectuals in the specific context of the country and African specificities. Consider these statements from LS, the black South African:

> In colonies of settlement like South Africa and America for instance where everyday relations are racialized, it is imperative that there be always a speaking black intellectual. . . . It is not what we achieve as public intellectuals per se but keeping the black voices alive . . . . I realized that reality is not organized according to disciplinary boundaries. What is political in the life of black people is at the same time and at once religious, social, and educational. Neither is it organized according to ideological compartments with hard walls separating them. For instance, what appears as a racial problem most of the time is at once an economic problem, a social problem, a political problem all at once at the same time . . . . In South Africa, the fractionalisation [among public intellectuals] is mostly along racial lines, black and white. White public intellectuals have styled themselves as defenders of white privilege. As black public intellectuals we find ourselves nor only having to do battle against the state but also against our white counterparts. (Interview with LS, 23 August 2020)

Contrast this with the following narrative on the same subject by SF, the white public intellectual:

> Identity politics in South Africa is interesting and more complicated . . . than what people think. Thus, the reality of the public intellectual terrain is more complex than Black versus White. There was a time when an exclusively white newspaper asked its readers who they thought were the most important persons in South Africa. The two top persons named were black people identified with viewpoints identical with what white people wanted. The black persons were conservatives (champions of hard work and discipline) and critical of the ANC. There was also the case of a black journalist with a business newspaper who was constantly writing about what whites liked to read. The journalist was taken up on one occasion by somebody who called him a disgrace and advised him to check what another Black journalist was writing about – but it so happened that the 'Black journalist' was actually a white academic. Me . . . . The development path chosen after the 1994 elections was one that divided society into insider and outsider . . . . The implication is that . . . it all boils down to a debate between insiders, themselves polarised, and outsiders. There is the need for public intellectuals who are committed to outsiders to speak more compared to those committed to insiders. (Interview with SF, 12 August 2020)

These viewpoints underscore the complexities of identities in racially divided societies when it comes to the role of the political scientist as a public intellectual. On the one hand, the salience of race is unquestionable. On the other hand, there are obvious limits to the heuristic value of race in the wider understanding of the realities of everyday life and of the perception of the roles of individuals and groups beyond the obvious categorizations of race to include socio-economic factors, religion, education, politics, ideological preferences, aspirations, pressures of caucuses and organizations/other groups, in the shaping of actions and reactions.

These currents underscore the extent to which the work of public intellectuals is cut out for them not only by universal and cross-temporal impulses but more importantly by the specificities of lived experiences and socially constructed contexts. It is important to bear this in mind as we examine the views of the African public intellectuals with political science backgrounds surveyed in this study on the relevance and influence of their training, political science traditions, and experience.

Relevance of training and political science traditions and philosophies

The majority of respondents believe that their training as political scientists, and their immersion in the traditions and philosophies of the discipline, have proved very relevant and useful in their task as public intellectuals. For them, it has provided a deep, critical and robust platform from which to expand their understanding of life beyond classroom foundations, ponder on public affairs, challenge elements of the status quo that may otherwise be hidden to the ordinary eye, as it were, and a sense of public duty. It has thus enabled them to better identify and appreciate public issues, governance matters, as well as the uses and abuses of power.

Within this general acknowledgement of their academic background, some underscore that the subject is more complex. For instance, interdisciplinary approaches are becoming more important in our increasingly complex world to the extent that one of the respondents notes that 'I don't think political science in and of itself is sufficient to facilitate either understanding or explication of the issues, subjects, and phenomena that interest me' (Interview with MO, 3 June 2020). In the same vein, CH (Interview, 19 August 2020) indicates that 'political science traditions and philosophies have not been key to me – my approach is interdisciplinary'. Another important intervention here is that

> in theory, training should be decisive; in reality, the media and the people that the public intellectual engages with are often not interested in what the public intellectual has to say . . . . The point: training is relevant in theory; in practice, not as much. (Interview with SF, 12 August 2020)

Role of national and regional professional associations

In general, the assessment of national and regional professional associations has not been very positive. For instance, EA (Interview, 29 May 2020) agrees with others on the state of the *Association of African Political Science* and offers more insight in this regard, noting that

> the association has been comatose for some time now. I know efforts were being made to revive the body and a conference was scheduled for 2020 to revive the body. This has been adversely affected by the COVID-19 lockdown and travel restrictions.

The association was founded in Dar es Salaam in 1974 as the continental group for political scientists. For several decades, it was the most formidable framework for various generations of political scientists, students and scholars from related disciplines interested in African governance, politics, economy, society and development. on the continent. Its biennial conferences and annual workshops helped to solidify pan-African scholarship and create/consolidate various schools of thought such as the famous Dar, Ibadan, Cairo and Harare Schools in conjunction with the Council for the Development of Social Science Research in Africa (CODESRIA). However, following a downturn in its funding, whose sources were mainly from outside Africa, AAPS began to witness decline at the beginning of the new millennium, up to 2017. Attempts to revive the Association started in earnest in 2018, with Professor Siphamandla emerging as Interim President. A virtual conference was in fact held in March 2021 in the wake of the Covid pandemic and it is hoped the initiative not only to revive but also re-energize the Association will wax stronger, with appropriate attention paid to expanding the Association's resource base to include African sources more than ever before. It was sad indeed that while it went into decline, the association could nor provide the kind of intellectual and policy leadership that it earlier provided the continent and new and aspiring political scientists through the path-breaking, Africa-rooted works of leading scholars such as Claude Ake.

Most of the national associations in countries covered by this study (Ghana, Nigeria, South Africa, Uganda) are reported either as being weak now or only recently recovering from their weak status over a long period of time. It is reported that the Ghana Political Science Association, barely a decade old, has been dormant over the years and was re-launched only in 2019. The case of the Nigerian Political Science Association is similar. Vibrant from the 1970s to the mid-1990s, it went comatose subsequently and was resuscitated only a few years ago. The lack of vibrancy and inclusiveness of the South African Political Science Association reflects key issues in the country's political history. On this, an informed observer, SF, notes (in interview on 12 August 2020):

> I am not aware of any role for SAPS in this regard; is it even their function to do that in South Africa? I am aware that some continental bodies (such as the Bar Association) are influential. However, the political science association is not very useful here. Why this is the case I cannot really say, but one fact is that the association remains the preserve of conservative people who do not really care about public intellectual work. Incidentally, the association is not very welcome to young Black South Africans. In essence, the association as

it is currently constituted tends to focus more on science, losing the political contexts of public life.

An apparent saving grace in this regard remains CODESRIA, committed to promoting Social Science and Humanities Research, teaching and learning in Africa consistently since the 1970s. Reflecting this is the statement that 'CODESRIA . . . provided opportunities for mentorship which I enjoyed. It also opened pathways to writing papers and publications which boosted my academic career'. (Interview with JI, 24 May 2020).

The state of democracy and development

Three statements are emblematic of the respondents' views on the state of democracy in Africa. First is the position:

> The quality of democratic life, in general, and governance, in particular, remain disappointingly low in the continent. Without doubt, most African countries have made some progress. The idea of military hijack of power and the 'legitimacy' of eternal presidency have come into disrepute – despite the surviving efforts of the Biyas, Nguemas, Nguessos, Musevenis, Kagames and Debys (Deby was killed in April 2021 while still in power). The 'eternal leaders' that remain in power forever no longer have the confidence and implicit assumptions of their legitimacy, or so I think. I don't think any of them are able to sleep well, if they sleep at all, any longer. We can be sure that when they all die, their 'eternity' in office will die with them. One of the things that is most worrying, despite the unprecedented mobilisation through, and possibilities of, the social media for democratic change, is the decline in the quality of civil and political societies since the triumph of democratic rule in the post-1989 era. (Interview with WA, 30 May 2020)

Next, it is suggested:

> Fiction is critical for us as political scientists, particularly regarding the debate and reality of democracy and development – and beyond. Larry Diamond's essay, 'Fiction as Political Thought' is also illustrative of why fiction constitutes one of most critical vehicles for understanding *the political*. I have argued that some (literary) writers have offered far more penetrating insights about certain socio-political configurations in the continent than even social scientists. (Interview with WA, 30 May 2020)

Third, is the more sympathetic position that

> the relationship between democracy and development is a complex one and it is often difficult to assess if and how one leads to the other. What I always

emphasise is that both democracy and development are core values and should be pursued in ways and manners that do the greatest good to the majority of the people and that 'the quality of democracy and governance are in constant flux and my task as a public intellectual is to continuously assess them'. (Interview with JI, 24 May 2020)

Self-assessment on engagement with government and others

The general image is that engagement between the public intellectuals on one hand and government and others could be better, given that this often depends more on the interests, preferences and priorities of those in positions of authority in government and elsewhere, as well as the extent to which public intellectuals actually seek sufficient and autonomous engagement. Thus, the lamentation is that while such countries as South Africa:

> Still have a reasonably vibrant public discourse . . . it is not necessarily the Political Scientists who are engaging or at the forefront of these debates. So we have little depth in the discussion about the nature of the state and why it produces the kind of politics we are seeing. Much more robust engagement was had before – we are no longer speaking among or to each other, more at each other. (Interview with CH, 19 August 2020)

On the latter, MO, a Nigerian in the diaspora, declares:

> Most Nigerian intellectuals are not sufficiently engaged. There's great evidence of cooptation, collaboration, and cooperation with the state and less evidence of friction and confrontation among public intellectuals on one hand and key actors in government . . . (and others) . . . . Most seem to be more intent in feathering their nests and collaborating with powerful elites and the state than in engaging in meaningful disputation. (Interview with MO, 3 June 2020)

Another line of argument is that there is some form of engagement, but the positive impact on democracy, good governance and development is minimal, if any. As indicated earlier, others blame the manipulative antics of the elite for this reality. Drawing from experience, one of the respondents, SF, states:

> In theory, advice should lead to policy. In fact, this is often a fiction. Government is often about power – personal and group advancement. There was an occasion when a Minister invited me to a meeting and then realised that I was not supporting his position. He quickly disbanded the meeting. In essence, therefore, if political scientists as public intellectuals have any influence, it is because (and when) they conform with the political agenda of the government. (Interview with SF, 12 August 2020)

Another view is:

> There is a huge interaction gap among the government, the organised private
> sector and academia in terms of engagement. This reduces the efficacy of the
> public intellectuals. It seems there are just too few public oriented intellectuals.
> Government officials are probably more attuned to dealing with motley of
> consultants and experts from multilateral organisations than to resort to domestic
> expertise . . . . The situation is such that the country [Nigeria] is approaching what
> can be described as 'cut and paste' policy making. (Interview with EA, 29 May 2020)

In terms of the high and low points of their role as public intellectuals, the interviewees
offer a range of interesting answers. For the high points, they identify bringing about
transformation in policy and practice, being approached for advice, being on platforms
across Africa where they are able to shape debates and influence decision-making,
being invited to occupy office, having their newspaper columns being followed by
many, and name and face recognition. For the low points, they finger state reprisals,
growing perception of talking to the deaf, and the feeling that nobody cares, and being
unjustly accused of being partisan.

Divisions among public intellectuals

It is the general consensus that there are divisions among public intellectuals and on
the dimensions of these divisions and what may be responsible for them. According
to EA:

> There is a near absence of serious ideological divide among public intellectuals
> in terms of the traditional left and right orientations, reflecting the nature
> of contemporary global politics. There are however variations in theoretical
> perspectives and individual philosophies often expressed in priorities and policy
> preferences. There are elements of grandstanding arising from deep sentiments,
> religious and ethno-linguistic affiliations and gender. These have stultified debates
> and reflected the various forms of authoritarianism that have come to characterise
> the ivory tower and the wider society. (Interview, 29 May 2020)

In the same vein elements of this viewpoint resonate with specific experiences. For
Ghana, it is indicated that 'factionalisation among public intellectuals is real' and
manifests along with gender, religious and ideological lines (Interview with GA, 25
May 2020). Two views on Nigeria are in agreement with this perspective. One, by FA
(Interview, 25 May 2020) laments that 'public intellectuals get easily sucked into the
vortex of some of the social issues they canvass against', including ethnic and religious
ones, and become 'indistinguishable from the issues they declaim'. MO weighs in with
the observation:

> There is significant factionalisation. I am disappointed and dismayed by the extent
> and depth of it. This is evident in ideological, ethnic, religious, gender, and regional

divides that are seen in Nigeria. Many respected and distinguished scholars are now ethnic jingoists. . . . Public intellectuals should be more active now than ever before. They have a significant role to play despite the turmoil in the body politic. However, there's need also for them to connect better to the popular masses and make their analysis digestible to them, in the sense of being organic intellectuals. (Interview, 3 June 2020)

The debate on this subject in the South African milieu has been reflected earlier, and it underscores the similarity of experiences across the continent, with the specific addition in that country of the racial divide.

Two comments of a general nature that echo MO's comment earlier on the need for public intellectuals to move towards becoming organic intellectuals need to be highlighted here, given their implications for the way forward. One, by CH (Interview, 19 August 2020), is to the effect that the divergences noted among intellectuals are in a sense healthy, given the increase in the number of public intellectuals on the continent. She goes on to add, however, that

we have to also have common agendas that we are working towards – what are the key questions that we as Political Scientists are trying to answer in this age and day? When and how do we get together to frame them and to collaborate on finding solutions? There is now more opportunity to do so but less of it actually happening.

Picking up this line of reasoning, WA says:

It is tragic that those that Gramsci would describe as 'organic intellectuals' in many African social formations often engage in fratricidal wars against themselves when they should unite to fight those who are responsible for Africa's infernal crises. 'Uniting' does not mean sharing the same ideas or belonging to similar organisations. It means leveraging common ideas about social progress through strategic thinking and strategic planning. Related to this is the ways in which cross-cutting ties (ideological, political, ethnic, religious, gender, etc) often disable rather than enable African public intellectuals in leveraging their skills to ensure social transformation. (Interview, 30 May 2020)

Conclusion: The imperatives of organic linkages

The opportunities and challenges that have been highlighted in the review of the experiences of a handful of political scientists serving as public intellectuals in African contexts have provided insights into the uncertainties in the theory and reality of the terrain for public intellectual work by political scientists in Africa, as well as the historical sociology of the enterprise. Building on an empirically grounded investigation of self-assessment of the terrain by thirteen of such political scientists engaged in the work of public intellectuals has provided us with insights on sets of options that offer pathways to a better future that are of course not necessarily exhaustive or definitive enough to be the last word on the topic. Nonetheless, those insights make a case for strengthening the relevance, relative autonomy, vibrancy and skills sets of those among the political science community in Africa so engaged in this strategic role. These desired goals can be pursued through the deliberate nurturing of two sets of linkages. One would comprise linkages with the African peoples where they live in their communities and civic terrains. The second set would involve developing effective ties with national, regional and global platforms for academic and professional networking among political and related social scientists and humanities intellectuals in manners that facilitate the resolution of local challenges and help to build on strengths and opportunities. This will better strengthen public intellectuals as they seek to advance the cause of democracy, development and good governance on the continent and make them more relevant to the everyday life of Africans.

15

Political scientists and intellectuals in the political evolution of Cameroon

1960–2020

Fabien Nkot, Hélène Amélie Molo and Isa Adamu

Introduction

This chapter examines the contribution of political scientists to the sociopolitical evolution of Cameroon since its independence in 1960 by studying the action of Cameroonian political scientists from the philosophical approach of two authors, namely Jean-Paul Sartre and Julien Benda. Sartre argues that an intellectual should transcend the theoretical aspects of his thought and be effectively engaged in politics to '[unmask] the fundamental contradictions of the society' (Sartre 1976: 245; also see 1972). Benda on the other hand believes that the intellectual should not intervene in praxis because:

> The 'clerk' is only strong if he is clearly conscious of his essential qualities and his true function and shows mankind that he is clearly conscious of them. In other words, he declares to them that his kingdom is not of this world, that the grandeur of his teaching lies precisely in this absence of practical value. (Benda 2007: 191; also see 1927)

Two entirely opposing ideas are advocated by these authors: one advocates committed and practical action by intellectuals, while the other suggests they should not intervene in the field. With regard to the deployment of Cameroonian political scientists in the construction of the main axes of the history of their country, we will see if their action aligns with the approach of Sartre or Benda.

Depending on their orientation, intellectuals choose to dwell on a specific conceptual or theoretical approach by formulating ideas that can contribute to social change. This is a first step and a type of commitment that is likely to contribute to 'awareness' and to the unmasking of the fundamental contradictions of the society: that is to say, the struggle between class and within the dominant class itself, the organic conflict between the truth the latter needs for its own purposes and the myths, values and traditions with which it seeks to infect other classes in order to ensure its hegemony. (Sartre 1972: 35)

In this first stage, the intellectual goes beyond the theoretical approach to properly experiment with the doctrines or ideologies with which he 'flirts' on paper. However, theory and practice are two completely different realities, so bringing them into coherence can prove to be difficult and can weaken the credibility of an excellent theoretician, who turns out to be a poor practitioner, as suggested by Benda: 'the "clerk's" defeat begins from the very moment when he claims to be practical' (2007: 190). In terms of this logic, intellectuals should refrain from being actors in the practical field. In Cameroon, however, social development in general and political developments in particular are largely the result of actions by intellectuals.

Since the creation of the University of Yaoundé in 1962, the presence of lecturers has been highly noticeable in the political arena and work shaping the role of the state (Ngwé et al. 2006: 182). While these intellectuals are recruited from all disciplines, political scientists deserve particular attention, since they represent the science of the state, of power or even, as Meynaud (1961: 95–114) argued, the structure of authority.

In terms of this logic, this chapter will investigate the impact of the activities of Cameroonian political scientists on the political evolution of the country. It is important to note their close relations to public law. The two disciplines are constantly 'overlapping, penetrating' (Houde and Lettre 1965: 79). Public law phenomena are political phenomena as 'many similar issues are covered by both public law and political science, none of them bearing exclusivity over those issues' (Houde and Lettre 1965: 74–5). The rapprochement between political science and public law in Cameroon should also be understood on a historical level. Originally, the first University (Yaoundé) had the faculty of laws and economics, where the law section offered political science. The restructuring in 1993 separated legal and political sciences from economics. Currently in Cameroon, these are organized under the faculties of legal and political sciences. This explains the large number of intellectuals who are graduates of both public law and political science. In this study, graduates of both public law and political science are considered political scientists. The focus will be on their role in the political evolution of Cameroon during the era of its first president; the presidential succession of 1982 in Cameroon and the adoption of the Constitution of 1996; the sociopolitical crisis in the North-West and South-West regions, which was generated by the so-called English-speaking problem in the country and the structuring of political opposition.

Early role of political scientists in public life

Intervention by political scientists in the public sphere was felt from the outset of the political life of independent Cameroon: in the (a) pre and post-independence process;

(b) reunification of the two 'Cameroons' and the advent of the unitary state; and (c) intervening in the administration and management of public affairs.

The pre- and post-independence process

During this period, very few Cameroonians had received formal political science training, but the general debate of the elite related to aspirations of independence and decolonization. It is worth noting that the first contact between the native population of Cameroon and European explorers, in this case the Portuguese, took place in 1472 (Owona 1973: 17). In 1884 Cameroon became a German protectorate following an agreement between the Douala Chiefs of the coastal city and the German Empire. Following the First and Second World Wars that marked the defeat of the Germans, the Cameroonian territory was placed first under the mandate of the League of Nations and then under UN trusteeship (1922–45). Four-fifths of Cameroonian territory was administered by France and one-fifth by Great Britain.

On the eve of independence, Cameroonian intellectuals participated in the decolonization process as individuals or through a student association. This was the case with François Sengat-Kuo who had obtained a law degree and a Diploma of Higher Studies with a Doctorate in Economic Sciences. His first revolutionary writings appeared in the 1950s under a pseudonym. Between 1957 and 1958, he was President of the Union of Kamerun Students in France, which had close ties to the Union of the Populations of Cameroon (UPC) (Nkot 2018: 198), a mythical anti-colonial party.

Augustin Frédérick Kodock was an intellectual who in 1955 joined the Basic Committee of the Union of the Populations of Cameroon of Toulouse, where he was a student. He penned revolutionary articles that appeared in publications such as 'The Student of Black Africa'. He had a degree and a diploma in in-depth studies in law as well as a Doctorate in economic sciences. He also obtained a diploma from the Toulouse Institute of Political Studies.

Cameroon gained its independence on 1 January 1960. The first president of independent Cameroon, Ahmadou Ahidjo, implemented a policy of rallying intellectuals to his vision and a number of Cameroonian political scientists joined the movement. Between 1960 and 1962, François Sengat-Kuo was director of Cabinet and technical advisor to the Minister of Foreign Affairs, and Minister Plenipotentiary to the Embassy of Cameroon at the United Nations. Augustin Frédérick Kodock was director of the ministry in charge of finance and the economy and involved in the development of the first five-year plan.

Abel Eyinga was another young intellectual. He studied at the Institute of Political Studies in Paris, where he obtained a doctorate in law. Upon his return to Cameroon in 1962, he was appointed Chief of Cabinet to Prime Minister Charles Assale (Tobner 2014). Kanga Victor entered the government in the 1960s. He earned a Doctor of Law from the Faculty of Law of Paris and was a graduate of the National School of Customs. He became Minister of State, Minister of National Economy in the Government in 1961, Minister of Finance, Planning and National Equipment in 1964, and Minister of Information and Tourism in 1966.

Although involved in the implementation of President Ahidjo's policy, some intellectuals, as Abel Eyinga, criticized the persistent hegemony of the West. He deplored the situation in which power was actually in the hands of the French Technical Advisers assigned to the Ministers (Deltombe, Domergue and Tatsitsa 2011: 389), and eventually resigned from his administrative post and left Cameroon. This highlighted the totalitarian inclination of the Ahidjo regime. In fact, after attempting to run in the 1970 presidential election against Ahidjo, an arrest warrant was issued against him. This case formed the basis of his book *Mandat d'arrêt pour cause d'élections: de la démocratie au Cameroun: 1970–1978* (Eyinga 1978).

In 1966, Kanga Victor was accused of disclosing false information about the regime through anonymously penned leaflets accusing the Head of State of financial scandals (Emagna 1996: 66). He was relieved of his duties on 23 November 1966, arrested and sentenced to four years in prison.

One of the political scientists who joined the Ahidjo administration after independence was Paul Biya, who had a bachelor's degree in public law, a diploma from the Paris Institute of Political Studies and a graduate diploma in public law. Upon his return to Cameroon in 1962, he was appointed Chargé de Mission at the Presidency of the Republic. In 1982, he became the second president of the Republic of Cameroon (Nkot 2018: 30).

Furthermore, political scientists and jurists have produced an abundance of publications that allows us to understand the role of intellectuals in the history of Cameroon. For example, Achille Mbembe (holder of a Diploma of Advanced Studies in Political Science from the Institute of Political Studies in Paris and a Doctorate in History from the University of Paris-Sorbonne) has highlighted the struggle of the Union des Populations du Cameroun (UPC) against colonialism. By contesting the criteria on which the colonial regime functioned, the UPC reshapes mentalities to disapprove of the colonial paradigm as such (Mbembe 1996: 363).

Abel Eyinga criticized the French authorities for interference in the internal affairs of Cameroon after the appointment of Mr Ramadier to the post of High Commissioner of France to Cameroon, the resignation of Mr André Marie Mbida and, above all, the appointment of Mr Ahidjo as Prime Minister (Nkot 2001: 31).

Reunification of the two 'Cameroons'

Independence of the eastern French-speaking region of Cameroon with the Constitution on 4 March 1960 was followed by its reunification with western English-speaking Cameroon and revision of the Constitution in 1961. Cameroon was then a federal republic with two federated states. This configuration was modified after the Referendum of 20 May 1972, whereby the people voted for the draft Constitution establishing a unitary state in Cameroon. This was the basis of the demands of a section of the English-speaking elite to denounce, in cultural terms, francization of the English-speaking community or, politically speaking, their marginalization from the most important political functions (Nkot 2001: 49).

An important doctrinal controversy concerned the validity of the Referendum of 20 May 1972 and whether it led to a constitutional revision or a new text. Among the political scientists and jurists who took part in the debate were Joseph Owona, Alain Didier Olinga, Lekene Donfack Etienne, François Mbome and Maurice Kamto (Nkot 2001: 53–69).

The government at the time of the referendum included eminent political scientists and jurists:

- Paul Biya, then Minister of State, Secretary General of the Presidency of the Republic;
- Bidias Ngon Bernard, the Minister of Finance. He had diplomas from the National School of Administration and the Institut des Hautes Etudes d'Outre-Mer in Paris, and a degree in law from the Federal University of Cameroon;
- François-Xavier Ngoubeyou, Minister of Youth and Sports. He had a law degree and was a graduate of the Institut des Hautes Études d'Outre-Mer in Paris;
- Fokam kamga Paul, Minister of Public Health. He had obtained a law degree from the Faculty of Law of Paris and was a graduate of the Institut d'Etudes Politiques de Paris, as well as l'Ecole Nationale de la France d'Outre-mer.

The government that oversaw the process leading to the 1972 referendum was staffed by experts in political and legal theory. Sengat-Kuo (graduate from the Faculty of Law in Paris and the National School of Administration), a scholar who joined the government on 3 July 1972 as deputy secretary general of the Presidency, was the main writer of the Constitution of 1972 (Nkot 2018: 199). At the same time, Paul Tessa (holder of a Degree in Public Law, a Diploma of Higher Studies in Public Law and a Diploma of Higher Studies in Political Science from the universities of Toulouse and Paris) (Echu 2010: 319) officiated at the Presidency of the Republic as Technical Advisor. President Ahidjo wanted to have a centralized executive in the country. This objective of the first president of Cameroon was considered by political scientists to be 'the inclination of a section of the English-speaking elite for compromise' (Nkot 2001: 258) based on the notion that certain scholars stated that the bourgeoisie of the Southern Cameroons betrayed the aspirations of the English-speaking populations (Nkot 2001: 181).

Intervening in the administration

Intellectuals assisted President Ahidjo to implement his various policies with violence (bullying, informing, humiliation, sham assassination etc.), advocacy (by campaigning domestically and abroad) and privileges, like promotions in political and administrative careers, and control over the university (Emagna 1996: 58–9).

In addition to the advisors in political and legal theory, several intellectuals joined the administration of the first president. One example is Adamou Ndam Njoya. He studied in Paris in the 1960s and obtained a degree in public law, a graduate diploma in political science, a state doctorate in public law and a diploma from the Institut des Hautes Etudes d'Outre-Mer. After returning to Cameroon in 1969, he occupied positions like secretary of foreign affairs, director of the Institute of International Relations, vice-minister of foreign affairs, minister delegate to the General Inspection of the State and of Administrative Reform, and minister of national education (Nkot 2018: 161). He left his mark in the last position in his quest for excellence in the school environment. In the arrangement of the Brevet des Etudes du Premier Cycle in 1980, this meant that students with low scores were suspended for a period of two years from examination – a measure which did not earn him friendships.

Augustin Frédérick Kodock became Secretary of State for Finance in July 1964. He was then seconded to the African Development Bank. Other intellectuals with qualifications in political studies and law also contributed to Mr Ahidjo's policy:

- Samuel Eboua (graduate of the Institut d'Etudes Politiques of the University of Paris); Ayang Luc (law degree from the University of Yaoundé in 1972 and Minister in charge of livestock since 1978);
- Ngome Kome Albert (degree in political and economic sciences from New York University and Master's degree in economic sciences from Lancaster University in Great Britain; occupied several administrative positions from 1969, Minister of Transport in 1979);
- Ntang Gilbert (holder of a law degree from the Faculty of Law and Economic Sciences of Caen, and a graduate of the l'Institut des hautes études d'Outre-mer; several positions of responsibility from 1963 and Minister of Finance in 1979);
- Joseph-Marie Bipoun Woum (law degree and Doctor of Law from the University of Toulouse; he graduated from the Institute of Political Studies and in 1972 was appointed Deputy Director of higher education at the Ministry of National Education, and in 1978 Director General of the Douala University Center);
- Joseph Owona (graduate diploma in political science, a state doctorate and Agrégation of public law, academic career between 1969 and 1982 serving as head of Department of Public Law at the University of Yaoundé, and Director of the Institute of International Relations of Cameroon).

Political scientists' role during the era of the second president

President Ahidjo left power on 4 November 1982. In his speech at the occasion, he called on all Cameroonians to 'give their wholehearted confidence, and to lend their support to [his] constitutional successor, Mr Paul Biya' (Nkot 2018: 190). The second president of Cameroon assured his predecessor of his 'loyalty'. However, during this transition part of the dignitaries did not want President Ahidjo to give up the power. The main debate was framed around a protocol controversy. While President Ahidjo had resigned as the head of state, he still remained the leader of Cameroon's single party (Cameroon National Union, UNC). The partisans of President Ahidjo were stating that the party is above the State and partisans of President Biya defended the opposite. This conflict led to the 1984 coup d'état.

The 1982 presidential succession

When taking power Paul Biya, a political scientist, had little room to manoeuvre in the institutional landscape demanding loyalty to the former president and the single party. Tsafack (2016: 5) argues that in resigning, Ahidjo thought that his status as the former president and incumbent President of the UNC, he be above the new head of state, which created a conflict between him and Paul Biya. In an interview with Jeune Afrique on 25 May 1983, Biya stated that he intended to exercise, without hindrance, all his constitutional responsibilities by firmly conducting the affairs of the state (Biya 1984: 291). Several political scientists and jurists backed his approach. For example, Joseph Owona and Jean-Pierre Fogui (Doctor of Political Science) collaborated on the special edition of the national daily dedicated to the first anniversary of the accession of President Paul Biya to power. Owona in an article '*Le parti et l'Etat : l'expérience camerounaise de la primauté de l'Etat*' and J-P Fogui in an article '*Le futur comme une attitude*' supported the idea of the primacy of the state over the party (Pokam 2010: 87).

The boldness and determination of President Biya prompted Ahidjo to resign as President of the CNU in September 1983. Following an attempted coup d'état on 6 April 1984, Paul Biya surround himself with loyal supporters, among these jurists and political scientists:

- Ngongang Ouandji – minister of state responsible for justice in 1984. He obtained a law degree at the Faculty of Law and Economic Sciences of the University of Bordeaux, as well as a DES in criminal sciences. He also studied political science at the Institut d'Etudes Politiques de Bordeaux;
- Sengat-Kuo François – minister of information and culture 1983, thought to be the editor of Paul Biya's speeches. He has a Bachelor of Laws degree;
- Zambo Joseph – graduated from the Institut des Hautes Etudes d'Outre-Mer in Paris in 1962 and obtained a degree in law and economic sciences from Yaoundé in 1966. Minister Delegate at the Presidency in Charge of Relations with Assemblies 1984;
- Ntsama Etienne – graduated from the Faculty of Law and Economic Sciences of Yaoundé, Minister of Finance in 1984.

Although Paul Biya took over the presidency of the UNC after Ahidjo's resignation, creating a new party was also on his agenda. At the CNU Congress held in Bamenda in 1985, the party changed its name and became the *Rassemblement Démocratique du Peuple Camerounais* (RDPC) /Cameroon Peoples' Democratic Movement (CPDM). Despite the emergence of several other political parties since the 1990s, the CPDM has dominated the political theatre with a strong participation of the intellectual elite, particularly the informed political scientists and jurists. Among the political and legal experts who have served as officials of the party are: the National President, Paul Biya; François Sengat-Kuo; Ekani Denis (Doctor of State in Law); Kontchou Kouomegni Augustin (BA in Public Law from the University of Yaoundé, diplomas in Public Law from the University of Paris II and in Political Science from the University of Paris I, as well a State Doctorate in Political Science from the University of Paris I, Panthéon Sorbonne); Eyebe Ayissi Henri (Degree in Public Law in 1978 and a Doctorate in Public Law obtained in 1981 from the University of Yaoundé); Messengue Avom Bernard (Doctor of Law from the University of

Law, Economics and Sciences of Aix-Marseille in France); Moukoko Mbonjo Pierre (Doctor of State in Political Science from the University of Paris I Sorbonne and graduate of the Institute of Political Studies of Paris); Ngolle Ngolle Elvis (BA in Political Science, International Relations option at More Head State University in the United States and a PhD in International Studies from the University of Denver in 1985); Sadi René Emmanuel (Law Degree from the University of Yaoundé); Antoine Zanga (degree from the University of Yaoundé, Diploma of Higher Studies in Public Law from the University of Social Sciences of Toulouse and a State Doctorate in Public Law from the University of Paris X-Nanterre). Narcisse Mouelle Kombi (Diploma of Advanced Studies in International Law, Diploma of Higher Studies in Political Science, Doctor of Law from the University of Paris V and Professor of Public Law and Political Science); Charlemagne Messanga Nyamding (Professor of Political Science and Public Law).

Contributions to the democratization process

At the beginning of the 1990s, Cameroon experienced sociopolitical turbulence resulting from the economic crisis which largely affected the educated middle classes already frustrated by slow political rotation. City dwellers were impoverished and threatened by mass layoffs, while the State was neither able to meet its obligations towards public servants, nor to provide employment to until then privileged young graduates (Bigombe Logo and Menthong 1996: 16). This led to social unrest and an uprising by certain politicians. Public opinion called for greater liberalization of political life, which resulted in the adoption of the laws on freedom of association, in 1990, allowing meetings and public demonstrations, and freedom of social communication. Several political scientists and jurists set up new political parties as an alternative to the regime in place. In 1991, Adamou Ndam Njoya founded the Democratic Union of Cameroon and Hameni Bielieu Victorin created the Union of Democratic Forces in Cameroon. The Union of Populations of Cameroon was created by Secretary-General Augustin Frédérick Kodock.

Despite these new parties, calm was not observed in sociopolitical life. The opposition parties sought to compel the government to convene a sovereign national conference. In October 1991, President Paul Biya nominated two commissions for the development of a draft electoral code and a media code and proposed legislative elections for early 1992 (Bigombe Logo and Menthong 1996: 17). The tripartite conference of government, political parties and independent personalities took place in Yaoundé, from 30 October to 18 November 1991. Several members were political scientists. Its Technical Committee comprised Augustin Kontchou Kouomegni, Bipoun Woum Joseph-Marie and Simon Munzu (who has a Doctorate in Law from the University of Cambridge). The Commission dedicated to the Electoral Code consisted of Joseph Owona, Roger Gabriel Nlep (Doctor of Law) Bernard Momo (Doctor of Law and specialist in Constitutional Law). The Human Rights Commission included Fogui Jean-Pierre and Ngongo Louis Paul (both with a Doctor of State in Political Science). The Constitutional Technical Committee included Ephraim Ngwafor (Bachelor of Laws from the University of Yaoundé, an LLM from the Dalhousie Law School in 1978 and a PhD from the University of London). Nicole Claire Ndoko (Doctor of Law) and Ewang Sone Andrew (Doctor of Law) also participated.

The decisions made at this tripartite conference helped to set Cameroon on the path of democratization. During this period Roger Gabriel Nlep conceptualized the theory of 'triangle équilatéral' for the three large ethnic complexes in Cameroon to become legitimate platforms for the exercise of state power (Nkot 2018: 224) and of the 'electoral village' to draw the attention of political actors to popular participation (Nkot 2018: 235).

An abundance of political and legal literature was produced analysing the events and their implications during that important moment in the history of Cameroon. For Luc Sindjoun, professor of political science, while the monolithic state had disappeared, 'the top' in control of the society remained to a very large extent the same. However, this hegemony was tainted with a devaluation of power (Courade and Sindjoun 1996: 6). Owona Nguini and Menthong noted that between the years 1990 and 2010, an electoral process opened up opportunities for new parties, such as the Social Democratic Front (SDF) led by Ni John Fru Ndi, the National Union for Democracy and Progress (UNDP) first led by Samuel Eboua and since 1991 by Maïgari Bello Bouba, or the Cameroon Democratic Union (UDC) since 1991 led since by Adamou Ndam Njoya (Owona Nguini and Menthong 2018: 101).

Referring to the place occupied by the university during the democratization process of the 1990s, Ngwe, Folefack, Mandjack and Pokam noted its prominence. Caught in the double dynamic of global restructuring of the state – redefining education at the international level, and socio-economic reconfiguration at the local level – it and its agents actively participated in the political processes of the 1990s. The political changes which crystallized at and on the university made it into an issue of struggle and established it as an arena between politicians and groups competing for the management of the country (Ngwé et al. 2006: 187–8).

Contributions to the consolidation of presidential power

The contribution made by political scientists and jurists to the consolidation of power by the second president was manifest in the drafting of the 1996 Constitution and their participation in the management of public affairs.

The 1996 Constitution

After the events of 1990 and the legislative and municipal elections of 1992, mechanisms were put in place for the next presidential elections. A broad national debate was convened in 1993 to examine the proposed changes to the new version of the Constitution. At the time, there was a general public debate on the constitution. The main issues at stake were (1) the constitutionalizing of the decentralization, with people in favour of a federation versus a unitary decentralized state; and (2) the terms limitation of the mandate of the President. The Technical Committee responsible for examining and refining the proposals in 1992 included three political scientists and jurists among its eleven members, namely Joseph Owona, Simon Munzu, Carlson Anyangwe (PhD in law from the University of London). Misunderstandings arose between the seven French and English speakers during the process.

The President of the Committee, Joseph Owona, gave a draft of the Constitution to the prime minister in March 1993. The English-speaking elites gathered for a Conference in April 1993 in Buea and set up its own Standing Committee that developed a draft Federal Constitution, which was submitted to the Technical Committee of the National Constitution in May 1993. The final Constitution of Cameroon was promulgated in January 1996.

When the process of revising the 1966 Constitution was carried out in 2008, Maurice Kamto (Doctor of Law from the University of Nice and agrégé of Law in 1988) was minister delegate to the minister of justice and keeper of the seals.

Political theorists and jurists have fuelled debates on the 1996 Constitution over the years. Some scholars stated that the text promulgated by the President of the Republic is a law revising the Constitution of 1972. It is a logical consequence that the Cameroonian approach of 1996 affirms its regularity, according to Kenfack Temfack (2005). For Sindjoun (1996: 13) the legal category of 'constitutional revision' does not restore all the originality and richness of the constituent act of 1996.

The idea that the text promulgated in 1996 is the new constitution of Cameroon is based on a series of arguments, in particular those of Kamto. This intellectual claimed that the draft submitted to the National Assembly did not indicate anything about the provisions that were to be modified. He argued that, as a result, virtually the entire 1972 Constitution has been revised. This is the same position as that adopted by Mr Donfack Sokeng, who affirmed that the law amending the Constitution of 1972 is the logical demonstration that the Cameroonian stride of 1996, approbates its consistency (Kenfack Temfack 2005).

For some, the constitutional revisions in Cameroon all had the same objective, namely the personalization of power, as argued by Matip and Koutouki (2009: 3). Donfack Sokeng (1996) considered it a manifestation of the relentless struggle of the forces present for the control of the supreme power of the state which was symbolized by the mastery of the constituent power.

Participation in the administration of the second president

As with the Ahidjo regime, political scientists and jurists widely embraced President Biya's policies. In addition to the intellectuals already mentioned, the following have served under the second president: Augustin Frédérick Kodock; Kontchou Kouomegni Augustin; Jean-Pierre Fogui; Ekani Denis; Monie John Nkengong; Enoch Kwayeb; Joseph Owona; Antoine Zanga; Rémy Zé Meka; Paul Tessa; Garga Haman Adji; Eyebe Ayissi Henri; Joseph-Marie Bipoun Woum; Kamto Maurice; Messengue Avom Bernard; Moukoko Mbonjo Pierre; Elvis Ngolle Ngolle; Ephraim Ngwafor; Lekene Donfack Etienne; Sadi René Emmanuel; Sindjoun Luc; Narcisse Mouelle Kombi; Ondoa Magloire; Nkot Pierre Fabien; and Bernard Momo.

Techniques used to consolidate President Biya's policies

In addition to participation in the management of public affairs, the aforementioned political and legal experts have supported the head of state during political meetings of the CPDM. However, they have also produced publications thwarting ideas that have embarrassed the existing regime. Intellectuals have participated in debates in the public fora, symposia and debates, to scrutinize the use of public power.

When French President Emmanuel Macron visited the Paris Agricultural Show on 22 February 2020, an individual of African descent reminded him of the ongoing genocide in the North-West and South-West regions of Cameroon. Narcisse Mouelle Kombi, Professor of Public Law and Political Science, released a statement stating that President Paul Biya, whose virtues of humanism, tolerance, patience and compassion are indisputable, had not stopped working for the definitive return to lasting peace and a normal resumption of activities in the North-West and South-West regions (Mouelle Kombi 2020).

Following the legislative elections in 2020, the ruling party secured 139 seats out of the total 167 (the polls were cancelled in 11 electoral districts due to due to the conflict in the North-West and South-West regions of the country). Manasse Aboya Endong, professor of political science at the University of Douala, commented on the results as follows: 'the result is a reflection of the balance of power in the Cameroonian political field'. Sindjoun (2020) spoke about the criticism of the organization of these legislative and municipal elections, arguing that discussion of the imperfections of the electoral code or the situation in the North-West and South-West regions as the causes of the boycott of the legislative and municipal elections were unfounded. According to him the discussion on the rate of participation in legislative and municipal elections was ill-informed about the general problems of electoral participation in democracy. Moreover, the discussion on the overwhelming majority of the political party, CPDM, was ignorant of the legitimate emergence of a dominant party in an electoral democracy.

The sociopolitical crisis of the North-West and South-West regions

The English-speaking question is the result of the historic route that the country has followed under the domination of the French and English powers. The unification that took place in 1972 under conditions that some have described as turbulent is the true starting point of this nagging question because the state changed from a federated format to a unitary format and saw the start of the assimilation of the English-speaking minority by the French-speaking majority (Nkot 2005).

The English-speaking problem

Among the intellectuals, there are contradictory hypotheses on various aspects of the English-speaking crisis. These issues relate to such matters as the validity of the referendum that enshrined the advent of the unitary state, and the legitimacy of the protest mobilized by the English-speaking population.

With regard to the validity of the referendum, the specific question is whether the constitution that established the unitary state was a new law or a revision of the 1961 text? Two theses compete. One sees it as a constitutional amendment. This approach is supported by political scientists and jurists such as Joseph Owona, Alain Didier Olinga, Lekene Donfack Etienne, François Mbome (Professor of Law). The other hypothesis that the question was about a new constitution is defended by Maurice Kamto (Nkot 2001: 53–69).

Mode of contestation

Mathias Eric Owona Nguini (Political Science graduate from the University of Bordeaux and Lecturer at the University of Yaoundé 2) criticized the seizure of arms by the separatists in the North-West and South-West regions, when he took part in a live TV broadcast on the programme 'Club d'élites' on Vision 4 in 2020. He disapproved of the claims of the 11 March 2020 edition of a local newspaper, 'le Messager' giving pride to the secessionist leader of the Virtual Republic of Ambazonia. Aboya Manasse Endong underlined 'the non-legitimacy of the street as a means of coming to power' during a conference organized by the Friedrich Ebert Stiftung, on 3 February 2020. Serge Banyongen (PhD in international relations) did not agree with the two previous intellectuals. He believed that the violent strategy was adopted because of the failure of other strategies (Banyongen 2017).

Solving the Anglophone problem

The corporatist claims of lawyers and teachers registered in the North-West and South-West regions in 2016 gave way to violent separatist conflict. In order to address this problem, the Head of State convened a Major National Dialogue in 2019. This Dialogue was preceded by preparatory consultations conducted by the Prime Minister. Several political scientists took part in these exchanges, including:

- Ntuda Ebode Joseph Vincent (Professor of Political Science and International Relations, and Coordinator of the Center for Research and Political and Strategic Studies of the University of Yaoundé 2) and Alain Didier Olinga in the delegation from the Center Region;
- Messanga Nyamding and James Mouangué Kobila (Professor of Public Law at the University of Douala) in the delegation from the Littoral Region;
- Ondoua Alain Franklin (Professor of Public Law, Dean of the Faculty of Law and Political Sciences of the University of Yaoundé II) and Machikou Ndzesop Nadine (Professor of Political Science) in the delegation from the University of Yaoundé II.

During the Major National Dialogue, political scientists and jurists worked in various bodies that had been set up.

- The commission dedicated to bilingualism, cultural diversity and social cohesion had Moukoko Mbonjo Pierre as Vice-President.
- The commission on the education system had in its team of rapporteurs Nguele Abada Marcelin (professor of public law).
- The commission that focused on the education system had as Vice-President Fogui Jean-Pierre and Rapporteur, James Mouangué Kobila.
- In the commission dedicated to the return of refugees, Elvis Ngolle Ngolle was vice-president.
- Nkene Blaise (associate professor of political science) officiated as Rapporteur in the Commission that worked on disarmament, demobilization and reintegration of ex-combatants.
- The Commission that examined the role of the diaspora in the crisis and its contribution to the development of the country had Machinkou Ndzesop Nadine as its Rapporteur.
- The Commission on Decentralization and Local Development had as Vice-President Lekene Donfack, and one of the rapporteurs was Cheuwa Jean Claude (professor of public law).
- In the team dedicated to the preparation of the General Report of the work, was Cheka Cosmas (professor of law at the University of Yaoundé 2).

Political scientists' contradictory approach to the regime in place

The focus of this chapter has been on the activities of political scientists who have supported the regimes in place. It has also noted the role of those who have criticized the regimes. Most of the latter are members of opposition political parties. From the outset, it emerged that these political opponents had worked for the political regime before adopting an opposing view. Among these intellectuals, who had been notably high-ranking officials in the administration, is Abel Eyinga. He founded the 'La Nationale' party (Nkot 2018: 94–95), under whose auspices he ran (unsuccessfully) in the 1996 municipal elections to be mayor of the city of Ebolowa. Other political figures who have opposed President Paul Biya include François Sengat-Kuo; Adamou Ndam Njoya, who was the founding president of the party 'Democratic Union of Cameroon', Garga Haman Hadji, Hameni Bielieu Victorin and Maurice Kamto.

The flexibility of these political scientists and intellectuals raises questions about their motivations, and it was suggested that this type of intellectual resembles either the figure of the Prince or that of the opponent. In their careers, as in the preparation for their retirement, they base their strategy (of career) on the alliance or antagonism with the Prince of the moment (Emagna 1996: 77). But one could also be tempted to think that if the policy implemented by the political regime no longer suits the aspirations of these opponents, they decide to stand out in an attempt to influence public opinion and obtain power.

Conclusion

This chapter has demonstrated that political scientists and jurists have intervened in the sociopolitical evolution of Cameroon. Therefore, they were inclined to follow the path of Jean-Paul Sartre. It is important to note the differentiated approach favoured by this category of intellectuals. Some remain in the comfort of their 'laboratories' and formulate ideas and theories to facilitate understanding of the political game or to provide knowledge to other actors in the field. The political leaders know how to capitalize the interests of these scholars to their advantage because the vocation of an educator is an awakening of conscience. By giving it legitimacy and additional credit the intellectual is a resource for the ruling regime. (Emagna 1996: 58).

At the same time, the intellectuals who opted to oppose the current regime are helping to animate the political game. Through their interpolative action, they oblige the political oligarchy to adjust its action in the direction of greater consideration of the general interest. If we focus on the strength of political scientists and jurists, both in the ruling group and in the opposition camp, we are tempted to believe that the political 'ring' in Cameroon is a battle between these types of intellectuals who oppose each other for the victory of their faction and, therefore, of their ideology. Using this logic, the question is about legitimization of the action of the protagonists in the arena or else to discredit the processes used by the opposing party. In any event, the recorded action-reaction dialectic contributes to thinking that, and as argued by Lamont (1982: 38), the interest of intellectuals is on the one hand to access institutions and institutional resources, and on the other hand to maximize the legitimacy of the institutions in which they are inserted.

16

A critical review of politics and the state of academic freedom in Ghana's public universities

From pre-independence till the Fourth Republic

Kwadwo Appiagyei-Atua

Introduction

At the institutional level, academic freedom is a defining characteristic of the health of universities. Similarly, at the societal level, academic freedom is indicative of the political cultural and democratic values within the wider community. This conclusion provides the premise to examine as the first issue in this chapter, what constitutes academic freedom followed by an analysis of the relationship between academic freedom and the respect for democracy.

Next, the work discusses the introduction of university education in the Gold Coast and later Ghana and the establishment of Ghana's first three public universities, namely, the University of Ghana (UG), the Kwame Nkrumah University of Science and Technology (KNUST) and the University of Cape Coast (UCC). In conjunction with that, the work devotes attention to a historical analysis of the respect for academic freedom in Ghana, which is broken up into phases influenced by the kind of political system that was/is in vogue. This analysis is done against the background of the democratic situation in the country in order to test the relationship between academic freedom and democracy.

The chapter subsequently focuses attention on the three case studies identified to examine academic freedom under threat under Ghana's Fourth Republic, namely the incident at the KNUST, the conversion of polytechnics into technical universities and controversies surrounding the Public University Bill (PUB) 2018. Finally, the work deals with the subject of managerialism embodied in neopatrimonialism as the basis for the PUB. Lastly, conclusion is drawn and recommendations are given in the context of the trends of the developments of academic freedom in the case of political changes in Ghana.

Defining academic freedom and establishing its relationship with democracy

As stated elsewhere, academic freedom is a concept that is characterized by variegated meanings (Gerber 2001; Latif 2014). In this chapter, unless the context otherwise indicates, academic freedom is defined as a freedom carved out for the academic community to provide access and opportunity for the conduct of scientific enquiry, the consequent production of knowledge and the dissemination of the knowledge or findings thereof. The dissemination is done principally through teaching, publication and the application of these findings to promote the full development of the human personality and other benefits to society. The enquiry, production of knowledge and its dissemination are done within the limits of public order, professional ethics and social responsibility and without restraint or the threat of sanctions by the government and other power brokers (Appiagyei-Atua, Beiter and Karran 2015). The generic definition is anchored on four pillars or freedoms which constitute the specific understandings of academic freedom. These are institutional autonomy, self-governance, individual rights and freedoms (for both academics and students) and tenure.[1]

Academic freedom does not take place in a vacuum. Largely, respect for, protection of and fulfilment of the exigencies of freedom is shaped by the democratic conditions in a particular state. Conceptions of democracy are based on the fundamental ideas of popular sovereignty, accountability and collective decision-making, all anchored in respect for human rights and fundamental freedoms. Therefore, the kind of democratic credentials of a country is determined by the variable incorporation of different rights protections. It follows then that in principle, the more democratic a society is, the higher the level of respect for academic freedom. That is to say, democracy should guarantee respect for academic freedom (and other rights and freedoms). Bergan (2002: 49) supports this view when he considers academic freedom to be the heart of a democratic society and, therefore, democracy is hardly conceivable without academic freedom.

Alternatively, academic freedom can be used as a vehicle to fight for greater respect for other rights and freedoms in the larger society. In this second scenario, because of the privileged position of academics and students (as a result of their ability to protect and enjoy at least some level of academic freedom within the university space), they are better placed to critique governments and the corporate sector and to ensure their accountability to the society. Appiagyei-Atua et al. espouse this second approach through the composite theory which talks about the dual benefit of academic freedom for society. First, the traditional benefit – when knowledge is produced to meet societal needs. Second, when academic freedom becomes the measuring rod for society to enjoy similar rights commensurate with its own needs, thereby invoking a duty on the academic community not to remain insular but to use its freedom to promote effective gown-town relationships (Appiagyei-Atua, Beiter and Karran 2015: 325–6). Busia and Degni-Segui also lend support to this second proposition by arguing that no serious

---

[1]   See below for a detailed discussion of these concepts.

analyst can deny the important implications of the protection of academic freedom for the broader democratic and human rights discourses and struggles, and even the quest for economic development in contemporary Africa (Busia and Degni-Segui 1996: 13).

However, at the same time, academic freedom is everywhere threatened by the rising trend of managerialism in higher education. The main changes occasioned by managerialism are represented by the loss of the universities of their shared governance, collegiality, academic tenure and professional autonomy (Deem 1998). This phenomenon has the tendency to muddy the waters and create some difficulty in using the democracy matrix to gauge the state of academic freedom in even more advanced democratic nations (Beiter, Karran and Appiagyei-Atua 2016).

Formation of UG, KNUST and UCC

The British colonial policy of promoting mercantilism, empire-building and hegemony (Gathii 2007) did not give room for the promotion of higher education in the colonies. A few mission schools were established to accomplish the *mission civilisatrice* agenda of the missionary churches. This entrenched colonial position began to take a different turn when decolonization became imminent and unavoidable (Boahen 1975; Madeira 2011; Enwo–Irem 2013). The policy goal to embrace higher education was, however, grounded in developing a core of Europeanized elite to maintain, after colonialism, the politico-economic framework put in place by the colonial enterprise (Mamdani 1994).

The Asquith Commission report (Asquith Report 1945)[2] which became Britain's 'blueprint for the export of universities to her people overseas' (Ashby and Anderson 1966: 214) saw the establishment of three main universities in Africa, including the University College of the Gold Coast in 1948 (Nwauwa 1997; Zeleza 2003), which was established through the University College of the Gold Coast Ordinance of August 11, 1948. The purpose for its establishment was, among others, to 'provid[e] for and promot[e] university education, learning and research' (University of Ghana n.d).

Four years after gaining independence from British colonial rule, UCG evolved into UG through an Act of Parliament – the University of Ghana Act, 1961 (Act 79) – which came into being on 1 October 1961.

The next public university to be established was the Kumasi College of Technology (KCT) in 1951 which started following a recommendation in the Watson Commission report to that effect (Colonial No 231, 1948). Like UCG, KCT was affiliated with the University of London. In 1961, the college was granted full university status and renamed the Kwame Nkrumah University of Science and Technology (KNUST), through the Kwame Nkrumah University of Science and Technology, Kumasi Act 80 (1961). The name was changed to the University of Science and Technology after the overthrow of Kwame Nkrumah, Ghana's first President, through a coup d'état on

2   In addition, there was the Commission on Higher Education in West Africa (the Elliot Commission) established by the British government to assess the future of higher education in Anglophone West Africa. The latter commission also called for the establishment of university colleges at Ibadan in Nigeria and the reorganization of the Fourah Bay College in Sierra Leone.

24 February 1966. However, another Act of Parliament, 1998 (Act 559) changed the name back to the Kwame Nkrumah University of Science and Technology.

The third university, UCC first opened as the University College of Cape Coast (UCCC) in 1962 and was affiliated with UG. It was set up to train graduate teachers for second cycle institutions in the country. The UCCC was reconstituted as the University College of Science Education in October 1964 and reverted to its original name after the coup of 1966. Finally, in 1971, it became a full-fledged university under the University of Cape Coast Act, 1971 (Act 390).

The state of academic freedom within the public universities,

1948–57

The British colonial authorities sought to entrench and protect the UCGC's right to academic freedom straight from its birth, though not embodied in the Ordinance establishing the institution itself. Governor Sir Gerald Creasy, the then colonial representative in the Gold Coast, at the opening of the university college, emphasized that the UCGC was 'an autonomous institution, entirely independent of the Government' (Agbodeka 1998: 6).

Yet, for the first thirteen years of its existence and until it was converted to a university, the UCGC looked up to two separate institutions in Great Britain: the Inter-Universities Council which served the UCGC in an advisory capacity and approved all academic appointments, in fulfilment of the requirements of the Asquith Commission.[3] The other was the University of London for approval and control of details of degree regulations. The latter arrangement placed the university college under the suzerainty of the University of London. The UCGC's first principal, Mr Mowbray Balme, criticized this arrangement as being 'singularly ill-suited because of its autocratic constitution in which the Vice-Chancellor, with the connivance of the professors, make absolute decisions' (Austin 1976: 170). In other words, the UCGC did not enjoy institutional autonomy due to the suzerain nature of the relationship it had with the University of London. The case with KCT was no different as it was also affiliated with the University of London.

African leaders initially unequivocally expressed the need to promote academic freedom within the universities (UNESCO 1962; Dlamini 2002). Dr Kwame Nkrumah, the first President of the Republic of Ghana, did the same (O'Brien 1964: 488). Thus, at the Tananarive Conference of 1962 organized by African States in conjunction with the United Nations Educational, Scientific and Cultural Organisation (UNESCO), to map out a strategy for African universities, academic freedom found its way into the communique issued at the end of the event (UNESCO 1962).

---

[3]   One of the recommendations of the Asquith Commission was that the British Government should set up an Inter-Universities Council to advise on all matters relating to Higher Education in the new British Colonies.

Yet, it did not take long for the honeymoon to be compromised when the Nkrumah government resorted to autocratic rule and was met with dissent on the university campuses. Events began to unravel when in 1960, Ghana declared itself a republic and jettisoned the 1957 Independence Constitution for the First Republic Constitution. Both constitutions did not guarantee respect for academic freedom. The 1960 Constitution saw a whittling down of the human rights provisions in the previous constitution to only trifling references to human rights contained under Article 13 thereof on 'Declaration of Fundamental principles'.

The coming into force of the 1960 Republican Constitution saw the downward spiral of Ghana's democracy towards a 'creeping dictatorship' (Walters 1993: 227). Consequently, Nkrumah is quoted as saying, 'if reforms do not come from within, we intend to impose them from outside, and no resort to the cry of academic freedom (for academic freedom does not mean irresponsibility) is going to [restrain] us' (qtd. Mkandawire 1997: 20).

The single party system which replaced the liberal democratic order that the departing colonialists sought to establish through the independence constitution of Ghana and other African countries, was built on the principle that there can be no dissent against any policy initiative taken by the leadership of the party. Therefore, the ruling party sought to suppress attempts by the academic community to create, in their words, 'a state within a state' and the urgent need to bring them under control and be incorporated into the party structure. The department of political science and the department of law were particularly critical of the Nkrumah regime.

As part of this dictatorial ambition, the Convention People's Party (CPP) regime of Nkrumah schemed to water down academic freedom in the University Acts for UG and KNUST. Among others, under Section 4 of the University of Ghana Act, the position of Chancellor of the University was reposed in the head of state, making Dr Kwame Nkrumah the first Chancellor of the university. The university council was given the power to appoint the vice-chancellor with the approval of the chancellor (S6 Act 79).

The Chairman of the University Council was appointed by the Chancellor and was vested with the power of acting as Chancellor in the absence of the Chancellor (S5 Act 79). Also, the Chancellor was part of the University Council. Thus, the towering presence of the Chancellor in the Council was conspicuous. Moreover, the council was packed with government officials or government appointees.[4] Further, under Section 10 of Act 79, the University Council was given broad powers 'to do or provide for any act or thing in relation to the University which it considers necessary or expedient in its capacity as the governing body'.[5]

As a result, violations of academic freedom in the three public universities, especially UG, campus were rife, among which were dismissal of some staff without due process, planting of spies in the classrooms to report on dissident' lecturers, co-opting of the national student (the National Union of Ghana Students (NUGS) and its replacement

---

[4] See similar provisions under sections 4, 5 and 6 of the KNUST Act.
[5] See a similar provision under section 7 of the KNUST Act.

by another body which was more compliant to the whims of Dr Nkrumah (Finlay 1968) and Kwapong 1966: 543).

1966–72

Following the overthrow of Nkrumah in the 1966 coup, the basic laws of the three existing public universities at the time remained in place. However, in general, the military regime that took over the reins of the government did not use the provisions of these laws to suppress academic freedom in practice The new Head of State and Chairman of the National Liberation Council (NLC), Lt-General Ankrah, assumed the position of Chancellor of the three universities between 1966 and 1967, a position he handed later over to the co-chair of the NLC, Brigadier Afrifa.

The *Legon Observer*, a fortnightly magazine, started publication with its base at the department of political science of UG and established itself as a critical voice against the NLC.

Ghana returned to constitutional rule in 1969 following the coming into force of the Second Republican Constitution. This Constitution, however, did not introduce any reform of the laws regulating the functioning of the public universities. Among the few innovations which affected the university directly was the establishment of a new office of the Ombudsman whose functions included investigating any action taken by, or on behalf of, public bodies, including higher education institutions (Article 11, Constitution of the Republic of Ghana 1969).

Also, under the Second Republic, Article 49 (b) of the Constitution vested the appointment of the Chairman and other members of the Council for higher education in the ceremonial president.[6] However, again relying on the 1961 Act for UG and for UST, Mr Akuffo-Addo, the then president of the Republic, was made the chairman of the University Council..

In the case of UCC, the 1971 Act establishing it as a full-fledged university under the second Republic, Section 9(3), the president was given the power, acting in accordance with the advice of the prime minister, to constitute the university council. The chancellor was appointed by the President in consultation with the university council (s5(1) of the UCC Act). Pro-chancellor as chair of council appointed by the president acting on the advice of the prime minister (S6(1) of the UCC Act). The vice-chancellor was appointed by the president on the advice of the prime minister and on the recommendation of the university council (S7(1) of the UCC Act).

1972–81

The 1969 Constitution was overthrown in 1972 by the National Redemption Council (NRC) headed by Col Kutu Acheampong who became the Chancellor of the three universities when he assumed power. When the NRC morphed into the Supreme Military Council, (SMC), it sought to introduce a new form of governance structure

---

6   The Second Republican Constitution followed the parliamentary model of governance with the position of President being ceremonial.

dubbed the 'Union Government' which was a power-sharing arrangement between civilian politicians, the police and the armed forces, thus doing away with partisan politics. The proposal was vehemently opposed by important stakeholders in the country, including university students who saw it as a surreptitious attempt by the military regime to perpetuate itself in power. The *Legon Observer* was used as a vehicle to express opposition to the machinations of the Acheampong regime. Therefore, the government banned it from 1974 until 1978 by withholding foreign exchange to import newsprint and also caused the arrested and detention of its editors. Through the application of these measures, academic freedom on UG premises suffered brutal repression.

Violent student demonstrations as a reaction led to the closure of Ghana's universities. In reaction, the government of the day sought to place the universities under the Ministry of Education to control and deny them their institutional autonomy.

The most promising change in the quest by Ghanaians for respect for academic freedom in the universities occurred in 1979 when under the Third Republican Constitution, Article 55(1) thereof granted the university the autonomy to appoint its own chancellor and barred the president, while he continued in office as president, from holding the office of the chancellor or head of any university in Ghana (Constitution of the Republic of Ghana 1979). However, a new chancellor could not be appointed in any of the three public universities during this period due to a lack of agreement among the university administration, the National Commission on Higher Education (NCHE) and the Attorney-General on what process to follow.

These were innovative and positive provisions that would have secured greater respect for academic freedom at public universities. However, that draft amendment never saw the light of day. Thus, between 1980 and 1981 when the Limann government was in power, there was no Chancellor for the three public universities.

Another relevant provision in the 1979 Constitution on academic freedom was article 157(8) which granted university councils the power to appoint their own chairman. However, again, the Council did not exercise that power but allowed the University of Ghana Act to regulate the appointment, which vested that power in the President. The same was the case with UST and UCC.

Thus, we see a situation where the return to democracy led to gradual and incremental attempts to open up the space for the reintroduction of respect for academic freedom. Yet, it looks like the universities were not ready to embrace these opportunities.

1981–92

The 1979 Constitution was overthrown two years later through another *coup d'état* led by Jerry John Rawlings who brought in the Provisional National Defence Council (PNDC). With the overthrow of the Constitution, Rawlings was made Chancellor of all the public universities. For example, in the University of Ghana (Amendment) Act (PNDCL 239) it was provided under section 1(1) thereof that 'the Head of State shall hold the office of Chancellor and as such shall be the head of the University'.

The same law, however, introduced some innovative steps under section 7(2) of PNDC Law 239 which saw the expansion of the list of memberships of the University Council, a positive move towards greater respect for self-governance within the university. However, the retrogressive part of the arrangement was that all the members of the Council were appointed by the PNDC (S7(1), PNDCL 239). Similar arrangements were made for UST and UCC.[7] In the case of UCC, a three-member interim administration committee body was appointed to serve as the University Council though the UCC Act was not abolished.[8]

1992–present

One of the constitutional reforms brought about in the 1992 Constitution is the explicit introduction of academic freedom in the Constitution. Thus, Article 21(1) (b) of the Fourth Republican Constitution of the Republic of Ghana 1992) provides (Constitution of the Republic of Ghana 1992):

> All persons shall have the right to freedom of thought, conscience and belief, which shall include academic freedom.

UG stands out among the three universities as the first and the only public university to institute changes to its basic laws in response to the 1992 Constitution by enacting a new Statute in 2004. However, the 1961 University of Ghana Act remained in force. Among the innovations introduced in the 2004 Statute was the power granted to the University Council to appoint its own Chancellor. The Chancellor in turn was vested with the authority to appoint the chairman of the University Council in consultation with the Executive Committee of the Academic Board (S 5(1) 2004 Statute, UG). This provision falls in line with Article 195(3) of the 1992 Constitution which vests the power of appointment of persons to hold office in a body of higher education, research or professional training, in the council or other governing body of that institution or body.

A new University of Ghana Act 806 finally came into force on 5 October 2010. A year later, a new Statute was enacted to replace that of 2004. The Act and Statute, however, reversed the procedure for the appointment of the chairperson of the university council to the President, in contravention of Article 195(3) of the 1992 Constitution.

Establishment of new universities

Under the Fourth Republic, starting in 1992, a number of universities have been set up while others have been upgraded to university status by the government. Ghana's fourth university, the University for Development Studies (UDS), was established in Tamale, the Northern regional capital, under the University for Development

---

[7]   See sections 5,6,9 on Chancellor, Chairman of Council and composition of Council P.N.D.C.L. 278, University of Cape Coast Act, 19921(1) continued in existence.
[8]   See University of Cape Coast (Interim Administration Committee) Law, 1990 PNDC Law 243.

Studies Act, 1992 (PNDC Law 279). The Ghana Institute of Management and Public Administration (GIMPA) was established by the Ghana Institute of Management and Public Administration Act, 2004 (Act 676). It started as a joint Ghana Government/United Nations (UN) special fund project in 1961. Under s2 of Act 676, GIMPA is established as a public tertiary institution. It is granted financial autonomy and academic autonomy subject to the provisions of the Act. The Rector is appointed by the Council. The chairperson and the other members of the Council are appointed by the President (S5(3) GIMPA Act).

The University of Education, Winneba (UEW) was established in September 1992 as a University College under PNDC Law 322. On 14th May 2004, the University of Education Act 672 was enacted to upgrade the status of the University College of Education of Winneba to the status of a full University. Under s12(1) of the Act, the council is given the power to appoint a Chancellor of the University. Also, Section 13(1) provides that there shall be a vice-chancellor or pro-vice-chancellor as the Council may determine who shall be appointed by the Council.

Other universities established within this time frame, among others, are the University of Professional Studies, Accra, which was set up under the University of Professional Studies Act, 2012 and the University of Energy and Natural Resources (UENR) that was established through the University of Energy and Natural Resources Act, 2011 (Act 830). The University of Mines and Technology (UMaT) became a full-fledged university in November 2004 through the University of Mines and Technology, Tarkwa Act, 2004 (Act 677). The University of Health and Allied Sciences, Ho (UHAS) was established by an Act of Parliament (Act 828). All these have similar governance structures as the above.

Academic freedom under threat (2016–20): Three case studies

Technical universities saga

In 2016, the Technical Universities Act, 2016 (Act 922) was enacted by the previous government which converted six of the ten polytechnics in the country into technical universities (TUs). Yet, the new government which came to power following the 2016 elections sought to place a number of stumbling blocks in the way of the TUs, most likely to prevent the operationalisation of the new Act.

Among other things, the National Council for Tertiary Education (NCTE) issued a number of draft documents (called the 'Harmonised Statutes') in a letter to the Governing Councils of the six TUs demanding that the documents be circulated as inputs for approval of the governing councils. The NCTE further directed the Governing Councils that no substantive appointments shall be made to positions in the Technical Universities until the proposed 'Harmonised Statutes' had been approved (Awini 2017).

These directives from the NCTE, however, contravened some provisions of the TU Act. The first is Section 26 of the Act which confers the power to enact Statutes on the Council of each TU. Therefore, the letter constituted the usurpation of the councils' powers by the NCTE. The directive to ratify the proposed 'harmonised' conditions of service also contravened Section 42 of the Labour Act, 2003 (Act 651) which relates to the right of workers to negotiate terms and conditions of employment in Ghana.

Following the opposition expressed by the TUs to the NCTE letter, including taking the matter to court, the Minister of Education came up with an amendment to the TU Act in December of the same year, seeking to regularize, by way of legislation, the very things the NCTE sought to do. For example, Clause 1 of the Amendment Bill provides that 'Section 14 of the Technical Universities Act, 2016 (Act 922) (which vests in the TU governing councils the power to appoint Chancellors for their institutions) is amended by the substitution for subsection (2) of the criteria and modalities for the nomination and election of the Chancellor shall be prescribed by the Statutes of the Technical University'. Then clause 6 of the Amendment Bill provides that the previously rejected Harmonised Statutes shall be what will regulate the TUs. According to a leading member of the joint Technical Universities Association, Peter Awini Seidu, the bill 'has the tendency to distort the stable and enduring governance processes, structure, culture and administration of public universities in the country' (Arthur 2018).

The KNUST Saga

The university authorities at KNUST decided in 2018 to convert the all-male Katanga Hall and Continental Hall into mixed halls, which was resisted by the students. The decision was not welcomed by the affected students who organized a peaceful night vigil to protest the decision. However, the event was violently disrupted by campus security forces leading to some alleged molestations against the students. In reaction, the students embarked on a peaceful demonstration which degenerated into violence, destruction of property and the subsequent closure of the university (Lartey 2018).

The government then decided to dissolve the KNUST governing council and, in its place, inaugurate a new interim governing council (IGC) to assume the powers of the governing council. The seven-member body included student representation but most conspicuously absent was representation from the University Teachers Association of Ghana (UTAG) and the Teachers Education Workers' Union (TEWU). The vice-chancellor was also asked to step aside.

However, all these decisions were not based on the KNUST Act. A strike action by the UTAG and TEWU led to a reversal of the government decisions, including the reinstatement of the university council.

The Public University Bill 2018

PUB represents, perhaps, the most pervasive attempt by a government to subject the university to its ultimate control and caprices as the Bill sought to affect all the four elements of academic freedom – institutional autonomy, self-governance, individual rights and freedoms for academics, tenure and students' academic freedom.

The first area of concern was that the composition of the university council had majority representation from the government, with the chairperson nominated by the president and the president having the right to appoint the membership by a dubious reference to Article 70 of the Constitution. Having a controlling stake in the university council would have empowered the government to influence university appointments, financial commitments, admission of students and the universities' relation with other external bodies as the council is ceased with the power to do these.

One spot was given to the various unions of the university to share on a rotating basis. This was later changed, but it would have constituted a serious violation of freedom of association and a denial of the role of UTAG, in particular, to take part in the self-governance of the university. Equally, the wide powers granted to the government would have compromised the management of the university and unduly affected research content, bidding for contracts and other matters, all of which would portend ill for the teaching and learning environment on university campuses.

At the end of the day, all three principal officers of a public university – the chancellor, pro-chancellor and vice-chancellor would be appointed directly or indirectly by the President of the Republic. The Bill also gave a substantial amount of power to the Minister of Education. For example, Clause 42 provided that the 'Minister may from time to time give policy directives through the National Council for Tertiary Education to the University and the University shall comply'.

Further, Clause 3(5) of the Bill gave the president the power to dissolve and reconstitute the Council in case of emergencies and appoint an interim council to operate for a stated period, without determining what constitutes an emergency.

Clause 41(1) is one of the positive provisions which seek to promote academic freedom, particularly, institutional autonomy and individual freedom for academics:

1. A public university, in performing its functions shall
   a) have the right and responsibility to preserve and promote the traditional principles of academic freedom in the conduct of its internal and external affairs;
   b) have the power to regulate its affairs in accordance with its independent ethos and traditions and in doing so it shall have regard to —
      i. the promotion and preservation of equality of opportunity and access;
      ii. effective and efficient use of resources and;
      iii. its obligations as to public accountability.
2. A member of the academic staff of a university shall have the freedom, within the law, in the member's teaching, research and any other activities either in or outside the university, to question and test received wisdom, to put forward new ideas and to state opinions, and shall not be disadvantaged, or subject to less favourable treatment by the university, for the exercise of that freedom.

However, many other provisions of the Bill operated as claw-back clauses to obliterate and make these provisions of no effect. Therefore, the mention of academic freedom here had no substance to it. It is also worth noting that the academic was only limited in the enjoyment of his/her freedoms against the university but not the government, the principal duty-bearer in the academic freedom equation.

After a hard fight, however, the academic community prevailed and the Bill did not live to see the light of day, though it is feared that the Bill may resurface.

Academic freedom vs. managerialism

The posture of the Ghana government in coming up with PUB represents a managerial, corporatist model of running universities which shifts the organizational structures gradually away from a collegial towards a more corporate model. Assessing such trends, Standler rightly comments that 'as in other areas of life, more management and control means less freedom' (Standler 2000).

In the case of many African countries where democracy was suppressed over a period of time until its re-emergence in the post–Cold War period, external factors also played their part to introduce managerialism into the university space. This includes the stringent International Monetary Fund (IMF) and World Bank structural adjustment conditionalities of the 1980s and 1990s, whose implementation enabled these Bretton Wood institutions to become the new dictators of education policies for Africa. The SAP obliged African governments to use the funding relationships with the IMF/WB to further limit institutional autonomy in universities through cuts to university spending (Kingston 2011).

Thus, the neoliberal globalization package of political and public sector reforms that were introduced in the political sphere (democracy and human rights), was extended to the university as well. This has in turn had a great impact on the management systems of the university and affected time or resources to conduct research and produce new knowledge (Rabah 2015).

Unfortunately, this approach is fraught with danger, being typically a positivistic approach to law-making (Green 1999). This process is akin to the practice of neo-patrimonialism, a blend of a political system in which the customs and patterns of patrimonialism – a style of authority which is personalized and shaped by the ruler's preferences rather than any codified system of law (Enweremadu 2013) – becomes the norm.

Conclusion and recommendations

The chapter has sought to undertake an analysis of academic freedom at Ghana's public universities in order to discuss it against the theory of establishing the correlation between democracy and the level of respect for academic freedom. The findings, in broad strokes, point to a poor picture of the state of academic freedom when Ghana moved from a liberal constitution at the time of independence to a dictatorial, one-party state and later military rule. The 1979 Constitution marked a watershed moment when the position of Chancellor reserved for sitting Heads of State was abolished though that Constitution did not live long to see that provision come into fruition. Ghana had to wait till 1992 before that provision was restored in the new Fourth Republican Constitution which has survived till today. However, the express recognition of academic freedom in the Constitution has not guaranteed a high level of respect for academic freedom, though the country has chalked some successes in its democracy rankings. The situation is attributed to the introduction of managerialism in university governance. This trend is crippling the respect for academic freedom which may have a ripple effect in the respect of democracy in the larger society while also hurting the research potential of the country's universities which is already quite low.

The chapter recommends a return from the managerialist approach to the collegial approach because, based on experience, the undue political intrusion of the university space leads to atrophy in African universities. States should, therefore, balance institutional autonomy and accountability and not control, but regulate, the university to ensure greater respect for academic freedom on university campuses.

17

The politics of political science in Africa

An afterword

Siphamandla Zondi

Introduction

Themes in political science in Africa are discussed with the hope that such a discussion reveals something significant about the politics of this science. This is inevitable because political science is a contentious science about contentious issues in society. Politics in Africa is particularly contested by various actors because the past, present and future of Africa are still very much up for grab. The discussions about them are still being shaped. Almost no debate on African politics can be considered to have been settled in a manner Europeans think about democracy or political theory.

So, writing about politics in Africa is to write about controversies. The politics of political science in Africa has many connected layers. One of these is the politics of knowledge related to who produces the knowledge about African politics, to what end, who is included and who is excluded. It is also about what gets talked about and what gets ignored, what is emphasized and what is de-emphasized. The production of knowledge for political science encounters controversies that the whole of Western knowledge is confronting increasingly today. Much of this controversy is about power relations really. This contestation is also old in the history of African scholarship. Sharp questions about knowledge produced by anthropology in the first part of the twentieth century being used in the service of the colonial project is one example (Nyoka 2012). The likes of Michael Crowder and Magema Fuze find the urge to write 'authentic' stories in the midst of distortions of the colonial civilized missions of the nineteenth century.

Re-centring Africa

More recently, authors have argued for re-centring Africa in the telling of its history and present gesture towards questioning the dominant politics of knowledge (Zeleza 2005a). They identify as a problem the de-centring of Africa's own aspirations, concerns and contributions in the story that is called Africa, that is, African history, politics, anthropology, sociology, literature and so forth. These debates question the continued dominance of the Western approaches in the choice about what questions to pose about Africa's story, the methodological tools by which we interpret African realties, the theoretical lens we use to name the problems and frame solutions, the concepts and terms we use to describe the African story. It seems all of this is borrowed from a world that is very different from Africa, actually the world that produced a marginalized and failing Africa, the Western world. Of course, this is what J.M. Blaut calls the colonizer's model of the world that describes its ways of objective (Blaut 1993), a hubris of zero point of departure or one that is a God's eye view uncontaminated by the real politics of power relations in which Africa is on the losing end (Mignolo 2009).

Another layer of this politics is one related to what then is African about the knowledge we talk about. What is African about African history, political science and so forth? What is African about the tools used to produce them? What is African about institutions where the bulk of this science is produced, the universities? Given that universities are born out of the making of a universe, a single way of the world at the expense of many, what is African about them beyond their physical location? This question has been linked to the making of knowledge that began with epistemicide through which African and other ways of knowing were decimated to make the way to this 'Universal' way of knowing at the expense of 'diversal' or 'multiversal' ways of knowing (Ndlovu-Gatsheni, Building and Africa 2015). This leads to the suggestion that perhaps we are not talking about African universities and African sciences here, but sciences in Africa and universities in Africa (Ndlovu-Gatsheni and Zondi 2016). This latter understanding helps us to acknowledge that Africans by definition are asked to contribute to a knowledge system of this colonizer's model of the world. They are being invited into what Paulin Hountondji calls extraverted discourses by which he means the use of African data to validate theories, concepts and lenses from the West (Hountondji 1997).

African political science

We are therefore talking here about political science in Africa rather than African political science. This is a science whose basic framing happened in Europe and North America, and it was not adapted to African conditions, but African realities are adapted to the 'universal' political science. The genealogy of this political science follows that of the universities in Africa, all part of what Ndlovu-Gatsheni calls the intrusion of cognitive empires (Ndlovu-Gatsheni 2015). It was imposed by Western political scientists and imported by African students of Western political science. This process of epistemic diffusion was near perfect because political theory in Africa is a mirror of Western one, comparative politics is too, so are international relations and political economy. Of course, the examples, the data and voices include African ones, but the framing mirrors the one from the metropole. The agency of Africans in this process is complex and multifarious, as is the case with the rest of the civilizing mission of the colonial empire.

This leads to another layer, whether we might want to talk about political science or political sciences. This question arises in recognition that the former reinforces the universalist pretensions of the discipline by which true diversity of thought is either prevented or minimized. The one political science fathers the permutations of the science in different locations such as Africa, but the frame comes from the dominant world. The idea of knowledge versus knowlegdes provides the context for this debate. There is talk about knowledges – otherwise, [LL1] the liberation of ways of knowing from the power of one-way or no-way (Escobar 2007).

Political sciences in this case means opening up to the possibilities that there may be ways of studying politics that is different from the mainstream, that may be inspired by the diversity of civilizations and propelled by epistemic justice and fairness. African political science would then emerge as one of the many political sciences in a world of knowledge that Amitav Acharya likes to a multiplex or what Ngugi wa Thiong'o calls a globalectic world of knowledge (Wa Thiong'o 2012). This diversity would be driven by dealing justly and authentically with contexts whose politics are being studied.

Another layer of this politics of the science about politics would be the idea of a science co-created with those who are on the margins of society, for whom it is a promise of a better life for all. This is a political science that is less professional and less elitist, but deeply inclusive and participatory. This possibility of elite working with the grassroots actors in horizontal relationships, curating together the stories that make African political science would deepen its Africanness in two ways. At a superficial level, its making would involve the Africans on the ground, and at a deeper level, it will increase the chances of filtering into the study of political views from below.

Themes in political science in Africa

It is clear from the chapters in this book that politics in and of Africa have been changing in many ways (Arowosegbe 2008). Many of these ways have not been accounted for sufficiently in the existing and rather disparate literature. It is literature that is spread across many themes, often treated in a manner that is not sufficiently conscious of inter-theme and cross-disciplinary meanings and implications of these themes. For instance, a rich literature on peace and security does not sufficiently consider the connection between hardcore academic questions about the nature and character of conflict with discussions taking place elsewhere on the evolution of public policy that is critical for thinking about how security ideas could best be turned into actionable policy interventions. Similarly, discussions on the politics of teaching politics may not be sufficiently drawing from the works on research methodologies that impinge on the study of politics in Africa.

While this book lays some ground towards achieving what we mention above, it does not actually do this interweaving of themes in individual chapters. In a way, we epitomize this fragmentation in thematic discussions, encouraged by the need to deepen our understanding of each theme as a factor in the appreciation of ways in which political science is evolving in Africa. What we achieve with depth may compensate for what we fail to achieve both in the completeness of a range of key themes on African politics and in the cross-pollinations of themes in African politics.

Because there have not been books looking at the state of political science generally for a long time, in doing this book we did not have the benefit of comprehensive cataloguing of themes, factors and developments in political science in Africa to draw from for a cross-pollination of themes and concerns showing how they interface to produce a nuanced picture of the current state of political science in Africa. What this book tries to do is to present discussion that should have been recorded over the past two decades and then tries to cover a variety of themes, old and new, in the hope that the connections, convergences and divergences will be apparent to a careful reader. This book may have to be followed by one that seeks to achieve a more integrated understanding of political science in Africa today by looking at intersections and connections a lot more deliberately.

Decolonization of political science

The age of decolonization of knowledge forces deep questions on us, some of which are dealt with in this book. These include what is being done to shift the centre of concerns in political science from Eurocentric imaginaries to those related to the African realities. This question required that this book be deliberate about inviting new thinking about the direction that political science in Africa is taking, including new methodological forays and new approach to teaching, including those of a greater use of new technologies to give students a critical reading of politics in Africa. Yet, this question forces us also to thinking explicitly and implicitly about what it means to decolonize political and political science in Africa. This is unavoidable because the practice of politics and the science of politics have in recent years been confronted with the need to reflect and act on decolonization, sometimes called second decolonization. The whole knowledge sector has been confronted with this task and so every area of knowledge has been invited into self-reflections and discussions that interpret the decolonial turn today.

The political science discipline as a whole has not taken this matter of decolonization as seriously as it has taken such issues as digitization, globalization or environmental politics on which the political science fraternity led by the International Political Science Association and other association have organized major conferences and publications. The subject of decolonization seems to have been left to scholars of the south to pursue through their 'own' meetings and panels in international conference. It has unfortunately been left to the margins both globally and in Africa. It is one of those debates the mainstream seems to tolerate without taking it seriously enough to foreground it. It will certainly not become mainstreamed because to do so would be disruptive, it would negate the very existence of mainstream political science both in the world and in Africa. This is because, as Mbembe has taught us, decolonization implies decommission the very essence of things, it is to disrupt in deep ways the way things have been (Mbembe 2018). It is reset the foundations on which knowledge is built. This subject is understandably too scary for the mainstream to contemplate; it will erode the very basis of our privileges, advantages and dominance of the study of politics as political scientists.

Digitization of the practice and science of politics

Digital politics feeds the growth of digital political science and vice versa. The advent of digital transformation alongside the fast growth of new technologies and their uses in the practice and science of politics is one of the major developments of the post–Cold War era (Saleh 2017). This is also the outgrowth of globalization with its search for new ways in which diffusion of its values, goods and services may be achieved that led to investment in science and innovation. The promise of new technologies is expressed in the use of the concept of transformation, digital transformation that is said to require adaptation and maturity. The introduction of online voting platforms in the world has spread to African countries with great speed; the use of social media to conduct basic political processes such as dialogue and public participation; and the emergence of online political persona all represent some of the ways in which digitization has happened in politics.

This development has received significant attention in mainstream political science including in the iconic international conferences of the International Political Science Association. This attention is ongoing, not every possible question on this development has been posed and answered, but the enthusiasm about it is higher than about decolonization or transformation of political science. We have seen growing interest in digital politics and digitization of political science too in Africa. Whether this digitization will help to transform in fundamental the ways how we understand how to cultivate knowledges in ways that are just to Africa is up for debate. Whether digitization will cultivate the decolonization of the discipline and practice of politics remains to be seen. Whether digitization will accelerate the processes of fundamental transformation of the ways we understand, study and discuss African politics is yet to be known. But certainly, there is an expectation that digitization should not undermine or overshadow the long-lasting conversations about how to reimagine the politics and the science of politics. Answers to these questions will come from what is said and done [LL3] in the integration of new technologies to enhance research methodology, classroom pedagogy or the epistemology of the discipline and its application.

Transdisciplinary forays and political science in Africa

The extent to which political science converses genuinely and deeply with other disciplines on shared concerns is a matter for discussion. Whether it reaches out to other disciplines in order to deepen our understanding of the whole of politics and its ramifications for the whole of society, is up for conjecture. Whether it is open enough to 360-degree understandings of political phenomena may have a bearing on the future of the discipline.

Transcending disciplinarity is to overcome the silos on which disciplines in the modern organization of knowledge are founded. Disciplines obviously have helped to guide our focused study of certain portions of the whole reality. But they have also produced a decadence, a failure to see the whole, the tendency to balkanize the whole so that we all only understand parts of it. This disciplinary decadence that Lewis R. Gordon has linked to Eurocentrism reproduces a structure of hierarchy that excludes and marginalizes much by design at the centre of modern knowledge even though we need the structure of circles that by design includes others (Gordon 2011).

But Western knowledge does not approve any other way of organizing knowledge beyond disciplines. While it has long been recognized that this was producing incomplete solutions and unhealthy relationships in knowledge cultivation, yet there is no contemplation of unknown alternatives. As a result, disciplinarians pay lip service to the idea of looking beyond disciplines, including by merely adding in knowledges of other disciplines and superficially integrating disciplines [LL4]. Much has been invested in disciplined knowledge, and the thought of undisciplined one is too unsettling for disciplinarians.

Political science is one of those disciplines that maintain the status quo of disciplined knowledge despite its claim to be liberating. It is true to its founders, who are a must-discuss theme in every foundational course in political science. These are the fathers of the discipline, which does not have mothers and natives or indigenes as its recognized creators, also in Africa. There is an unspoken rule to begin it by understanding Plato and Aristotle and then realists in North America, idealists in North America and Europe, and constructivists also in the West. Marxism and political economy are perspectives that emerged from the eastern front of the West. All these are archives from which African political scientists frame their discussion from. Political science in Africa is political science taken to Africa.

Engendering political science

The gender question has also given growing attention in political science circles the world over. It is true of all disciplines and the whole of Western knowledge. Feminists have succeeded in getting political scientists to recognize the gendered nature of politics and political science and their implications. They have forced on the discipline the need to confront gender and politics. This has led to the expansion of the field of gender politics or gender and politics in the mainstream, also inspired by the works of African feminists in the past fifty years (Adésínà 2010).

The question of gender has been on a political science whose structuring is patriarchal in deep ways. Not only are disciplines ascribed to fathers who are men from about five Western countries but its assumed world, its interlocutors, its theories and its framing are patriarchal by design. This is why the gender questions and feminist concerns are only slowly receiving attention, while the risk of these being cocooned into a corner is big.

Political science in Africa is making efforts to accommodate feminist perspectives without abandoning the patriarchal frames and meanings of the discipline. A sort of a rainbow of patriarchal and feminist perspectives co-existing is being framed. It seems that as in the mainstream, among African political scientists the task to champion and use the gendered lens on politics is left to sisters as if women were the only gendered people (McFadden 2011). This also serves to maintain rather than decommission the hierarchies that make up the discipline by having the gender layer somewhere at the bottom of the disciplinary ladder. This is also a failure because without decommissioning political science as we know it, recolouring its components simply makes it attractive to various audiences without re-presenting it as a liberating discourse.

Whither political science in Africa

The direction that political science in Africa is taking seems to be tied to the direction that mainstream political science takes going forward. It is tied to whether political science will respond to or ignore the call for its decommissioning as a Eurocentric science and recommissioning it as a multiversal/diversal area of study. It is about whether the discipline will save itself from irrelevance and extinction by responding to the pertinent questions about its ability to authentically and diversally address the issues the whole society in Africa has with politics. It is about what is done to shift paradigms and to confront coloniality within political science, the colonizer's model of the world, of knowledge and of power handed down to Africa over centuries.

The future of African politics is online, and the future of its science includes significant digitalization. Yet this is meaningless, if it is not done on the basis of a discipline undergoing fundamental transformation in order to enable a multiplex of political sciences. The online is meaningless if it is not disruptive at a deep epistemological level. If it is only about adopting technologies, then it becomes another form of commodification of knowledge.

Future has women, youth and children at the centre of the production of political science and the exercise of politics as a form of practice, not as tokenism to save patriarch from its outdatedness. It should be about co-creation of knowledge in sites and platforms that are non-patriarchal [LL5]. The contribution to this eventuality means that current work on the role and position of women in African politics tells us how to move firmly towards de-patriarchization of politics and political science.

The future of political science may influence the future direction of African politics. The two are linked. As political pundits, we have in many ways produced the kind of formal politics we witness today. We will also contribute to re-imagining the political perhaps through process long explained by Catherine Odora-Hoppers and Richards (2012) as unlearning in order to relearn. This requires the rethinking of the thinking itself. As we do this, it may be that we will inspire the practitioners of politics to do the same. There has been a revolving door between the science of politics and the practice of politics with many political scientists becoming politicians in a number of African countries. But it is also possible that the change in one will not lead to similar change in the other [LL6]. Liberation or emancipation from the margins is not an automatic process – it requires political will and sometimes struggles, too.

References

Abbas, S. (2010), 'The Sudanese Women's Movement and the Mobilisation for the 2008 Legislative Quota and its Aftermath', *IDS Bulletin*, 41(5): 100–8.

Acemoglu, D., T. Reed and J. A. Robinson (2014), 'Chiefs: Economic Development and Elite Control of Civil Society in Sierra Leone', *Journal of Political Economy*, 122(2): 319–68.

Acemoglu, D. and J. A. Robinson (2012), *Why Nations Fail: The Origins of Power, Prosperity and Poverty*, New York: Crown Publishing Group.

Achebe, C. (2009), *The Education of a British-Protected Child: Essays*, London: Penguin Books.

Achebe, N. (2020), *Female Monarchs and Merchant Queens in Africa. Ohio Short Histories of Africa*, Athens: Ohio University Press.

Achebe, N. and C. C. Robertson (2019), *Holding the World Together: African Women in Changing Perspective*. Madison, Wisconsin: The University of Wisconsin Press.

Acholonu, C. (1995), *Motherism – An Afrocentric Alternative to Feminism*, Abuja: Afa Publications.

Acholonu, R. (1995), *Family Love in Nigerian Fiction: Feminist Perspectives*, Owerri: Achisons Publications.

Adar, K. G. (1998), 'Ethnicity and Ethnic Kings: The Enduring Dual Constraint in Kenya's Multiethnic Democratic Electoral Experiment', *The Journal of Third World Spectrum*, 5(2): 71–96.

Adebanwi, W. (ed.) (2014), *Public Intellectual, the Public Sphere and the Public Spirit*, Ibadan: Ibadan University Press.

Adem, S. (2014), 'Ali A. Mazrui, the Postcolonial Theorist', *African Studies Review*, 57(1): 135–52.

Adesanmi, P. (2004), '"Nous les Colonisés": Reflections on the Territorial Integrity of Oppression', *Social Text*, 22(1): 35–58.

Adésínà, J. O. (2006), 'Sociology Beyond Despair: Recovery Of Nerve, Endogeneity, And Epistemic Intervention', *South African Review of Sociology*, 37(2): 241–59.

Adésínà, J. O. (2010), 'Re-appropriating Matrifocality: Endogeneity and African Gender Scholarship', *African Sociological Review / Revue Africaine de Sociologie*, 14(1): 2–19.

Adetula, V. A. (2011), 'Measuring Democracy and "Good Governance" in Africa: A Critique of Assumptions and Methods', in K. Kondlo and C. Ejiogu (eds), *Governance in the 21st Century*, 10–25. Cape Town: HSRC Press.

Adeyemi, S. (2017), 'Lecturers' Variables as Predictors of Academic Performance in Universities', *Journal of Social Sciences*, 50(1–3): 14–26.

Afolabi, O. S. (2018), 'Research, Political Methodology and Power in Nigeria', presented at the Workshop: Reflections on Regions, Policy Coherence and Quality of Democracy, Medellin. Columbia.

Afolabi, O. S. (2020), 'Conducting Focus Group Discussion in Africa: Researching the Nexus Between the State and Election Administration', *SAGE Open* (accessed 10 January 2020).

Afolabi, O. S. (2019), 'Leadership Challenges of Middle-Level Academics in Universities in Nigeria', *Journal of Higher Education in Africa*, 17(1–2): 1–18.

Afolabi, O. S. and H. A. Idowu (2020), 'African Universities Quality Management Challenges and Higher Education Agenda', in M. Sony, K. T. Karingada and N. Baporikar (eds), *Quality Management Implementation in Higher Education: Practices, Models, and Case Studies*, Hershey: IGI Global.

Afrobarometer (2017), *Round 7 Survey Manual*, Cape Town: Afrobarometer Network.

Agbalajobi, D. T. (2021), *Promoting Gender Equality in Political Participation: New Perspectives on Nigeria. Africa: Past, Present & Prospects*, London and New York: Rowman & Littlefield.

Agbodeka, F. (1998), *A History of University of Ghana: Half a Century of Higher Education (1948–1998)*, Accra: Woeli Publishing Services.

Agbu, O. A. (2011), *Ethnicity and Democratisation in Africa Challenges for Politics and Development*, Uppsala: Nordic Africa Institute.

Ahikire, J. (2007), *Localised or Localising Democracy: Gender and Politics of Decentralisation in Contemporary Uganda*. Fountain series in gender studies, Kampala: Fountain Publishers.

Aiyede, E. R. and E. A. Udalla (2013), 'Values: Intellectuals and Policy Process in Nigeria: A Theoretical Cum Ideological Explanation', *Public Policy and Administration Research*, 3(10): 22–32.

Ajulu, R. (1995), 'The Left and the Question of Democratic Transition in Kenya: A Reply to Mwakenya', *Review of African Political Economy*, 22(64): 229–35.

Ajulu, R. (2000), 'Thinking Through the Crisis of Democratisation in Kenya: A Response to Adar and Murunga', *African Sociological Review / Revue Africaine de Sociologie*, 4(2): 133–57.

Ake, C. (1982), *Social Science as Imperialism: The Theory of Political Development*, 2nd edn, Ibadan: Ibadan University Press.

Ake, C. (1994), *Democratization of Disempowerment in Africa*, Lagos: Malthouse Press.

Ake, C. (1996), *Democracy and Development in Africa*, Washington, D.C.: The Brookings Institution.

Alasuutari, P. and A. Qadir (2016), 'Imageries of the Social World in Epistemic Governance', *International Sociology*, 31(6): 633–52.

Albertyn, C. (2005), 'Defending and Securing Rights through Law: Feminism, Law and the Courts in South Africa', *Politikon*, 32(2): 217–37.

Alcoff, L. M. (2002), 'Does the Public Intellectual Have Intellectual Integrity?', *Metaphilosophy*, 33(5): 521–34.

Allen, F. (2016), 'Decolonising African Political Science and the Question of the Relevance of the Discipline for Development', in S. J. Ndlovu-Gatsheni and S. Zondi (eds), *Decolonizing the University, Knowledge Systems and Disciplines in Africa*, mmxvi, 181–93, Durham: Carolina Academic Press.

Almond, G. A. (1956), 'Comparative Political Systems', *The Journal of Politics*, 18(3): 391–409.

Almond, G. A. and J. S. Coleman (1960), *The Politics of the Developing Areas*, Princeton: Princeton University Press.

Ambler, C. (2011), '"A School in the Interior" African Studies: Engagement and Interdisciplinarity', *African Studies Review*, 54(1): 1–17.

Amin, A. A. and A. Ntembe (2021), 'Sub-Saharan Africa's Higher Education: Financing, Growth and Employment', *International Journal of Higher Education*, 10(1): 14–23.

Amin, S. (1976), *Neo-Colonialism in West Africa*, New York: Monthly Review Press.

Amin, S. (1989), *Eurocentrism*, London: Zed Books.

Amin, S. (1990a), *Delinking: Towards a Polycentric World*, London: Zed Books.

Amin, S. (1990b), *Maldevelopment: Anatomy of a Global Failure*, London: Zed Books.

Amin, S. (1996), *Imperialism and Unequal Development*, New York: Monthly Review Press.

Ampofo, A. A., J. Beoku-Betts, W. N. Njambi and M. Osirim (2004), 'Women's and Gender Studies in English-Speaking Sub-Saharan Africa: A Review of Research in the Social Sciences', *Gender and Society*, 18(6): 685–714.

Amuwo, A. K. (2002), 'Between Intellectual Responsibility and Political Commodification of Knowledge: Nigeria's Academic Political Scientists under the Babangida Military Junta, 1985–1993', *African Studies Review*, 45(2): 93–121.

Anber, P. (1967), 'Modernisation and Political Disintegration: Nigeria and the Ibos', *The Journal of Modern African Studies*, 5(2): 163–79.

Anugwom, E. E. (2000), 'Ethnic Conflict and Democracy in Nigeria: The Marginalisation Question', *Journal of Social Development in Africa*, 15(1): 61–78.

Apata, G. O. (2019), 'Corruption And The Postcolonial State: How The West Invented African Corruption', *Journal of Contemporary African Studies*, 37(1): 43–56.

Appiagyei-Atua, K. (2019), 'Students' Academic Freedom in African Universities and Democratic Enhancement', *African Human Rights Law Journal*, 19(1): 151–66.

Appiagyei-Atua, K., K. D. Beiter and T. Karran (2015), 'The Composite Theory: An African Contribution to the Academic Freedom Discourse', *South African Journal on Human Rights*, 31(2): 315–29.

Appiagyei-Atua, K., K. D. Beiter and T. Karran (2016), 'A Review of Academic Freedom in African Universities through the Prism of the 1997 ILO/UNESCO Recommendation', *AAUP Journal of Academic Freedom*, 7: 1–23.

Apter, D. (2009), 'An Approach to Interdisciplinarity', *International Social Science Journal*, 60(196): 183–93.

Armitage, D. (2013), 'The International Turn in Intellectual History', in S. Moyn and D. M. McMahon (eds), *Rethinking Modern European Intellectual History*, 232–52. New York: Oxford University Press.

Arnfred, S. and A.A. Ampofo, eds (2009), *African Feminist Politics of Knowledge: Tensions, Challenges, Possibilities*, Uppsala: Nordiska Afrikainstitutet.

Arowosegbe, J. O. (2008), 'Decolonising the social sciences in the global South: Claude Ake and the praxis of knowledge production in Africa', *ASC Working Paper Series*, 79: 1–42.

Arthur, K. E. (2018), 'Technical Universities Calls for the Immediate Withdrawal of the Amendment Bill 2017 of the Technical Universities Act 2016 (Act 922)', *Beach Fm Online*, https://beachfmonline.com/2018-02-13-technical-universities-calls-for-the-immediate-withdrawal-of-the-amendment-bill-2017-of-the-technical-universities-act-2016-act-922/ (accessed 19 April 2021).

Asante, M. K. (1991), 'The Afrocentric Idea in Education', *The Journal of Negro Education*, 60(2): 170–80.

Ashby, E. and M. Anderson (1966), *Universities: British, Indian, African — A Study in the Ecology of Higher Education*, First Edition, London: Weidenfeld and Nicolson.

Ashcroft, B., G. Griffiths and H. Tiffin (eds) (1995), *The Post-Colonial Studies Reader*, London: Routledge.

Ashcroft, B., G. Griffiths and H. Tiffin (1998), *Post-Colonial Studies: The Key Concepts*, London and New York: Routledge.

Asquith Report (1945), Report of the Commission on Higher Education in the Colonies 1945 (Asquith Report), London: His Majesty's Stationary Office.

Austin, D. (1976), *Ghana Observed: Essays on the Politics of a West African Republic*, Manchester and New York: Manchester University Press; Africana Publishing Company.

Awa, E. (1983), 'Teaching Political Science in African Universities: A Problem-Solving Approach', in Y. R. Barongo (ed.), *Political Science in Africa: A Critical Review*, 27–36, London and Ibadan: Zed Press; Progressive and Socialist Books Depot.

Awe, B. (1977), 'Reflections on the Conference on Women and Development: I', in Wellesley Editorial Committee (ed.), *Women and the National Development: The Complexities of Change*, 314–16, Chicago and London: University of Chicago Press.

Awini, P. (2017), 'Take Your Hands Off Technical Universities - TUTAG Cautions NCTE', *MyjoyOnline.Com*, https://www.myjoyonline.com/take-your-hands-off-technical -universities-tutag-cautions-ncte/ (accessed 20 April 2021).

Ayandele, E. A. (1974), *The Educated Elite in the Nigerian Society*, Ibadan: Ibadan University Press.

Ayee, J. R. A. and M. A. A. Gyekye-Jandoh (2014), 'The Vicissitudes of Political Science in Ghana', in S. Agyei-Mensah, J. A. Ayee and A. D. Oduro (eds), *Changing Perspectives on the Social Sciences in Ghana*, 159–92, Dordrecht: Springer.

Ayisi, E. O. (1979), *An Introduction to the Study of African Culture*, 2nd edn, London: Heinemann.

Badrī, B. Y. and A. M. Tripp (2017), *Women's Activism in Africa: Struggles for Rights and Representation*, London: Zed Books Ltd.

Baert, P. and J. Isaac (2011), 'Intellectuals and Society: Sociological and Historical Perspectives', in G. Delanty and S. P. Turner (eds), *Routledge International Handbook of Contemporary Social and Political Theory*, 200–11, London: Routledge.

Baldwin, K. (2013), 'Why Vote with the Chief? Political Connections and Public Goods Provision in Zambia', *American Journal of Political Science*, 57(4): 794–809.

Banda, F. (2005), *Women, Law and Human Rights: An African Perspective*, Oxford and Portland: Hart Publishing.

Bandola-Gill, J., M. Flinders and A. Anderson (2021), 'Co-option, Control and Criticality: The Politics of Relevance Regimes for the Future of Political Science', *European Political Science*, 20(1): 218–36.

Banyongen, S. (2017), 'Crise anglophone: les errements des politologues camerounais', *Journal du Cameroun*, 23 February, https://www.journalducameroun.com/crise -anglophone-errements-politologues-camerounais/ (accessed 2 May 2020).

Barbour, J. D. (2007), 'Edward Said and the Space of Exile', *Literature & Theology*, 21(3): 293–301.

Barkan, J. D. (2009), *Legislative Power in Emerging African Democracies*, Boulder: Lynne Rienner Publishers.

Barongo, Y. R. (1980), *Neocolonialism and African Politics: A Survey of the Impact of Neocolonialism on African Political Behavior*, New York: Vantage Press.

Barongo, Y. R. (1983a), 'Introduction', in Y. R. Barongo (ed.), *Political Science in Africa: A Critical Review*, 1–4, London: Zed Books.

Barongo, Y. R., ed. (1983b), *Political Science in Africa: A Critical Review*, London: Zed Books.

Bates, R. H. (1981), *Markets and States in Tropical Africa: The Political Basis of Agricultural Policies*, Berkeley: University of California Press.

Beck, N. L. (2000), 'Political Methodology: A Welcoming Discipline', *Journal of the American Statistical Association*, 95(450): 651–54.

Beckman, B. and A. Jega (1995), 'Scholars and Democratic Politics in Nigeria', *Review of African Political Economy*, 22(64): 167–81.

Beissinger, M. R. (2008), 'A New Look at Ethnicity and Democratization', *Journal of Democracy*, 19(3): 85–97.

Beiter, K. D., T. Karran and K. Appiagyei-Atua (2016), 'Measuring the Erosion of Academic Freedom as an International Human Right: A Report on the Legal Protection of Academic Freedom in Europe', *Vanderbilt Journal of Transnational Law*, 49(3): 597–692.

Bell, D. (1962), *The End of Ideology: On the Exhaustion of Political Ideas in the Fifties, with "The Resumption of History in the New Century"*, Cambridge, MA: Harvard University Press.

Bellagamba, A. and G. Klute (eds) (2008), *Beside the State: Emergent Powers in Contemporary Africa*, Köln: Rüdiger Köppe Verlag.

Benda, J. (1927), *La trahison des clercs*, 1st edn, Paris: B. Grasset.

Benda, J. (2007), *The Treason of the Intellectuals*, New Brunswick: Transaction Publishers.

Beoku-Betts, J. (2021), 'African Feminist and Gender Scholarship: Contemporary Standpoints and Sites of Activism', in A. A. Ampofo and J. Beoku-Betts (eds), *Producing Inclusive Feminist Knowledge: Positionalities and Discourses in the Global South (Advances in Gender Research, Vol. 31)*, 43–64, Bingley: Emerald Publishing Limited.

Beoku-Betts, J. and F. A. O. M'Cormack-Hale, eds (2022), *War, Women and Post-conflict Empowerment: Lessons from Sierra Leone. Politics and Development in Contemporary Africa*, London and New York: Zed; Bloomsbury Publishing.

Beoku-Betts, J. and W. N. Njambi (2005), 'African Feminist Scholars in Women's Studies: Negotiating Spaces of Dislocation and Transformation in the Study of Women', *Meridians*, 6(1): 113–32.

Bergan, S. (2002), 'Institutional Autonomy between Myth and Responsibility', in *Autonomy and Responsibility: The University's Obligations for the XXIst Century*, Proceedings of the Launch Event for the Magna Charta Observatory, 49–66, Bologna: Bononia University Press.

Berndtson, E. (1991), 'The Development of Political Science: Methodological Problems of Comparative Research', in D. Easton, J. Gunnell and L. Graziano (eds), *The Development of Political Science: A Comparative Survey*, 34–58, London: Taylor & Francis Group.

Bhabha, H. K. (1994), *The Location of Culture*, London: Routledge.

Bierschenk, T. and J.-P. Olivier de Sardan (2019), 'How to Study Bureaucracies Ethnographically?', *Critique of Anthropology*, 39(2): 243–57.

Bigombe Logo, P. and H.-L. Menthong (1996), 'Crise de légitimité et évidence de la continuité politique', *Politique Africaine*, 62: 15–23.

Biya, P. (1984), Le message du renouveau: Discours et interviews du président Paul Biya, Yaoundé: SOPECAM.

Bjørnskov, C. and M. Rode (2020), 'Regime Types and Regime Change: A New Dataset on Democracy, Coups, and Political Institutions', *The Review of International Organizations*, 15(2): 531–51.

Blaney, D. L. and A. B. Tickner (2017), 'Worlding, Ontological Politics and the Possibility of a Decolonial IR', *Millennium: Journal of International Studies*, 45(3): 293–311.

Blaut, J. M. (1993), *The Colonizer's Model of the World: Geographical Diffusionism and Eurocentric History*, New York: Guilford Press.

Blundo, G. (2015), 'The King is not a Kinsman: Multiple Accountabilities and Practical Norms in West African Bureaucracies', in J.-P. Olivier de Sardan and T. De Herdt (eds),

Real Governance and Practical Norms in Sub-Saharan Africa: The Game of the Rules, 142–59, London: Routledge.

Boahen, A. A. (1975), *Ghana: Evolution and Change in the Nineteenth and Twentieth Centuries*, London: Longman.

Bob-Milliar, G. M. (2009), 'Chieftaincy, Diaspora, and Development: The Institution of Nkosuohene in Ghana', *African Affairs*, 108(433): 541–58.

Boden, R. and D. Epstein (2011), 'A Flat Earth Society? Imagining Academic Freedom', *The Sociological Review*, 59(3): 476–95.

Boko, S. H., M. Baliamoune-Lutz and S. R. Kimuna (eds) (2005), *Women in African Development: The Challenges of Globalization and Liberalization in the 21st Century*, Trenton: Africa World Press.

Bond, J. R. (2007), 'The Scientification of the Study of Politics: Some Observations on the Behavioral Evolution in Political Science', *The Journal of Politics*, 69(4): 897–907.

Booysen, S. and A. van Nieuwkerk (1998), 'Political Studies in South Africa: An Assessment of the Discipline and the Profession', *Politikon*, 25(1): 3–29.

Börzel, T. A. and T. Risse (2016), 'Dysfunctional State Institutions, Trust, and Governance in Areas of Limited Statehood', *Regulation & Governance*, 10(2): 149–60.

Bose, S. (2004), 'Decolonization and state building in South Asia', *Journal of International Affairs*, 58(1): 95–113.

Botchwey, K. (1977), 'Marxism And The Analysis Of The African Reality', *Africa Development / Afrique et Développement*, 2(1): 9–16.

Bouilly, E., O. Rillon and H. Cross (2016), 'African Women's Struggles in a Gender Perspective', *Review of African Political Economy*, 43(149): 338–49.

Box-Steffensmeier, J. M., H. E. Brady and D. Collier (eds) (2008), *The Oxford Handbook of Political Methodology*, Oxford: Oxford University Press.

Braimah, A. I., R. H. Kilu and N. K. Annin-Bonsu (2014), 'The Politics of Public Policy and Problems of Implementation in Africa: An Appraisal of Ghana's National Health Insurance Scheme in Ga East District', *International Journal of Humanities and Social Science*, 4(4): 193–207.

Bratton, M. (2007), 'Formal Versus Informal Institutions in Africa', *Journal of Democracy*, 18(3): 96–110.

Bratton, M. and C. Logan (2006), 'Voters but not yet Citizens: The Weak Demand for Political Accountability in Africa's Unclaimed Democracies', *Afrobarometer Working Papers*, 63: 29.

Bratton, M. and N. Van de Walle (1997), *Democratic Experiments in Africa: Regime Transitions in Comparative Perspective*, Cambridge: Cambridge University Press.

Briggs, R. C. and Weathers, S. (2016), 'Gender and Location in African Politics Scholarship: The Other White Man's Burden?', *African Affairs*, 115(460): 466–89.

Brinkerhoff, D. W., A. Wetterberg and E. Wibbels (2018), 'Distance, Services, and Citizen Perceptions of the State in Rural Africa', *Governance*, 31(1): 103–24.

Bryceson, D. F. (2012), 'Discovery And Denial: Social Science Theory And Interdisciplinarity In African Studies', *African Affairs*, 111(443): 281–302.

Budd, E. (2004), *Democratization, Development, and the Patrimonial State in the Age of Globalization*, Lanham: Lexington Books.

Bujra, A. S. and T. Mkandawire (1980), 'The Evolution of Social Science in Africa Problems and Prospects', *Africa Development / Afrique et Développement*, 5(4): 21–40.

Burawoy, M. (2013), 'Sociology and Interdisciplinarity: The Promise and the Perils', *Philippine Sociological Review*, 61(1): 7–19.

Busia, N. K. A. and R. Degni-Segui (1996), *The State of Academic Freedom in Africa 1995*, Dakar: Codesria.

Butler, J. (2004), *Precarious Life: The Powers of Mourning and Violence*, Reprint edition, London and New York: Verso.

Butler, J. (2016), *Frames of War: When Is Life Grievable?*, London and New York: Verso.

Buur, L. and H. M. Kyed (2006), 'Contested Sources of Authority: Re-claiming State Sovereignty by Formalizing Traditional Authority in Mozambique', *Development and Change*, 37(4): 847–69.

Callaghy, T. M. (1994), 'Civil Society, Democracy, and Economic Change in Africa: A Dissenting Opinion about Resurgent Societies', in N. Chazan, J. W. Harbeson and D. S. Rothchild (eds), *Civil Society and the State in Africa*, 231–53, Boulder: Lynne Rienner Publishers.

Campbell, H. (1989), 'The Teaching and Research of Political Economy in Africa with Specific Reference to East Africa', in W. O. Oyugi (ed.), *The Teaching and Research of Political Science in Eastern Africa*, 107–32, Addis Ababa: OSSREA.

Cardoso, F. H. (1977), 'The Consumption of Dependency Theory in the United States', *Latin American Research Review*, 12(3): 7–24.

Carter, G. M. (1959), 'A Political Scientist in Africa', *African Studies Bulletin*, 2(4): 1–12.

Castro-Gómez, S. (2005), *La Hybris Del Punto Cero: Ciencia, Raza e Ilustración En La Nueva Granada (1750–1816)*, Bogotá: Pontificia Universidad Javeriana.

Chabal, P. and J.-P. Daloz (1999), *Africa Works: Disorder as Political Instrument*, Oxford: James Currey.

Chakrabarty, D. (2000), *Provincializing Europe: Postcolonial Thought and Historical Difference*, Princeton: Princeton University Press.

Charrad, M. (2001), *States and Women's Rights: The Making of Postcolonial Tunisia, Algeria, and Morocco*, Berkeley: University of California Press.

Chatterjee, P. (1986), *Nationalist Thought and the Colonial World: A Derivative Discourse?* London: Zed for The United Nations University.

Chazan, N. (1983), *An Anatomy of Ghanaian Politics: Managing Political Recession, 1969–1982*, Boulder: Westview Press.

Cheeseman, N. (2018), 'Introduction: Understanding African Politics: Bringing the State Back in', in N. Cheeseman (ed.), *Institutions and Democracy in Africa: How the Rules of the Game Shape Political Developments*, 1–38, Cambridge: Cambridge University Press.

Cheeseman, N., C. Death and L. Whitfield (2017), 'Notes on Researching Africa', *African Affairs*, 121(485): 1–5.

Chege, M. (1997), 'The Social Science Area Studies Controversy from the Continental African Standpoint', *Africa Today*, 44(2): 133–42.

Cheibub, J. A. (2007), *Presidentialism, Parliamentarism, and Democracy*, Cambridge: Cambridge University Press.

Cheibub, J. A., J. Gandhi and J. R. Vreeland (2010), 'Democracy and Dictatorship Revisited', *Public choice*, 143: 67–101.

Cheru, F. (1989), *The Silent Revolution in Africa: Debt, Development and Democracy*, London: Zed Books.

Chidza, R. (2017), 'Jonathan Moyo, Political Turncoat Par-excellence….would-be Kingmaker that Never Was', *NewsDay Zimbabwe*, https://www.newsday.co.zw/2017/11/jonathan-moyo-political-turncoat-par-excellence-kingmaker-never/ (accessed 5 March 2021).

Chikwendu, E. (1983), 'The African Peasantry: Neglected by African Political Science', in Y. R. Barongo (ed.), *Political Science in Africa: A Critical Review*, 37–47, London and Ibadan: Zed Press; Progressive and Socialist Books Depot.

Choat, S. (2020), 'Decolonising the Political Theory Curriculum', *Politics*, 41(3): 404–20.

Chole, E. and J. Ibrahim, (eds) (1995), *Democratisation Processes in Africa: Problems and Prospects*, Dakar: Codesria.

Christianse, Y. (2003), 'Passing Away: The Unspeakable (Losses) of Postapartheid South Africa', in D. Eng and D. Kazanjian (eds), *Loss: The Politics of Mourning*, 372–95, London: University of California Press.

Chuku, G. (2009), 'Igbo Women and Political Participation in Nigeria, 1800s-2005', *International Journal of African Historical Studies*, 42(1): 81–103.

Chweya, L. J., J. K. Tuta, S. K. Akivaga and B. Sihanya (2005), *Control of Corruption in Kenya: Legal and Political Dimensions*, Nairobi: Claripress.

Clark, S. G. and R. L. Wallace (2015), 'Integration and Interdisciplinarity: Concepts, Frameworks, and Education', *Policy Sciences*, 48(2): 233–55.

Cliffe, L. and J. S. Saul (1973), *Socialism in Tanzania: An Interdisciplinary Reader*, Nairobi: East African Publishing House.

CODESRIA (2014), 'CODESRIA Methodology Workshop Series: Training the Trainers Theme: Quantitative and Qualitative Methods in Social Science Research', Codesria, https://www.codesria.org/spip.php?article1744 (accessed 14 April 2021).

Coleman, F. (2009), 'Gender Equality and the Rule of Law in Liberia: Statutory Law, Customary Law, and the Status of Women', in S. Hoffman Williams (ed.), *Constituting Equality: Gender Equality and Comparative Constitutional Law*, 195–214, New York: Cambridge University Press.

Coleman, J. S. (1958), *Nigeria: Background to Nationalism*, Berkeley: University of California Press.

Coleman, J. S. and C. R. D. Halisi (1983), 'American Political Science and Tropical Africa: Universalism vs. Relativism', *African Studies Review*, 26(3/4): 25–62.

Collier, P. (1998), 'The Political Economy of Ethnicity', *CSAE Working Paper Series*, 1998(08): 1–14.

Collier, P. and A. Hoeffler (2004), 'Greed and Grievance in Civil War', *Oxford Economic Papers*, 56(4): 563–95.

Colonial No 231 (1948), Commission of Enquiry into Disturbances in the Gold Coast, Watson Commission, 1948.

Constitution of the Republic of Ghana (1969), Accra, Ghana: Ghana Publishing Corporation.

Constitution of the Republic of Ghana (1979), Accra, Ghana: Ghana Publishing Corporation.

Constitution of the Republic of Ghana (1992), Accra, Ghana: Ghana Publishing Corporation.

Coppedge, M., J. Gerring, C. H. Knutsen, J. Teorell, K. L. Marquardt, J. Medzihorsky, et al. (2020), 'V-Dem Methodology v10', Gothenburg: University of Gothenburg, Varieties of Democracy Institute.

Cornwall, A. and D. Eade, (eds) (2010), *Deconstructing Development Discourse: Buzzwords and Fuzzwords*, Warwickshire: Practical Action Publishing.

Courade, G. and L. Sindjoun (1996), 'Le Cameroun dans l'entre-deux: Introduction au thème', *Politique Africaine*, 62: 3–14.

Crawford, G. (2009), '"Making Democracy a Reality"? The Politics of Decentralisation and the Limits to Local Democracy in Ghana', *Journal of Contemporary African Studies*, 27(1): 57–83.

Crook, R. C. (2003), 'Decentralisation and Poverty Reduction in Africa: The Politics of Local-Central Relations', *Public Administration & Development*, 23(1): 77–88.

Crouch, H. (1993), 'Democratic Prospects in Indonesia', *Asian Journal of Political Science*, 1(2): 77–92.

Dahl, R. A. (1971), *Polyarchy: Participation and Opposition*, New Haven: Yale University Press.

Dahrendorf, R. (1976), *Class and Class Conflict in Industrial Society*, London: Routledge.

Darbon, D., R. Nakanabo Diallo, O. Provini and S. Schlimmer (2019), 'Un état de la littérature sur l'analyse des politiques publiques en Afrique', *Papiers de Recherche AFD*, 98: 1–36.

Darkwah, A., S. Tonah and M. Assimeng (2014), 'The Development of Sociology and Anthropology in Ghana and Future Trends', in S. Agyei-Mensah, J. A. Ayee and A. D. Oduro (eds), *Changing Perspectives on the Social Sciences in Ghana*, 95–112, Dordrecht: Springer.

Das, V. (2001), 'Violence and Translation', *Anthropological Quarterly*, 75(1): 105–12.

Dawuni, J. and G. Bauer (eds) (2016), *Gender and the Judiciary in Africa: Moving from Obscurity to Parity?*, New York: Routledge.

Dawuni, J. and A. Kang (2015), 'Her Ladyship Chief Justice: The Rise of Female Leaders in the Judiciary in Africa', *Africa Today*, 65(2): 44–69.

Debrah, E. (2009), 'The Economy and Regime Change in Ghana, 1992–2004', *Ghana Social Science Journal*, 5–6(1–2): 84–113.

Debrah, E., S. Alidu and I. Owusu-Mensah (2016), 'The Cost of Inter-Ethnic Conflicts in Ghana's Northern Region: The Case of the Nawuri-Gonja Conflicts', *Journal of African Conflicts and Peace Studies*, 3(1): 1–27.

Deem, R. (1998), '"New Managerialism" and Higher Education: The Management of Performances and Cultures in Universities in the United Kingdom', *International Studies in Sociology of Education*, 8(1): 47–70.

Deltombe, T., M. Domergue and J. Tatsitsa (2011), *Kamerun! Une guerre cachée aux origines de la Françafrique (1948–1971)*, Paris: La Découverte.

Desch, M. C., ed. (2016), *Public Intellectuals in the Global Arena: Professors or Pundits?*, Notre Dame: University of Notre Dame Press.

Diabate, N. (2020), *Naked Agency: Genital Cursing and Biopolitics in Africa*, Durham: Duke University Press.

Diamond, L. (1988), *Class, Ethnicity, and Democracy in Nigeria: The Failure of the First Republic*, 1st edn, Syracuse: Syracuse University Press.

Diamond, L., J. J. Linz and S. M. Lipset, eds (1988), *Democracy in Developing Countries, Vol. II: Africa*, Boulder: Lynne Rienner Publishers.

Diop, C. A. (1991), *Civilization or Barbarism: An Authentic Anthropology*, Chicago: Chicago Review Press.

Diouf, M. (1994), 'The Intelligentsia in the Democratic Transition', in M. Mamdani and M. Diouf (eds), *Academic Freedom in Africa*, 327–36, Dakar: Codesria.

Diouf, M. and M. Mamdani, eds (1994), *Academic Freedom in Africa*, Dakar: Codesria.

Dipholo, K. B., E. Mafema and N. Tshishonga (2014), 'Traditional Leadership in Botswana: Opportunities', *The Journal of African and Asian Local Government Studies*, 3(2): 17–28.

Dlamini, C. (2002), 'University Autonomy and Academic Freedom in Africa: Ex Africa Semper Aliquid Novi?', *The Comparative and International Law Journal of Southern Africa*, 35(1): 77–98.

Doka, K. J. (1999), 'Disenfranchised Grief', *Bereavement Care*, 18(3): 37–9.

Donfack Sokeng, L. (1996), 'Les ambiguïtés de la "'révision constitutionnelle'" du 18 janvier 1996 au Cameroun', in S. Melone, A. Minkoa She and L. Sindjoun (eds), *La Réforme Constitutionnelle du 18 janvier 1996 au Cameroun: Aspects juridiques et politiques*, 34–52, Yaoundé: Association Africaine de Science Politique (Section Camerounaise, GRAP).

Duermeijer, C., M. Amir and L. Schoombee (2018), 'Africa Generates Less than 1% of the World's Research; Data Analytics can Change that', *Elsevier Connect*, https://www.elsevier.com/connect/africa-generates-less-than-1-of-the-worlds-research-data-analytics-can-change-that (accessed 25 June 2020).

Dunn, J. and A. F. Robertson (1973), *Dependence and Opportunity: Political Change in Ahafo*, London and New York: Cambridge University Press.

Dunne, T., L. Hansen and C. Wight (2013), 'The End of International Relations Theory?' *European Journal of International Relations*, 19(3): 405–25.

Durkheim, E. (1902 [1893]), *De la division du travail social*, 2nd edn, Paris: F. Alcan.

Dye, T. R. (2013), *Understanding Public Policy*, 14th edn, Upper Saddle River: Pearson.

Easton, D. (1969), 'The New Revolution in Political Science', *The American Political Science Review*, 63(4): 1051–61.

Easton, D., J. G. Gunnell and M. B. Stein (eds) (1995), *Regime and Discipline: Democracy and the Development of Political Science*, Ann Arbor: University of Michigan Press.

Eboko, F. (2005), 'Politique publique et sida en Afrique: De l'anthropologie à la science politique (Public Policy and AIDS in Africa: From Anthropology to Political Science)', *Cahiers d'Études Africaines*, 45(178): 351–87.

Echu, G. (2010), *Who's who au Cameroun: Recueil biographique des personnalités du Cameroun*, Yaoundé: Africana Publications.

Edgren, G. (2003), *Donorship, Ownership and Partnership: Issues Arising from Four Sida Studies of Donor-Recipient Relations*, Stockholm: Sida, https://publikationer.sida.se/contentassets/9eb50ac50e7d4494bdccd4ef52d09fa7/13364.pdf (accessed 26 March 2021).

Eggen, Ø. (2011), 'Chiefs and Everyday Governance: Parallel State Organisations in Malawi', *Journal of Southern African Studies*, 37(2): 313–31.

Eisenstadt, S. N. and L. Roniger (1984), *Patrons, Clients and Friends: Interpersonal Relations and the Structure of Trust in Society*, Cambridge: Cambridge University Press.

EIU (2020), *Democracy Index 2019: A Year of Democratic Setbacks and Popular Protest*, London: The Economist Intelligence Unit.

Ejembi, H. I. (1983), 'Science vs. Philosophy: The Need for a Relevant Political Science', in Y. R. Barongo (ed.), *Political Science in Africa: A Critical Review*, 17–26, London: Zed Books.

Ekeh, P. P. (1975), 'Colonialism and the Two Publics in Africa: A Theoretical Statement', *Comparative Studies in Society and History*, 17(1): 91–112.

Ekeh, P. P. (1983), *Colonialism and Social Structure. An Inaugural Lecture*, Ibadan: University of Ibadan.

Ekeh, P. P. (1997), 'The Concept of Second Liberation and the Prospects of Democracy in Africa: A Nigerian Context', in P. A. Beckett and C. Young (eds), *Dilemmas of Democracy in Nigeria*, 83–110, Rochester: University of Rochester Press.

Elebute, A. and S. Ocheni (2020), 'Ellen Johnson-Sirleaf Political Communication into Liberia Presidency', in S.A. Omotoso (ed.), *Women's Political Communication in Africa*, 99–118, Cham: Springer.

Elias, N. (1978), *The Civilizing Process*, Oxford: Blackwell.

Emagna, M. (1996), 'Les intellectuels camerounais sous le regime Ahidjo (1958–1982)', *Afrika Focus*, 12(1–3): 51–83.

Engels, B. and M. Müller (2019), 'Northern Theories, Southern Movements? Contentious Politics in Africa through the Lens of Social Movement Theory', *Journal of Contemporary African Studies*, 37(1): 72–92,.

Engels, F. (1973), *Dialectics of Nature*, New York: International Publishers.

Englebert, P. (2002), 'Born-again Buganda or the Limits of Traditional Resurgence in Africa', *The Journal of Modern African Studies*, 40(3): 345–68.

Enweremadu, D. U. (2013), 'The Struggle against Corruption in Nigeria: The Role of the National Anti-Corruption Commission (ICPC) under the Fourth Republic', in *IFRA Special Research Issue Vol. 2*, 41–66, Ibadan: French Institute for Research in Africa.

Enwo–Irem, I. N. (2013), 'Colonialism and Education: The Challenges for Sustainable Development in Nigeria', *Mediterranean Journal of Social Sciences*, 4(5): 163–8.

Escobar, A. (2007), 'Worlds and Knowledges Otherwise', *Cultural Studies*, 21(2–3): 179–210.

Esman, M. J. (1994), *Ethnic Politics*, Ithaca: Cornell University Press.

Eweka, O. (2020), 'Working Behind the Scenes: Rethinking Peace and Development in the First Lady Illusory Continuum of Afropolicom', in S. A. Omotoso (ed.), *Women's Political Communication in Africa*, 133–154, Cham: Springer.

Eyinga, A. (1978), *Mandat d'arrêt pour cause d'élections: de la démocratie au Cameroun 1970–1978*, Paris: L'Harmattan.

Eyoh, D. (1998), 'African Perspectives on Democracy and the Dilemmas of Postcolonial Intellectuals', *Africa Today*, 45(3/4): 281–306.

Faber, J. and W. J. Scheper (1997), 'Interdisciplinary Social Science: a Methodological Analysis', *Quality and Quantity*, 31(1): 37–56.

Faculty of Arts Handbook (2015), *Faculty of Arts Handbook*, KwaDlangezwa: University of Zululand.

Faculty of Social Sciences (2012a), *Academic Curriculum Handbook*, Ile-Ife: Obafemi Awolowo University Press.

Faculty of Social Sciences (2012b), *Academic Curriculum Handbook*, Benin City: University of Benin.

Faculty of Social Sciences (2012c), *Academic Curriculum Handbook*, Ibadan: University of Ibadan.

Falola, T., ed. (2002), *African Politics in Postimperial Times: The Essays of Richard L. Sklar*, Trenton: Africa World Press.

Falola, T. (2021), 'Teaching Women's Studies in Africa', in O. Yacob-Haliso and T. Falola (eds), *The Palgrave Handbook of African Women's Studies*, 235–92, Cham: Palgrave Macmillan.

Fanon, F. (2001 [1963]), *The Wretched of the Earth*, London: Penguin Books.

Finlay, D. J. (1968), 'Students and Politics in Ghana', *Daedalus*, 97(1): 51–69.

Fischer, F. (2003), *Reframing Public Policy: Discursive Politics and Deliberative Practices*, Oxford: Oxford University Press.

Fortes, M. and E. E. Evans-Pritchard, eds (1940), *African Political Systems*, Oxford: Oxford University Press.

Foucault, M. (1979), *Discipline and Punish: The Birth of the Prison*, New York: Vintage Books.

Frank, A. G. (1967), *Capitalism and Underdevelopment in Latin America: Historical Studies of Chile and Brazil*, New York: Monthly Review Press.

Frank, A. G. (1970), 'The Development of Underdevelopment', in R. I. Rhodes (ed.), *Imperialism and Underdevelopment: A Reader*, 4–17, New York: Monthly Review Press.

Frank, A. G. (1972), 'Economic Dependence, Class Structure, and Underdevelopment Policy', in J. D. Cockcroft, A. G. Frank and D. L. Johnson (eds), *Dependence and Underdevelopment: Latin America's Political Economy*, 19–45, Garden City: Anchor Books.

Freedom House (2021), 'Freedom in the World 2021: Democracy under Siege', Washington, DC: Freedom House.

Freeman, L. (2015), 'Phenomenology of Racial Oppression', *Knowledge Cultures*, 3(1): 24–44.

Freire, P. (1972 [1968]), *Pedagogy of the Oppressed*, trans. M. B. Ramos, New York: Herder and Herder.

Frempong, A. K. D. (2001), 'Ghana's Election 2000: The Ethnic Undercurrents', in J. R. A. Ayee (ed.), *Deepening Democracy in Ghana: The Politics of the 2000 Elections*, i, 140–59, Accra: Freedom Publications.

Frempong, A. K. D. (2014), 'Ethnicity, Democracy and Ghana's Election 2004', in E. Debrah, E. Gyimah-Boadi, A. Essuman-Johnson and K. A. Ninsin (eds), *Ghana: Essays in the Study of Political Science*, 73–89, Legon-Accra: Sub-Saharan Publishers.

Frempong, A. K. D. (2017), *Elections in Ghana (1951–2016)*, Tema: DigiBooks Publishing.

Fridy, K. S. and W. M. Myers (2019), 'Challenges to Decentralisation in Ghana: Where do Citizens Seek Assistance?' *Commonwealth & Comparative Politics*, 57(1): 71–92.

Fukuyama, F. (1989), 'The End of History?', *The National Interest*, 16: 3–18.

Gathii, J. T. (2007), 'Imperialism, Colonialism, and International Law', *Buffalo Law Review*, 54(4): 1013–66.

Gerber, L. G. (2001), '"Inextricably Linked": Shared Governance and Academic Freedom', *Academe*, 87(3): 22–4.

Gerring, J. (2015), 'The Relevance of Relevance', in G. Stoker, B. G. Peters and J. Pierre (eds), *The Relevance of Political Science*, 36–49, London: Red Globe Press.

Gibbon, P. (1995), *Markets, Civil Society and Democracy in Kenya*, Uppsala: Nordic Africa Institute.

Gibbon, P., Y. Bangura and A. Ofstad, (eds) (1992), *Authoritarianism, Democracy and Adjustment: The Politics of Economic Reform in Africa*, Uppsala: Nordic Africa Institute.

Giroux, H. A. (1995), 'Beyond the Ivory Tower: Public Intellectuals and the Crisis of Higher Education', in C. Nelson and M. Berube (eds), *Higher Education Under Fire: Politics, Economics, and the Crisis of the Humanities*, 238–58, New York: Routledge.

Glickman, H. (ed.) (1995), *Ethnic Conflict and Democratization in Africa*, Atlanta: African Studies Association.

Global Integrity (2019), 'Africa Integrity Indicators – Project Summary & Methodology', Washington, DC: Global Integrity.

Goggin, M. L. (1986), 'The "Too Few Cases/Too Many Variables" Problem in Implementation Research', *The Western Political Quarterly*, 39(2): 328–47.

Goody, J. (2006), *The Theft of History*, Cambridge: Cambridge University Press.

Gordon, A. A. (1996), *Transforming Capitalism and Patriarchy: Gender and Development in Africa*, Boulder: Lynne Rienner.

Gordon, L. R. (2011), 'Shifting the Geography of Reason in an Age of Disciplinary Decadence', *Transmodernity*, 1(2): 95–103.

Gouws, A., J. S. Kotze and J.-A. Van Wyk (2013), 'Celebrating 40 Years: The State of Political Science in South Africa in 2014', *Politikon*, 40(3): 393–423.

Green, L. (1999), 'Positivism and Conventionalism', *Canadian Journal of Law and Jurisprudence*, 12(1): 35–52.

Grischow, J. D. (2008), 'Rural "Community", Chiefs and Social Capital: The Case of Southern Ghana', *Journal of Agrarian Change*, 8(1): 64–93.

Grosfoguel, R. (2013), 'The Structure of Knowledge in Westernized Universities: Epistemic Racism/Sexism and the Four Genocides/Epistemicides of the Long 16th Century', Human Architecture: *Journal of the Sociology of Self-Knowledge*, 11(1): 73–90.

Gwagwa, N. N. (1991), 'Women in Local Government: Towards a Future South Africa', *Environment and Urbanization*, 3(1): 70–8.

Habermas, J. (1989), *The Structural Transformation of the Public Sphere*, Cambridge: Polity Press.

Halpern, C., P. Hassenteufel and P. Zittoun, (eds) (2018), *Policy Analysis in* France, Bristol: Policy Press.

Hansen, G. E. (1969), 'Intellect and Power: Some Notes on the Intellectual as a Political Type', *The Journal of Politics*, 31(2): 311–28.

Harbeson, J. W., D. S. Rothchild and N. Chazan (eds) (1994), *Civil Society and the State in Africa*, Boulder: Lynne Rienner Publishers.

Hardgrave, R. L. (1994), 'India: The Dilemmas of Diversity', in L. Diamond and M. F. Plattner (eds), *Nationalism, Ethnic Conflict, and Democracy*, 71–85, Baltimore: Johns Hopkins University Press.

Harrison, G. (2004), *The World Bank and Africa: The Construction of Governance States*, London: Routledge.

Hartlaub, S. G. and F. A. Lancaster (2008), 'Teacher Characteristics and Pedagogy in Political Science', *Journal of Political Science Education*, 4(4): 377–93.

Hasselskog, M. and I. Schierenbeck (2015), 'National Policy in Local Practice: The Case of Rwanda', *Third World Quarterly*, 36(5): 950–66.

Hassim, S. (2006), *Women's Organizations and Democracy in South Africa: Contesting Authority. Women in Africa and the Diaspora*, Madison: University of Wisconsin Press.

Hassim, S. (2014a), *The ANC Women's League: Sex, Gender and Politics. Ohio Short Histories of Africa*, Athens: Ohio University Press.

Hassim, S. (2014b), 'A Life of Refusal. Winnie Madikizela-Mandela and Violence in South Africa', *Storia delle Donne*, 10: 55–77.

Hausner, S. L. (2019), 'The Division of Labour after Durkheim', in L. Spillman (ed.), *Oxford Bibliographies in Sociology*, Online, Oxford and New York: Oxford University Press.

Hay, C. (2002), *Political Analysis: A Critical Introduction*, New York: Palgrave.

Hay, C. (2015), 'Relevant to Whom? Relevant for what? The Role and Public Responsibility of the Political Analyst', in G. Stoker, B. G. Peters and J. Pierre (eds), *The Relevance of Political Science*, 50–64, London: Red Globe Press.

Hayes, G. (2016), 'Chabani Manganyi: Black Intellectual and Psychologist', *Psychology in Society*, 52: 73–9.

Headley, J. M. (2007), *The Europeanization of the World: On the Origins of Human Rights and Democracy*, Princeton: Princeton University Press.

Hegel, G. W. F. (1971 [1894]), *Philosophy of Mind*, trans. W. Wallace, Oxford: Clarendon Press.

Heidegger, M. (1962), *Being and Time*, trans. J. Macquarrie and E. S. Robinson, New York: Harper Collins.

Helmke, G. and S. Levitsky (2004), 'Informal Institutions and Comparative Politics: A Research Agenda', *Perspectives on Politics*, 2(4): 725–40.

Herbst, J. (2000), *States and Power in Africa: Comparative Lessons in Authority and Control*, Princeton: Princeton University Press.

Hicken, A. (2011), 'Clientelism', *Annual Review of Political Science*, 14(1): 289–310.

Hindess, B. (1997), 'Antipolitical Motifs in Western Political Discourse', in A. Schedler (ed.), *The End of Politics? Explorations into Modern Antipolitics*, 21–39, London: Palgrave Macmillan.

Hirschman, A. O. (1981), *Essays in Trespassing: Economics to Politics and Beyond*, Cambridge: Cambridge University Press.

Holub, R. C. (1991), *Jürgen Habermas: Critic in the Public Sphere*, London: Routledge.

Holzinger, K., F. G. Kern and D. Kromrey (2016), 'The Dualism of Contemporary Traditional Governance and the State: Institutional Setups and Political Consequences', *Political Research Quarterly*, 69(3): 469–81.

Hooker, J. R. (1963), 'The Anthropologists' Frontier: The Last Phase of African Exploitation', *The Journal of Modern African Studies*, 1(4): 455–9.

Hope, K. R. Sr. (2001), 'The New Public Management: Context and Practice in Africa', *International Public Management Journal*, 4(2): 119–34

Horowitz, D. L. (1985), *Ethnic Groups in Conflict*, Berkeley: University of California Press.

Houde, J. and B. Lettre (1965), 'Droit public et science politique', *Les Cahiers de droit*, 6(2): 71–9.

Hountondji, P. (1990). 'Scientific Dependence in Africa Today', *Research in African Literatures*, 21(3): 5–15.

Hountondji, P., ed. (1997), *Endogenous Knowledge: Research Trails*, Dakar: Codesria.

Hountondji, P. (2009), 'Knowledge of Africa, Knowledge by Africans: Two Perspectives on African Studies', *RCCS Annual Review*.

Huggins, C. (2017), *Agricultural Reform in Rwanda: Authoritarianism, Markets and Zones of Governance*, London: Zed Books.

Hughes, J. A. and W. W. Sharrock (1997), *The Philosophy of Social Research*, 3rd edn, London: Routledge.

Hultin, M. (1985), *Skill Development for Self Reliance: Regional Project in Eastern and Southern Africa*, Stockholm: Sida.

Huntington, S. P. (1965), 'Political Development and Political Decay', *World Politics*, 17(3): 386–430.

Huntington, S. P. (1968), *Political Order in Changing Societies*, New Haven: Yale University Press.

Huntington, S. P. (1991), *The Third Wave: Democratization in the Late Twentieth Century*, Norman: University of Oklahoma Press.

Huntington, S. P. (1996), *The Clash of Civilizations and the Remaking of World Order*, New York: Simon & Schuster.

Hyden, G. (1974), 'Co-operative Education and Co-operative Development: The Tanzanian Experience', *Agricultural Administration*, 1(1): 35–50.

Hyden, G. (1975), 'Ujamaa, Villagisation and Rural Development in Tanzania', *Development Policy Review*, A8(1): 53–72.

Hyden, G. (1989), 'Political Science in Post Independence Africa', in W. O. Oyugi (ed.), *The Teaching and Research of Political Science in Eastern Africa*, 13–32, Addis Ababa: OSSREA.

Hyden, G. (2019a), 'Comparative Analysis in African Politics', in *Oxford Research Encyclopedia of Politics*, Oxford: Oxford University Press.

Hyden, G. (2019b), 'Democracy in African Governance: Seeing and Doing It Differently', Stockholm: Expertgruppen för biståndsanalys.

Ibrahim, F. A. (2000), 'Sudanese Women under Repression, and the Shortest Way to Equality', in M. R. Waller and J. Rycenga, *Frontline Feminisms: Women, War, and Resistance*, pp. 129–39, London: Taylor & Francis.

Ibrahim, J. (1997), *Expanding Democratic Space in Nigeria*, Dakar: Codesria.

Ibrahim, J. (1998), 'Political Scientists and the Subversion of Democracy in Nigeria', in G. Nzongola-Ntalaja and M. C. Lee (eds), *The State and Democracy in Africa*, 114–24, Trenton and Asmara: Africa World Press.

Ibrahim, J. (2004), 'The First Lady Syndrome and the Marginalisation of Women from Power: Opportunities or Compromises for Gender Equality?', *Feminist Africa* 3: 48–69.

Idahosa, G. E. (2021), 'African Women in University Management and Leadership', in O. Yacob-Haliso and T. Falola (eds), *The Palgrave Handbook of African Women's Studies*, 1–17, Cham: Palgrave Macmillan.

Ihonvbere, J. O. (1996), 'Where Is the Third Wave? A Critical Evaluation of Africa's Non-Transition to Democracy', *Africa Today*, 43(4): 343–67.

Isike, C. (2019), 'Digitalization and Political Science in South Africa', in M. Kneuer and H. V. Milner (eds), *Political Science and Digitalization – Global Perspectives*, 271–83, Leverkusen Opladen: Verlag Barbara Budrich.

Jacobs, J. A. and S. Frickel (2009), 'Interdisciplinarity: A Critical Assessment', *Annual Review of Sociology*, 35: 43–65.

Jacobs, S. (2022), 'Where is Black Feminism? An Interview with Desiree Lewis', *Buala/Africa is a Country*, 28 April 2022.

Jega, A. (1995), 'Nigerian Universities and Academic Staff under Military Rule', *Review of African Political Economy*, 22(64): 251–6.

Jinadu, L. A. (1987), 'The Institutional Development of Political Science in Nigeria: Trends, Problems and Prospects', *International Political Science Review*, 8(1): 59–72.

Jinadu, L. A. (2000), 'The Globalisation of Political Science: An African Perspective: Presidential Address, June 22, 1999', *African Journal of Political Science / Revue Africaine de Science Politique*, 5(1): 1–13.

Jinadu, L. A. (2002), 'AAPS, African Political Science and Globalisation: Which Way Forward?', *African Journal of Political Science*, 7(2): 1–10.

Jinadu, L. A. (2004), 'Explaining and Managing Ethnic Conflict in Africa: Towards a Cultural Theory of Democracy', *African Journal of Political Science*, 9(1): 1–26.

Johnson, C. A. (2004), *The Sorrows of Empire: Militarism, Secrecy, and the End of the Republic*, London: Verso.

Johnsson, A. I., K. Nyström and R. Sundén (1983), *Adult Education in Tanzania: A Review*, Stockholm: Sida.

Jose, J. and S. C. Motta (2017), 'Reoccupying The Political: transforming Political Science', *Social Identities*, 23(6): 651–60.

Joseph, R., ed. (1999), *State, Conflict, and Democracy in Africa*, Boulder: Lynne Rienner.

Juma, C. and N. Clark (1995), 'Policy Research in Sub-Saharan Africa: An Exploration', *Public Administration & Development*, 15(2): 121–37.

Kabira, W. M. (2012), *Time for Harvest: Women and Constitution Making in Kenya*, Nairobi: University of Nairobi Press.

Kabira, W. M., J. Adhiambo-Oduol and M. Nzomo (1993), *Democratic Change in Africa: Women's Perspective*, Nairobi: Association of African Women for Research and Development; ACTS Gender Institute, African Centre for Technology Studies.

Kampala Declaration (1990), 'The Kampala Declaration on Intellectual Freedom and Social Responsibility (1990)', https://digitallibrary.un.org/record/520822 (accessed 20 April 2021).

Kaplan, R. D. (1993), *Balkan Ghosts: A Journey Through History*, Manhattan and London: St. Martin's Press and Macmillan.

Karlström, M. (1996), 'Imagining Democracy: Political Culture and Democratisation in Buganda', *Africa: Journal of the International African Institute*, 66(4): 485–505.

Kaufmann, D., A. Kraay and M. Mastruzzi (2010), 'The Worldwide Governance Indicators: Methodology and Analytical Issues', *Policy Research Working Paper: The World Bank*, 5430, https://openknowledge.worldbank.org/handle/10986/3913

Kelsall, T. (2011), 'Going with the Grain in African Development?', *Development Policy Review*, 29(1): 223–51.

Kenfack Temfack, E. (2005), 'L'autorité de la norme constitutionnelle au Cameroun', Université de Douala.

Kenny, M. E., L. A. K. Simon, K. Kiley-Brabeck and R. M. Lerner (eds) (2001), *Learning to Serve: Promoting Civil Society Through Service Learning*, Norwell: Kluwer Academic Publishers.

Khan, M. H. (2004), 'State Failure in Developing Countries and Institutional Reform Strategies', presented at the Annual World Bank Conference on Development Economics – Europe 2003, Paris: World Bank, https://eprints.soas.ac.uk/3683/1/State_Failure.pdf

Kibwana, K. (2001), 'Women, Politics and Gender Politiking: Questions from Kenya', in J. Oloka-Onyango, *Constitutionalism in Africa: Creating Opportunities, Facing Challenges*, 194–210, Kampala: Fountain Press.

Kimambo, I. N. (1971), *A Political History of the Pare of Tanzania*, New York: International Publishers.

Kingston, K. G. (2011), 'The Impacts of the World Bank and IMF Structural Adjustment Programmes on Africa: The Case Study of Cote D'Ivoire, Senegal, Uganda, and Zimbabwe', *Sacha Journal of Policy and Strategic Studies*, 1(2): 110–30.

Kirk-Greene, A. H. M. (1967), 'The Peoples of Nigeria: The Cultural Background to the Crisis', *African Affairs*, 66(262): 3–11.

Kirst, S. (2020), '"Chiefs do not Talk Law, most of them Talk Power." Traditional Authorities in Conflicts over Land Grabbing in Ghana', *Canadian Journal of African Studies / Revue Canadienne Des Études Africaines*, 54(3): 519–39.

Kleinberg, R. B. and J. A. Clark, eds (2000), *Economic Liberalization, Democratization and Civil Society in the Developing World*, London: Palgrave Macmillan UK.

Kleist, N. (2011), 'Modern Chiefs: Tradition, Development and Return among Traditional Authorities in Ghana', *African Affairs*, 110(441): 629–47.

Korff, R., V. Korff and P. Manakit (2006), 'Patronage, Activists and Repression: A Comparison of Minority Conflicts in Northern and Southern Thailand', *European Journal of East Asian Studies*, 5(1): 71–100.

Krasner, S. D. (2009), *Power, the State, and Sovereignty: Essays on International Relations*, London and New York: Routledge.

Kubler, D. and J. de Maillard (2009), *Analyser les politiques publiques*, Grenoble: Presses Universitaires de Grenoble.

Kwachou, M. (2022), 'In response to Acker: Black and African Feminist Theories on Gender and Education', *Comparative Education*, 59(2): 169-192.

Kwapong, A. (1966), 'Address by the Vice-chancellor, Dr. Alexander Kwapong, to Congregation of the University of Ghana', *Minerva*, 4(4): 542–54.

Kwarteng, K. (2012), *Ghosts of Empire: Britain's Legacies in the New World*, London: Bloomsbury Publishing.

Kwesiga, J. C. (2003), 'The National Machinery for Gender Equality in Uganda: Institutionalised Gesture Politics?' In *Mainstreaming Gender, Democratizing the State?: Institutional Mechanisms for the Advancement of Women* ed. S. Rai. Manchester: Manchester University Press.

Lake, D. A. and D. Rothchild (1998), 'Spreading Fear: The Genesis of Transnational Ethnic Conflict', in D. A. Lake and D. Rothchild (eds), *The International Spread of Ethnic Conflict: Fear, Diffusion, and Escalation*, 3–32, Princeton: Princeton University Press.

Lambach, D. (2007), 'Close Encounters in the Third Dimension: The Regional Effects of State Failure', in T. Debiel and D. Lambach (eds), *State Failure Revisited I: Globalization of Security and Neighborhood Effects*, 32–52, Duisburg: Institute for Development and Peace.

Lambsdorff, J. G. (2006), 'The Methodology of the Corruption Perceptions Index 2006', Transparency International (TI) and University of Passau, 1–12, https://images .transparencycdn.org/images/2006_CPI_LongMethodology_EN_200407_141551.pdf

Lamont, M. (1982), 'Le Pouvoir des intellectuels', *Politique*, 1(1): 19–46.

Lartey, N. L. (2018), 'REGSEC Orders Closure of KNUST, Imposes Curfew after Violent Protest', *Citinewsroom*, https://citinewsroom.com/2018/10/regsec-orders-closure-of -knust-imposes-curfew-after-violent-protest/ (accessed 19 April 2021).

Latif, M. M. M. A. (2014), 'Academic Freedom: Problems in Conceptualization and Research', *Higher Education Research & Development*, 33(2): 399–401.

Lauer, H. and K. Anyidoho (eds) (2012), *Reclaiming the Human Sciences and Humanities through African Perspectives*, Accra: Sub-Saharan Publishers.

Lauth, H.-J. (2000), 'Informal Institutions and Democracy', *Democratization*, 7(4): 21–50.

Lavigne Delville, P. (2017), 'Pour une socio-anthropologie de l'action publique dans les pays "sous régime d'aide"', *Anthropologie & développement*, 45: 33–64.

Lavigne Delville, P. and S. Ayimpam (2018), 'Public Policy and Public Action in Africa, between Practical Norms, Political Dynamics and Outside Influences', *Anthropologie & Développement*, 48–49: 7–23.

Lemarchand, R. (1972), 'Political Clientelism and Ethnicity in Tropical Africa: Competing Solidarities in Nation-Building', *The American Political Science Review*, 66(1): 68–90.

Lentz, C. (2006), 'Decentralization, the State and Conflicts over Local Boundaries in Northern Ghana', *Development and Change*, 37(4): 901–19.

Le Roy, M. K. (2013), *Research Methods in Political Science (with MicroCase Printed Access Card)*, Belmont: Cengage.

Lewis, D. (2002), *African Feminist Studies: 1980–2002*. Review essay for the African Gender Institute's 'Strengthening Gender and Women's Studies for Africa's Social Transformation' Project, http://www.gwsafrica.org/knowledge/africa.

Lewis, D. and G. Baderoon (2021), *Surfacing: On Being Black and Feminist in South Africa*, Johannesburg: Wits University Press.

Leys, C. (1975), *Underdevelopment in Kenya: The Political Economy of Neo-Colonialism*, London: Heinemann.

Lijphart, A. (1971), 'Comparative Politics and the Comparative Method', *The American Political Science Review*, 65(3): 682–93.

Lijphart, A. (1977), *Democracy in Plural Societies: A Comparative Exploration*, New Haven: Yale University Press.

Lindberg, S. I. (2006), *Democracy and Elections in Africa*, Baltimore: Johns Hopkins University Press.

Lindberg, S. I. (2013), 'Have the Cake and Eat It: The Rational Voter in Africa', *Party Politics*, 19(6): 945–61.

Lindberg, S. I. and M. K. C. Morrison (2008), 'Are African Voters Really Ethnic or Clientelistic? Survey Evidence from Ghana', *Political Science Quarterly*, 123(1): 95–122.

Livsey, T (2017), *Nigeria's University Age: Reframing Decolonization and Development*, Cambridge Imperial and Post-colonial Studies Series, 300, London: Palgrave Macmillan.

Lofchie, M. F. (1968), 'Political Theory and African Politics', *The Journal of Modern African Studies*, 6(1): 3–15.

Long, N. (2001), *Development Sociology: Actor Perspectives*, New York: Routledge.

Lovejoy, A. O. (1940), 'Reflections on the History of Ideas', *Journal of the History of Ideas*, 1(1): 3–23.

Lowe Morna, C., ed. (2004), *Ringing up the Changes: Gender in Southern African Politics*, Johannesburg: Gender Links.

Luhmann, N. (1986), 'The Autopoiesis of Social Systems', in F. Geyer and J. van der Zouwen (eds), *Sociocybernetic Paradoxes*, 172–92, London: Sage Publications.

Lumumba-Kasongo, T. (1999), *The Dynamics of Economic and Political Relations between Africa and Foreign Powers: A Study in International Relations*, Westport: Praeger.

Lumumba-Kasongo, T. (2002), 'Reconceptualizing the State as the Leading Agent of Development in the Context of Globalization in Africa', *African Journal of Political Science*, 7(1): 79–108.

Lumumba-Kasongo, T. (2017), 'Pan-African Curriculum in Higher Education: A Reflection', in M. Cross and A. Ndofirepi (eds), *Knowledge and Change in African Universities: Volume 2 – Re-Imagining the Terrain*, 43–66, Rotterdam: Sense Publishers.

Lund, C. (2006), 'Twilight Institutions: Public Authority and Local Politics in Africa', *Development and Change*, 37(4): 685–705.

Lushaba, L. S. (2009), *Development as Modernity, Modernity as Development*, Dakar: Codesria.

Mackenzie, W. J. M. (1971), 'The Political Science of Political Science', *Government and Opposition*, 6(3): 277–302.

MacLean, L. M. (2004), 'Mediating Ethnic Conflict at the Grassroots: The Role of Local Associational Life in Shaping Political Values in Côte d'Ivoire and Ghana', *The Journal of Modern African Studies*, 42(4): 589–617.

Madeira, A. I. (2011), 'Popular Education and Republican Ideals: The Portuguese lay Missions in Colonial Africa, 1917–1927', *Paedagogica Historica*, 47(1–2): 123–38.

Mafeje, A. (1976), 'The Problem of Anthropology in Historical Perspective: An Inquiry into the Growth of the Social Sciences', *Canadian Journal of African Studies*, 10(2): 307–33.

Mafeje, A. (1994), 'African Intellectuals: An Inquiry into their Genesis and Social Options', in M. Diouf and M. Mamdani (eds), *Academic Freedom in Africa*, 193–211, Dakar: Codesria.

Mafeje, A. (1995), 'Benign Recolonization and Malignant Minds in the Service of Imperialism', *Codesria Bulletin*, 2: 17–20.

Mafeje, A. (1998), 'The Beast and the Icon: No End to Ali Mazrui's Pax-Africana Muddles', *Codesria Bulletin*, 2: 9–11.

Mafeje, A. (2000), 'Africanity: A Combative Ontology', *Codesria Bulletin*, 1 & 4: 66–71.

Mafeje, A. (2011), 'Africanity: A Combative Ontology', in R. Devisch and F. B. Nyamnjoh (eds), *The Postcolonial Turn: Re-Imagining Anthropology and Africa*, 31–44, Bemenda: Langaa RPCIG.

Magubane, B. and J. C. Faris (1985), 'On the Political Relevance of Anthropology', *Dialectical Anthropology*, 9(1/4): 91–104.

Maldonado-Torres, N. (2011), 'Thinking through the Decolonial Turn: Post-continental Interventions in Theory, Philosophy, and Critique—An Introduction', *Transmodernity*, 1(2): 1–15.

Mama, A. (1995), 'Feminism or Femocracy? State Feminism and Democratisation in Nigeria', *Africa Development*, 20(1): 37–58.

Mama, A. (2007), 'Is it Ethical to Study Africa? Preliminary thoughts on Scholarship and Freedom', *African Studies Review*, 50(1): 1–26.

Mama, A. (2019), 'African Feminist Thought', in *Oxford Research Encyclopedia of African History*, https://doi.org/10.1093/acrefore/9780190277734.013.504

Mamdani, M. (1994), 'The Intelligentsia, the State and Social Movements in Africa', in M. Mamdani and M. Diouf (eds), *Academic Freedom in Africa*, 247–61, Dakar: Codesria.

Mamdani, M. (1996), *Citizen and Subject: Contemporary Africa and the Legacy of Late Colonialism*, Princeton: Princeton University Press.

Mamdani, M. (2007), *Scholars in the Marketplace: The Dilemmas of Neo-Liberal Reform at Makerere University, 1989-2005*, Dakar: Codesria.

Mamdani, M. (2019), 'Decolonising Universities', in J. D. Jansen (ed.), *Decolonisation in Universities: The Politics of Knowledge*, 15–28, Johannesburg: Wits University Press.

Mamdani, M. and E. Wamba-dia-Wamba, eds (1995), *African Studies in Social Movements and Democracy*, Dakar: Codesria.

Manning, C. (2002), *The Politics of Peace in Mozambique: Post-Conflict Democratization, 1992-2000*, Westport: Praeger.

Maringe, F. (2017), 'Transforming Knowledge Production Systems in the New African University', in M. Cross and A. Ndofirepi (eds), *Knowledge and Change in African Universities: Volume 2 – Re-Imagining the Terrain*, 1–18, Rotterdam: Sense Publishers.

Marshall, M. G., T. R. Gurr and K. Jaggers (2019), 'Polity IV Project: Political Regime Characteristics and Transitions, 1800–2018. Dataset Users' Manual', Center for Systemic Peace, 86, http://www.systemicpeace.org/inscr/p4manualv2018.pdf

Masaiti, G. (2015), 'Effectiveness and Viability of Revenue Diversification in Sub-Saharan Africa's Higher Education: Examining Zambia's Public Universities', *International Journal of Humanities Social Sciences and Education*, 2(5): 33–44.

Masaiti, G. and H. Shen (2013), 'Cost Sharing in Zambia's Public Universities: Prospects and Challenges', *European Journal of Educational Research*, 2(1): 1–15.

Mate, N. (2009), 'Factors Affecting Political Participation in Zambia', presented at the 2009 Afrobarometer Summer School, University of Cape Town (UCT) South Africa.

Mate, N. (2014), 'Emerging Knowledge and Approaches in Measuring Democratic Quality', presented at the Making Gains and Counting Losses in 20 years of Democracy: A Roundtable on Perspectives on Democratic Accountability in South Africa, Pretoria.

Matembe, M. R. K. and N. R. Dorsey (2002), *Miria Matembe: Gender, politics, and constitution making in Uganda*. Fountain Series in Gender Studies, Kampala: Fountain Publishers.

Matip, N. F. and K. Koutouki (2009), 'Cameroun: Une Analyse Juridique de la Mutation Constitutionnelle du 10 Avril 2008', *Institute for Security Studies*, 1–11.

Mazrui, A. A. (1966), 'Nkrumah: The Leninist Czar', *Transition*, 26: 8–17.

Mazrui, A. A. (1968), 'From Social Darwinism to Current Theories of Modernization: A Tradition of Analysis', *World Politics*, 21(1): 69–83.

Mazrui, A. A. (1970), 'An African's New Guinea', *New Guinea*, 5(3): 54–5.

Mazrui, A. A. (1980), *The African Condition: A Political Diagnosis*, London: Heinemann.

Mazrui, A. A. (1986), *The Africans: A Triple Heritage*, 1st American edition, Boston: Little Brown & Company.

Mazrui, A. A. (1994), 'Decaying Parts of Africa need Benign Colonisation', *International Herald Tribune*, 4 August, 23–44.

Mazrui, A. A. (1995a), 'Self-Colonization and the Search for Pax Africana: A Rejoinder', *Codesria Bulletin*, 2: 20–22.

Mazrui, A. A. (1995b), 'Pax-Africana: Between the State and the Intellectuals', *Codesria Bulletin*, 3: 19–22.

Mazrui, A. A. (2004a), *Islam: Between Globalization & Counter-Terrorism*, Trenton: Africa World Press.

Mazrui, A. A. (2004b), *The African Predicament and the American Experience: A Tale of Two Edens*, Westport: Praeger.

Mazrui, A. A. (2006), *A Tale of Two Africas: Nigeria and South Africa as Contrasting Visions*, ed. J. N. Karioki, London: Adonis & Abbey Publishers.

Mazrui, A. A. (2014), *The Politics of Gender and the Culture of Sexuality: Western, Islamic, and African Perspectives*, ed. E. Anwar, Lanham: University Press of America.

Mbaku, J. M. and J. O. Ihonvbere, eds (2003), *The Transition to Democratic Governance in Africa: The Continuing Struggle*, Westport: Praeger.

Mbalibulha, S. B. B. (2013), 'The History of Makerere Institute of Social Research (MISR) and her Place in the Study of the Social Sciences in Africa', *Journal of Higher Education in Africa / Revue de l'enseignement Supérieur En Afrique*, 11(1–2): 121–42.

Mbembe, A. (1996), *La naissance du maquis dans le Sud-Cameroun (1920–1960): histoire des usages de la raison en colonie*, Paris: Karthala.

Mbembe, A. (2001), *On the Postcolony*, Berkeley: University of California Press.

Mbembe, A. (2002), 'African Modes of Self-Writing', trans. S. Rendall, *Public Culture*, 14(1): 239–73.

Mbembe, A. (2003), 'Necropolitics', *Public Culture*, 15(1): 11–40.

Mbembe, A. (2018), 'Decolonizing African Studies', *African Studies Review*, 61(3): 1–7.

Mbembe, A. (2019), 'Future Knowledges and Their Implications for the Decolonisation Project', in J. D. Jansen (ed.), *Decolonisation in Universities: The Politics of Knowledge*, 239–54, Johannesburg: Wits University Press.

McFadden, P. (2011), 'Re-crafting Citizenship in the Postcolonial Moment: A Focus on Southern Africa', *Works and Days*, 29(57/58): 265–79.

McKay, V. (1968), 'The Research Climate in Eastern Africa (Report on a Mission for the Research Liaison Committee of the African Studies Association, July–September, 1967)', *African Studies Bulletin*, 11(1): 1–17.

McRobbie, A. (2006), 'Vulnerability, Violence and (cosmopolitan) Ethics: Butler's Precarious Life', *The British Journal of Sociology*, 57(1): 69–86.

Medie, P. A. and A. J. Kang (2018), 'Power, Knowledge and the Politics of Gender in the Global South', *European Journal of Politics and Gender*, 1(1–2): 37–54.

Meena, R. and M. Mbilinyi (1991) 'Women's Research and Documentation Project (Tanzania)', *Signs*, 16(4): 852–9.

Mengisteab, K. (2008), 'Globalization and State–Society Relations in Africa', *Africa Development*, 33(2): 37–65.

Mengisteab, K. and C. Daddieh, eds (1999), *State Building and Democratization in Africa: Faith, Hope, and Realities*, Westport: Praeger.

Mernissi, F., N. El Saadawi and M. Vajrathon (1978), 'A Critical Look at the Wellesley Conference', *Quest: A Feminist Quarterly*, 4(2): 101–8.

Metuge, W. (1983), 'Class Interests in the Teaching of Political Science in African Universities', in Y. R. Barongo (ed.), *Political Science in Africa: A Critical Review*, 48–55, London and Ibadan: Zed Press; Progressive and Socialist Books Depot.

Meynaud, J. (1961), *Introduction à la science politique*, 2nd edn, Paris: Librairie Armand Colin.

Migdal, J. S. (1988), *Strong Societies and Weak States: State-Society Relations and State Capabilities in the Third World*, Princeton: Princeton University Press.

Mignolo, W. D. (2009), 'Epistemic Disobedience, Independent Thought and Decolonial Freedom', *Theory, Culture & Society*, 26(7–8): 159–81.

Mill, J. S. (1958 [1861]), *Considerations on Representative Government*, New York: Liberal Arts Press.

Miti, K. N. (1989), 'On Research and Teaching of Political Theory in East Africa', in W. O. Oyugi (ed.), *The Teaching and Research of Political Science in Eastern Africa*, 52–62, Addis Ababa: OSSREA.

Mkandawire, T. (1997), 'The Social Sciences in Africa: Breaking Local Barriers and Negotiating International Presence. The Bashorun M. K. O. Abiola Distinguished Lecture Presented to the 1996 African Studies Association Annual Meeting', *African Studies Review*, 40(2): 15–36.

Mkandawire, T. (2001), 'Thinking about Developmental States in Africa', *Cambridge Journal of Economics*, 25(3): 289–314.

Mkandawire, T., ed. (2004), *Social Policy in a Development Context*, London: Palgrave Macmillan.

Mkandawire, T., ed. (2005), *African Intellectuals: Rethinking Politics, Language, Gender and Development*, Dakar and London: Codesria; Zed Books.

Mkandawire, T. (2011), 'Running While Others Walk: Knowledge and the Challenge of Africa's Development', *Africa Development*, 36(2): 1–36.

Mkandawire, T. (2015), 'Neopatrimonialism and the Political Economy of Economic Performance in Africa: Critical Reflections', *World Politics*, 67(3): 563–612.

Mkandawire, T. and A. O. Olukoshi, eds (1995), *Between Liberalisation and Oppression: The Politics of Structural Adjustment in Africa*, Dakar: CODESRIA.

Mkandawire, T. and C. C. Soludo (1999), *Our Continent, Our Future: African Perspectives on Structural Adjustment*, Trenton: Africa World Press.

Mngomezulu, B. R. and S. Hadebe (2018), 'What Would the Decolonisation of a Political Science Curriculum Entail? Lessons to be Learnt From the East African Experience at the Federal University of East Africa', *Politikon*, 45(1): 66–80.

Moahi, K. H. (2010), 'Research Issues in the Humanities and Social Sciences in Africa in the 21st Century: Challenges and Opportunities', *Inkanyiso: Journal of Humanities and Social Sciences*, 2(2): 78–85.

Mohamedbhai, G. (2008), *The Effects of Massification on Higher Education in Africa*, Accra: Association of African University Press.

Mohanty, C. T. (1991), 'Under Western Eyes: Feminist Scholarship and Colonial Discourses', in C. Mohanty, D. Russo and L. Torres (eds), *Third World Women and the Politics of Feminism*, 51–80, Bloomington: Indiana University Press.

Mo Ibrahim Foundation (2019), *Agendas 2063 & 2030: Is Africa on Track?*, London: Mo Ibrahim Foundation.

Mokoena, D. A. (2020), 'Women of Marikana in the Media: Decolonial Analysis of Gendered Representations', in S. A. Omotoso, *Women's Political Communication in Africa* 27–42, Cham: Springer.

Monga, C. (1996), *The Anthropology of Anger: Civil Society and Democracy in Africa*, Boulder: Lynne Rienner Publishers.

Mouelle Kombi, N. (2020), 'Qu'est ce que le génocide?', *Cameroon Tribune*, 25 February.

Moyo, J. N. (1992), *Voting for Democracy: A Study of Electoral Politics in Zimbabwe*, Harare: University of Zimbabwe Publications.

Muggah, R. (2006), *No Refuge: The Crisis of Refugee Militarization in Africa*, London: Zed Books.

Mujaju, A. B. (1989), 'Research and Teaching of Comparative Politics in the Eastern African Region', in W. O. Oyugi (ed.), *The Teaching and Research of Political Science in Eastern Africa*, 63–84, Addis Ababa: OSSREA.

Murunga, G. R. (2000), 'review of *Civil Society and the Democratic Experience in Kenya: A Review of Constitution-Making from the Middle: Civil Society and Transition Politics in Kenya, 1992-1997*, W. Mutunga', *African Sociological Review*, 4(1): 97–118.

Murunga, G. R. (2002), 'African Women in the Academy and Beyond: Review Essay', *Jenda: A Journal of Culture and African Women Studies*, 2(1).

Murunga, G. R. (2007), 'Governance and the Politics of Structural Adjustment in Kenya', in G. R. Murunga and S. W. Nasong'o (eds), *Kenya: The Struggle for Democracy*, 263–300, London and Dakar: Zed Books; Codesria.

Murunga, G. R. and S. W. Nasong'o (2006), 'Bent on Self-destruction: The Kibaki Regime in Kenya', *Journal of Contemporary African Studies*, 24(1): 1–28.

Murunga, G. R. and S. W. Nasong'o eds. (2007), *Kenya: The Struggle for Democracy*, London and Dakar: Zed Books; Codesria.

Mustapha, A. R. (2006), 'Rethinking Africanist Political Science', *CODESRIA Bulletin*, 3–4: 3–10.

Myers, W. M. and K. S. Fridy (2017), 'Formal versus Traditional Institutions: Evidence from Ghana', *Democratization*, 24(2): 367–82.

Nabudere, D. W. (1977), *The Political Economy of Imperialism: Its Theoretical and Polemical Treatment from Mercantilist to Multilateral Imperialism*, Dar es Salaam: Tanzania Publishing House.

Nabudere, D. W. (1979), *Essays on the Theory and Practice of Imperialism*, London: Onyx Press.

Nabudere, D. W. (2006), 'The Frantz Fanon Blog: Walter Rodney, The Dar es Salaam School and the Current Situation', *The Frantz Fanon Blog*, http://readingfanon.blogspot.com/2011/12/walter-rodney-dar-essalaamschool-and.html (accessed 24 March 2021).

Napier, C. J. and P. Labuschagne (2018), 'The Study Of Political Science In South Africa And Beyond: the Search For Relevance', *Africa Review*, 10(2): 188–205.

Napier, C. J. and P. Mtimkulu (2013), 'The Idea of Africa in South African Political Science', *Politikon*, 40(3): 467–78.

Narayan, U. (1997), *Dislocating Cultures: Third World Feminism and the Politics of Knowledge*, London: Routledge.

Nasong'o, S. W. (2004), 'From Political Dictatorship to Authoritarian Economism: Plural Politics and Free Market Reforms in Africa', *Journal of Third World Studies*, 21(2): 107–25.

Nasong'o, S. W. (2005), *Contending Political Paradigms in Africa: Rationality and the Politics of Democratization in Kenya and Zambia*, New York: Routledge

Nasong'o, S. W. (2007), 'Negotiating New Rules of the Game: Social Movements, Civil Society and the Kenyan Transition', in G. R. Murunga and S. W. Nasong'o (eds), *Kenya: The Struggle for Democracy*, 19–57, London and Dakar: Zed Books; Codesria.

Nasong'o, S. W. (2008), 'Shifting Modes of Politics in Africa: Theoretical and Conceptual Imperatives', in S. W. Nasong'o (ed.) *The African Search for Stable Forms of Statehood: Essays in Political Criticism*, 19–44, Lewiston: Edwin Mellen Press.

Nasong'o, S. W. (2017), 'Global Citizen, Dialectical Thinker: Ali Mazrui and the Analytical Potency of Mazruiana', in D. N. Wachanga (ed.), *Growing up in a Shrinking World: How Politics, Culture and the Nuclear Age Defined the Biography of Ali A. Mazrui*, 137–53, Trenton: Africa World Press.

Nasong'o, S. W. (2018), 'Man in the Mirror: Echoes of Jomo in Uhuru', *The Elephant*, https://www.theelephant.info/features/2018/11/01/man-in-the-mirror-echoes-of-jomo -in-uhuru/ (accessed 24 March 2021).

Nasong'o, S. W. (2019), 'Rethinking Africa's Development Models: Between Modernization and Dependency Paradigms', *Journal of African Interdisciplinary Studies*, 3(1): 33–40.

Nasong'o, S. W. and T. A. Ayot (2007), 'Women in Kenya's Politics of Transition and Democratisation', in G. R. Murunga and S. W. Nasong'o (eds), *Kenya: The Struggle for Democracy*, 164–96, Dakar and London: Zed.

Ndegwa, S. N. (1996), *The Two Faces of Civil Society: NGOs and Politics in Africa. Kumarian Press Books on International Development*, West Hartford: Kumarian Press.

Ndlovu-Gatsheni, S. J. (2007), 'Giving Africa Voice within Global Governance: Oral History, Human Rights and the United Nations (UN) Human Rights Council', *ASC Working Paper Series*, 73: 1–30.

Ndlovu-Gatsheni, S. J. (2013), *Coloniality of Power in Postcolonial Africa: Myths of Decolonization*, Dakar: Codesria.

Ndlovu-Gatsheni, S. J. (2015), 'Decoloniality in Africa: A Continuing Search for a New World Order', *The Australasian Review of African Studies*, 36(2): 22–50.

Ndlovu-Gatsheni, S. J. (2018), *Epistemic Freedom in Africa: Deprovincialization and Decolonization*, London: Routledge.

Ndlovu-Gatsheni, S. J., R. S. Building and S. Africa (2015), 'Beyond "Clash of Civilizations" Towards "Pluriversality": Paper presented at Cairo Conference on Culture, Egypt', June 2015.

Ndlovu-Gatsheni, S. J. and S. Zondi, eds (2016), *Decolonizing the University, Knowledge Systems and Disciplines in Africa*, Durham: Carolina Academic Press.

Neubert, D. (1999), 'Demokratisierung ohne Zivilgesellschaft? Zur Rolle von Patron-Klient-Beziehungen in den neuen afrikanischen Mehrparteiensystemen', in H.-J. Lauth and U. Liebert (eds), *Im Schatten Demokratischer Legitimität: Informelle Institutionen Und Politische Partizipation Im Interkulturellen Demokratievergleich*, 258–76, Opladen: Westdeutscher Verlag.

Neubert, D. (2004), 'Globalisierung der Demokratie? Klientelismus in Mehrparteiensystemen in Afrika südlich der Sahara', in V. Luhr, A. Kohls and D. Kumitz (eds), *Sozialwissenschaftliche Perspektiven auf Afrika: Festschrift für Manfred Schulz*, 207–23, Münster: LIT.

Neubert, D. (2008), 'Academic Cooperation between Germany and Africa – Challenges and Some Lessons Learnt', in E. W. Schamp and S. Stefan (eds), *Academic Cooperation with Africa: Lessons for Partnership in Higher Education*, 80–93, Münster: LIT.

Neubert, D. (2009), 'Local and Regional Non-State Actors on the Margins of Public Policy in Africa', in A. Peters, L. Koechlin, T. Förster and G. Fenner Zinkernagel (eds), *Non-State Actors as Standard Setters*, 35–60, Cambridge: Cambridge University Press.

Neubert, D. (2020), 'Sociology of Development: Sociology, Development Studies or Already Dead?', in S. Kurfurst and S. Wehner (eds), *Southeast Asian Transformations - Urban and Rural Developments in the 21st Century*, 25–40, Bielefeld: Transcript Verlag.

Nevers, de R. (1993), 'Democratization and Ethnic Conflict', *Survival*, 35(2): 31–48.

Ng, D. and K. Litzenberg (2019), 'Overcoming Disciplinary Divides in Higher Education: The case of Agricultural Economics', *Palgrave Communications*, 5(26): 1–7.

Ngcaweni, W. and B. Ngcaweni, eds (2018), *We Are No Longer at Ease: The Struggle for #FeesMustFall*, Auckland Park, South Africa: Jacana.

Ng'ethe, N. (1977), 'Harambee and Rural Development in Kenya towards a Political/ Administrative Re-interpretation', Institute for Development Studies, University of Nairobi, Working paper:302, 3–24, https://opendocs.ids.ac.uk/opendocs/handle/20 .500.12413/1174

Ngwé, L., H. De Prince Pokam, A. Mandjack and E. Folefack (2006), 'L'université et les universitaires dans les mutations politiques et éducatives au Cameroun', *Cahiers de la recherche sur l'éducation et les savoirs*, 5: 169–91.

Ninsin, K. A. (1998), *Ghana: Transition to Democracy*, Dakar: Codesria.

Nisbet, R. A. (1969), *Social Change and History: Aspects of the Western Theory of Development*, New York: Oxford University Press.

Nkom, S. A. (1993), 'Competing Paradigms in the Search for a More Relevant Social Science in Nigeria', *Journal of Third World Studies*, 10(1): 196–224.

Nkot, P. F. (2001), 'Perversion politique du droit et construction de l'État unitaire au Cameroun', Université Laval, https://www.giersa.ulaval.ca/perversion-politique-du -droit-et-construction-de-letat-unitaire-au-cameroun

Nkot, P. F. (2005), *Usages Politiques du droit en Afrique. Le cas du Cameroun*, Brussels: Bruylant.

Nkot, P. F. (2018), *Dictionnaire de la politique au Cameroun*, 2nd edn, Quebec: Presses de l'Université Laval.

Nmoma, V. (1995), 'Ethnic Conflict, Constitutional Engineering and Democracy in Nigeria', in H. Glickman (ed.), *Ethnic Conflict and Democratization in Africa*, 311–50, Atlanta: African Studies Association Press.

Nnaemeka, O., ed. (1998), *Sisterhood, Feminisms and Power: From Africa to the Diaspora*, Trenton: Africa World Press.

Nnaemeka, O. (2004), 'Nego Feminism: Theorizing, Practicing, and Pruning Africa's Way', *Signs: Journal of Women in Culture and Society*, 29(2): 357–85.

Nnoli, O. (1998), *Ethnic Conflicts in Africa*, Dakar: Codesria.

Nwauwa, A. O. (1997), *Imperialism, Academe and Nationalism: Britain and University Education for Africans 1860–1960*, London: Routledge.

Nyamnjoh, F. B. (2016), *#RhodesMustFall: Nibbling at Resilient Colonialism in South Africa*, Bamenda: Langaa RPCIG.

Nyangira, N. (1987), 'Ethnicity, Class, and Politics in Kenya', in M. G. Schatzberg (ed.), *The Political Economy of Kenya*, 15–31, New York: Praeger.

Nyarota, G. (2018), *The Graceless Fall of Robert Mugabe: The End of a Dictator's Reign*, Cape Town: Penguin Books.

Nye, J. S. (2009), 'The Question of Relevance', in G. King, K. L. Schlozman and N. H. Nie (eds), *The Future of Political Science: 100 Perspectives*, 252–54, New York: Routledge.

Nyere, C., J. Van Wyk and A. Muresan (2020), 'African First Ladies, Politics and the State', *Politeia*, 37(2): 1–20.

Nyoka, B. (2012), 'Mafeje and "Authentic Interlocutors": An Appraisal of His Epistemology', *African Sociological Review*, 16(1): 4–18.

Nyoka, B. (2013), 'Negation and Affirmation: A Critique of Sociology in South Africa', *African Sociological Review*, 17(1): 2–24, http://www.jstor.org/stable/24487528

Nyong'o, P. A., ed. (1987), *Popular Struggles for Democracy in Africa: Studies in African Political Economy*, London: Zed Books.

Nyong'o, P. A. (1989), 'State and Society in Kenya: The Disintegration of the Nationalist Coalitions and the Rise of Presidential Authoritarianism 1963–78', *African Affairs*, 88(351): 229–51.

Nyong'o, P. A. (1992a), 'Africa: The Failure of One-Party Rule', *Journal of Democracy*, 3(1): 90–6.

Nyong'o, P. A. (1992b), *30 Years of Independence in Africa: The Lost Decades?* Nairobi: Academy Science Publishers.

Nyong'o, P. A. (2002), *The Study of African Politics: A Critical Appreciation of a Heritage*, Nairobi: Heinrich Böll Foundation.

Nzegwu, N. (1995), 'Recovering Igbo Traditions: A Case for Indigenous Women's Organizations in Development', in M. Nussbaum and J. Glover, *Women, Culture and Development: A Study of Human Capabilities*, 81–102, Oxford: Clarendon Press.

Nzongola-Ntalaja, G. (1987), *Revolution and Counter-Revolution in Africa: Essays in Contemporary Politics*, London: Zed Books.

Nzongola-Ntalaja, G. (1997), 'The Role of Intellectuals in the Struggle for Democracy, Peace and Reconstruction in Africa', *African Journal of Political Science*, 2(2): 1–14, https://www.jstor.org/stable/23493572

Nzongola-Ntalaja, G. and M. C. Lee (1998), *The State and Democracy in Africa*, Trenton: Africa World Press.

O'Brien (1964), 'Speech Delivered by Nkrumah in February 1963'.

Obudho, R. A. (1983), *Urbanization in Kenya: A Bottom-up Approach to Development Policy*, Illustrated edition, New York: University Press of America.

Odora-Hoppers, C. and H. Richards (2012), *Rethinking Thinking: Modernity's "Other" and the Transformation of the University*, Pretoria: Unisa Press.

Ogundipe-Leslie, M. (1994), *Re-Creating Ourselves: African Women & Critical Transformations*, Trenton: Africa World Press.

Ojo, O. J. B. (1983), 'Towards a Development Oriented Political Science Curriculum', in Y. R. Barongo (ed.), *Political Science in Africa: A Critical Review*, 56–69, London and Ibadan: Zed Press; Progressive and Socialist Books Depot.

Oketch, M. (2016), 'Financing Higher Education in Sub-Saharan Africa: Some Reflections and Implications for Sustainable Development', *Higher Education*, 72: 525–39.

Okonjo, K. (1976), 'The Dual-Sex Political System in Operation: Igbo Women and Community Politics in Midwestern Nigeria', in N. J. Hafkin and E. G. Bay (eds), *Women in Africa: Studies in Social Economic Change*, 45–58, Stanford: Stanford University Press.

Olivier de Sardan, J.-P. (2015), 'Abandoning the Neo-Patrimonialist Paradigm: For a Pluralist Approach to the Bureaucratic Mode of Governance in Africa', in L. Koechlin and T. Förster (eds), *The Politics of Governance: Actors and Articulations in Africa and Beyond*, 75–92, New York: Routledge.

Olonisakin, F. and A. Okech (eds) (2011), *Women's Security Governance in Africa*, Dakar, Nairobi: Pambazuka Press.

Oloruntoba, S. (2015), 'Pan-Africanism, Knowledge Production and the Third Liberation of Africa', *International Journal of African Renaissance Studies*, 10(1): 7–24.

Olufadewa, I. I., M. A. Adesina and T. Ayorinde (2020), 'From Africa to the World: Reimagining Africa's Research Capacity and Culture in the Global Knowledge Economy', *Journal of Global Health*, 10(1): 1–3.

Olukoshi, A. O. (ed.) (1998), *The Politics of Opposition in Contemporary Africa*, Uppsala: Nordic Africa Institute.

Olukoshi, A. O. (1999), 'State, Conflict and Democracy in Africa: The Complex Process of Renewal', in R. Joseph (ed.), *State, Conflict, and Democracy in Africa*, 451–65, Boulder: Lynne Rienner.

Omar, A. (2016), 'Moving Beyond the Canon: Reflections of a Young African Scholar of Political Theory', *Arts and Humanities in Higher Education*, 15(1): 153–59.

Omotoso, S. A. (ed.) (2020), *Women's Political Communication in Africa*, Cham: Springer.

Omotoso, S. A. and O. M. Fanyiyi (2020), 'Women's Recipe for the African Policom Stew', in S. A. Omotoso, *Women's Political Communication in Africa*, 1–8, Cham: Springer.

Onoge, O. (1977), 'Revolutionary Imperatives in African Sociology', in P. C. W. Gutkind and P. Waterman (eds), *African Social Studies: A Radical Reader*, 32–43, London: Heinemann.

Osaghae, E. E. (1993), 'Colonialism and African Political Thought', *Journal of Asian and African Studies*, 45: 22–38.

Osaghae, E. E. (1994), *Ethnicity and Its Management in Africa: The Democratization Link*, Lagos: Malthouse Press.

Osaghae, E. E. (1995), 'The Study of Political Transitions in Africa', *Review of African Political Economy*, 22(64): 183–97.

Osaghae, E. E. (1999), 'Democratization in sub-Saharan Africa: Faltering Prospects, New Hopes', *Journal of Contemporary African Studies*, 17(1): 5–28.

Osaghae, E. E. (2005), 'The State of Africa's Second Liberation', *Interventions: International Journal of Postcolonial Studies*, 7(1): 1–20.

Osaghae, E. E. (2007), 'Fragile States', *Development in Practice*, 17(4/5): 691–9.

Osaghae, E. E. (2015), 'A State of Our Own: Second Independence, Federalism and the Decolonisation of the State in Africa', University of London Inaugural Lecture, Ibadan: Bookcraft.

Osha, S. (2018), *Dani Nabudere's Afrikology: A Quest for African Holism*, Dakar: Codesria.

Osinulu, C. and N. E. Mba (1996), *Nigerian Women in Politics, 1986–1993*, Ikeja and Lagos State: Malthouse Press.

Owona, A. (1973), 'La naissance du Cameroun (1884–1914)', *Cahiers d'Études africaines*, 13(49): 16–36.

Owona Nguini, M. É. and H.-L. Menthong (2018), '"Gouvernement perpétuel" et démocratisation janusienne au Cameroun (1990–2018)', *Politique africaine*, 150(2): 97–114.

Oyewumi, O. (1997), *The Invention of Women: Making an African Sense of Western Gender Discourses*, Minneapolis: University of Minnesota Press.

Oyewumi, O., ed. (2005), *African Gender Studies: A Reader*, 1st edn, New York: Palgrave Macmillan.

Oyovbaire, S. E. (1980), 'The Responsibility of Political Science in Nigeria', *Nigerian Journal of Political Science*, 2(2): 23–24.

Oyovbaire, S. E. (1983), 'The Tyranny of Borrowed Paradigms and the Responsibility of Political Science: The Nigerian Experience', in Y. Barongo (ed.), *Political Science in Africa: A Critical Review*, 239–54, London: Zed Books.

Oyugi, W. O., A. K. Gitonga, M. Chege and A. Odhiambo, eds (1988), *Democratic Theory & Practice in Africa*, Enl. edn, Nairobi: Heinemann.

Oyugi, W. O., P. Wanyande and C. Odhiambo-Mbai (eds) (2003), *The Politics of Transition in Kenya: From KANU to NARC*, Nairobi: Heinrich Böll Foundation.

Paden, J. N. (1971), 'Communal Competition, Conflict and Violence in Kano', in H. Wolpe (ed.), *Nigeria: Modernization and the Politics of Communalism*, 113–44, East Lansing: Michigan State University Press.

Padonou, O. (2019), 'Où sont les intellectuels africains?', *Jeune Afrique* (Paris, 31 March): 18–19.

Park, P. (1988), 'Toward an Emancipatory Sociology: Abandoning Universalism for True Indigenisation', *International Sociology*, 3(2): 161–70.

Parpart, J. L. and K. A. Staudt, eds (1990), *Women and the State in Africa*, Boulder: Lynne Rienner Publishers.

Pereira, C. (2001), 'Culture, Gender and Constitutional Restructuring in Nigeria', in J. Oloka-Onyango, ed. *Constitutionalism in Africa: Creating Opportunities, Facing Challenges*, 146–72, Kampala: Fountain Press.

Pereira, C. (2002), 'Between Knowing and Imagining: What Space for Feminism in Scholarship on Africa?' *Feminist Africa* 1: 9–33.

Perkin, E. and J. Court (2005), 'Networks and Policy Processes in International Development: A Literature Review', Overseas Development Institute: Working Paper, Working paper, https://www.files.ethz.ch/isn/22716/wp252.pdf

Petchenkine, Y. (1992), *Ghana: In Search of Stability, 1957–92*, Westport: Praeger.

Peters, B. G. (1999), *Institutional Theory in Political Science: The 'New Institutionalism'*, London: Pinter.

Peters, M. A. (2015), 'Why is my curriculum white?' *Educational Philosophy and Theory*, 47(7): 641–46.

Peters, S. J., T. R. Alter and T. J. Shaffer (eds) (2018), *Jumping into Civic Life: Stories of Public Work from Extension Professionals*, Dayton: Kettering Foundation Press.

Petiteville, F. and A. Smith (2006), 'Analyser les politiques publiques internationales', *Revue Française de Science Politique*, 56(3): 357–66.

Pierson, P. (2000), 'The Limits of Design: Explaining Institutional Origins and Change', *Governance*, 13(4): 475–99.

Pitcher, A., M. H. Moran and M. Johnston (2009), 'Rethinking Patrimonialism and Neopatrimonialism in Africa', *African Studies Review*, 52(1): 125–56.

Pokam, H. de P. (2010), 'La participation des universitaires au processus de construction/reconstruction de l'espace public au Cameroun', *African Anthropologist*, 17(1–2): 81–116.

Pollard, A. and J. Court (2005), 'How Civil Society Organisations use Evidence to Influence Policy Processes: A Literature Review', Overseas Development Institute: Working Paper, 249, https://www.files.ethz.ch/isn/22707/wp249.pdf

Post, K. W. J. (1963), *The Nigerian Federal Election of 1959: Politics and Administration in a Developing Political System*, London: Oxford University Press.

Post, R. C. (2012), *Democracy, Expertise, and Academic Freedom: A First Amendment Jurisprudence for the Modern State*, New Haven: Yale University Press.

Przeworski, A. and H. Teune (1970), *The Logic of Comparative Social Inquiry*, New York: Wiley-Interscience.

Przeworski, A., M. E. Alvarez, J. A. Cheibub and F. Limongi (2000), *Democracy and Development: Political Institutions and Well-Being in the World, 1950–1990*, Cambridge: Cambridge University Press.

Przeworski, A., S. C. Stokes and B. Manin, eds (1999), *Democracy, Accountability, and Representation*, Cambridge: Cambridge University Press.

Pul, H. A. S. (2003), 'Exclusion, Association and Violence: Trends and Triggers in Northern Ghana's Konkomba-Dagomba Wars', *African Anthropologist*, 10(1): 39–82.

QoG (2021), Quality of Government Institute, Gothernburg University, Retrieved from: https://www.gu.se/en/quality-government

Quijano, A. (2000), 'Coloniality of Power, Eurocentrism, and Latin America', *Nepantla: Views from South*, 1(3): 533–80, muse.jhu.edu/article/23906

Rabah, I. (2015), 'Introduction of Managerialism into University Administration: Erosion of the Collegial Model, Shared Governance, and Academic Tenure', *Global Journal of Management and Business Research*, 15(12): 24–36.

Rabushka, A. and K. A. Shepsle (1972), *Politics in Plural Societies: A Theory of Democratic Instability*, 1st edn, Columbus: Merrill.

Ransome-Kuti, F. (1947/2011), 'We had Equality Till Britain Came', in T. K. Wayne (ed.), *Feminist Writings from Ancient Times to the Modern World: A Global Sourcebook and History*, 544–9, Santa Barbara: ABC-CLIO.

Rasheed, S. (1994), 'Social Sciences and Policy Making in Africa: A Critical Review', *Africa Development / Afrique et Développement*, 19(1): 91–118.

Ray, D. I. (2003), 'Ghana: Traditional Leadership and Rural Local Governance', in D. I. Ray and P. S. Reddy (eds), *Grassroots Governance? Chiefs in Africa and the Afro-Caribbean*, 83–122, Calgary: University of Calgary Press.

Reilly, B. (2001), 'Democracy, Ethnic Fragmentation, and Internal Conflict: Confused Theories, Faulty Data, and the "Crucial Case" of Papua New Guinea', *International Security*, 25(3): 162–85.

Reno, W. (1995), *Corruption and State Politics in Sierra Leone*, Cambridge: Cambridge University Press.

Reno, W. (1998), *Warlord Politics and African States*, Boulder: Lynne Rienner Publishers.

Reynal-Querol, M. (2002), 'Ethnicity, Political Systems, And Civil Wars', *The Journal of Conflict Resolution*, 46(1): 29–54.

Robinson, P. (2015), 'Students Take to Social Media an Analysis of #FeesMustFall Infographics', *The Meltwater Blog*, https://www.meltwater.com/blog/feesmustfall/ (accessed 10 August 2018).

Rodney, W. (1972), *How Europe Underdeveloped Africa*, London and Dar-Es-Salaam: Bogle-L'Ouverture Publications; Tanzanian Publishing House.

Rodney, W. (1981), How Europe Underdeveloped Africa, Washington, DC: Howard University Press.

Rodney, W. (2012 [1972]), *How Europe Underdeveloped Africa*, Rev. edn, Cape Town: Pambazuka Press.

Rodriguez, C. R., D. Tsikata and A. A. Ampofo (2015), *Transatlantic Feminisms: Women and Gender Studies in Africa and the Diaspora*, Lanham: Lexington Books.

Rogowski, R. (2013), 'Shooting (or Ignoring) the Messenger', *Political Studies Review*, 11(2): 216–21.

Rose, A. W. (1966), 'Sociology and the Transitional African Societies: An Important Encounter', *The American Journal of Economics and Sociology*, 25(2): 181–99.

Roseman, C., C. G. Mayo and F. B. Collinge (eds) (1966), *Dimensions of Political Analysis: An Introduction to the Contemporary Study of Politics*, Englewood Cliffs: Prentice-Hall.

Rosenberg, A. (1988), *Philosophy of Social Science*, Oxford: Clarendon Press.

Rostow, W. W. (1960), *The Stages of Economic Growth: A Non-Communist Manifesto*, Cambridge: Cambridge University Press.

Rothchild, D. (1997), *Managing Ethnic Conflict in Africa: Pressures and Incentives for Cooperation*, Washington, D.C: Brookings Institution Press.

Rothchild, D. and N. Chazan (eds) (1988), *The Precarious Balance: State and Society in Africa*, Boulder: Westview Press.

Rothchild, D. and R. L. Curry Jr. (1979), *Scarcity, Choice, and Public Policy in Middle Africa*, Berkeley: University of California Press.

Rothchild, D. and V. A. Olorunsola (eds) (1983), *State Versus Ethnic Claims: African Policy Dilemmas*, 1st edn, Boulder: Westview Press.

Rudolph, S. H. and L. I. Rudolph (1967), *The Modernity of Tradition: Political Development in India*, Chicago: University of Chicago Press.

Sabbi, M. (2018), 'Who Runs the Municipality? The Intractable Interest of Neo-traditional Actors in Ghana's Local State', University of Bayreuth African Studies Working Papers, 22, https://epub.uni-bayreuth.de/4082/1/WP22_Sabbi_final.pdf

Sabbi, M., L. Doumbia and D. Neubert (2020), 'Dynamics of Everyday Life within Municipal Administrations in Francophone and Anglophone Africa', *Africa Spectrum*, 55: 73–85.

Sabbi, M. and C. A. Mensah (2016), 'Juggling Administrative Institutions: Local State Actors and the Management of Urban Space in Kumasi, Ghana', *Urban Forum*, 27(1): 59–78.

Sadie, Y. (2013), 'The State of Comparative Politics in South Africa', *Politikon*, 40(3): 501–16.

Sadiqi, F. (2008), 'Facing Challenges and Pioneering Feminist and Gender Studies: Women in Postcolonial and Today's Maghrib', *African and Asian Studies*, 7(4): 447–70.

Said, E. W. (1978), *Orientalism: Western Conceptions of the Orient*, London: Routledge.

Said, E. W. (1993), *Culture and Imperialism*, New York: Vintage Books.

Said, E. W. (1999), *Out of Place: A Memoir*, New York: Vintage Books.

Said, E. W. (2000), *Reflections on Exile and Other Essays*, Cambridge, MA: Harvard University Press.

Saleh, I. (2017), 'Digital Politics in North Africa: Possibilities to Reverse Subversion', in S. Fuller (ed.), *North Africa: Social, Environmental and Political Issues*, Hauppauge: Nova Science Publishers, 73–96.

Sall, E. (ed.) (2000), *Women in Academia: Gender and Academic Freedom in Africa*, Dakar: Codesria.

Salter, L. and A. M. V. Hearn (1996), *Outside the Lines: Issues in Interdisciplinary Research*, Montreal and Kingston: McGill-Queen's University Press.

SAR (2020), 'Academic Freedom Monitoring Project', *Scholars at Risk*, https://www.scholarsatrisk.org/academic-freedom-monitoring-project-index/ (accessed 12 March 2021).

Sartre, J.-P. (1972), *Plaidoyer pour les intellectuels*, Paris: Gallimard.

Sartre, J.-P. (1976), *Between Existentialism and Marxism*, trans. J. Mathews, New York: William Morrow.

Schedler, A. and C. Mudde (2008), 'The Use of Datasets in Comparative Politics Paper', presented at the European Consortium of Political Research Workshop, The Numbers We Use, the World We See: Evaluating Cross-National Datasets in Comparative Politics, Rennes, France.

Schraeder, P. J. (2004), *African Politics and Society: A Mosaic in Transformation*, 2nd edn, Belmont: Thomson Wadsworth.

Schumpeter, J. A. (1950), *Capitalism, Socialism, and Democracy*, New York: Harper and Brothers.

Shaw, T. M. (1991), 'Reformism, Revisionism, and Radicalism in African Political Economy during the 1990s', *The Journal of Modern African Studies*, 29(2): 191–212.

Shils, E. (1963), 'On the Comparative Study of the New States', in C. Geertz (ed.), *Old Societies and New States; the Quest for Modernity in Asia and Africa*, 1–26, Glencoe: The Free Press.

Sindjoun, L. (1996), 'Identité nationale et "révision constitutionnelle" du 18 janvier 1996. Comment constitutionnalise-t-on le "nous" au Cameroun dans l'État post-unitaire?', *Polis*, 1: 10–24.

Sindjoun, L. (2020), 'Le crépuscule de l'imposture', *Cameroon Tribune*, 10 March, 10–11.

Sklar, R. L. (1979), 'The Nature of Class Domination in Africa', *The Journal of Modern African Studies*, 17(4): 531–52.

Sklar, R. L. (1983), 'Democracy in Africa', *African Studies Review*, 26 (3–4), 11–24.

Sklar, R. L. (1985), 'The Colonial Imprint on African Political Thought', in G. M. Carter and P. O'Meara (eds), *African Independence: The First Twenty-Five Years*, Bloomington and London: Indiana University Press; Hutchinson.

Sklar, R. L. and D. G. Becker (eds) (1999), *Postimperialism and World Politics*, First edition, Westport: Praeger.

Smith, A. D. (1981), *The Ethnic Revival*, Cambridge: Cambridge University Press.

Smith, H. E. (1990), 'Sociology and the Study of Non-Western Societies', *The American Sociologist*, 21(2): 150–63.

Smith, M. G. (1982), 'Ethnicity and Ethnic Groups in America: The View from Harvard', *Ethnic and Racial Studies*, 5(1): 1–22.

Snyder, J. (2000), *From Voting to Violence: Democratization and Nationalist Conflict*, New York: W.W. Norton.

Sofola, Z. (1998), 'Feminism and African Womanhood', in O. Nnaemeka (ed.), *Sisterhood, Feminisms and Power in Africa: From Africa to the Diaspora*, 51–64, Trenton: Africa World Press.

Southall, R. (2019), 'The Decolonisation of the Political Science Curriculum in East Africa: A Reply to Mngomezulu and Sakhile Hadebe', *Politikon*, 46(2): 240–51.

Soyinka, W., S. Amin, T. Mkandawire, B. H. Selassie and G. Mugo (2015), *Reimagining Pan-Africanism: Distinguished Mwalimu Nyerere Lecture Series 2009–2013*, Dar es Salaam: Mkuki na Nyota Publishers.

Standler, R. B. (2000), 'Academic Freedom in the USA', My Essays About Education Law http://www.rbs2.com/afree.htm (accessed 20 April 2021).

Steady, F. C. (2006), *Women and Collective Action in Africa: Development, Democratization, and Empowerment, with Special Focus on Sierra Leone*, 1st edn, New York: Palgrave Macmillan.

Steinmo, S., K. A. Thelen and F. Longstreth (eds) (1992), *Structuring Politics: Historical Institutionalism in Comparative Analysis*, Cambridge: Cambridge University Press.

Stoker, G., G. B. Peters and J. Pierre (2015), 'Introduction', in G. Stoker, G. B. Peters and J. Pierre (eds), *The Relevance of Political Science*, 1–16, London: Palgrave Macmillan.

Stone, D. and S. Ladi (2015), 'Global Public Policy and Transnational Administration', *Public Administration*, 93(4): 839–55.

Stone, D. and K. Moloney (eds) (2019), *The Oxford Handbook of Global Policy and Transnational Administration*, Oxford: Oxford University Press.

Suberu, R. T. (1990), 'Federalism and Instability in Nigeria', *Plural Societies*, 19(2–3): 145–61.

Sueyoshi, K. C. (2018), 'Five Limitations: Political Science Applied to The Non-West', *Global Politics Review*, 4(1): 78–86.

Tamale, S. (1999), *When Hens Begin to Crow: Gender and Parliamentary Politics in Uganda*, Boulder: Westview.

Tamale, S. (2001), 'Gender and Affirmative Action in Post-1995 Uganda: A New Dispensation, or Business as Usual?' in J. Oloka-Onyango (ed.), *Constitutionalism in Africa: Creating Opportunities, Facing Challenges*, 211–34, Kampala, Uganda: Fountain Press.

Tamale, S. (2011), *African Sexualities: A Reader*, Cape Town: Pambazuka Press.

Tamale, S. (2020), *Decolonization and Afro-Feminism*, Wakefield: Daraja Press.

Tandon, Y., ed. (1982), *University of Dar Es Salaam: Debate on Class, State and Imperialism*, Dar es Salaam: Tanzania Publishing House.

Tandon, Y. (1984), 'Arguments within African Marxism: The Dar es Salaam Debates', *Journal of African Marxists*, 5(5): 31–43.

Tandon, Y. (1989), 'Research on and Teaching of International Relations in Eastern Africa', in W. O. Oyugi (ed.), *The Teaching and Research of Political Science in Eastern Africa*, 85–106, Addis Ababa: OSSREA.

Temu, A. and B. Swai (1981), *Historians and Africanist History: A Critique*, London: Zed Books.

Tendi, M. B. (2020), *The Army and politics in Zimbabwe: Mujuru, the Liberation Fighter and Kingmaker*, Cambridge: Cambridge University Press.

Tettey, W. J. and K. P. Puplampu (2000), 'Social Science Research and the Africanist: The Need for Intellectual and Attitudinal Reconfiguration', *African Studies Review*, 43(3): 81–102.

'The Kampala Declaration on Intellectual Freedom and Social Responsibility' (1990), Codesria, Article 22, http://abahlali.org/files/Kampala%20Declaration.pdf

Tieleman, J. and J. Uitermark (2019), 'Chiefs in the City: Traditional Authority in the Modern State', *Sociology*, 53(4): 707–23.

Tipps, D. C. (1973), 'Modernization Theory and the Comparative Study of Societies: A Critical Perspective', *Comparative Studies in Society and History*, 15(2): 199–226.

Tobner, O. (2014), 'Dr Abel Eyinga: Vie et mort d'un juste', *Journal du Cameroun*, https://www.journalducameroun.com/dr-abel-eyinga-vie-et-mort-dun-juste/ (accessed 9 April 2021).

Todes, A., P. Sithole and A. Williamson (2007), *Local Government, Gender and Integrated Development Planning*, Cape Town: Human Sciences Research Council.

Tolmay, S. and C. Lowe Morna (eds.) (2010), *At the Coalface: Gender and Local Government in Zimbabwe*, Johannesburg: Gender Links.

Tripp, A., I. Casimiro, J. Kwesiga and A. Mungwa (2009), *African Women's Movements: Transforming Political Landscapes*, New York: Cambridge University Press.

Tripp, A. M. (2016), 'Comparative Perspectives on Concepts of Gender, Ethnicity, and Race', *Politics, Groups, and Identities*, 4(2): 307–24.

Tripp, A. M. (forthcoming), 'Fatema Mernissi Challenges Transnational Feminism', in F. Sadiqi, M. Badran and R. Rhouni, *Fatema Mernissi*.

Tripp, A. M. and J. C. Kwesiga (2002). *The Women's Movement in Uganda: History, Challenges, and Prospects*, Kampala: Fountain Publishers.

Tsafack, D. (2016), 'Rassemblement démocratique du peuple camerounais (RDPC): Radioscopie et trajectoire d'un parti présidentiel', Direction générale des relations internationales et de la stratégie, 35, https://www.academia.edu/30871091/RDPC _radioscopie_et_trajectoire_dun_parti_pr%C3%A9sidentiel_Note_du_GRIP

Tshuma, L. A. (2020), 'ZANU-PF Women's League and the (Re)configuration of Political Power in Influencing Succession Politics in Zimbabwe', in S. A. Omotoso (ed.), *Women's Political Communication in Africa*, 61–76, Cham: Springer.

Tsikata, Dzodzi (2000), *LipService and Peanuts: The State and National Machinery for Women in Africa*. National Machinery Series 11. Accra, Ghana: Third World NetworkAfrica.

Twumasi, Y. (2014), 'The 1969 Election', in E. Debrah, E. Gyimah-Boadi, A. Essuman-Johnson and K. A. Ninsin (eds), *Ghana: Essays in the Study of Political Science*, 45–58, Legon-Accra: Sub-Saharan Publishers.

Ubink, J. (2007), 'Traditional Authority Revisited: Popular Perceptions of Chiefs and Chieftaincy in Peri-Urban Kumasi, Ghana', *The Journal of Legal Pluralism and Unofficial Law*, 39(55): 123–61.

Uchendu, E. (2007), *Women and Conflict in the Nigerian Civil War*, Trenton: Africa World Press.

Udogu, E. I. (1999), 'The Issue of Ethnicity and Democratization in Africa: Toward the Millennium', *Journal of Black Studies*, 29(6): 790–808.

Udogu, E. I. (2018), *Ethnicity and Democracy in Sub-Saharan Africa*, London: Routledge.

Ugbem, C. E. (2019), 'Ethnicity, Democracy and the Development Nexus in Nigeria', *The International Journal of Social Sciences and Humanities Invention*, 6(4): 5400–6.

Umoren, J. A. (1996), *Democracy and Ethnic Diversity in Nigeria*, Lanham: University Press of America.

UNESCO (1962), 'The Development of Higher Education in Africa', Report of the Conference on the Development of Higher Education in Africa, Tananarive, 3–12 September 1962, Paris: UNESCO.

UNESCO (1997), 'Recommendation Concerning the Status of Higher-Education Teaching Personnel', http://portal.unesco.org/en/ev.php-URL_ID=13144&URL_DO=DO_TOPIC&URL_SECTION=201.html (accessed 20 April 2021).

University of Ghana (2011), 'Code of Conduct for Academic Staff of the University of Ghana March 2011', *University of Ghana Special Reporter No. 798*, 49(4): 1–12, http://www.ug.edu.gh/paddocs/CodeofConductionforAcademicStaff.pdf

University of Johannesburg (n.d.), 'Home', https://www.uj.ac.za:443/ (accessed 30 April 2021).

University of KwaZulu-Natal (2013), *College of Humanities Academic Curriculum Handbook*, Pietermaritzburg: UKZN Press.

University of Zambia (n.d.), 'Home', https://www.unza.zm/ (accessed 30 April 2021).

Usman, Y. B. (1980), 'The Elementary Responsibility of Political and Other Sciences in Nigeria', *Nigerian Journal of Political Science*, 2(2): 20–6.

van de Walle, N. (2003), 'Presidentialism and Clientelism in Africa's Emerging Party Systems', *The Journal of Modern African Studies*, 41(2): 297–321.

Vanhanen, T. (1999), 'Domestic Ethnic Conflict and Ethnic Nepotism: A Comparative Analysis', *Journal of Peace Research*, 36(1): 55–73.

Vanhanen, T. (2000), 'A New Dataset for Measuring Democracy, 1810–1998', *Journal of Peace Research*, 37(2): 251–65.

van Wyk, J. A. (2017), 'The First Ladies of Southern Africa: Trophies or Trailblazers?' *Politikon: South African Journal of Political Studies*, 44(1): 1–16.

von Freyhold, M. (1979), *Ujamaa Villages in Tanzania: Analysis of a Social Experiment*, London: Heinemann.

Vorrath, J. and L. F. Krebs (2009), 'Democratisation and Conflict in Ethnically Divided Societies', *Living Reviews in Democracy*, 1(1): 1–8.

Wagner, C. (2016), 'Reflections on the State of Social Science Research on the African Continent', *Bulletin of Sociological Methodology / Bulletin de Méthodologie Sociologique*, 130: 90–6.

Wallerstein, I. (1976), 'The Three Stages of African Involvement in the World Economy', in P. C. W. Gutkind and I. Wallerstein (eds), *The Political Economy of Contemporary Africa*, 30–57, Beverly Hills: Sage Publications.

Wallerstein, I. (1979), *The Capitalist World-Economy*, Cambridge: Cambridge University Press.

Walters, R. W. (1993), *Pan Africanism in the African Diaspora: An Analysis of Modern Afrocentric Political Movements*, Detroit: Wayne State University Press.

Warren, C. L. (2018), *Ontological Terror: Blackness, Nihilism, and Emancipation*, Illustrated edition, Durham: Duke University Press Books.

Wa Thiong'o, N. (1986), *Decolonising the Mind: The Politics of Language in African Literature*, Nairobi: Heinemann.

Wa Thiong'o, N. (1993), *Moving the Centre: The Struggle for Cultural Freedoms*, London: James Currey Publishers.

Wa Thiong'o, N. (2009), *Something Torn and New: An African Renaissance*, New York: Basic Civitas Books.

Wa Thiong'o, N. (2012), *Globalectics: Theory and the Politics of Knowing*, New York: Columbia University Press.

Watson, J. and A. Gouws (2019), *Nasty Women Talk Back*, South Africa: LAPA Publishers.

Weaver, R. K. and B. A. Rockman (eds) (1993), *Do Institutions Matter? Government Capabilities in the United States and Abroad*, Washington: The Brookings Institution.

Weiner, M. (1996), 'Bad Neighbors, Bad Neighborhoods: An Inquiry into the Causes of Refugee Flows', *International Security*, 21(1): 5–42.

Whitaker Jr., C. S. (1970), *The Politics of Tradition: Continuity and Change in Northern Nigeria, 1946–1966*, Princeton: Princeton University Press.

Wilderson, F. B. (2008), 'Biko and the Problematic of Presence', in A. Mngxitama, A. Alexander and N. Gibson (eds), *Biko Lives!: Contesting the Legacies of Steve Biko*, 95–114, New York: Palgrave Macmillan.

Wilmot, P. F. (1973), 'Introduction', in P. F. Wilmot (ed.), *Sociology in Africa: A Book of Readings, Volume 1*, 1–10, Zaria: Ahmadu Bello University.

Wilmot, P. F. (2005), *Seeing Double*, London: Jonathan Cape.

Woodson, C. G. (2012), *The Miseducation of the Negro*, New York: Start Publishing.

World Bank (1981), Accelerated Development in Sub-Saharan Africa: An Agenda for Action, Washington, DC: The World Bank, http://documents1.worldbank.org/curated/en/702471468768312009/pdf/multi-page.pdf

World Bank (2010), *Financing Higher Education in Africa*, Washington, DC: The World Bank.

Wright, W. J. (2019), 'The Public Is Intellectual', *The Professional Geographer*, 71(1): 172–8.

Yacob-Haliso, O. and T. Falola (eds) (2021a), *The Palgrave Handbook of African Women's Studies*, Cham: Palgrave Macmillan.

Yacob-Haliso, O. and T. Falola (2021b), 'Conclusion: Charting Future Paths for African Women's Studies', in O. Yacob-Haliso and T. Falola (eds), *The Palgrave Handbook of African Women's Studies*, Cham: Palgrave Macmillan.

Yancy, G. (2008), 'Colonial Gazing: The Production of the Body as "Other"', *The Western Journal of Black Studies*, 32(1): 1–15.

Yancy, G. and J. Butler (2015), 'What's Wrong With "All Lives Matter"?' *Opinionator*, https://shifter-magazine.com/wp-content/uploads/2015/01/Whats-Wrong-With-All -Lives-Matter.pdf (accessed 18 October 2021).

Young, C. (1976), *The Politics of Cultural Pluralism*, Madison: University of Wisconsin Press.

Young, C. (1994), *The African Colonial State in Comparative Perspective*, New Haven: Yale University Press.

Young, C. (2012), *The Post-Colonial State in Africa: Fifty Years of Independence 1960–2010*, Madison: University of Wisconsin Press.

Yountae, A. (2017), *The Decolonial Abyss: Mysticism and Cosmopolitics from the Ruins*, New York: Fordham University Press.

Zegeye, A. and M. Vambe (2006), 'Knowledge Production and Publishing in Africa', *Development Southern Africa*, 23(3): 333–49.

Zeleza, P. T. (1997), *Manufacturing African Studies and Crises*, Dakar: Codesria.

Zeleza, P. T. (2002), 'The Politics of Historical and Social Science Research in Africa', *Journal of Southern African Studies*, 28(1): 9–23.

Zeleza, P. T. (2003), 'Academic Freedom in the Neo-Liberal Order: Governments, Globalization, Governance, and Gender', *Journal of Higher Education in Africa*, 1(1): 149–94, http://www.jstor.org/stable/24486118

Zeleza, P. T. (2005a), 'Banishing the Silences: Towards the Globalization of African History', Paper presented at the 11th General Assembly of CODESRIA, Maputo, December 6 - 10.

Zeleza, P. T. (2005b), 'The Politics and Poetics of Exile: Edward Said in Africa', *Research in African Literatures*, 36(3): 1–22.

Zeleza, P. T. (2005c), 'Transnational Education and African Universities', *Journal of Higher Education in Africa*, 3(1): 1–28, http://www.jstor.org/stable/24486240

Zeleza, P. T. (2006a), *The Study of Africa Volume 1: Disciplinary and Interdisciplinary Encounters*, Dakar: Codesria.

Zeleza, P. T. (2006b), 'The Disciplinary, Interdisciplinary and Global Dimensions of African Studies', *International Journal of African Renaissance Studies*, 1(2): 195–220.

Zolberg, A. R. (1966), *Creating Political Order: The Party-States of West Africa*, Chicago: Rand McNally.

Zondi, S. (2018), 'Decolonising International Relations and Its Theory: A Critical Conceptual Meditation', *Politikon*, 45(1): 16–31.

Index